The Foreign Office and British
Diplomacy in the Twentieth Century

The Foreign Office and British Diplomacy in the Twentieth Century

Edited by
Gaynor Johnson

Routledge
Taylor & Francis Group

LONDON AND NEW YORK

First published 2005 by Routledge, an imprint of Tayor & Francis
2 Park Square, Milton Park, Abingdon, Oxon, OX14 4RN

Simultaneously published in the USA and Canada
by Routledge
270 Madison Ave, New York, NY 10016

Routledge is an imprint of the Taylor & Francis Group

Transferred to Digital Printing 2009

Typeset in Times 10/12pt in Europe by Alden Group, Oxford

British Library Catalouging in Publication Data
A catalogue record for this book is available from
the British Library

Library of Congress Cataloging in Publication Data

ISBN10: 0-714-65679-8 (hbk)
ISBN10: 0-415-56831-5 (pbk)

ISBN13: 978-0-714-65679-3 (hbk)
ISBN13: 978-0-415-56831-9 (pbk)

CONTENTS

Acknowledgements

I would like to thank Bolton Institute, the British International History Group, the Foreign and Commonwealth Office and the Institute of Contemporary British History for their generous support for the project on which this book is based. In particular, He is grateful to Eamonn Clifford, Keith Hamilton, Michael Kandiah, Dr Martin Longden, Heather Yasamee, Professor John Young and Sir Michael Jay, the present Permanent Under-Secretary at the Foreign and Commonwealth Office. Andrew Humphreys and Cathy Jennings at Frank Cass/Taylor and Francis have provided prompt and good-humoured advice as have the editors of *Contemporary British History*, Kevin Ruane and Peter Catterall. I would also like to extend a public word of thanks to Baron Owen of Plymouth for agreeing to write the preface to this volume.

GAYNOR JOHNSON
Bolton Institute
February 2004

Notes on Contributors

Alyson J.K. Bailes, CMG, is Director of the Stockholm International Peace Research Institute (SIPRI). She was a member of Her Majesty's Diplomatic Service from 1969 to 2002, ending her career as British Ambassador to Helsinki. Her other postings included Budapest, the British Delegation to NATO, Bonn, Beijing and Oslo. She also spent periods on loan to the Ministry of Defence, the Western European Union in Brussels and the East West Institute in New York.

Sir Alan Campbell, CMG, KCMG, GCMG. Among his appointments, Sir Alan was Ambassador to Ethiopia, 1969–72; Assistant Under-Secretary at the Foreign and Commonwealth Office, 1972–74; Deputy Under-Secretary, 1974–76; Ambassador to Italy, 1976–79 and Director of National Westminster Bank, 1979–89. He is the author of *Colleagues and Friends* (1988) and has contributed articles to *International Affairs* and to the *New Dictionary of National Biography*.

John Charmley is Dean of the School of History at the University of East Anglia, where he has taught since 1979. He is author of eight books, including the controversial *Churchill: The End of Glory* (1993) and, most recently, *Splendid Isolation? Britain and the Balance of Power 1874–1914* (1999). He is currently working on a book on Princess Lieven and British foreign policy, 1812–34.

James Ellison is Lecturer in Modern and Contemporary History at Queen Mary, University of London. He teaches and researches post-1945 British foreign policy and has particular interest in Britain's relations with Europe and the United States. He is the author of *Threatening Europe: Britain and the Creation of the European Community, 1955–1958* (2000) and is currently writing a book about Anglo-American relations and Europe in the 1960s.

Sean Greenwood is a Research Professor in Modern History at Canterbury Christ Church University College, where he was the Head of the Department of History until 2003. He has published on a range of topics dealing with British foreign policy since the 1930s, most recently a contribution to a Nobel Symposium assessing the last ten years of the Cold War. Currently he is engaged in writing a biography of the distinguished diplomat Lord Gladwyn.

Keith Hamilton is Senior Editor of *Documents on British Policy Overseas* and historian in the Foreign and Commonwealth Office. His publications include *Bertie of Thame: Edwardian Ambassador* (1990), *The Practice of*

Diplomacy: Its Evolution, Theory and Administration (1995, with Richard Langhorne), and *The Last Cold War Warriors: Britain, Détente and the CSCE, 1972–1975* (1999). He is currently editing a collection of British documents on *The Year of Europe: America, Europe and the Energy Crisis, 1972–74*, the first part of which will be published in 2005 on CD-ROM.

Gaynor Johnson is Senior Lecturer at the Bolton Institute. She is the author of *The Berlin Embassy of Lord D'Abernon, 1920–1926* (2002); the editor of *Locarno Revisited: European Diplomacy, 1920–1929* (2004); *Our Man in Berlin: The Diary of Sir Eric Phipps 1933–1937* (2004); and with Matthew Hughes, *Fanaticism in the Modern Era* (2004). She is currently writing a biography of Viscount Cecil of Chelwood.

Richard Langhorne is Director of the Center for Global Change and Governance at Rutgers University. He was previously Director of Wilton Park, Foreign and Commonwealth Office, 1993–96. He is the author of *The Collapse of the Concert of Europe* (1982), *The Practice of Diplomacy* (1995, with Keith Hamilton), *The Coming of Globalization* (2001), and has edited the *Guide to Diplomacy and International Relations* (2002).

B.J.C. McKercher is Professor of International History and Chair of War Studies at the Royal Military College of Canada. An expert on inter-war British foreign policy, and his major books include *Esme Howard: A Diplomatic Biography* (1989) and *Transition of Power: Britain's Loss of Global Pre-Eminence to the United States, 1930–1945* (1999). With Erik Goldstein, he edited and contributed to *Power and Stability: British Foreign Policy, 1865–1965* (2003).

Peter Neville teaches history at the University of East Anglia. He is the author of *Appeasing Hitler: The Diplomacy of Sir Nevile Henderson 1937–9* (2000), and a contributor to the *Munich Crisis: Prelude to World War Two* (1999). His latest book is *Mussolini* (2003).

T.G. Otte is a Lecturer in Diplomatic/International History at the University of East Anglia. He is editor of *The Makers of British Foreign Policy: from Pitt to Thatcher* (2002) and *Classic Guides to Diplomacy from Machiavelli to Kissinger* (2001). He has just finished a monograph on Britain, the Great Powers and the China Question, 1894–1905.

Lord David Owen was Secretary of State for Foreign and Commonwealth Affairs 1977–79. A co-founder of the Social Democrat Party, with Shirley Williams (Baroness Williams of Crosby) and Roy Jenkins (the late Lord Jenkins of Hillhead), he was deputy leader of the party 1982–83 and leader 1983–1987. A member of the Independent Commission on Disarmament and Security Issues and the Independent Commission on International

Humanitarian Issues in the 1980s, Lord Owen became European Union co-chairman of the International Conference on the Former Yugoslavia 1992–95. His publications include *Time to Declare* (1991) and *Balkan Odyssey* (1995).

Kevin Ruane is a Reader in Modern History at Canterbury Christ Church University College. His publications include *The Rise and Fall of the European Defence Community: Anglo-American Relations and the Crisis of European Defence 1950–55* (2000) and *The Vietnam Wars* (2000). He is currently working on a study of Anglo-American relations during the Indo-China war.

Alan Sharp is Professor of International Studies and Head of the School of History and International Affairs at the University of Ulster. His major research and publishing interests are in British foreign policy after the First World War, with a particular focus on Lord Curzon's tenure of the Foreign Office and the career of James Headlam-Morley. He is author of *The Versailles Settlement: Peacemaking in Paris 1919* (1991), and editor with Glyn Stone of a collection of essays, *Anglo-French Relations in the Twentieth Century: Rivalry and Cooperation* (2000).

Zara Steiner is an Emeritus Fellow, New Hall, University of Cambridge. The author of a number of studies of British foreign policy in the first half of the twentieth century, her most recent works include a revised edition of *Britain and the Origins of the First World War* (2003), co-authored with Keith Neilson, and 'British Power and Stability: The Historical Record', *Diplomacy and Statecraft*, 14/2 (2003).

Preface

LORD DAVID OWEN, PC CH

Just as after the 1956 Suez debacle, so over the invasion of Iraq in 2003, there will have to be a fresh attempt to chart a new course for British foreign policy and British diplomacy. In stark contrast to the 1990–91 Gulf War, in 2002–3 there have been over the invasion of Iraq fundamental errors and poor judgements, not just in the field of intelligence but above all for us in Britain in the handling of the detailed diplomacy from 10 Downing Street. Nevertheless, once the United States was ready after 11 September 2001 to send troops back to the Gulf to topple Saddam Hussein, I believe the British government was correct to offer military support and that France and Germany made a mistake in opposing the war.

A good place to start a rethink in Britain about the twenty-first century is to absorb the many wisdoms contained in this series of essays from the twentieth century. They are a mixture of vignettes of history and relevant modern experience. At first sight, looking at the titles, they may appear too disparate but on closer reading I found to a surprising extent an inner coherence, particularly since the excellent referencing of the inevitably compressed text provides a fascinating additional reading list.

Given the dominant position in foreign policy of the prime minister, Tony Blair, it is not a bad starting place to examine Lloyd George's post-war period as prime minister and his relationship with Curzon, the foreign secretary, not least the period when Curzon was the acting foreign secretary during the Paris Peace Conference. In 1920, the radical weekly *New Europe* asserted, 'We are in the hands of a Prime Minister who has usurped the functions of the Foreign Secretary... The Foreign Office seems incapable of asserting its right to control policy, and has irresponsible competitors, not only in the Garden Suburb of Downing Street'.[1] That sounds very familiar.

One of the casualties of Iraq will, I hope, be the demise of the totally new Overseas and Defence Secretariat inside Number 10, created after the General Election in 2001, as well as the transfer back to the Cabinet Office of the European Secretariat from Number 10. Not since 1956 when Anthony Eden's wife commented that the Suez Canal ran through her sitting room in 10 Downing Street have we seen such a concentration of detailed decision making in the hands of the prime minister. Predictably such a highly personalised structure of government leads to ill-judged decisions which are less likely to win support amongst public and professional opinion. Eden's 'Suezide' forms the background to an important essay analysing 'power by proxy' in relation to the United States which concludes that both Eden and Macmillan by the 1960s felt for different reasons that the American proxy was not the solution.

The role of the permanent under-secretary in the Foreign Office is now much diminished, yet it was very important, particularly when Hardinge was the Grand Panjundrum and forged with the Foreign Secretary a partnership 'of equals . . . unique in Foreign Office history'.[2] We cannot turn back the clock to the decade before the Great War which saw the Foreign Office reach the zenith of its power and influence. Prime ministerial involvement and interference is part of globalisation and membership of the European Union. Yet still cabinet government emerges to challenge prime ministerial government as Margaret Thatcher learnt to her cost and Tony Blair is now encountering.

The Foreign Office will always have its enemies, not just critics. They are reminded in one essay that Henderson's period as pre-war ambassador in Berlin and the appeasement period was preceded by a robust analysis, particularly with Rumbold's dissection of *Mein Kampf* and his final report to the Foreign Office in 1933 in which he said Hitler, Goring and Goebbels were 'notoriously pathological cases' and the Nazi leadership as a whole, he warned, was made up of 'fantastic hooligans and eccentrics'.[3] It is also salutary to note that a generation of diplomats had been recruited in an atmosphere when the diplomatic secretary, a certain Theo Russell, could in 1918 express his alarm that men without a public school background might be accepted into the Diplomatic Service and even worse they might be 'Jews, coloured men and infidels who are British subjects'.[4]

I never knew that Gladwyn Jebb, one of the Foreign Office's foremost European federalists, was actually a late convert. Also that on 18 June 1960, in a conversation with de Gaulle, who was still involved with Algeria, the general seemed to see a possible opening for Britain to be a part of a European confederation, only for the British cabinet on 13 July to decide not to seek entry. A tantalising 'what if' unfolds here if Britain had been part of the Fouchet Plan for limiting European integration.

The essays of two fairly recent diplomats, Alan Campbell and Alyson Bailes, interestingly reflect what is, I believe, the reality of the twenty-first century diplomat. The Foreign Office is now recruited from a much broader spectrum; it is modern in its attitudes and in its working habits; and with inter-change in postings with civil service departments it is poised to be an effective participant in any new foreign policy. Oddly perhaps in this context, the saga of how the Foreign Office was not knocked down but brilliantly renovated and how Wilton Park survived every vicissitude are also relevant essays.

The almost naïve zealotry when the Office was totally dominated by European integrationists is hopefully over. It is now more rooted in public opinion in Britain which has seen off simplistic economic and political arguments for membership of the eurozone. The Foreign Office is an instrument ready to be played by the politicians if they know how to in order to develop a realistic working relationship with the United States, which cannot exclude France and Germany.

We do not need new structures; in particular Tony Blair should not seek to build a tripartite structure within the European Union. It is far better for Britain to be free to forge different alliances on different topics with the 24 other European Union nations. We have had the false dawn of Europe's euphoria in 1991 over the Balkans. We have, I suspect, passed in 2003 the high-water mark of American triumphalism. We need to forget all the 'isms' and just focus on practical delivery.

I believe the structure which could be revived is the quadripartite mechanism. That focused on Berlin and handled the necessary secrecy and strains of the Cold War very well. Its credibility was knocked by Margaret Thatcher's opposition to German reunification and by Chancellor Schroeder's and President Chirac's stance over Iraq. A new unifying theme for its private diplomacy could be the war against international terrorism, and a better balance might be achieved if it was open at any time for the national security adviser to the American president to attend as well as the American Secretary of State.

These four nations working privately and quietly together, can more easily nudge a complex world towards greater prosperity and better governance. NATO is emerging as a global military alliance. The Security Council can do things which not even the neo-conservatives now seem ready to advocate the United States doing alone, for example United Nations involvement in elections and constitution building in Iraq and peacekeeping in Haiti. In G8, with the addition of China and a return to the initial fireside chats and fewer, if any, press releases, helpful guidance can flow out once a year to the United Nations, International Monetary Fund, World Bank and World Trade Organisation. Regional groupings envisaged in San Francisco and enshrined in the United Nations Charter can contribute more positively than in previous times. As always, we can learn from the past.

NOTES

1. *The New Europe*, 28 Oct. 1920.
2. V Cromwell and Z. Steiner, 'The Foreign Office before 1914: A Study in Resistance', in G. Sutherland (ed.), *Studies in the Growth of Nineteenth-Century Government* (London: Routledge, 1972), p.188.
3. E L. Woodard and R. Butler (eds), *Documents on British Foreign Policy 1919–1939*, Second Series, Vol. V (London: HMSO, 1956), Rumbold to Simon, 30 Apr. 1933, pp.384–90.
4. United Kingdom National Archives (formerly the Public Record Office), London: FO 366/780, Note, 14 Jun. 1918.

Introduction: The Foreign Office and British Diplomacy in the Twentieth Century

GAYNOR JOHNSON

Harold Nicolson, in his seminal study of diplomatic theory, warned his reader against using the word 'diplomacy' as a synonym for 'foreign policy' or for 'negotiation'. Further travesties of meaning he pointed to include a shorthand way of referring to a relation in the Diplomatic Service, as in 'my nephew is working for diplomacy', or in a more elliptic sense, in its adjectival form meaning tactful or discrete. Its proper use, Nicolson reminds us, is to signify 'the process and machinery by which ... negotiation is carried out'.[1] It is hoped that the contents of this volume live up to Nicolson's definition. One of the principal objectives of the project on which it is based is to trace the way in which the decision-making process in British foreign policy evolved during the twentieth century. This has been a comparatively lightly trodden path among historians, and has tended to fall between the stools of diplomatic theory and the much larger realm of international history.[2] That is, the extent to which the operation of the Foreign Office (used here also as a shorthand for the Foreign and Commonwealth Office) and Diplomatic Service reflected the enormous changes that took place in the international arena during this period, many of which had a profound bearing on Britain's status as a world and imperial power.

A second purpose of this volume is to illustrate the connection between diplomacy and the foreign policy of British governments of the twentieth century. Specifically, it aims to look at this process from two points of view: from the position of the policy makers – a group including ministers and civil servants – and from the perspective of those charged with putting foreign policy strategies into operation and interpreting them to other powers. In particular, the role of ambassadorial diplomacy will be considered, both before the Second World War, and after, through a mixture of academic discussion and by first-hand insights by a recently retired ambassador.

Nicolson's definition of diplomacy does much to encourage a distinction between the theoretical application of the word and a separate study of foreign policy. He is quite clear: diplomacy is not the same as foreign policy. Yet while few would dispute this claim, this approach is not entirely helpful.

Diplomacy as a concept, or as a description of process, cannot exist meaningfully within an intellectual vacuum. Its fullest significance is only revealed when applied to a specific context. If diplomacy is about the process and machinery of negotiation, they will be determined in part by the unique circumstances of individual situations. That, in turn, leads to evolution of strategy, which prompts either adaptation or resistance from those engaged in the process. This volume demonstrates that the history of diplomacy as practised by Britain in the twentieth century was irrevocably bound to the changing international climate that sometimes worked in favour of the promotion of British interests, but more often did not. The diplomatic strategies expounded by Nicolson had at their heart the assumption that Britain would dictate the international agenda in the twentieth century as she had done in the past two centuries. But that was not to be the case.

The volume covers a period that saw Britain's decline as a world and imperial power. There have been a number of important studies of this subject within the last twenty years, but these have been primarily from the point of view of grand strategy, and certainly have not been from the perspective of one government department.[3] Yet it is self-evident to suggest that the operation of the Foreign Office during this period, and an analysis of the priorities of its policy-makers, provides one of the most important ways of studying this decline. The picture was not entirely bleak. Foreign Office personnel proved to be both inventive and adaptable when faced by the challenges posed particularly by diplomacy after 1945. But these characteristics always worked within a carefully constructed and clearly defined method of working, which as Alyson Bailes points out, may have become highly bureaucratic by the end of the century, but which continued to operate efficiently. The greater professional mobility open to Foreign Office and Diplomatic Service staff, in which women could rise to the rank of ambassador – something Curzon would have thought risible half a century earlier – and non-Oxbridge graduates could aspire to become senior civil servants, was partially facilitated by an obsession with method and procedure that began with the Hardinge reforms of 1905. Yet the operational framework was sufficiently rigid to offer reassuring permanence of hierarchy but contained sufficient flexibility to enable Foreign Office *modus operandi* to move with the times, whether in relation to international affairs or the technical challenges posed by computers and e-mail.

Most of the volume is based on papers given at an international conference held at the Institute of Contemporary British History, University of London, in June 2003. The contributors are a mix of academic historians from Britain and North America and highly experienced foreign policy practitioners. They include some of the foremost authorities on diplomacy and British foreign policy. The essays aim as closely as possible to cover the whole of the twentieth century, a period that has been taken to be from c.1890 to 2000. Some, such as those by John Charmley and Zara Steiner, are designed to provide an overview of a wider period of up to half a century, in order to give context to the more detailed studies of specific decades and individuals. These essays also help the volume avoid the oft-quoted criticism that diplomatic history is simply what one Foreign Office official said to another.

The volume also provides a further demonstration that foreign policy cannot be understood unless placed in its wider economic and political context. At no time has this been more true than during the twentieth century. Medieval monarchs paid for wars by raising taxation. Such a simple strategy was impossible in the twentieth century. The mechanisation of warfare born out of the industrial revolution and the enormous implications waging war had on Britain's industrial infrastructure and manpower gave an added importance to the use of diplomacy to avoid conflict, or at least to postpone it to the most economically advantageous time. This issue has obvious resonance in the period leading up to the two world wars, but took on an entirely different dimension after 1945, with the advent of the Cold War and the nuclear arms race. The uncertainty surrounding the relationship between foreign policy and defence capability is reflected in essays spanning the entire the twentieth century, and includes discussion of the priorities of the British government in foreign affairs after the collapse of communism in 1989.

Many introductions to volumes of this nature simply summarise the contents of the essays. This approach is not entirely without merit, but can discourage the reader from making a more detailed scrutiny of the work as a whole. As it is, this volume works on three levels. First, from the perspective of the essay, each offers a short, self-contained, detailed study of the operation of the Foreign Office and its impact on British foreign policy during a comparatively short chronological period. Second, the volume in its entirety enables the tracing of more general themes over a longer chronological period. Finally, the volume has a clear academic rationale that sits well within the existing historiography on the subject. This has already been touched on, but merits more detailed discussion.

It would be impossible to do justice here to the depth and range of scholarship on British foreign policy in the twentieth century. The historiographical debates surrounding the four pivotal events of the century – the origins and consequences of the two world wars, the Cold War and the collapse of communism – are all vast and closely interlinked, with studies of the role of Britain at the heart of most of them. Inevitably, given the enormous scope of the subject, the contributions to this volume represent only a fraction of the range of topics that have been studied. As indicated above, a much smaller area of historical investigation has been the history of the Foreign Office, its operation, and its impact on British foreign policy. Another feature of this subject is the overwhelming concentration on the pre-Second World War period. There has yet to be a substantial academic study of the Foreign Office in the second half of the century.[4] This is a major gap, and one, of course, partly caused by legislation covering access to government papers. The task of rectifying this situation fully will therefore fall to the next generation of historians. Nevertheless, the essay by Keith Hamilton indicates the rich veins of information that have survived and the potential for a monograph study of the subject. It is also telling that Wilton Park, established after the Second World War – and which now owes its existence to the Foreign Office – has been the subject of a detailed history, discussed here by Richard Langhorne, but its 'parent' body in Whitehall has not.[5]

The history of the Foreign Office before the Second World War has been dominated, amongst others, by the work of Zara Steiner, Valerie Cromwell and Michael Dockrill.[6] They describe a dichotomous situation, where the influence of the Foreign Office as the primary driving force behind British foreign policy was systematically eroded through the impact of government ministers and the contingencies of modern warfare and diplomacy, yet produced civil servants and diplomats whose professionalism and knowledge of foreign affairs was considerably in excess of that which had existed at the end of the nineteenth century. Part of that process, as Thomas Otte's essay illustrates, was borne out of a desire within the Foreign Office itself to modernise and formalise its procedures, but most of the changes in working practices and in the selection of staff were imposed by the need to react to external pressures, either from within Whitehall or international events. Indeed, the 1905 Hardinge reforms chronicled by Otte here and in Steiner's classic study, *The Foreign Office*, represent a rare occasion when a wide-ranging programme of change was instigated from within the Foreign Office. Hence the history of the modernisation of the working practices of the Foreign Office and Diplomatic Service is dominated by the feelings of resentment and bewilderment of those who had to endure the changes. Even those who more readily embraced change, such as Alyson Bailes and Sir Alan Campbell, whose reminiscences are included here, expressed astonishment at their speed during the final thirty years of the twentieth century. It would, of course, be nonsense to suggest that bureaucratic conservatism was the preserve of the Foreign Office. As Peter Hennessy has shown, there were plenty of other examples within Whitehall during this period.[7] But what makes the position of the Foreign Office of particular interest is that of all the departments of government, it was this institution's *raison d'être* that underwent the greatest change in the twentieth century.

There are some important consistencies, but these are relatively few in number. The role of the political head of the Foreign Office, the Foreign Secretary, has at least as much significance at the beginning of the twenty-first century as it did at the start of the twentieth. The post was, and remains, one worthy of senior Cabinet rank, although the social background of the incumbent has changed from that of the aristocracy at the beginning of the century to a mixture of lower and upper middle-class by the century's end. This trend is also true of other Cabinet positions, including that of Prime Minister, and reflects the impact of the massive socio-economic changes of the century that removed many of the class barriers to professional advancement that had hitherto been in place. Nevertheless, political convention still has it that the post of Foreign Secretary is a grooming stage in the careers of those marked out for the premiership, although in fact the evidence does not bear this out. Of the thirty-three holders of the post in the twentieth century, ironically, only a small percentage went on to become Prime Minister. Exceptions include Anthony Eden, Alec Douglas-Home and John Major. Arthur Balfour is in the unique category of being a former Prime Minister who later became Foreign Secretary, again indicating the importance accorded to the post. There were a number who aspired to be Prime Minister but who were defeated by circumstance. In this category, one would include George Curzon, Austen Chamberlain and Douglas Hurd, among others. The principal change in the role of Foreign Secretary in the twentieth century has been an expansion in the volume and range of tasks that the office holder is expected to perform. Among the causes of this have been the blurring of the demarcation between the work of the Foreign and Colonial Office, particularly after the First World War, heightened after 1945 and formalised in the late 1960s with the creation of a single Foreign and Commonwealth Office (FCO), British membership of bodies such as the European Union and NATO and the electronic information revolution in the last fifteen years. These are issues highlighted by all of the essays, but especially those by Gaynor Johnson, Alan Sharp, Kevin Ruane and James Ellison, Alyson Bailes, Sir Alan Campbell and Sean Greenwood. These changes have a number of implications for the international historian. While the wealth of information generated is now unprecedented and will enrich the study of the operation of the Foreign Office and British foreign policy in the fullness of time, the situation is not entirely unproblematic. As Zara Steiner points out here, any reliance by the FCO on less permanent means of communication such as e-mail and other forms of electronic messaging as a substitute for the minute sheet on which, in times past, mandarins recorded their views, will have a significant impact on the way in which future generations write the history of foreign policy.

However, those seeking continuity in the operation of government should not look to the political head of department but to the civil service. One of the most neglected topics of historical investigation is the role of the departmental head of the civil service, the Permanent Under-Secretary (PUS). In the twentieth century, the Foreign Office had more than its share of able and colourful characters who filled this role and who shaped the way in which the Office ran, its approach to diplomacy, its impact on foreign policy and relationships with other departments, secretaries of state and prime ministers. Yet there is no single study of either the role of the Foreign Secretary or the Permanent Under-Secretary in twentieth century British foreign policy. Inevitably the picture of the former is more complete through biographies and detailed studies of foreign policy problems than the picture of the latter. The only PUS of the twentieth century about which a substantial amount has been written is Robert Vansittart, who held the post between 1930 and 1937. Interest in his period as head of the Foreign Office civil service continues unabated and is reflected in Brian McKercher's essay in this volume. Although McKercher is careful to trace the influences of his predecessors on Vansittart's attitudes towards diplomacy, in general historians' interest has stemmed more from a fascination with Neville Chamberlain and the appeasement of Hitler than from an interest in the role of PUS.[8] Vansittart was also much more of a self-publicist than other PUSs.[9] Although their impact on the operation of the Foreign Office in the long term as well as the short term was arguably greater than that of Vansittart, both Hardinge and Eyre Crowe have only one biographer each.[10] Most of the other PUSs have been accorded little more than a brief mention by international historians.[11]

The significance of the continuity provided by the Foreign Office PUS and other senior officials can be seen in the wider context of British foreign policy in the twentieth century. As indicated above, much has been written about the decline of British influence in world affairs, and this is one of the most important themes in international history. While it would be absurd to suggest that Britain's status in world events was the same at the end of the century as it was at the start, all the essays in this volume demonstrate that the Foreign Office's general approach to Britain's role in international affairs did not change fundamentally in the course of the century. The cautious approach towards large-scale British involvement in European affairs implicit in the words of Harold Wilson and of diplomats such as Gladwyn Jebb about entry into the Common Market in the 1960s, discussed in Sean Greenwood's essay, would have been recognisable to Curzon as Foreign Secretary (1919–23), and to a range of PUSs, especially Eyre Crowe (1920–25) and William Tyrrell (1925–28). Lord Gladwyn later became convinced of the merits of membership of the Common Market, albeit primarily because of the advantages it offered to British trade; he was not a federalist. Throughout the twentieth century, successive British governments have sought ways of avoiding making concrete offers of financial or military support to European neighbours under threat, to the Empire and later to the Commonwealth. The strategy has always been one of strictly limited involvement. Most concessions to this have been made grudgingly and often only when few alternatives existed or the prospect of war appeared inevitable. The stormy history of the *Entente Cordiale* provides an example of this.[12] The haggling that has taken place in Brussels and elsewhere about the terms under which the British government will sign European Union treaties in the last thirty years is also part of this mindset and appears to be set to continue. It is tempting to ask whether it is appropriate or advisable for Britain to adopt a similar strategy when the climate of international affairs has changed so radically over the last century. Suggestions could be made about failing to move with the times. However, that would be to miss the point. The strategy of limited involvement has always been based on a general assessment of where Britain's vested interests lie, and that has changed little in the last hundred years. While the international status that the empire once gave Britain may have changed, the Commonwealth still exists, and British governments still have to balance commitment to that with relations with other states.

The theme of readjustment of status is central to Britain's relationship with the United States in the twentieth century. A number of essays comment on this long and frequently painful process, and it forms the basis of the contribution by Ruane and Ellison. As they suggest, it is tempting to regard the 'special relationship' forged by Margaret Thatcher and Ronald Reagan in the 1980s, and the close partnership during the recent Second Gulf War, as a general indicator of a cordial bond between Britain and the United States. Although by no means as rocky as relations with Europe, the Anglo-American relationship was fraught with tensions, particularly in the first half of the twentieth century, over issues concerning American entry into the two world wars, and the economic and diplomatic consequences of peacemaking after the First World War. But there were wider diplomatic reasons for this tension. The principal cause was that the first two decades of the century saw the United States overtake Britain as the world's most economically powerful state. The economic arrangements that were necessary between the Allies during the First World War confirmed that situation. In the remainder of the century, the gap between the two countries in terms of their power on the world stage steadily widened. As one of only two of the world's superpowers, the United States was able to influence the way in which international diplomacy was conducted in a way that less militarily and economically powerful nations such as Britain were not. And the approach adopted by the United States was very similar to that exercised by Britain in the nineteenth century – balance of power diplomacy. This method of neutralising the threat to international security lingered on in the minds of Foreign Office officials as the preferred basis for British foreign policy well into the twentieth century. But by the middle of the century, Britain lacked the necessary resources to be regarded as an important player in the adoption of this type of strategy, and, unlike the United States, had become embroiled in European issues that had only peripheral importance to maintaining status as a Great Power. In this respect, it is important to compare American involvement in European affairs after 1945, where the advent of the Cold War meant that Europe became of strategic importance to the United States and Britain was relegated to the role of an ally. Ruane and Ellison demonstrate how the British government rationalised the reversal of roles in international affairs between Britain and the United States in the 1950s by 'encouraging' its more powerful ally to act in Britain's best interests. Some initiatives were more successful than others, but the psychology behind the strategy is interesting: the assumption that the Foreign Office was better able to read and offer advice on the international situation than its counterpart in Washington. What Britain lacked in military and economic power was significantly counterbalanced within the relationship with the United States by experience, knowledge and insight.

The final theme that can be identified is the Foreign Office's reactions to the changing patterns of diplomatic interaction between states. Mention has already been made of British fondness for balance of power diplomacy. Nevertheless, it would be misleading to suggest that the only reason why foreign secretaries held such store by it was through a romantic affection for the days when Britain had been the world's dominant power. Few in the Foreign Office could entertain any other method of conducting diplomacy. Although the alliance system was regarded by the peacemakers of 1919 as an important cause of the war, balance of power diplomacy had given Europe a period of more-or-less unbroken peace for almost a century since 1815. Many such as Crowe believed that war had broken out in 1914 because the system had been undermined by Germany. Once the German threat had been eliminated, there was little reason to believe that equilibrium could not be restored to the international order. These are issues that form the core of the essays by Gaynor Johnson and Alan Sharp. As is well known, the Prime Minister, Lloyd George, had other ideas about the conduct of diplomacy, preferring to refer differences between states to the arbitration of international bodies such as the League of Nations or specially convened international conferences. The interwar period as a whole saw concerted efforts to wrest the initiative in the conduct of British foreign policy away from prime ministerial or inter-departmental interference and return the task to the Foreign Office. But at the heart of this process was the belief that maintaining the balance of power remained the optimum method of conducting diplomacy.

It could be claimed, however, that the great era of balance of power diplomacy in the twentieth century was in the half century that followed the Second World War, because of the increasingly apocalyptic implications should war break out. But this was only the policy of choice when the British government was in a position to play an instrumental role in brokering where the balance of power lay. As indicated above, this was not possible because of the rise of the superpowers, the United States and the Soviet Union. Nor did Britain have a natural affinity with the growing economic and political closeness of recent enemies, Germany and France, fostered by the Treaty of Rome of 1957. The scepticism behind the policies of Wilson and Macmillan in the 1960s, discussed by Sean Greenwood, stemmed partly from concerns about a return to 1920s-style conference diplomacy implied in the collectivist approach to problem solving within the embryonic European Union that had had such painful consequences for the Foreign Office in the early interwar period.

As indicated above, one of the rationales for the project on which this volume is based was to examine British foreign policy and diplomatic strategies from the point of view of those who have made academic study of these subjects, but also from the perspective of individuals who have 'hands on' experience of interpreting and acting on instructions from the Foreign Office in the field. As with the role of Foreign Secretary and PUS, there is no general study of the impact of ambassadors on British foreign policy in the twentieth century. In recent years, there has been a marked increase in the number of studies of individual ambassadors, but the view that they give is inevitably constricted by tight chronology and concentration on Britain's relations with just one country.[13] The essay by Peter Neville on a trio of ambassadors to Berlin in the interwar period offers a rare exception.[14] The study of ambassadorial diplomacy is important not only because it offers an opportunity to examine the impact and effect of diplomatic strategies but also to view foreign secretaries, Foreign Office officials and the British government as a whole from the perspective of a foreign power. It provides proof of the old adage that theory and practice seldom prove to be the same thing.

This was particularly true in the post-1945 period where, as Alyson Bailes argues in the present volume and many of her colleagues have illustrated in their memoirs, the role of ambassador has changed beyond recognition, especially in the last thirty years.[15] Long gone are the days when an ambassadorial appointment depended on social connection, perhaps friendship with the Foreign Secretary or Prime Minister of the day, or on strict adherence to a Diplomatic Service pecking order. Although her essay is not entirely about the role of women in diplomacy and their appointment as ambassadors, Bailes does suggest that it is they rather than their male counterparts who have more readily embraced the speed and nature of the changes in diplomatic practice and in international affairs. Female diplomats of any rank, and certainly ones occupying senior diplomatic positions, would have been unthinkable at the start of the twentieth century. And while their number had considerably increased by the end of the century, senior female Foreign Office officials and diplomats continued to make up a disproportionately small percentage of FCO and Diplomatic Service personnel. There is scope for research as to why that has been the case and of the women who have proved to be the exception.[16]

The analyses of the development and role of the Foreign Office in the conduct of British foreign policy in the twentieth century contained within this volume not only demonstrate the importance of the subjects to the study of international history, but illustrate the considerable potential for wider research of the individual dimensions of the foreign policy-making process away from their country-specific applications. However, to assess changes in the role of Foreign Secretary, the office of PUS and the post of ambassador during the last century would be a massive task. It is hoped that these essays provide at least a partial map for this process.

NOTES

1. H. Nicolson, *Diplomacy* (London: Oxford University Press, 1963), pp.3–4.
2. Notable exceptions include: Z.S. Steiner, *The Foreign Office and Foreign Policy, 1898–1914* (Cambridge: Cambridge University Press, 1969); R.A. Jones, *The British Diplomatic Service, 1815–1914* (Gerrards Cross: Smythe, 1983); A. Bosco and C. Navari (eds.), *Chatham House and British Foreign Policy 1919–1945: The Royal Institute of International Affairs in the Inter-War Period* (London: Lothian Foundation Press, 1994); R. Bullen (ed.), *The Foreign Office, 1782–1982* (Frederick, MD: University Publications of America, 1984); R. Warman, 'The Erosion of Foreign Office Influence in the Making of Foreign Policy, 1916–1918', *The Historical Journal*, 15/1 (1972), pp.133–59; E. Maisel, *The Foreign Office and Foreign Policy, 1919–1926* (Brighton: Sussex University Press, 1994); E. Goldstein, *Winning the Peace: British Diplomatic Strategy, Peace Planning, and the Paris Peace Conference, 1916–1920* (Oxford: Clarendon Press, 1991); C. Larner, 'The Amalgamation of the Diplomatic Service with the Foreign Office', *Journal of Contemporary History*, 7/1–2 (1972), pp.107–26; A. Sharp, 'The Foreign Office in Eclipse, 1919–1922', *History*, 61/2 (1976), pp.198–218.
3. One of the most influential being P. Kennedy, *The Realities Behind Diplomacy: Background Influences on British External Policy 1865–1980* (London: Fontana, 1981); P. Kennedy, *The Rise and Fall of the Great Powers: Economic Change and Military Conflict from 1500–2000* (New York: Random House, 1987).
4. A partial exception is J. Connell, *The 'Office': A Study of British Foreign Policy and its Makers, 1919–1951* (London: Allan Wingate, 1958). However, important work on Colonial and Foreign Office policy towards the Empire and the Commonwealth has been done by Lorna Lloyd. See L. Lloyd, '"What's in a Name?" The Curious Tale of the Office of High Commissioner', *Diplomacy and Statecraft*, 11/1 (2000), pp.47–78; L. Lloyd, '"Us and Them": The Changing Nature of Commonwealth Diplomacy, 1880–1973', *Commonwealth and Comparative Politics*, 39/3 (2001), pp.9–30. Also J. Zametica (ed.), *British Officials and British Foreign Policy 1945–1950* (Leicester: Leicester University Press, 1990); N. Henderson, *The Private Office Revisited: A Personal Account of Life in the Private Office of Five Secretaries of State for Foreign Affairs, and an Inside View of that Office and of Subsequent Ministers seen in Recent Times* (London: Profile, 2001); R. Dudley Edwards, *True Brits: Inside the Foreign Office* (London: BBC books, 1994).
5. R. Mayne, *In Victory, Magnanimity, In Peace, Goodwill: A History of Wilton Park* (London: Whitehall History Publishing in association with Frank Cass, 2003).
6. Z.S. Steiner, *The Foreign Office*; V. Cromwell and Z.S. Steiner, 'The Foreign Office before 1914: A Study in Resistance', in G. Sutherland (ed.), *Studies in the Growth of Nineteenth-Century Government* (London: Routledge, 1972); Z.S. Steiner and M.L. Dockrill, 'The Foreign Office and the Paris Peace Conference of 1919', *International History Review*, 2/2 (1980), pp.55–86; Z. S. Steiner, 'Elitism and Foreign Policy: The Foreign Office before

the Great War', in B.J.C. McKercher and D.J. Moss (eds.), *Shadow and Substance in British Foreign Policy, 1895–1939: Memorial Essays Honouring C.J. Lowe* (Edmonton: University of Alberta Press, 1984). Other important studies include E. Goldstein, *Winning the Peace*.

7. P. Hennessy, *Whitehall* (London: Secker and Warburg, 1989).

8. I. Colvin, *Vansittart in Office* (London: Gollancz, 1965); N. Rose, *Vansittart: Portrait of a Diplomat* (London: Heinemann, 1977); M. Roi, *Alternative to Appeasement: Sir Robert Vansittart and Alliance Diplomacy, 1934–1937* (Westport, CT: Praeger, 1997); A.L. Goldman, 'Sir Robert Vansittart's Search for Italian Cooperation against Hitler, 1933–1936', *Journal of Contemporary History*, 9/2 (1974), pp.93–130; B.J.C. McKercher, 'The Last Old Diplomat: Sir Robert Vansittart and the Verities of British Foreign Policy, 1903–1930', *Diplomacy and Statecraft*, 6/1 (1995), pp.1–38; C. Morrisey and M.A. Ramsay, '"Giving a Lead in the Right Direction": Sir Robert Vansittart and the Defence Requirements Sub-Committee', *Diplomacy and Statecraft*, 6/3 (1995), pp.39–60; S. Bourette-Knowles, 'The Global Micawber: Sir Robert Vansittart, the Treasury and the Global Balance of Power 1933–1935', *Diplomacy and Statecraft*, 6/1 (1995), pp.91–121; M. Roi, 'From the Stresa Front to the Triple Entente: Sir Robert Vansittart, the Abyssinian Crisis, and the Containment of Germany', *Diplomacy and Statecraft*, 6/3 (1995), pp.61–90.

9. R. Vansittart, *Mist Procession* (London: Hutchinson, 1958).

10. S. Crowe and E.T. Corp, *Our Ablest Public Servant: Sir Eyre Crowe, GCB, GCMG, KCB, KCMG, 1864–1925* (Braunton: Merlin, 1993), although S.E. Crowe, 'Sir Eyre Crowe and the Locarno Pact', *The English Historical Review*, 87/1 (1972), pp.49–72, is more balanced; B.C. Busch, *Hardinge of Penshurst: A Study in the Old Diplomacy* (Hamden, CT: Archon, 1980).

11. An important exception being E.T. Corp, 'Sir William Tyrrell: The *Eminence Grise* of the British Foreign Office', *The Historical Journal*, 25/4 (1982), pp.697–708.

12. P.M.H. Bell, *France and Britain 1900–1940: Entente and Estrangement* (London: Longman, 1996); P.M.H. Bell, *France and Britain 1940–1990: The Long Separation* (London: Longman, 1997).

13. See M. Gilbert, *Sir Horace Rumbold: Portrait of A Diplomat* (London: Heinemann), 1973; P. Neville, *Appeasing Hitler. The Diplomacy of Sir Nevile Henderson 1937–9* (Basingstoke; Palgrave Macmillan, 2000); G. Johnson, *The Berlin Embassy of Lord D'Abernon, 1920–1926* (Basingstoke: Palgrave Macmillan, 2002); G. Protheroe, 'Sir George Clerk and the Struggle for British Influence in Central Europe, 1919–26', *Diplomacy and Statecraft*, 12/2 (2001), pp.39–64, and his forthcoming biography of Clerk, to be published by Taylor & Francis Diplomats Series, 2004; K. Urbach, *Bismarck's Favourite Englishman: Lord Odo Russell's Mission to Berlin* (London: IB Tauris, 1999); K. Hamilton, *Bertie of Thame: Edwardian Ambassador* (Woodbridge: Royal Historical Society, 1990); D. Gillies, *Radical Diplomat: The Life of Archibald Clark Kerr, Lord Inverchapel, 1882–1951* (London: IB Tauris, 1999); B. J.C. McKercher, *Esme Howard: A Diplomatic Biography* (Cambridge: Cambridge University Press, 1989).

14. Cf. B. Willson, *Friendly Relations: a Narrative of Britain's Ministers and Ambassadors to America, 1791–1930* (London: Dickson and Thompson, 1934); F.L. Ford, 'Three Observers in Berlin: Rumbold, Dodd and François-Poncet', C.E. Schorske, 'Two German Ambassadors: Dirksen and Schulenburg', F. Gilbert, 'Two British Ambassadors: Perth and Henderson', and W.W. Kaufmann, 'Two American Ambassadors: Bullitt and Kennedy', all in G.A. Craig and F. Gilbert (eds.), *The Diplomats, 1919–1939* (Princeton: Princeton University Press, 1953); W.-A. van't Padje, 'At the Heart of the Growing Anglo-Imperialist Rivalry: Two British Ambassadors in Berlin, 1884–1908', unpublished D.Phil thesis, Oxford University, 2001.

15. The already large body of diplomatic memoirs from this period include D. Scott, *Three Years as British Ambassador in South Africa* (Braamfontein: South African Institute of International Affairs, 1980); H. Brind, *Lying Abroad: Diplomatic Memoirs* (London: Radcliffe, 1999); H. Phillips, *Envoy Extraordinary: A Most Unlikely Ambassador* (London: Radcliffe, 1995); W. Hugh-Jones, *Diplomacy to Politics: By Way of the Jungle* (Spennymoor: Memoir Club, 2002); B. Burrows, *Diplomat in a Changing World* (Spennymoor: Memoir Club, 2001); R. Faber, *A Chain of Cities: Diplomacy at the End of*

Empire (London: Radcliffe, 2000); J. Reeve, *Cocktails, Crises and Cockroaches* (London: Radcliffe, 1999); I. Lucas, *A Road to Damascus: Mainly Diplomatic Memoirs from the Middle East* (London: Radcliffe, 1997); D. Owen, *Balkan Odyssey* (London: Gollancz, 1995); S. Falle, *My Lucky Life: In War, Revolution, Peace and Diplomacy* (Lewes: Book Guild, 1996); C.H. Philips, *Beyond the Ivory Tower: The Autobiography of Sir Cyril Philips* (London: Radcliffe, 1995); P. Cradock, *Experiences of China* (London: John Murray, 1994); N. Elliott, *Never Judge a Man by his Umbrella* (Wilton: Russell, 1991); F. Roberts, *Dealing with Dictators: The Destruction and Revival of Europe, 1930– 1970* (London: Weidenfeld and Nicolson, 1991); C. Parrott, *The Serpent and the Nightingale* (London: Faber, 1977); W.G. Hayter, *The Kremlin and the Embassy* (London: Hodder and Stoughton, 1966) and G. Rendel, *The Sword and the Olive: Recollections of Diplomacy and the Foreign Service, 1913–1954* (London: John Murray, 1957).

16. For example, M. West, *Catching the Bag: Who'd be a Woman Diplomat?* (Edinburgh: Pentland Press, 2000).

The Foreign and Commonwealth Office: Resistance and Adaptation to Changing Times

ZARA STEINER

The collective noun, Foreign and Commonwealth Office (FCO), is a convenient and useful shorthand that covers both the Foreign Secretary and members of the Foreign Service serving at home and abroad. In a sense, this usage represents a fiction, for the people who constitute the FCO are individuals with their own personalities, ideas and actions. They are men and women (at least since 1946) who do not always act in unison nor present a collective view. There are times when the Foreign Secretary and his officials disagree over policy or when the latter recommend alternative options, the famous 'hands', so disliked by some statesmen, which will leave some dissatisfied when the final decision is made. Ambassadors may offer advice which the Foreign Secretary ignores or home officials contradict. The diplomat abroad may act on his or her own without consultation with London. Any historical survey of the role and influence of the FCO must acknowledge this diversity which may affect both the formulation and execution of foreign policy. In the past, British historians have been fortunate in being able to trace the decision-making process. They have been assisted by the clarity of the British Cabinet structure and by the system of docketing and minuting not usually found in other European foreign ministries. Traditionally, Foreign Secretaries have controlled the conduct of British foreign affairs. They have enjoyed a position of special importance in the Cabinet, second in prestige only to the Prime Minister (and some went from one position to the other).

They have tended to stay in office longer than most of their other Cabinet colleagues and returned to the Foreign Office when their party wins an election. Only the Prime Minister or at most two or three colleagues have checked their authority. Occasionally, as in the 1930s, an inner cabinet of which the Foreign Secretary is usually a member, plays a special role in the conduct of foreign affairs. Other ministers lack both the time and interest to keep a watching brief over the daily business of the Foreign Secretary. Foreign Office officials were well aware that ministers did not read the Foreign Office documents that were sent them. It was undoubtedly true that in the past and still today, the Cabinet was the final ministerial authority on fundamental questions. It was here that the decisions to enter both the world wars, to send the task force to the Falklands in 1982 and troops to Iraq in 2003 have been taken. In the past, however, the Foreign Secretary had a fairly free hand in steering the country through foreign waters.

The second feature of the British system, the practice regularised after the introduction of the Foreign Office reforms of 1905, of minuted dispatches moving up the departmental hierarchy, has given historians a unique opportunity to trace the decision-making process within the Office. There are studies of the influence of permanent officials in the Quai d'Orsay or German foreign ministry but the process of reconstruction is far more difficult in the absence of such evidence.[1] We know a great deal about the advice given to the Foreign Secretary and who had had his ear. We can document the decisions that he actually took with or without the advice of the Office. Ernest Bevin, no great lover or reader of papers, often liked a full verbal argument and consultation with one or two senior people before resolving a problem so at times the record may be more difficult to reconstruct. He wrote out his decision, usually in red ink (the only red ink allowed in the Office) and expected his staff to carry it out. George Brown, despite the many stories about his time as Foreign Secretary, was industrious and well organised. He read the papers, took soundings, and recorded his decisions that were implemented by his staff even if they had argued against it. This was not always the case in the American Department of State; Henry Kissinger repeatedly complained of the frustrations of giving orders and discovering that they were not implemented. Going through the papers available at the National Archives (formerly the Public Record Office), albeit under the thirty-year rule, historians can trace the course of internal debate and make informed judgements about the reason for the decision taken at whatever level that this was done. The papers did not necessarily have to go to the top, and decisions on matters of secondary importance could be made by senior clerks, the Assistant Under-Secretary or the Permanent Under-Secretary without referral to the Foreign Secretary. We have come a long way since the time when the author of this essay was assured by the Foreign Office librarian, C.H. Fone,

in the 1960s that officials only carried out the policies determined by the
Foreign Secretary and had little influence over their formulation.

Developments since 1945 have complicated the process of decision-
making. Among the more recent changes, the expansion of the Prime
Minister's office as an alternative source of policy-making, the development
of the Cabinet Office's committee system as the centre of inter-departmental
co-ordination, and the communications revolution require special note. In
each case, the FCO has had to adapt itself, willingly or not, to their
consequences. Some have historical roots. There is nothing new about the role
of the Prime Minister in the making of foreign policy or about clashes between
Prime Minister and Foreign Secretaries. The case of Lloyd George and his
'Garden Suburb' is well known.[2] Differences in background and temperament
added to the difficulties of Lloyd George's relationship with Lord Curzon, the
former intent on making foreign policy himself and highly suspicious of
professional diplomats, and the latter believing that he was far more qualified
than the Prime Minister to handle Britain's foreign affairs. Despite policy
differences, some provoking one of Curzon's frequent threats to resign, it is
probably true that when it came to European questions, the two men agreed
more than they disagreed.

The most celebrated example of the 1930s was the clash between Anthony
Eden and Neville Chamberlain that led to the former's resignation in 1937.
Policy conflicts over Italy and the United States were considerably
exacerbated by Chamberlain's clear intention to take over the conduct of
diplomacy and Eden's sensitivity about maintaining his position. He was to
find Chamberlain's interventions a personal as well as a professional affront.
Over the key problem of how to handle Hitler, there were fewer differences
between the two men than recorded by Eden in his memoirs where he paints an
exaggerated picture of himself as a consistent anti-appeaser. In the post-war
period, the disagreements between Attlee and Bevin led to the former giving
way. Attlee regarded the Foreign Office's emphasis on Britain's great power
role and its traditional interests excessive given the country's serious
economic difficulties. He objected, too, to Bevin's increasingly rigid and
ideologically based anti-Soviet attitudes. At the beginning of 1947, there was
a standoff battle over the Middle East; faced with the opposition of the
Chiefs of Staff as well as the Foreign Office, Attlee stood down. For the most
part, while Prime Minister, he was content to leave the conduct of foreign
affairs in Bevin's hands. The case of Suez is yet another example not only of
Prime Ministerial control over foreign and defence policy but Eden's ability to
keep most of the Foreign Office (though not the Foreign Secretary) in
ignorance of what he was doing. The development of summit diplomacy and
the increasing importance of multinational negotiations have involved the
Prime Minister as well as the Foreign Secretary in diplomatic negotiations

which before 1914 would have been left to resident heads of missions to handle. With or without the Foreign Secretary present, Prime Minister represents the country at the negotiating table. Membership of the European Community requires the Prime Minister's presence at its most important gatherings. While the involvement of the Prime Minister in foreign negotiations is hardly new, it is argued, nevertheless, that under Margaret Thatcher, and even more clearly under Tony Blair, a more radical re-ordering of the relationship between the Prime Minister's office and the FCO has taken place. It is not at all clear whether this is due to the personalities of the incumbents and so only a temporary shift in the policy-making process or whether the state of current diplomacy will make this a more common feature of future prime ministerships. At the time that Margaret Thatcher selected Anthony Parsons, formerly Ambassador to the United Nations, and subsequently Sir Percy Craddock, another Foreign Office professional, as her personal foreign policy adviser at Number 10 Downing Street, anxious diplomats were assured that she did not intend to develop an alternative source of information and advice in her own office. The appointment of Sir Geoffrey Howe, a strong Foreign Secretary who enjoyed a close working relationship with Margaret Thatcher, confirmed this reading of her interests. Howe was opposed to any development that would give the government or the Prime Minister 'a free-standing set of advice' from 'somewhere else, somewhere out in outer space'.[3] Yet in picking able Foreign Office men as her private secretaries, Margaret Thatcher opened new channels for making her own foreign policy decisions. Charles Powell, plucked by Margaret Thatcher from the Foreign Office, wielded considerable influence both in determining what information came to Margaret Thatcher's attention and whose advice should be heeded. 'He could mark your card', one former Deputy Under-Secretary told the author. After Margaret Thatcher resigned, Powell left the Foreign Service and went into business. During the Falklands crisis, Margaret Thatcher, perhaps surprised by the extent and potential for British influence, caught the 'foreign policy bug'. Some of her interventions in foreign affairs were the natural result of Britain's membership in the European Union, but her policies were often her own and not those favoured by her Foreign Office advisers. Special briefings before European Union meetings were often nerve-racking affairs for Foreign Office officials; there was no guarantee that they affected her decisions. Her 'special relationship' with Ronald Reagan enhanced the Prime Minister's reputation on the world stage and opened possibilities for private initiatives outside the normal diplomatic channels.

It is too early to judge the consequences of the present close relationship between Britain and the United States. Critics claim that Tony Blair and his personal advisers have far surpassed Margaret Thatcher in establishing alternative sources of information in conducting foreign affairs, with the help of personal advisers. It is said that while Downing Street gets all the information that comes to the Foreign Office, the reverse seems not to be true. Blair's two senior diplomatic advisers in 2003 were Sir David Manning, ambassador-designate to Washington, and Sir Stephen Walls; each had their own staff. Manning, a senior diplomat, was in constant direct communication with Condoleezza Rice, George W. Bush's National Security Adviser. Manning often travelled with the Prime Minister when the latter went abroad. Blair's diplomatic private secretaries can anticipate going to major posts abroad. This is hardly a new practice. Robert Vansittart, home or private secretary to both Prime Ministers, Stanley Baldwin and Ramsay MacDonald, became Permanent Under-Secretary in the Foreign Office in 1930. The future ambassador may have his own line to Downing Street. While private secretary, he will have the advantage of constant contact with the Prime Minister. Rather than liaise with the FCO, they may become part of the Downing Street team. According to some sources, the present expansion of the Prime Minister's private office is deeply resented by diplomats at the Foreign Office. It was widely reported in the press that while Blair's diplomatic advisers supported the Prime Minister's Iraq policies (though there is no confirming evidence) there was considerable opposition from the FCO and from some of the European and Middle Eastern embassies. It is a sign of the contemporary situation that two of the Cabinet Office committees dealing with foreign affairs were moved into Downing Street.

While these problems may be of a transitory nature, this is hardly true of the need to adjust the Foreign Service to the multi-departmental character of diplomacy today. This has led to a number of initiatives, in part as a result of outside pressure. Diplomats are specifically recruited or trained to deal with issues that cross the domestic-foreign divide. Women and men are assigned to other government departments and outside agencies and some home civil servants have temporary appointments in the Foreign Office. The work of Peter Hennessy and the publication of the Franks Report on the Falklands crisis have shown how central the Cabinet Office and the Cabinet Secretary has become to the running of the British government and to the whole process of coordination. The Cabinet Office system of committees, ministerial, official and mixed, and the Cabinet Office secretariats that service them, provide the mechanism for inter-departmental decision-making.[4] The first Cabinet Secretary, the powerful Maurice Hankey, was only appointed in 1916, and the multiplication of Cabinet committees began during the inter-war period. It was their massive quantitative expansion after the Second World War that has led to the development of the contemporary structure. By the time Labour left office in 1951, there were some 148 standing committees and 213 *ad hoc* committees in existence. These were doing much of the work that the Cabinet no longer could handle. All post-war Prime Ministers have tried to deal with this administrative overload; only a few (Churchill, a strong Cabinet man, for one) have succeeded in slimming down the number of committees. First orally in 1979 and subsequently in a written reply to a parliamentary question in 1983, Margaret Thatcher referred to the main standing and *ad hoc* committees that operate under the general direction of the Cabinet Secretary. Of key importance for the Foreign Office is the Overseas and Defence Committee with its many sub-committees and the Intelligence and Security Committee which includes the Joint Intelligence Committee that prepares and circulates intelligence assessments from all the intelligence sources. It is in committees composed of civil servants that efforts are made to resolve differences so that ministers attending the Overseas and Defence Committee will have only to settle questions of the highest importance. The FCO has fully recognised the importance of being strongly represented in the Cabinet Office and senior officials spend a great deal of their time there. The FCO has managed to defend its turf and remains the chief co-ordinating department but there is a good deal of give and take with domestic civil servants. The outcome of committee discussions can depend on the ability of its officials to represent the views of the FCO, which claims to represent the national as distinct from departmental interests. The Cabinet no longer functions as it did before the First World War. Published ministerial diaries have shown how little time is actually spent in the Cabinet discussing foreign policy.[5] The great majority of such questions, including European Union issues, never reach the Cabinet. Some Foreign Secretaries, Lord Carrington for one, relied on written communications; he disliked bringing contentious matters to the Overseas and Defence Committee.[6] In many respects, the Cabinet Office has become the government's engine room. The author of this essay has written elsewhere about the negative consequences of the consensual style of committee decision-making in foreign affairs.[7] The emphasis on agreement and compromise does not necessarily produce the best solution but rather the one which everyone will accept. As conflicts of interest are resolved in London, delegations abroad find they have little negotiating room. This makes for consistency of policy (British delegates play the same hand in different situations) but it can also lead to rigidity when engaged in multinational bargaining. The Cabinet structure is, moreover, a closed one dominated by the civil servants; there is no or little room for a fresh breath of non-Whitehall air. For the student of foreign affairs, the shift from the Cabinet to the Cabinet Office has complicated the task of illuminating the decision-making process.

The frequent travels of Foreign Secretaries and officials, both from the Foreign Office and other domestic departments, have altered the balance between London and the missions abroad. The former, as they set out for a set of negotiations may well read the papers that have been assembled for their use or consult with those who accompany them. The resident ambassador will have a few minutes on the way from the airport, or more usefully, a longer meeting at the embassy to bring them up to date. When the Foreign Secretary leaves, it will be the embassy that will finish the job, tying up the loose ends left by the minister. It is the visitor, however, who is the chief negotiator. The technological revolution has reinforced the central role of the London offices. The new telephone-satellite based system had immensely speeded up the speed of communication. As messages and faxes fly back and forth between London and even the most distant post, the room for initiative and independent action is reduced. The ambassador may have only a few hours, while their London masters are asleep, when they are freed from the tyranny of the airwaves. All the European Union offices in the member countries are in direct communication with each other; lateral decision-making has become common. An Emergency Unit has direct lines to key departments in Whitehall and to all the relevant posts abroad; a vast improvement over the cumbersome system of communication in the past. The new system has its drawbacks. There is little time for thought; queries and answers follow in relatively short progression. A form of 'Cherokee English' had replaced the rich prose of the hand-written or typed despatches of the past. The FCO still prides itself on the drafting skills of its diplomats. It may be that the use of e-mail encourages clarity of expression and incisiveness. There are doubters. Historians wonder whether in the future they will be able to trace the decision-making process in the traditional manner. It may well be that they will have to learn to ask different questions.

Since the Second World War, all foreign ministers have had to adapt to momentous changes in the nature of diplomacy. The diplomatic map has expanded beyond recognition in terms of the number of countries involved and the subjects of multinational negotiation. The number of international organisations has also increased and many have developed their own institutional frameworks not unlike those of national governments. There have been special problems for the Foreign and Commonwealth Office. It has had to adjust to Britain's reduction in world status which has meant re-shaping an inherited diplomatic machine. Many diplomats feel that the FCO had managed this adjustment surprisingly well and that only France rivals Britain in the excellence of its diplomatic service. In 1973, Eric Clark wrote in his book *Corps Diplomatique*, 'British diplomacy has a reputation developed during the country's days as a great power. It is still highly regarded; its own diplomats, certainly, almost universally regard it as the best. British diplomats impress as being unbeatable in crisis situations. They rarely take pains to impress; boasting or displaying abilities are, somehow, not good form. Often they act and look like men born to be sleeping behind copies of *The Times* in a London club, but they seem well-informed and they are highly respected for their skills by their "opponents"'.[8] Percy Craddock, an experienced FCO official, claimed that 'We exercise disproportionate influence for a medium rank power. We come to the table with certain cards having been dealt and the skill in the game in making use of the cards and playing them as well, as forcefully, as cleverly as we can'.

These high opinions of the British Foreign Service have not been shared by all, either at home or abroad. Diplomats live in a world where their professional claims are constantly being questioned. As a result, they have been forced to take part in self-examination exercises. The reputation, adaptability and capability of the British Foreign Service have come under repeated attack in the Commons, in the press and even in government circles. The FCO has been the subject of numerous investigations. The members of the Royal Commission on the Civil Service which investigated the Foreign Office, Diplomatic and Consular Service in 1914 complained that the British Foreign Service was the second most expensive in the world and the most snobbish. They pointed out that it was recruited from too narrow a social base. There were too many peers' sons and Etonians, no non-conformists, Scots or Ulster Presbyterians and no one with radical or socialist leanings. The Diplomatic Service, an entirely separate service, was even worse, more exclusive than the Foreign Office in social background and education. Diplomats spent almost all of their professional lives abroad, moved only in restricted social circles and took little or no interest in commercial affairs. The consular service was very much the 'Cinderella service' with regard to prestige, recruitment and career structures. With but a few outstanding exceptions, consuls were rarely appointed to diplomatic posts. Nor were they invited to grace the ambassador's or minister's table even in relatively isolated posts. The commissioners concluded that the whole existing system could hardly serve the needs of a country dependent on world trade for its influence and prosperity. Many concrete recommendations were made; some were implemented in the immediate post-war period. Steps were taken to enlarge the membership of the Selection Board which was to interview candidates only after the examination which, for the first time, was to be opened at all. Examinations were made the same as for the home civil service but with special provision for foreign languages. Separate entry into the Foreign Office and Diplomatic Service was abolished and the income qualification for diplomats abolished. Plans were made to amalgamate the two services but resistance was strong on both sides and the Treasury slow and niggardly about meeting the expenses the reforms necessitated. The joint seniority list was reduced to a joint list of only second and third secretaries.

By 1930, nonetheless, only a minority of clerks and diplomats were considered non-interchangeable, a decided improvement on the pre-1914 situation. Despite the opening up of the examination system, the educational and social exclusiveness of the Service were still subject of continual public criticism. In the years 1925–29, there were nine Etonian entrants from a total of thirty-eight successful candidates. In 1932, only one successful candidate came from Eton in a group of seven recruits. In 1938, three of the eleven recruits were Etonians.[9] What was noticeable was the more varied list of public schools and the appearance of a handful of successful candidates from state grammar schools. Almost all the men (and they were only men) who entered the service between the two world wars had attended Oxford and Cambridge, but it had become very rare for anyone to sit the examination who had not been to university at all. William Strang, who rose to become Permanent Under-Secretary after the Second World War, was still seen as a somewhat exceptional recruit. He entered the Foreign Office through the special examinations held in 1919 intended to attract ex-service men to the seriously understaffed service. The son of a farmer, he had attended a country grammar school and University College, London, followed by some time in Paris preparing to do a Ph.D before the war intervened. Though he had some postings abroad, he spent, mainly by choice, most of his professional life at the Foreign Office. In the inter-war period, too, the social pool from which candidates were recruited was somewhat broadened; a higher proportion of recruits came from professional families (some were the grandsons or great grandsons of landed families) but still very few entrants came from the business classes. Quite apart from the Bolshevik moles, political views may have grown more varied.

Increasingly public criticism and a series of parliamentary questions during the 1930s finally led to the major changes introduced by the Eden reforms of 1943. Due mainly to the efforts of Sir David Scott, the pre-war head of the Consular Department, the Consular Service was brought in from the cold. As part of the general reform programme proposed in 1941, the Foreign Office, Diplomatic Service, Consular Service and commercial diplomatic service were to be made part of a single unified Foreign Service. Other reforms included provisions for broadening the field of entry and for making the terms of service more attractive. Special retirement provisions allowed staff not suited for promotion to the highest ranks of the profession to leave the service. As so often is the case, the intentions of the reformers were only partly fulfilled. Older patterns and prejudices died slowly and later enquiries, Plowden in 1963 and Duncan in 1968–69, still found differences and distinctions between types of posts and the kinds of people who filled them. Members of both committees complained of the lack of sympathy in the diplomatic establishment for the commercial requirements of a 'major power of the second order' and a misplaced emphasis among diplomats on the purely political work of the service.

Critiques of elitism continued throughout the 1970s and 1980s and are still heard today. The FCO intake has broadened. In the 1950s, only one in seven of the administrative entry (the highest level of entry) came from a state school and only one in ten had not attended Oxford or Cambridge. By the 1970s, one in two came from a state school and one in three had not attended either Oxford or Cambridge. The merger in 1968 of the Commonwealth Office with the Foreign Office created new problems (different forms of recruitment and different standards) of integration that took time to sort out, and which left a residue of ill-feeling among those transferred. In more recent decades, the battle to vary the mixture of schools and universities and to attract candidates of different backgrounds has continued as have efforts, including the sanctioning of BBC radio and television programmes, to change the public image of the FCO. Though Oxford and Cambridge still contribute a disproportionate number of successful candidates in the 'fast stream' entry for which non-social reasons are blamed, other universities are represented too. The proportions of state and independent schools vary from year to year, but as late as 1993, two-thirds of fast-stream entrants came from independent schools. Beyond a general middle-class bias (hardly different from that found in the senior ranks of the Treasury) and a tendency for some Foreign Service sons to follow in their father's footsteps, the Foreign Service is hardly the socially exclusive club of the past. Image and reality did not necessarily correspond. In a book by Ruth Dudley Edwards, *True Brits: Inside the Foreign Office*, that accompanied the television series on the Foreign Office screened in 1994, the author notes in her preface that during her travels she met 'a large number of unexpected people from unexpected backgrounds with expected accents. They came from Glasgow, Newcastle, Glamorgan and Antrim as well as the Home Counties'.[10] Subsequent chapters suggest that the mixture is richer in the so-called main stream than in the fast stream, which constitutes the top levels of the service.

The Foreign Office has conducted extensive campaigns to enlarge its net of recruitment. It has recognised the need to attract different sorts of people into the service. It needs an elite, not of breeding or wealth, but of talent. It must have men and women who are well educated, knowledgeable, flexible, independent-minded and ambitious. It also needs, and in greater number, men and women with practical intelligence and good common sense, people who, in FCO jargon, may have fewer 'policy capable' skills. The problem for selectors is to identify the numbers and kinds of recruits that are required and to encourage transfers between streams (the word streaming has been dropped but the practice remains) when appropriate. In a service where the number of top posts is limited and where promotion blockage in middle levels is not uncommon, the tendency towards bureaucratic conservatism is strong. The FCO insists that the Foreign Service requires different talents from those found in the home civil service. The Canadian experiment with a single service is now used to buttress its claims. It is not without significance, however, that the major departmental growth at King Charles Street has been in the functional and administrative departments. The need for specialist skills not unlike those found in the home civil service has become obvious. The FCO rarely has the reserves necessary to provide the specialist training required, both in London and abroad, and so depends on using its 'main stream' to fill these positions. Diplomats insist, however, that representing Britain abroad demands different talents than those found in the home civil service. It is true that the Foreign Office attracts men and women who have read a far wider variety of subjects at university that their predecessors. When the author asked for a breakdown some years ago, it was amusing to find that the two most successful candidates had read theology. Post-entry training in languages and area studies has been successfully implemented; parallel programmes in other specialised fields seems more difficult to arrange. Some specialists enter at mid-career levels and FCO people have been encouraged (when they can be spared) to serve in other government departments and non-official agencies, dealing with a variety of subjects such as defence, finance, commerce and ecology, which are all subjects of international negotiations.

Informed critics of the service still complain that though recruitment procedures have been improved, the Foreign Office ethos has scarcely changed. Once entering the Foreign Service, a process of acculturalisation takes place. There is a FCO style which entrants, whatever their backgrounds, appear to acquire. Pride in Britain's political institutions and past performance often translates into that assumption of superiority that so annoys some domestic civil servants and many foreigners. Only the French diplomatic service provokes similar reactions, not least among their British counterparts. The pressure of the diplomatic environment is strong. The mission heads of today (apart from the women) are not vastly different from those of a previous generation. The very existence of an interchangeable, hierarchical and closed career service promotes a kind of 'group think'. Service abroad rubs off the rough edges and encourages conformity. Diplomats are not expected to rock the boat. Some critics claim that in inter-departmental committees, you know what the Foreign Office representative is going to say before he or she speaks. Specialist language training and regional postings can generate forms of 'localitis' though the FCO is acutely aware of the danger. Sir David Gore Booth, expecting to build on his 'O' Level in Russian, was sent to the Middle East Centre for Arab Studies (MECAS), located in a village near Beirut. He was hardly the only one who, in the course of his training, became part of a select cadre. Beyond the identifying school tie, the nicknames and reunions (some ten years after the school was disbanded) the members of the 'Camel Corps' developed a distinctive view of Middle Eastern politics. An Arabist would try, according to Gore-Booth, 'to put himself into the mindset of the Arabs and not to become an Arab or behave like one but to be able to predict or judge how Arabs would react in certain circumstances'.[11] It is too easy to assume that these men, many of whom went on to become ambassadors in the Middle East or went to senior positions in the FCO, thought alike, particularly as their countries of assignment had different points of view but they were marked by their common experiences. A Jak cartoon from the time of the 1973 war between Egypt and Israel which featured Sir Alec Douglas-Home and a collection of officials, dressed in Arab robes, pausing to look at a small perplexed colleague in a suit and bowler hat was not very far from its target. The caption ran, 'Oh come on, Cohen. Everyone at the Foreign Office dresses like this these days'. MECAS no longer exists; training is in London and Cairo and the influence of the Middle Easterners has diminished. Shifts in Foreign Office attitudes take place but they do so slowly. They may result from changes in political leadership, from generational differences, and from practical experience. A study of attitudes towards the European Union would be highly welcome. Some departments become identified with particular styles or policies, though the rotational system to some degree counteracts this tendency. Those who serve in international bodies (and there is considerable pressure to lengthen their service) can fall victim to the organisational virus. Like those who served in Geneva during the inter-war period, they can begin to look through institutionally tinted glass, or the reverse.

It was not only its social and educational exclusiveness that condemned the FCO to criticism. One of the most difficult challenges that the service faced resulted from the changing public attitude towards the role of women and the increasing pressure from outside the Foreign Office for their entry into the Foreign Service. The first 'lady typewriter' was only introduced into the office of the Foreign Secretary's Private Secretary in 1889. By 1914 Mrs Fulcher had a department of eleven. No one at that time thought it reasonable to employ women in other capacities ('the bag work in the registry would be too tough for a girl'). It was after the Great War and following wartime experiences with temporary staff in 1921 that women were first engaged on a permanent basis as clerical and executive officers. The resistance to female entry into the political establishment was strong and lasting. As late as 1941, Anthony Eden, no great enthusiast for female recruitment, was able to postpone the question of women's entry until the end of the war. Despite a well-timed question from Lady Astor when Eden first declared his intention of introducing Foreign Office reforms and an avalanche of representations from various women's groups, the Foreign Secretary promised only that a committee would review the question when the war ended. Practical considerations forced Eden to agree to the temporary appointment of women to the Foreign Office during wartime 'if no suitable male candidate could be found'. Contrary to the hopes of some in the Foreign Office, the women stayed the course and made a success of the wartime experiment.

Further resistance proved impossible. Women were allowed to enter the Foreign Service in 1946 but under special rules. Their number was limited to ten per cent of the total intake, they were to be paid twenty per cent less than men doing the same job and they had to resign when they married. The story provides rich pickings for the stand-up comic. Equal pay was conceded in 1955 (fully implemented only in 1961) and, since almost half the women who had entered the service resigned, the marriage bar was rescinded in 1972. Change has come if slowly. Not only are women entering the FCO top stream in greater numbers but they are advancing to become Heads of Posts and Heads of Mission. The number of women in the Senior Management Staff (the equivalent of the old fast stream) has increased from 24 (5.2 per cent) in April 1995 to 59 (12.5 per cent) in April 2003. In January 1998, there were eleven female Heads of Post; in 2003 there were twenty. Among ambassadors and high commissioners, there were three in 1994 and fourteen in April 2003. The figures tell only part of the story. Women still have not been given the top diplomatic jobs (Paula Neville Jones, an acknowledged high flier, turned down Bonn because she felt that she deserved Paris, symbolically still the plum of the service) as a breakdown of last year's postings suggest.[12] It cannot be too long, however, given appointments made elsewhere, before a woman will get a major embassy or its equivalent. There are problems. Many of the women in senior grades are unmarried. Twin careers in the Diplomatic Service are almost impossible to arrange and even joint postings are difficult. Some, admittedly a minority, claim that the Foreign Office still resembles an all-male boarding school which had taken in a handful of girls in the sixth form, a larger number in the first form, and a handful of token teachers. To be recruited into the fast stream, women have to be quite tough. Humour and physical courage are basic requirements. Life as an ambassador in Mozambique or in Lebanon (Maeve Fort served as ambassador in both) is not for the timid. As in other professions too, there can be a high degree of wastage. There will always be special factors that contribute to the relative shortage of women in the senior grades that have little to do with male attitudes. In a sense, the more pressing problem for personnel offices, because of the number of people involved, is the position of spouses, still mainly wives. Highly educated wives who have to give up careers of their own to follow their husbands find the restricted life in some missions abroad unbelievably boring. Many are unsettled by the prospects of sending children off to boarding school in the time-honoured way. While acknowledging that wives cannot be treated in the same manner as their predecessors (though there were rebels in the past), solutions to some of these problems have proved elusive. Almost all foreign services face the same difficulties; they are one of the major sources of mid-career discontent and may account for the high drop-out rate reported by some personnel chiefs. Domestic problems are an additional reason (for there are many) why many diplomats, despite the attractions of service abroad, prefer to be in London. Male spouses too, pose difficulties; 'fortunately', one informer commented, 'they are still rather rare'.

Though not unconnected with the problems of recruitment, most post-1945 investigating committees have concentrated on the need to adapt the Foreign Office to the needs of a country of the second rank. It was unfortunate that this adaptation had to take place when there had been a massive expansion of the diplomatic map. Expectations of savings led to drives for economy and extensive cuts in the diplomatic budget. Both the Plowden Committee on Representational Service Overseas (1962) and the Duncan Review Committee on Overseas Representation (1968–69) sought to reshape the Foreign Office in accordance with Britain's reduced status without any outlay of funds.[13] The Duncan enquiry was aimed specifically at the need to find economies in overseas representation. It recommended a two-tier diplomatic operation; an Area of Concentration (Europe and North America) and an Outer Area where savings in personnel and resources could be made. The proposal was a non-starter. Members of both enquiries criticised the continued political bias of the political establishment. Plowden insisted that commercial work 'must be regarded as a first charge in the resources of the overseas service' and expressed the hope that every ambassador and high commissioner in the future would have served in a commercial capacity. These injunctions were not without effect. In the 1970s, commercial postings became the 'flavour of the month' for the high fliers. The impulse died some years later and when stung by the failure of its embassy in Iran to predict the downfall of the Shah, the FCO stressed that the collection and analysis of political information should take pride of place in the work of most embassies. More recently, the pendulum had again swung again in the commercial direction. It was expected in the 1990s that most fast-streamers would spend some time doing commercial work, and that people who had spent much of their careers in commercial posts could move to the top diplomatic positions. It is now rare for any ambassador not to have had some experience in handling economic and commercial issues. Heads of missions, even in large embassies with separate commercial sections, fulfil a variety of functions. Sir Brian Fall, the Ambassador to Moscow in 1993, commented: 'I hate it when I have to fill in the form once a year, where I have to say how much political work, how much information work, how much economic work, how much commercial work I do, because this [job] has been a sort of wonderful mixture of all four'.[14] There is still no shortage of criticism about the commercial competence (or incompetence) of British diplomats. It should be said that the same complaints are made abroad of Foreign Services that are held up to the FCO as role models.

A new offensive in these same directions was launched by the Central Policy Review Staff in 1977. The CPRS, which had previously dealt exclusively with domestic policy, reported that the heart of Britain's external relations was economic in character and that its institutional machinery should be organised to meet this pressing need. The report still brings gasps of indignation from old-timers, for the investigators recommended that the Diplomatic Service should lose its separate identity and be merged into a Foreign Service group which would include members of the home civil service, military and other government agencies. Claiming that reporting, representational and negotiating skills were vastly overrated, the staff concluded that 'the work was done to an unjustifiably high standard. This is particularly true of the Diplomatic Service which, in our view, tends to err on the side of perfectionism in work whose importance is not always commensurate with the human and material resources devoted to it'.[15] Once the storm had passed and the incumbents of the FCO and its outside supporters had buried the possibility of extinction, many of the other CPRS recommendations were adopted, partly because of the pressure to economise but also because some were based on accurate observations of the foreign policy scene. Many domestic departments and agencies are involved in overseas policy and steps had to be taken to improve inter-departmental communication and coordination both in London and abroad. Specialisation in functional as distinct from linguistic skills had become essential if the diplomats were to perform effectively in the expanded diplomatic arena. The FCO has recognised the need to adapt itself to the new situation, particularly to the need to work closely with other departments on a whole range of foreign policy issues. The senior staff of the permanent delegation to the European Union, for instance, is a mixed one with almost half its members coming from home departments. In London, too, strong ties have been forged between the functional departments and other government departments both formally and informally. The Cabinet Office committee structure encourages such encounters. Not only have the functional departments multiplied in number but in some cases they have come to dwarf the old geographical departments which formerly constituted the heart of the FCO. The whole issue of specialisation is still one that provokes debate as it will continue to do in the future given the nature of contemporary diplomacy. The FCO cannot claim to speak for the national interest unless it can claim a degree of competence in the non-political (even the term 'political' has expanded in meaning) areas of overseas policies. The CPRS critique of the excessive professionalism of the Diplomatic Service has not gone unnoticed. More than one FCO official has complained that 'we still have too many Rolls Royces doing the work of Fords'.[16] It is one of the perennial problems of the Service.

The Plowden, Duncan and CPRS investigators each noted that the FCO finds it difficult to identify the longer trends in international affairs or to define and order its policy objectives. The Policy Planning Staff, an outgrowth of the Planning Staff created in 1964, was intended to strengthen the Foreign Office's capacity for forward planning. It has gained in prestige and attracts many of the most imaginative and creative men and women in the service. The staff has access to the Permanent Under-Secretary and Deputy Under-Secretaries, the latter the real work horses of the FCO, but a great deal of its influence must be exerted informally which can be a hit-and-miss proposition. Its members, moreover, have been swamped by demands for background papers on current questions and for material for ministerial speeches. The need for adequate planning resources, reinforced by membership in the European Union, is obvious, yet there is still a general feeling in the FCO that 'planning', in the usual sense of the word, is of restricted usefulness in international affairs and that forecasting, in order to be at all creditable, must be limited in time (five years appears to be the accepted limit). Other departments engaged in overseas operations, for instance the defence services, must project their future requirements over longer spans of time.

The FCO needs to make its contribution to the government's middle and longer range strategic planning. The unwillingness to anticipate international developments or to provide a coherent and realistic set of national objectives had reinforced a tendency to allow policies to evolve from the cumulative effect of decisions reached by what the late James Cable called 'conditioned reflex'. Few Foreign Secretaries are prepared to think about the intellectual foundations upon which their policies are founded. Such an analytic approach would go against the whole pragmatic tradition of British diplomacy. Not only is there a deep distrust of theory and system among FCO officials but also a fondness for customary ways of doing things and for the cult of common sense. Too often in the past, British diplomacy has been reactive rather than innovative.

The FCO is a natural target for criticism, above all for economising politicians. Though a relatively inexpensive department, few outsiders will sound the alarm bells when cuts are made. The FCO cannot boast of its achievements; its failures are far more newsworthy. It is a cumbersome machine but the shortage of funds only reinforces its rigidity and reluctance to experiment. There will be further cuts and amalgamation of posts; entertainment allowances will continue to be severely scrutinised. In the mid 1970s, the ambassador in Algeria unilaterally cut his embassy complement by two-thirds. He was hardly loved in London for his actions but it saved a lot of money. Such savings represent drops in the bucket and are often more expensive in loss of capability than they are worth. In the end, the survival of the FCO in its present form will depend on its success in convincing its political masters that it is an increasingly efficient bureaucracy that is giving value for money.

Like the edifice in which, after much discussion, it continues to be housed, the FCO presents an image of a traditional organisation that has failed to move with the times. The case can be made that the reality is different. As another contributor to this collection of essays shows, the re-modelling of the interior of Sir Gilbert Scott's Venetian palace has been surprisingly successful and has cost less than the building of a far more functional (and ugly) office building. The building still has its drawbacks as a place in which to work, and the Locarno reception rooms so lovingly restored may strike visitors as symbolic of Britain's unfortunate love affair with its Victorian past. Is it not a hopeful sign that on the beautiful desk of one of the restored offices there sits a twenty-first century computer alongside a copy of *Private Eye*?

NOTES

1. See, for example, G. Dethan, 'The Ministry of Foreign Affairs since the Nineteenth Century' and K. Doβ, 'The History of the German Foreign Office' in Z. Steiner (ed.), *The Times Survey of Foreign Ministries of the World* (London: Times Books, 1982).
2. K.O. Morgan, *Consensus and Disunity: the Lloyd George Coalition, 1918–1922* (Oxford: Oxford University Press, 1982), pp.17, 112, 260.
3. Quoted in S. Jenkins and A. Sloman, *With Respect, Ambassador: An Inquiry into the Foreign Office* (London: BBC books, 1985), p.117.
4. P. Hennessy, 'The Quality of Cabinet Government in Britain', *Policy Studies*, 6/2 (1985), pp.47–61, is a seminal article on the subject; Cmd 8787, *Falklands Islands Review*, Report of a Committee of Privy Counsellors, (London: HMSO, 1983).
5. See, for example, B. Castle, *The Castle Diaries, 1974–1978* (London: Weidenfeld & Nicolson, 1980).
6. Hennessy, 'Quality of Cabinet Government', p.37.
7. Z. Steiner, 'Decision-making in American and British Foreign Policy: An Open and Shut Case', *Review of International Studies*, 13/2 (1987), p.6.
8. E. Clark, *Corps Diplomatique* (London: Allen Lane, 1973), p.21.
9. V. Cromwell, 'The United Kingdom', in Steiner (ed.), *The Times Survey of Foreign Ministers of the World*, p.559.
10. R. Dudley Edwards, *True Brits: Inside the Foreign Office* (London: BBC Books, 1994), p.10.
11. Quoted in Edwards, *True Brits*, p.120.
12.

Women Heads of Post	
Consul General	Chongqing
Consul General	Ekaterinburg
Ambassador	Holy See (Vatican)
Ambassador	Kigali
Consul General	Lille
Ambassador	Lisbon
Ambassador	Mexico City
Consul General	Montreal
Ambassador	Oslo

– CONTINUED

Women Heads of Post	
Ambassador	Prague
High Commissioner	Pretoria
Ambassador	Rangoon
Ambassador	San Jose
Ambassador	Sana'a
Resident Representative	St Johns
Consul General	St Petersburg
Ambassador	Tallinn
Ambassador	Tbilisi
Ambassador	Tegucigalpa
Ambassador	Yerevan

The chart and the figures contained within this section were supplied by the FCO. I am particularly indebted to Dr Keith Hamilton for his assistance in securing this information.

13. Cmnd. 2276, *Report of the Committee on Representational Services Overseas, 1962–3* [Plowden Report] (London: HMSO 1964); Cmnd 4107, *Report of the Review Committee on Overseas Representation 1968–9* [Duncan Report] (London: HMSO, 1969).
14. Quoted in Dudley Edwards, *True Brits*, p.203.
15. *Review of Overseas Representation* (Report of the Central Policy Review Staff: London: HMSO, 1977), p.xiii.
16. Steiner, 'Decision-making in American and British Foreign Policy', p.10.

Old Diplomacy: Reflections on the Foreign Office before 1914

T.G. OTTE

In the immediate aftermath of the Great War, impelled by revulsion at the carnage of that conflict, generations of historians identified 'old' or 'secret diplomacy' as a major factor leading to war. The pre-1914 Foreign Office, in particular, appeared to be the epitome of 'old diplomacy'.[1] A closer examination of the archival evidence, however, would suggest a more complex picture in terms of administrative history, the Foreign Office's place within the policy-making process of late-Victorian and Edwardian Britain, and the country's diplomatic strategy. No doubt, late-nineteenth century commentators described it as a 'somewhat leisurely and aristocratic place'.[2] In the words of one critic: 'As a house of call to gossip and smoke, and read the morning papers, the Foreign Office is a most admirable institution. It so nicely takes up the time between the one o'clock lunch and the seven o'clock dinner'. More of a gentleman's club than an effective part of the British government, 'one can hardly term it a house of business'.[3] The author, Charles Marvin, whose indiscretions gave rise to the Official Secrets legislation, was perhaps not the most objective observer. Nevertheless, his comments reflected the sentiments of a wider Victorian and Edwardian public. Another contemporary quip likened Foreign Office clerks to the fountains in Trafalgar Square, because they played from ten to five. The tag attributed to Professor J.S. Phillimore, that the Foreign Office was 'the last choice preserve of administration pursued as a sport', still gained currency when the 1914

Royal Commission under Schomberg McDonnell enquired into the Civil Service.[4] Like all light sarcasm, such quips reveal an element of truth, but also disguise a more complex reality.

Unlike the domestic departments, the Foreign Office was less exposed to external pressure, and so 'better equipped for resistance' to change.[5] In contrast to the rest of Whitehall, the Foreign Office and the still separate diplomatic service were also relatively cheap. Interference by the Treasury was, therefore, largely limited to staffing, pension and other administrative matters.[6] An exception was politically significant foreign loans, especially those issued to China and Latin America. Here the need to obtain the consent of 'the cursed Treasury' restricted the Foreign Office's freedom of action.[7] Nevertheless, even amongst the older, traditional departments such as the Colonial, India and Home Offices, whose chiefs were usually senior Cabinet ministers, the Foreign Office enjoyed a superior status. This was a function of hierarchy. 'The Foreign Office is usually considered . . . to be the chief of all offices', Lord Rosebery noted on being offered its seals for the first time.[8] Within the Cabinet even a neophyte Foreign Secretary like Rosebery enjoyed considerable autonomy. To some extent this reflected the notion that foreign affairs were part of the royal prerogative. In foreign affairs, the liberal-leaning journalist and constitutional commentator Sidney Low complained in 1912 that the nascent 'Cabinet autocracy is exhibited with the least reserve'.[9] This was an overstatement, for in reality the Cabinet was no effective check on the powers of the Foreign Secretary. Although Salisbury or Grey acknowledged that the final decision-making power rested with the Cabinet, its involvement in foreign affairs was intermittent at best, the fissiparous Asquith administration notwithstanding. Most Cabinet ministers, in fact, took little or no interest in foreign affairs.[10] As a matter of routine, the two service ministers, the Colonial and India secretaries, and the Chancellor of the Exchequer were kept abreast of diplomatic developments, as well as the odd senior elder statesman, who had a special interest or expertise in foreign and imperial matters, such as the Duke of Devonshire during the Unionist administrations of the 1890s and early 1900s, or the Marquess of Ripon in the Campbell-Bannerman government. Central to the foreign policy-making process was the relationship between Foreign Secretary and Prime Minister. In Lord Granville's words, the Prime Minister 'should only appear as a Deus ex machinâ', intervening at the crucial moment to facilitate the solution of a complicated problem.[11] There were exceptions, such as Salisbury's *de facto* supervision of Iddesleigh's ill-starred five months at the Foreign Office in 1886–87, or Beaconsfield's surreptitious attempts to undermine Derby in 1877–78 with the aid of his Lord Chancellor, Earl Cairns, and his India Secretary, Salisbury.

The relative autonomy and exclusivity of the Foreign Secretaryship was also reflected in the small number of politicians who served in that post. There were only thirteen Foreign Secretaries between the 1830s and 1914. Many of them held the office several times: Salisbury four times; Palmerston, Clarendon and Granville three times; John Russell, Rosebery, Malmesbury, Derby and Aberdeen held it twice. The exceptions were Iddesleigh, whose appointment owed more to the parlous state of the Conservative front bench; Kimberley, who had, however, served in diplomatic functions previously and had headed the India Office;[12] and Lansdowne and Grey. The latter two filled the post for lengthy periods (five and eleven years respectively), and had earlier served in imperial administration or in a junior role at the Foreign Office. Aberdeen, Palmerston, Salisbury and Rosebery went on to the premiership. Conversely, the Foreign Office was seen as an appropriate office for a former Prime Minister, for example Lord John Russell's tenure 1859–65. Although the office of the Prime Minister ranked higher, many relinquished the seals of the Foreign Office only reluctantly.[13]

Just as the Foreign Secretary enjoyed relative autonomy within the Cabinet, so foreign affairs were a branch of politics still relatively shielded from public or parliamentary interference. Despite the campaigns got up by the Atrocitarians during the Great Eastern crisis of 1875–78 or the Armenian massacres of 1895, E.D. Morel's Congo reform agitation in response to the Belgian king's repressive regime 1903–10, or the strong Jingo groundswell at the end of the Far Eastern crisis of 1897–98, there are few instances of real and direct interference. Nevertheless, the extensions of the franchise had created a new environment to which foreign secretaries had to adapt. A successful foreign policy, Salisbury observed, had to take account of 'the swing of the pendulum at home'.[14]

If there were fewer politicians serving as Foreign Secretary, then the Foreign Office also was one of the smallest departments in Whitehall. Throughout the first half of the nineteenth century the Foreign Office remained 'an uncomplicated, compact organisation easily controlled by the Secretary of State'.[15] In fact, it remained practically static for the remainder of the century. Thus, at its creation in 1782 the Foreign Office had a staff of fourteen; in 1848 it had risen to forty-four; by 1914 there were fifty-one (first-division) clerks employed at the Foreign Office. As the 1914 Royal Commission concluded, 'The diplomatic establishment of the Foreign Office is the same as it was 50 years ago'.[16] The gradual increase in personnel strength, however, did not at all correspond to the exponential rise in the volume of its business, as measured in the number of papers received:[17]

1821	6,193
1830	11,546
1842	23,760
1853	35,104
1870	53,794
1880	77,236
1898	102,000
1906	143,208

While personnel quadrupled between 1782 and 1914, there was a twenty-threefold increase in the volume of correspondence. The acute pressure of work thus generated was widely acknowledged. Lord Malmesbury estimated that he spent an average of ten hours a day on Foreign Office business.[18]

The increasing workload also placed a premium on the recruitment of able and well-qualified clerks. Sir Charles Dilke, former Parliamentary Under-Secretary at the Foreign Office, noted in giving evidence to the 1890 Royal Commission on the Civil Establishment that the Foreign Office attracted a better class of men than the separate diplomatic service.[19] Gladstone regarded the Diplomatic Service 'as an egregious failure. It cuts off its members from the free atmosphere of British public life. It dwarfs them by running their ideas in the groove of their single subject... Besides egregious honours and advantages, they have the highest pay in the civil service, with (except in rare cases) the lowest capacity'.[20] Salisbury, too, had a low opinion of the Diplomatic Service. 'The Service is hardly good enough', was his not infrequent complaint.[21]

Recruitment remained a constant preoccupation for the Foreign Office. In 1892, the Foreign Office and Diplomatic Service entrance examinations became identical, though the lists of candidates remained separate.[22] In 1905, in the context of the general reorganisation and reform of the Foreign Office, Lord Lansdowne instituted further changes by adopting the new scheme of examination for the Home Civil Service, 'with a view to making the Foreign Office and Diplomatic Service more accessible to University men'.[23] Emphasis on proficiency in French and German was the only concession to the special nature of diplomatic work. The changes were meant 'to eliminate the crammer'.[24] Generations of candidates had previously passed through the hands of the crammer Mr. Scoones, who coached them at Garrick Chambers, next door to the Garrick Club, and who 'enjoyed a complete monopoly as regards candidates for the Foreign Office, Diplomatic and Consular Services'.[25] In 1907 further changes to the entrance examination were decided upon. Greater emphasis was laid on modern history (1763–1878). This had been consistently urged by Eyre Crowe who, in 1905, observed that 'one of our real needs is the application of a little more historical spirit'.[26]

Significantly, the power to give a candidate the prerequisite nomination was devolved from the Secretary of State to a Board of Selection, consisting of the Permanent Under-Secretary (PUS), the Private Secretary and two further senior clerks, who met biennially.[27] Although nominations were technically still given in the Secretary of State's name, the change abolished his powers of patronage. Academic qualifications, especially a good honours degree, were now the *sine qua non* for entering the diplomatic profession. This marked a significant shift from the recruitment patterns in the Victorian period, when few clerks achieved academic distinction. Most had been educated privately, often abroad, fewer at public school, and fewer still attended university and, if so, did not take a degree. There were, of course, a few exceptions: Edmund Monson, who took first class honours in Law and History and was a Fellow of All Souls; Charles Kennedy, for many years head of the commercial department, who obtained a first in Moral Sciences at Cambridge; Robert Morier, Jowett's pet at Balliol, even though he attained only a second class in *literae humaniorae*; and Conynghame Greene and Arthur Hardinge, another Fellow of All Souls, who both graduated first class in Honours Moderations.

The emphasis on academic attainment cannot, of course, completely be dissociated from a candidate's social background.[28] In reality, only men from certain social backgrounds tended to apply for nomination. The Foreign Office, one observer noted in the 1880s, was run by 'a fraternity of gentlemen clerks, born and brought up in the official purple'.[29] Little changed over the next three decades. Despite William Tyrrell's best efforts at dissimulation before the 1914 Royal Commission, the Foreign Office still recruited chiefly amongst Etonians: 16 out of the 21 entrants between 1907 and 1913 were educated at Eton.[30] Little wonder that Liberal critics, such as Noel Buxton, opined that 'The upper class, which has long lost its administrative domination over home government, retains it in foreign affairs'.[31] In terms of its social composition, both Office and Diplomatic Service were predominantly aristocratic or gentry, but not exclusively so.[32] The Diplomatic Service remained a 'stronghold of privileges and prerogatives which have again and again beaten off or buffeted the assaults of democracy', largely because of the continued requirement for candidates for the diplomatic service to have an annual income allowance of £400.[33] At the Foreign Office, however, members of the professional middle classes played a larger role, as is exemplified by the careers of Eyre Crowe and William Tyrrell, though the real breakthrough came only after the war, when men like Duff Cooper, David Kelly or Pierson Dixon rose to senior positions. A special exception was made regarding the employment of candidates of foreign extraction; a stipulation that blighted the career of the brilliant but undersung Francis Oppenheimer.[34]

The greater emphasis on academic achievement notwithstanding, the work of Foreign Office clerks was 'largely mechanical', docketing, indexing, ciphering and deciphering.[35] As J.D. Gregory complained, it 'stultified their education, dulled their wits and deprived them of every kind of initiative'.[36] But too much notice should not be accorded to such statements. 'Red Tape', as Thomas Sanderson observed, 'like drill in the army, is only the means to an end. It is the method by which a huge machine is made to move – rather ponderously – but steadily and without confusion. It is our duty to make ourselves masters of it, in order that the directions of our chiefs may be carried out properly in their details'.[37] This has some significance for the historian. It is not a plea for the study of how one pile of papers was shuffled from one desk to another as an end itself. The bureaucratisation of advanced industrial societies in the nineteenth century had political consequences. Examining the interstices of the Foreign Office yields further insights into the policy-making process. In modern sociological parlance, the Foreign Office was a knowledge-based organisation.[38] Efficient information management pro-cedures, guaranteeing a controlled information flow, had to be devised, properly maintained and constantly revised, geared towards the needs of informed policy-making and decisive action.

In this context, historians have tended to focus on the 1905 Crowe-Hardinge reforms. No doubt, the creation of the new registry and the introduction of the FO 371 general correspondence series, and more especially the minute sheets, form a landmark in the Foreign Office's history. Still, there are strong elements of continuity which ought not to be overlooked. The refining of the complex registration and indexing system to ensure the efficient management of the information flow remained a key concern for the Foreign Office throughout the period.[39] Francis Villiers and Eyre Crowe played significant roles in this process. In 1883–84, Villiers had advocated 'a complete revolution of the indexing system', though the final outcome was somewhat less radical.[40] Two decades later, noting the 'want of proper facilities for collecting, coordinating, selecting, focussing [sic], and thus making available for actual use the vast material annually accumulating in its pigeon-holes and stately volumes', Crowe devised the card index, which did revolutionise information management at the Foreign Office.[41] He supervised the introduction in January 1906 of the Central Registry and its three sub-registries, and continued to monitor its working in practice with a view to further improvements.[42] Crowe also was instrumental in devising the annual reports by heads of missions abroad as a further means of collating relevant supplementary information.[43] From now on, the Central Registry was the institutionalised memory bank of the Foreign Office, where policy-relevant information could be stored and (usually) retrieved.

The Crowe reform undoubtedly made the Foreign Office more professional. Yet, it had important antecedents. In October 1900, Arthur Ponsonby, a junior clerk of a few years' standing, informed the PUS, Sir Thomas Sanderson, that 'reform is in the air', and submitted a detailed memorandum outlining reforms in the service which he deemed necessary. Sanderson was not amused, and certainly did not act on his suggestions, as Ponsonby did not fail to mention when giving evidence to the 1914 Royal Commission.[44] This, as well as the self-serving statements by Francis Bertie and Charles Hardinge, have earned Sanderson the reputation of 'belong[ing] emphatically to the old School'.[45] Valentine Chirol, former clerk in the Foreign Office and by then *The Times*' distinguished foreign affairs editor, opined, 'Sanderson has made the Foreign Office for so many years a one-man show, that when he goes the rather obsolete and defective machinery he has kept going by his own motive power will collapse altogether'.[46] Bertie, no friend of Sanderson's, identified the 'red tape of Sanderson, Villiers and Co.' as holding the Foreign Office back; and Hardinge also accused these two men of acting as a brake on efforts to introduce much needed reforms.[47]

Closer scrutiny of the archival evidence suggests a more complex picture. The need to gather accurate information and to administer it efficiently provided a constant impetus for reform. In mid-century, Palmerston relished applying 'a vigorous and unsparing Pruning Knife' to any unseemly service offshoots.[48] In 1870, Granville and his PUS Hammond adapted the service to the changed international landscape by reducing the number of minor missions in Germany.[49] Despite Robert Morier's stigmatisation of the Gladstone-Granville duo as hostile to reforms, Granville in particular, under the guidance of Hammond's two successors, Lord Tenterden and Julian Pauncefote, proved to be something of a reforming Foreign Secretary.[50] In 1890, the Royal Commission under Sir Matthew Ridley recommended the amalgamation of Foreign Office and Diplomatic Service, though this was ultimately not adopted.[51] Intriguingly, Villiers, whom Hardinge later accused of being the 'champion' of some form of bureaucratic 'trade unionism', was a leading proponent of the scheme. It was political opposition, first by Salisbury and, later in 1895, by Kimberley that ultimately scuppered such plans.[52] Indeed, during his four spells at the Foreign Office Salisbury showed little interest in reform, with the exception of banning red boxes with handles and introducing colour-coded labels 'to show the urgency or importance of the papers'.[53] Again, it was Villiers who set the ball rolling with regards to the 1905 reform, urging upon Sanderson in the spring of 1903 a scheme to free junior clerks from some of their clerical chores, and to reform the registering and indexing of papers.[54] Lansdowne, generally supportive of calls for a major reform, appointed a departmental committee under Chauncy Cartwright, the Foreign Office's chief clerk, to enquire into the matter. In May 1904 the Cartwright committee recommended the establishment of a General Registry on the model developed by the Colonial Office. In this way paper-keeping was devolved away from the 'Executive Departments' into the hands of 'a specially trained staff', the second-division clerks.[55] The minute sheets were another innovation copied from the Colonial Office.[56] Admittedly, Villiers and Sanderson preferred a more cautious approach to the question of reform, but they did not seek to block it, as Bertie and Hardinge claimed. Crucially, the Bertie-Hardinge faction was ruthless in exploiting Sanderson's serious illness in 1904 to shunt Villiers from the Foreign Office into the diplomatic sidings at Lisbon, forcing out the chief clerk of the Western Department, Charles Augustus Hopwood, and so further sidelining Sanderson.[57]

The extent and character of the 1905 reforms have been examined by Zara Steiner. They were much more than a clerical revolution. Their significance lay in that the Foreign Office was now more involved in the policy-making process. Junior clerks were encouraged to acquire expert knowledge in specialist fields. They now also had the opportunity to record their views on permanent minute sheets (as opposed to the provisional sheets under the old system, which were routinely destroyed when the papers were bound up).[58] Nevertheless, however lengthy their minutes, the role of junior clerks remained limited, while the senior clerks took a larger share in framing policy. Insofar as the junior clerks were concerned, the minute sheets were playing fields for future policy advisers.

Historians of the period tend to view the 1905 reforms in the context of the rise to influential positions of an anti-German coterie around Bertie and Hardinge.[59] This development, however, was only incidental to the history of the reforms. The momentum in favour of reform preceded the rise of the Anglo-German antagonism, and stood in direct relation to the external pressure on Britain around the turn of the century. The reforms were a function of increased Great Power competition, and reflected the formative experience of a new generation of diplomats, the period of the country's international 'isolation'. To an extent they also reflected the contemporary clamour for 'national efficiency'.[60] Once the slow and ponderous machine, described so vividly in the early 1890s by Sanderson, had formulated its response to the late 1890s, it had to deal with the new environment of the cold war between two nations once thought to be kindred.

Despite the many changes wrought by the reforms of 1905, many patterns of conduct remained unaltered. Within the Foreign Office's hierarchy, the Under-Secretaries (one Permanent and up to three Assistant) retained their powerful positions. Much continued to depend on their personalities and their relationship with the Foreign Secretary. There were other interesting continuities. Of the seven Permanent Under-Secretaries since the appointment in 1854 of Edmund Hammond, the first modern PUS, six were Peers or baronets or were descended from one, the exception being Hammond, whose father, however, had been PUS (1795–1806). Five had risen through the ranks of the Foreign Office; only two, Charles Hardinge and Arthur Nicolson, were career diplomats. Crucially, five of the seven had previously been in charge of relations with Russia: Hardinge and Nicolson, both protégés of the Marquess of Dufferin and Ava, as ambassadors at St. Petersburg; Hammond as head of the Oriental Department; and Philip Currie and Sanderson as senior clerks of the Turkish Department and its successor the Eastern Department respectively. Only Tenterden and Pauncefote had little Russian experience. They were appointed in 1873 and 1882, largely on account of their legal acumen, at a time when Russia was relatively weak. Thus, the personnel arrangements at the top of the Foreign Office reflected the importance of Russia for Britain's foreign and imperial relations throughout the long nineteenth century.[61] Furthermore, they ensured that relations with Russia remained a key concern for the Foreign

Office. No wonder also that the Eastern department, as Sir John Tilley reflected, 'gave itself airs and considered itself "smart"'.[62]

The office of PUS, in its modern form, was fashioned by Edmund Hammond. He 'was the Foreign Office; ... direct[ing], single-handed, the whole current work of the department'.[63] The post was what its holder chose to make it. This became particularly apparent under Hardinge. Already Rosebery had elevated the PUS (or an Assistant Under-Secretary) to deputy Foreign Secretary with the power to lead the department, within certain limits, in the Secretary of State's absence.[64] Sanderson certainly conducted a good deal of semi-official correspondence with diplomats abroad and received foreign ambassadors in London, but he also took a more active role in the formulation and conduct of policy.[65] His successor Hardinge, an imperial statesman *manqué* rather than a Whitehall mandarin, extended the role of the PUS further. Within two days of taking office Hardinge took steps to concentrate power in his hands. Whilst encouraging heads of departments to develop 'a sense of self-reliant responsibility' and junior clerks 'to take an active interest in their work and to develop political initiative', Hardinge monopolised all lines of communication with the Foreign Secretary.[66] Thus, the decision of what was politically important lay with Hardinge, 'the Grand Panjundrum'.[67] His steady rise to the top of the profession owed much to a streak of ruthlessness in his character and dealings, but equally to his administrative ability and capacity for hard work. His Court connections, as well as Bertie's championing of his cause, meant that he had always been 'one of the favoured ones' in the service.[68] Hardinge was often accused of exercising an unwholesome influence over Grey – that, in fact, he was the true master of the Foreign Office.[69] Hardinge undoubtedly influenced Grey's decisions on particular problems. Yet, it was a genuine partnership 'of equals ... unique in Foreign Office history'.[70]

The unique character of Hardinge's position in the Foreign Office was demonstrated by the contrast with his successor as PUS, Sir Arthur Nicolson. Appointed in 1910, at the age of 61, he was at the peak of his career. Like Hardinge, his principal interest was in Eastern politics.[71] Unlike Hardinge, however, he was not well equipped for the role of Whitehall mandarin. He also never established the rapport with Grey that his predecessor had enjoyed. By 1911–12 Grey's diplomacy had reached the zenith of its influence, and his personal standing in Europe was high, making him less dependent on expert advice from within the Foreign Office.[72] Differences over policy towards Russia and, more importantly, Nicolson's open hostility towards the Liberal government's leaning towards Irish Home Rule led to a further deterioration in relations between PUS and Foreign Secretary. Indeed, by the spring of 1914, Nicolson was widely tipped to be moved to the Paris embassy.[73]

The Foreign Office in the decade before the Great War, then, had a clearly structured, though by no means rigid, hierarchy. The conduct of business lay

in the hands of a select, socially and educationally relatively homogenous
élite. The high degree of social homogeneity created a special sense of
a 'brotherhood'.[74] It helped to produce some degree of uniformity of outlook,
a firm, though not always fully articulated understanding of the basic
principles of British foreign policy, the 'Foreign Office mind'.[75] Although
these basic assumptions reflected a continuity in official foreign policy
thinking, there were generational shifts. The characteristics of any age are
revealed not merely in political deeds and social developments. They are
revealed also 'by the manner in which contemporaries tried to explain their
situation in time and place and by the language and concepts in which such
explanations are formulated'. These concepts and 'cognitive maps', upon
which policy decisions were based, require historical calibration.[76] Of course,
it would be dangerous to assume too much uniformity or systematic thought,
or fail to make allowance for deviation. Policy-making may be more
haphazard and less consistent than later reconstructions often suggest.

Nevertheless, there are certain elements that define the 'Edwardian
generation'. First coined by the Earl of Onslow, this slightly impressionistic
phrase is usually defined in terms of differing attitudes towards Germany as the
demarcation between Victorians and Edwardians. No doubt, deep suspicions of
German policy were a characteristic of the Edwardians. At the close of the
nineteenth century Germany exploited Britain's difficulties with France and
Russia to extract concessions for herself in return for often limited and mostly
doubtful support. A minute by Grey in the spring of 1909 bears testimony to the
impact of this experience.[77] When in the autumn of 1912 Crowe warned that
concluding an agreement with Germany would lead to a renewed 'policy of
political blackmail' by the German Foreign Ministry, Grey concurred: 'I have
always felt that this was the real reason of the change of our policy'.[78] The
perceived dangers entailed in a return to Britain's exposed international
position before 1904 were a recurrent theme in Foreign Office thinking. Already
Lansdowne had noted Germany's tendency to 'put a spoke in our wheels'
whenever possible.[79] The ever-pessimistic Nicolson warned that, if Britain were
ever isolated again, she would be 'compelled to attach [herself] as a satellite to
some powerful European combination'.[80]

Suspicions of Germany, however, were only one characteristic of the
Edwardians in office. Grey and his senior officials were haunted by the spectre
of a return to isolation. The French entente and the Anglo-Russian convention
of 1907 were seen in this context. As a political instrument, the entente was
merely a 'frame of mind'. In the event of 'ultimate emergencies it may be
found to have no substance at all'.[81] The agreement with France was not seen
as committing Britain to any prescribed course of action. Maintaining it was
dictated by two key considerations: the notion of the balance of power in
Europe and Britain's place amongst the Powers within the European and

Asiatic contexts. If Paris ever came to the conclusion that British support for France was lacking, Nicolson warned during the second Moroccan crisis of 1911 (the Agadir crisis), 'she would probably make terms with Germany irrespective of us ... This would mean we should have a triumphant Germany, and an unfriendly France and Russia and our policy since 1904 of preserving the equilibrium and consequently the peace of Europe would be wrecked'.[82] It was this that Grey had in mind when, shortly before becoming Foreign Secretary, he declared 'that the spirit of the agreement is more important than the letter of the agreement'.[83] This did not entail an unconditional commitment to France. Unreserved support for independent action by France, Grey was only too aware, would have 'change[d] the Entente into an Alliance – and Alliances, especially continental ones are not in accordance with our traditions'.[84] To an extent this was written for consumption by the French Foreign Ministry in an effort to keep France pliable. Yet, it reflected a genuine sense that peacetime alliances had to be avoided. There were, then, strong elements of continuity with the Salisbury and Lansdowne periods. Hardinge and Grey agreed that 'The present elastic situation is more satisfactory for us'. Moreover, Germany might make an alliance with France a pretext for an attack on France, 'while Russia is helpless'.[85] Some younger diplomats, like William Tyrrell and Cecil Spring-Rice, took a more extreme stance, criticising 'the weakness of a policy which looks upon treaties & agreements as substitutes for armies & navies'. Yet, even they admitted that 'we are better off' with the French and Russian agreements.[86]

Historical assumptions about a tradition of eschewing alliances apart, the potentially entangling nature of such combinations, and their unintended consequences, were clearly demonstrated to the Foreign Office by the two Anglo-Japanese alliances of 1902 and 1905. The 1902 compact had not produced the financial savings that Lansdowne and the Admiralty had anticipated at the time of its conclusion.[87] A decision not to renew it, however, ran the risk of losing regional influence to a more assertive Japan. Its eventual renewal, despite its expansion in substance and scope, committed Britain to maintaining an unnecessary strategic presence in Northern China, whilst not fully allaying concerns about Japan's ambitions in Asia.[88] As regards the French and Russian ententes, however, it was accepted that, as Gerald Spicer minuted, 'The "Ententes" will have ... a tendency towards becoming alliances in proportion as the Powers concerned have grounds to fear that Germany desires to play the predominant part in Europe'.[89] This was a perceptive comment. Already the first Moroccan crisis in 1905 had transformed the entente into something more than a purely colonial agreement. The second Moroccan crisis further hardened it into a 'virtual diplomatic alliance'. The staff talks, initiated in 1905–06 to instil into the French a degree of confidence in Britain's reliability, but languishing since then, were resumed. No doubt, Bertie and

Nicolson supported the idea of more far-reaching naval and military arrangements with France, 'unless we prefer to run the risk of being stranded in splendid isolation'.[90] Grey was opposed to 'something like an alliance'; and the Anglo-French notes of November 1912 merely confirmed that naval talks had taken place, but that no commitments had been entered into by either side.[91] There was disenchantment with aspects of French policy. French reluctance to curb Russian policy in the Balkans was one bone of contention; France's recalcitrance on smaller overseas issues was another.[92]

The fact that Nicolson pressed for a firmer commitment to France was symptomatic of the breakdown of his relations with Grey. It also reflected policy differences within the Foreign Office as to relations with Germany as well as Tyrrell's rise. Grey's 'very papal Private Secretary' encouraged the Foreign Secretary to utilise the improved international situation in 1912–13 to seek a détente with Berlin, without however giving up the general entente with France.[93] These were differences of degree, although magnified by Tyrrell's efforts to jockey for position in anticipation of Nicolson's appointment to the Paris embassy at some stage in 1914.

From the beginning, the French entente had also been judged by its value in bringing Russia closer to Britain. Both ententes, indeed, served a combination of British interests in Europe and overseas. The 1907 accord with Russia, as Hardinge explained, reduced some of Britain's most pressing problems in Central Asia: 'Russia will inevitably be drawn into paying greater attention to her position in the Near East & there she will constantly find herself in conflict with Germany and not in opposition to us ... the best possible relations with Russia ... must always be of the greatest advantage to us'.[94] But hopes to utilise the situation created by the Anglo-Russian convention to develop railway communications in southern Persia soon ran into the buffers of Russian prevarication and obstruction.[95] Despite the friendly noise emanating from St. Petersburg, the 1907 arrangement could not prevent the aggressive tactics employed by Russian representatives especially in Persia. By 1914, Russian pressure on the Shah's dominions was mounting.[96] Nevertheless, the importance of Russia for British strategy and the degree of Russian obstructionism did not entail some form 'appeasement' of Russia for the sake of British interests in Central Asia.[97] On the contrary, up to 1914, Grey's policy towards Russia was constant and consistently even-handed. It was of necessity reactive, since Grey 'could neither compel Anglo-Russian relations to be cordial, nor force Russo-German relations to be distant'.[98] Neither in the Bosnian crisis of 1908–09 which was prompted by the annexation of Bosnia by Austria-Hungary, nor later, did he yield to attempts at political blackmail, despite Nicolson's efforts to convince him of the need to strengthen ties with St Petersburg.[99] Grey and his advisers did not commit Britain to a continental war in 1914 for the sake of British interests in Central Asia. In fact, it is tempting to speculate whether the visible improvement in Anglo-Germans relations around 1913–14 was, in part, an attempt by Grey to ameliorate the anticipated fallout of the possible collapse of negotiations with Russia for the renewal of the 1907 convention;[100] or to block a Russo-German rapprochement by signalling a Western option to Berlin. Certainly, Nicolson judged the 'new factors' at St. Petersburg 'not [to] be indisposed to listen to [German] overtures, especially having regard to the internal situation both here & in France'. In reality, however, indications of a Russo-German rapprochement were sufficient only to kindle the PUS's unease, but not properly to improve relations between the two Eastern monarchies.[101]

There were other difficulties with St. Petersburg in the last years before 1914. The Russian occupation of Kashgar in July 1912 and increased pressure on Mongolia seemed to presage renewed instability in Central Asia.[102] In the Balkans, Russian prolixity over Albanian independence caused even Nicolson, the warmest supporter of closest ties with Russia, to doubt her reliability.[103] The obstreperous attitude of Sergei Sazonov, the Russian Foreign Minister, over the future of Spitzbergen as well as the naval talks in the first half of 1914 caused further friction.[104] It would be misleading, however, to assume too a high degree of uniformity of outlook on this point. Nicolson and Crowe remained wary of Germany. An understanding with Berlin, Crowe warned, 'would checkmate one of two formidable obstacles in the way of Germany's predominance'.[105]

Whatever the difficulties with Russia in the geostrategic periphery, Grey and his senior clerks saw her as essential to the balance of power in Europe. Russia's defeat in the Far East in 1905 had disabled the Franco-Russian alliance, and so tipped the balance of power in Germany's favour, with the Moroccan crisis the natural result of this. On taking office Grey was anxious 'to see Russia restored in the councils of Europe, & I hope on better terms with us'. Russia had to be 're-established as a factor in European politics. Whether we shall get an arrangement with her about Asiatic questions remains to be seen'.[106] Clearly, then, Grey saw Russia in a European as well as an Asiatic context. But he did not necessarily see a linkage between the two. Significantly, he judged the equilibrium in Europe to be disturbed. Concern for Russia as a key factor in the European balance of power remained constant until 1914. In a memorandum, penned in the aftermath of the Bosnian crisis, Hardinge noted the weakness of the Franco-Russian combination in relation to the German-led Triple Alliance. In the absence of British support in a future Balkans stand-off with Austria-Hungary, Russia would disengage and seek a compromise with the Austro-German group, and so ensure Germany's 'position of predominance in Europe'. An alliance with Russia was fraught with risks domestically as well as in regard to Germany.[107] Britain, therefore, had to continue her equilibrist policy. As Louis Mallet, first Lansdowne and then Grey's Private Secretary, observed, 'If we stick close to France ... we can hold Russia'.[108] The ties with France had implications beyond Anglo-Russian relations. The 1904 agreement, as Mallet observed, and as the German chancellor, Prince Bülow, admitted, 'has put us in a position which Germany has held for many years, and we must do everything in our power to keep it'.[109] This was the *beau idéal* of most Edwardians: Britain was 'the country holding the balance between the Dual and Triple Alliance'.[110] As Hardinge observed: 'By the two alliances and our "entente" with France the balance of power is fairly maintained'.[111] It was the British variant of a neo-Bismarckian diplomatic strategy. A central plank of this strategy was maintenance of the ententes with France and Russia: 'If France is left in the lurch an agreement or an alliance between France, Germany and Russia in the near future is certain'.[112]

If the ententes remained intact, then Britain's position as the linchpin of European politics would also be secure. The corresponding plank was a policy aiming at stabilising Germany's weakening combination with Italy and Austria-Hungary. The existence of a strong Germany was essential to a viable balance of power. Britain's 'interests would not be served by Germany being reduced to the rank of a weak Power, as this might easily lead to a Franco-Russian predominance equally, if not more, formidable to the British Empire'.[113] The Foreign Office, therefore, blocked attempts by the French ambassador at Rome, Camille Barrère, to 'paralyse German influence in Mediterranean affairs' by prising Italy away from her northern alliance partner. The quadripartite Mediterranean league that Barrère had suggested, Hardinge warned, would lead to the break-up of the Triple Alliance and 'would open up possibilities of other combinations which might prove more dangerous than those actually existent'.[114] The continued existence of the Triple Alliance was a British strategic interest, as Hardinge elaborated in early 1909: 'It is very much to the interest of France & England that Italy should continue as a source of weakness to the Triple Alliance. It would be a misfortune if the Alliance were denounced. Should the "Drei Kaiserbund" ever be re-established Italy must inevitably lean on France & England'.[115]

Indeed, Italy's Tripolitanian campaign in 1911 further reduced her alliance value for the two Germanic Powers: 'With Egypt on one side and Tunis on the other the good will of Great Britain and France will be of paramount importance to [Italy]'.[116] Despite Italy's strategic vulnerability to potential British pressure, efforts continued to do 'all we can to meet the Italians'.[117] At the same time, Italy's 'opt-out' out of her alliance obligations towards Berlin and Vienna under the Barrère-Prinetti 'agreement' of 1902 finally became known in London at that time.[118] Combined with an invigorated Franco-Russian alliance, this had the ironic effect of underlining Britain's position as the link to the weakening Triple Alliance.[119] The anxiety displayed by some German politicians for a détente seemed to confirm the correctness of this policy.

As with Italy, so with Austria. Fairfax Cartwright's idea of weaning Austria off Germany was blocked immediately by the Foreign Office: 'The balance of power in Europe would be completely upset and Germany left without even her nominal allies. Is it not more likely that she would consider this humiliating position intolerable and risk everything in defence of her honour, dragging Europe into what would be the most terrible war in all history?' Grey confirmed the equilibrist line of his policy: 'At present there is a fair equilibrium & we should not try to make a break between Germany & Austria'.[120] Any attempt to decouple the original Dual Alliance 'might easily bring about a very dangerous situation, for if Germany is deserted by [Austria] ... she will ... regard this as the final link in the "Einkreisung" policy of Great Britain, & may be seriously tempted to resort to the fortunes of war to burst through the iron ring encircling her'.[121]

Although loath to disrupt the Austro-German alliance, the Foreign Office and Grey were anxious 'practically [to] spell checkmate to Aehrenthal's policy of obtaining Austrian's supremacy in the Balkans', as this was seen as having a potentially destabilising effect on Europe.[122] There was, in fact, a marked shift of opinion against the Dual Monarchy within the Foreign Office. In the last years before the war the *Ballhausplatz*, with its propensity for 'manufactured rumours' was increasingly seen as the font of much mischief in European diplomacy.[123]

In the decade before the Great War the Foreign Office had reached the zenith of its power and influence. Like other institutions of the Edwardian state, it was also under assault domestically. Unlike other institutions, it had developed effective methods of dealing with such pressures. The notion of continually refining its administrative procedures was deeply ingrained in the Foreign Office, going back to mid-Victorian days. On the other hand, in its social composition and modes of behaviour it retained a somewhat old-worldly courtliness. That was 'already something of a handicap in July 1914'.[124] Nevertheless, it would be fallacious to conclude that the Foreign Office was staffed by the Bertie Wooster characters that populate the pages of a recent book on the First World War.[125] The 'Edwardian generation' at the Foreign Office pursued a diplomatic strategy designed in response to the formative experience of the 1890s. International 'isolation' implied vulnerability to political blackmail, arising out of Britain's inability adequately to defend Britain's overseas interests. There seemed to be no credible alternative to playing an active role in European politics, especially in light of Russia's weakness until around 1912.

For all the talk about the threat posed by Germany,[126] and the tension generated by the Anglo-German antagonism, Britain and Germany were primarily locked into a 'diplomatic duel'. Both pursued a neo-Bismarckian strategy.[127] As the Bosnian crisis or the naval and political talks with Germany in 1909–10 and 1912 demonstrated, both aimed to be the 'honest broker' without whom no international question could be settled, though they had rather different notions of what constituted honesty in international dealings.[128] Maintaining a finely balanced continental equilibrium meant that Britain was the linchpin of Great Power politics, and so well placed to protect her global interests. It required a careful reading of the shifts in the balance of power, and entailed subtle efforts to influence the diplomatic dynamic of European politics. Arguably, though, during the last years before 1914, the effectiveness of British foreign policy was limited by the failure to 'read' Germany accurately. By temperament and inclination, Britain's last pre-war ambassador, Sir Edward Goschen, was neither willing nor capable to cultivate closer contacts within the ruling circles at Berlin. The quality of diplomatic reporting declined, and with it the quality of policy-making towards Germany. Sanderson's ponderous machine still moved along smoothly, but the policy decisions it ground out were affected by the deficient information that was fed into it.[129] That the awful prospect of war had long ceased to deter elements around the Kaiser caught London by surprise. When German diplomacy took the calculated risk to let the iron dice roll, it marked the end also of Britain's old diplomacy.

NOTES

All references to Cabinet (CAB), Foreign Office (FO) or Treasury (T) documents relate to materials held at the National Archives, London (formerly the Public Record Office) unless otherwise stated.

1. A.J.P. Taylor, *The Trouble Makers: Dissent over Foreign Policy, 1792–1939* (London: Hamilton, 1957), pp.167–200. But see also H. Nicolson, *Sir Arthur Nicolson, Bart., First Lord Carnock: A Study in the Old Diplomacy* (London: Constable, 1930), pp.ix–x.
2. R.B. Mowat, *The Life of Lord Pauncefote: First Ambassador to the United States* (London: Constable, 1929), p.33.
3. C. Marvin, *Our Public Offices: Embodying an Account of the Disclosure of the Anglo-Russian Agreement and the Unrevealed Secret Treaty of May 31st, 1878* (London: Anderson, 1882), pp.206–7.
4. *Appendix to the 5th Report of the Royal Commission on the Civil Service (1914): Minutes of Evidence* (Cmd. 7749), 40579; Sir L. Collier, 'The Old Foreign Office', *Twentieth Century*, (1970), p.256. The hours of business were 11–6. See G.E.P. Hertslet (ed.), *The Foreign Office List and Diplomatic and Consular Yearbook for 1914* (London: HMSO, 1914), p.5.
5. V. Cromwell and Z.S. Steiner, 'The Foreign Office before 1914: A Study in Resistance', in G. Sutherland (ed.), *Studies in the Growth of Nineteenth-Century Government* (London: Routledge, 1972), p.167.
6. FO 366/449, minute by Lingen, 22 May 1882; T1/13229/5227, Treasury minute, 5 Apr. 1854.
7. Curzon Papers, India Office Library, Mss Eur. F.112/1B, Salisbury to Curzon, 23 Dec. 1897; see also D.C.M. Platt, *Finance, Trade, and Politics in British Foreign Policy, 1815–1914* (Oxford: Oxford University Press, 1968), pp.20–22.
8. Gladstone Papers, British Library, Add. Mss 44289, Rosebery to Gladstone, 2 Feb. 1886; also Lady G. Cecil, *Life of Robert, Marquess of Salisbury* (London: Hodder & Stoughton, 1931), Vol. 3, pp.200–201.

9. S. Low, 'The Foreign Office Autocracy', *Fortnightly Review*, 41/541 (Jan. 1912), pp.3, 5.
10. This author once found the Cabinet papers relating to the Anglo-French entente in the original, sealed envelope amongst the Walter Long Mss, Wiltshire Record Office. See also K.G. Robbins, 'The Foreign Secretary, the Cabinet, Parliament and the Parties', in F.H. Hinsley (ed.), *British Foreign Policy under Sir Edward Grey* (Cambridge: Cambridge University Press, 1977), pp.3–21.
11. Granville to Gladstone, 29 Oct. 1870, in A. Ramm (ed.), *Gladstone-Granville Correspondence, 1868–1876* (London: Royal Historical Society, 1952), Vol.I, No.351; also Lord E. Fitzmaurice, *The Life of George Leveson Gower, Second Earl of Granville, KG, 1815–1891* (London: Longman, 1905), Vol.II, p.64.
12. Kimberley was thought by senior diplomats the most likely successor to Clarendon. See FO 391/23 (Hammond Papers), Paget to Hammond, 28 Jun. 1870.
13. Hamilton Papers, British Library, Add. Mss 48612B, Rosebery to Hamilton, 14 May 1894. The Prime Minister, though, was still ranked below the two Anglican Archbishops. See CAB 37/75/48 Cabinet memorandum 'The Prime Minister's Precedence', 20 Mar. 1905.
14. Curzon Papers, Mss Eur F/112/B, Salisbury to Curzon, 23 Dec. 1897.
15. C.R. Middleton, *The Administration of British Foreign Policy, 1782–1846* (Durham, NC: Duke University Press, 1977), p.154.
16. *Fifth Report of the Royal Commission on the Civil Service, 1914* (Cmd. 7748), p.8.
17. Figures compiled from: FO 366/677, Hertslet, 20 Jan. 1871; FO 881/4905, Hertslet, 15 Jan. 1884; FO 881/5458, Hertslet, Jan. 1884, Enclosure 5; *Fifth Report of the Royal Commission* (Cmd. 7748), pp.8, 12; Sir J. Tilley and S. Gaselee, *The Foreign Office* (London: Putnam, 1933), pp.47, 66, 315.
18. Earl of Malmesbury, *Memoirs of an Ex-Minister: An Autobiography* (London: Longman, 1884), Vol.2, p.310; also Cecil, *Life of Salisbury*, Vol.3, p.203.
19. *Fourth Report of the Civil Establishment Commission, 1890* (Cmd. 6172), 29197.
20. Kimberley Papers, Bodleian Library, Mss Eng. c.4383, Gladstone to Kimberley, 12 May 1894.
21. FO 800/2 (Sanderson Papers), minute by Salisbury, c. 22 Mar. 1897. The feeling was wholeheartedly reciprocated. See C.H.D. Howard (ed.), *The Diary of Sir Edward Goschen* (London: Cambridge University Press, 1980), p.9.
22. *Fifth Report of the Royal Commission* (Cmd. 7748), p.9; A. Cecil, 'The Foreign Office', in A.W. Ward and G.P. Gooch (eds), *The Cambridge History of British Foreign Policy, 1783–1919* (Cambridge: Cambridge University Press, 1921–2), Vol.3, p.614.
23. FO 366/761, minute by Lansdowne, 16 Mar. 1905, and further correspondence. See also A.C. Ewald, *The Complete Guide to the Home Civil Service* (London: Frederick Warne, 13th edn., 1881), pp.48–50.
24. *Appendix 5th Report of the Royal Commission, 1914: Minutes of Evidence* (Cmd. 7749), 40880. For a sample consular entrance examination, see *Foreign Office List 1914*, pp.554–8.
25. Sir L. Oliphant, *Ambassador in Bonds* (London: Putnam, 1946), p.10.
26. T1/10369/4480, memorandum by Crowe, 5 Jan. 1905.
27. FO 366/1141/3735, Leathes (Civil Service Commission) to Hardinge, 1 Feb. 1907; FO 366/786/4779, 'Examinations for the Foreign Office and Diplomatic and Consular Services', 29 Nov. 1911; *Appendix 5th Report, 1914* (Cmd. 7749), 40783, 40796, 40882.
28. For Cecil's argument see Collier, 'Foreign Office', p.616. In general, the Order-in-Council of 4 June 1870 resulted in higher educational standards in all grades of the Civil Service. See V. Cromwell, *Revolution or Evolution? British Government in the Nineteenth Century* (London: Longman, 1977), p.155.
29. Anon., *Foreign Office, Diplomatic and Consular Sketches: Reprinted from Vanity Fair* (London: Allen, 1883), p.4.
30. *Fifth Report of Royal Commission, 1914, Minutes of Evidence* (Cmd. 7749), 40972, 41018-24 and Appendix 84, pp.306–7; Z.S. Steiner, *The Foreign Office and Foreign Policy, 1898–1914* (Cambridge: Cambridge University Press, 1969), pp.220–21.

31. Quoted in T.P. Conwell-Evans, *Foreign Policy from a Back Bench, 1904–1918* (Oxford: Oxford University Press, 1932), pp.78–9.

32. *Fifth Report of Royal Commission* (Cmd. 7749), 41018-24. For useful statistics see R. Jones, 'The Social Structure of the British Diplomatic Service, 1815–1914', *Histoire Sociale*, 14/27 (1981), pp.49–66, though he subsumes both branches of diplomacy under the label of diplomatic service. The same also applies to R.T. Nightingale, *The Personnel of the British Foreign Office and Diplomatic Service, 1851–1929* (London: The Fabian Society, 1930) (Tract No.232).

33. Sir G. Young, *Diplomacy, Old and New* (London: Swarthmore International Handbooks, 1921), p.31; FO 366/786/50765, parliamentary question, Noel Buxton, and minute by Cartwright, 14 Dec. 1911.

34. FO 366/1145/10867, minutes by Cartwright and Maycock, 30 and 31 Mar. 1908; see also. Oppenheimer's bitter memoirs *Stranger Within* (London: Faber, 1961).

35. A.H. Hardinge, *A Diplomatist in Europe* (London: Jonathan Cape, 1927), p.32; J.R. Rodd, *Social and Diplomatic Memories* (London: Arnold, 1922), Vol.1, p.40.

36. J.D. Gregory, *On the Edge of Diplomacy: Rambles and Reflections, 1902–1928* (London: Hutchinson, 1929), p.28; see also FO 881/7038*, Foreign Office memorandum, 'Departmental Instructions', 10 May 1898.

37. Memorandum by Sanderson, 'Observations on the Use and Abuse of Red Tape for the Juniors in the Eastern, Western, and American Departments', Oct. 1891, copy in FCO Library.

38. N. Stehrs, *Knowledge Societies* (London: Sage, 1994), pp.91–119.

39. FO 366/724, minute and memorandum by Currie, 'Instructions for Index-Makers', Dec. 1890; T1/11278/5434memorandum by Hiscock and Behrens, [c.10 May 1911].

40. FO 881/5452, memoranda by Villiers, 10 Nov. 1883 and 7 Jan. 1884. At the end of 1883 the arrears of papers awaiting registration amounted to 563,703; and this figure did not include papers after 1880. Villiers estimated that it would take ten clerks five years to work off the arrears.

41. T1/10369/4480, memorandum by Crowe, 5 Jan. 1905.

42. FO 366/761, minutes by Sanderson and Grey, 15 Jan. 1906; FO 371/799/16051, minute by Crowe, 28 Apr. on memoranda by Brand and Dickie, 15 and 24 Apr. 1909; FO 366/786/40089, minute by Crowe, 7 Aug. 1914; see also Steiner, *Foreign Office*, pp.80–82; S.E. Crowe and E.T. Corp, *Our Ablest Public Servant: Sir Eyre Crowe, 1864–1925* (Braunston: Merlin, 1993), pp.88–93.

43. FO 371/1557/11104, minute Crowe, 15 Mar. 1912.

44. Ponsonby Papers, Bodleian Library, Oxford, Ms.Eng.hist. c. 652, Ponsonby to Sanderson, 17 Oct. 1900, and memorandum Ponsonby, 'Suggestions for reforms in the diplomatic service', Oct. 1900; see also *Fifth Report of the Royal Commission* (Cmd. 7749), esp.39393-400. The memorandum is reproduced in Steiner, *Foreign Office*, pp.222–8; see also R.A. Jones, *The British Diplomatic Service, 1815–1914* (Gerrards Cross: Smythe, 1983), p.164.

45. Sir J. Tilley, *London to Tokyo* (London: Hutchinson, 1942), p.69.

46. Hardinge Papers, Cambridge University Library, Vol.7, Chirol to Hardinge, 18 Oct. 1904.

47. Hardinge Papers, Vol.3, Bertie to Hardinge, 4 Jun. 1902; Corbett Papers, Hampshire RO, Winchester, 17M78/151, Hardinge to Corbett, 17 Aug. [1905]. The collusion between Bertie and Hardinge is comprehensively treated in Steiner, *Foreign Office*, pp.70–78.

48. As quoted in H. Roseveare, *The Treasury, 1660–1870: The Foundations of Control* (London: Allen and Unwin, 1973), p.67.

49. Granville Papers (National Archives, London) PRO 30/29/104, minutes by Granville, n.d., and Hammond, 7 Oct. 1870; R. Wemyss, *Memoirs and Letters of the Rt. Hon. Sir Robert Morier, GCB, 1826–1876* (London: Arnold, 1911), p.247. An exception, however, was made for Darmstadt and Coburg, in deference to the Queen's family ties there, thus also confirming Royal prerogative in foreign policy.

50. FO 366/678, minute Granville, 21 Dec. 1882. Details of the reorganisations of 1881 and 1882 can be gleaned from the memoranda 'Establishment of the Foreign Office' and 'Diplomatic Establishment', both 10 May 1889, in FO 95/505.

51. *Fourth Report of the Royal Commission appointed to inquire into the Civil Establishments of the different offices at home and abroad, 1890* (Cmd. 6172), p.9; see also R. Moses, *The Civil Service in Great Britain* (New York: Columbia University Press, 1966), pp.159–81.

52. FO 800/1 (Sanderson Papers), memorandum by Villiers, 'Amalgamation of Foreign Office and Diplomatic Service', 4 Jul. 1891, and minutes by Currie and Salisbury, 2 Jul. 1892. Kimberley's position is outlined in memorandum by Kimberley, May 1895, ibid. and incorporated in memorandum by Mowatt, Sanderson and Hervey, May 1895, in FO 366/760. For Hardinge's views see for example Bertie Papers, British Library, Add. Mss 63015, Hardinge to Bertie, 25 May 1903.

53. FO 366/678, minute by Lister, 18 Apr. 1878; see also T.G. Otte, '"Floating Downstream": Lord Salisbury and British Foreign Policy, 1878–1902', in T.G. Otte (ed.), *The Makers of British Foreign Policy: From Pitt to Thatcher* (London: Palgrave Macmillan, 2002), pp.101–3.

54. Villiers to Sanderson, 27 Apr. 1903, in R. Jones, *The Nineteenth Century Foreign Office: Administrative History* (London: Weidenfeld & Nicolson, 1971), p.237.

55. Report of the Cartwright committee (W.C. Cartwright, A.H. Oakes, R.P. Maxwell, W. Langley), 18 May 1904, and memorandum 'Summary of Recommendations made by the Committee on Registration and Keeping of Papers', n.d..

56. T1/10369/4480, memorandum by Crowe, 7 Mar. 1905; FO 366/761, minutes by Sanderson and Grey, 15 Jan. 1906.

57. Bertie Papers, Add. Mss 63016, Hardinge to Bertie, 9 Jun. 1904; Hardinge Papers, Vol. 7, Bertie to Hardinge, 5 Jul. 1905. For a comprehensive treatment of their manoeuvres see Steiner, *Foreign Office*, pp.73–6.

58. H. Knatchbull-Hugessen, *Diplomat in Peace and War* (London: John Murray, 1949), pp.11–13. On the latter point see memorandum by Sanderson, 'Observations on the Use and Abuse of Red Tape for the Juniors in the Eastern, Western, and American Departments', Oct. 1891, copy in FCO Library.

59. M.L. Dockrill, 'The Formation of a Continental Foreign Policy by Great Britain, 1908–1912', unpublished Ph.D. diss., London, 1969, p.15; Z.S. Steiner, 'Foreign Office Views, Germany and the Great War, in R.J. Bullen et al. (eds), *Ideas and Politics: Aspects of European History* (London: Croom Helm, 1984), pp.38–41.

60. B. Semmel, *Imperialism and Social Reform* (London: Allen & Unwin, 1960), pp.3–7; G.R. Searle, *The Quest for National Efficiency: A Study in British Politics and Political Thought, 1899–1914* (London: Blackwell, 1990), pp.67-80.

61. The thrust of K. Neilson's *Britain and the Last Tsar: British Policy and Russia, 1894–1914* (Oxford: Clarendon Press, 1995).

62. Tilley and Gaselee, *Foreign Office*, p.131; for a useful snapshot of its predecessor, the Turkish Department under Currie, in the early 1880s, see Howard-von Recum Papers, Library of Congress, Washington DC, cont. 1, Howard diary, 1 Jan.–13 Jun. 1881.

63. Lord Redesdale, *Memories* (London: Hutchinson, 1915), Vol.1, pp.110–11; see also M.A. Anderson, 'Edmund Hammond: Permanent Under Secretary for Foreign Affairs, 1854–1973', unpublished Ph.D. diss., London, 1953, especially pp.227–71.

64. FO 366/760, minute by Rosebery, 31 Dec. 1893. This did not always work well in practice. See *I Documenti Diplomatici Italiani*, Second series, Vol.26, No.597, Tornielli to Blanc, 5 Oct. 1894.

65. Churchill Archives Centre, Churchill College, Cambridge, O'Conor Papers, OCON 6/1/15, Sanderson to O'Conor, 6 Jul. 1898.

66. FO 366/761 and 1136, minutes Hardinge, 3 Feb. 1906. See also Lord Hardinge of Penshurst, *Old Diplomacy* (London: John Murray, 1947), p.98: 'My theory in the service was that "power" was the first aim'.

67. Rumbold Papers, Bodleian Library, Oxford, Rumbold dep. 13, Rumbold jr. to Rumbold sr., 15 Feb. 1908.

68. Satow Papers (National Archives, London) PRO 30/33/5/5, Paget to Satow, 22 Aug. 1898. For his debt to Bertie see Bertie Papers, Add. Mss 63025, Hardinge to Bertie, 14 Sep. 1910;

also B.C. Busch, *Hardinge of Penshurst: A Study in the Old Diplomacy* (Hamden, CT: Archon, 1980), pp.43–71.

69. W.T. Stead's verdict, see Steiner, *Foreign Office*, p.103; also Ripon Papers, British Library, Add. Mss 43543, Fitzmaurice to Ripon, 18 Apr. 1906.

70. Cromwell and Steiner, 'Foreign Office before 1914', p.188.

71. Kimberley Papers, Ms.Eng.c.4401, Dufferin to Kimberley, 22 Apr. 1894.

72. T.G. Otte, '"Almost a Law of Nature"? Sir Edward Grey, the Foreign Office and the Balance of Power in Europe, 1905–1912', in B.J.C. McKercher and E. Goldstein (eds), *Power and Stability: British Foreign Policy, 1865–1965* (London: Frank Cass, 2003), pp.107–8; K. Neilson, '"My beloved Russians": Sir Arthur Nicolson and Russia, 1906–16', *International History Review* 9/4 (1987), especially pp.526–36.

73. Hardinge Papers, Vol. 93, Mallet to Hardinge, 11 Aug. 1913; E.T. Corp, 'Sir William Tyrrell: The *Eminence Grise* of the British Foreign Office', *The Historical Journal*, 25/4 (1982), pp.697–708.

74. O. O'Malley, *The Phantom Caravan* (London: John Murray, 1954), p.157; see also Z.S. Steiner, 'Elitism and Foreign Policy: The Foreign Office before the Great War', in B.J. C. McKercher and D.J. Moss (eds), *Shadow and Substance in British Foreign Policy, 1895–1939* (Edmonton: University of Alberta Press, 1984), pp.19–55.

75. The phrase is usually attributed to Harold Nicolson, though it was already in use in the 1880s. See anon, *Foreign Office Sketches*, p.3.

76. K.T. Hoppen, *The Mid-Victorian Generation, 1846–1886* (Oxford: Clarendon, 1998), p.92. For the concept of 'cognitive maps' see A.K. Henrikson, 'The Geographical "Mental Maps" of American Foreign Policy-Makers', *International Political Science Review*, 1/4 (1980), pp.495–530; T.G. Otte, 'Eyre Crowe and British Foreign Policy: A Cognitive Map' in T.G. Otte and C.A. Pagedas (eds), *Personalities, War and Diplomacy: Essays in International History* (London: Frank Cass, 1997), pp.14–16.

77. FO 371/673/14511, minute by Grey, n.d., on Goschen to Grey, 16 Apr. 1909; see also Earl of Onslow, *Sixty-Three Years* (London: Hutchinson, 1944), pp.133–4; Neilson, *Last Tsar*, pp.48–50.

78. FO 371/1371/38804, minutes by Grey and Crowe, 17 Sep. 1912, on Granville to Grey, 12 Sep. 1912.

79. Balfour Papers, British Library Add. Mss 49729, Lansdowne to Balfour, 23 Apr. 1905; see also G.W. Monger, *The End of Isolation: British Foreign Policy, 1900–1907* (London: Nelson, 1963), pp.187–92.

80. Rodd Papers, Bodleian Library, Oxford, box 14, Nicolson to Rodd, 27 Feb. 1911.

81. FO 371/1117/3884, minute by Crowe, 2 Feb. 1911; T.G. Otte, 'The Elusive Balance: British Foreign Policy and the French Entente before the First World War', in A. Sharp and G. Stone (eds), *Anglo-French Relations in the Twentieth Century: Rivalry and Cooperation* (London: Routledge, 2000), pp.23–4.

82. Minute by Nicolson, 21 Jul. 1911, in G.P. Gooch and H.W.V. Temperley (eds), *British Documents on the Origins of the War, 1898–1914* (London: HMSO, 1927–38), Vol.7, No.409.

83. The 'City Speech' of 20 Oct. 1905, quoted in G.M. Trevelyan, *Grey of Fallodon* (London: Longman, 1943), pp.90–92.

84. Bertie Papers, Add. Mss 63018, Grey to Bertie, 15 Jan. 1906.

85. FO 371/74/38956, minutes by Hardinge and Grey, n.d., on memorandum by Pearson, 18 Sep. 1906.

86. FO 800/241 (Spring-Rice Papers), Tyrrell to Spring-Rice, 2 Jun. 1907.

87. CAB 37/63/143 and 170, memorandum by Selborne, 'Naval Estimates, 1903–4', 10 Oct. 1902, and memorandum Ritchie, 'Public Finances', 23 Dec. 1902.

88. Balfour Papers, Add. Mss 49747, Percy to Balfour, 18 Jan. 1905; T.G. Otte, '"Wee ah wee"?: Britain at Weihaiwei, 1898–1930', in G. Kennedy (ed.), *British Maritime Strategy East of Suez, 1898–2000* (London: Frank Cass, forthcoming 2004).

89. FO 371/599/5138, minute by Spicer, 8 Feb. 1909, on Cartwright to Grey, 9 Feb. 1909.

90. Bertie to Nicolson, 9 May 1912, in G.P. Gooch, H.W.V. Temperley (eds), *British Documents on the Origins of the War, 1898–1914* (London: HMSO, 1927–38), Vol.10/2, No.388; FO 800/364 (Nicolson Papers), Nicolson to Goschen, 11 Mar. 1913.
91. Bertie Papers, Add. Mss 63029, memorandum by Bertie, n.d. [25 Jul. 1912]; see also P.G. Halperin, *The Mediterranean Situation, 1908–1914* (Cambridge, MA: Harvard University Press, 1971), pp.99–109.
92. Rodd Papers, box 14, Nicolson to Rodd, 30 Nov. 1912; FO 371/2023/33449, minute by Crowe, 23 Jul. 1914, on A. Hardinge to Crowe, 20 Jul. 1914; FO 371/2045/12291, White to Grey, 11 Mar. 1914.
93. Rumbold Papers, dep. 13, Rumbold jr. to Rumbold sr., 15 Feb. 1908; Ponsonby Papers, Mss English history c. 659 and 660, Tyrrell to Ponsonby, 10 Jan. 1913 and 29 Jul. 1914.
94. FO 800/340 (Nicolson Papers), Hardinge to Nicolson, 25 Nov. 1907.
95. FO 371/503/23132, Marling to Grey, 17 Jun. 1908, and memorandum by Loraine, 16 Jun. 1908; D. McLean, *Britain and Her Buffer State: The Collapse of the Persian Empire, 1890–1914* (London: Royal Historical Society, 1979), pp.111–16.
96. Nicolson to Buchanan, 5 Dec. 1911, in G.P. Gooch, H.W.V. Temperley (eds), *British Documents on the Origins of the War, 1898–1914* (London: HMSO, 1927–38), Vol.10/1, No.898; FO 371/2066/6896, Townley to Grey, 5 Feb. 1914; FO 371/2073/22510, memorandum by Clerk, 'Anglo-Russian Relations in Persia', 23 Jul. 1914; J. Siegel, *Endgame: Britain, Russia and the Final Struggle for Central Asia, 1907–1914* (London: IB Tauris, 2002), pp.175–96.
97. The main thrust of K. Wilson, *The Policy of the Entente* (Cambridge: Cambridge University Press, 1985), pp.82–4.
98. Neilson, *Last Tsar*, pp.289–90.
99. FO 800/73 (Grey Papers), Grey to Nicolson, 24 Feb. 1909; FO/371/2094/32814, minute by Nicolson, n.d., on Granville to Grey, 18 Jul. 1914.
100. FO 371/1987/5608, Goschen to Grey, 5 Feb. 1914. For the negotiations, see Neilson, *Last Tsar*, pp.334–40, and Siegel, *Endgame*, pp.186–96.
101. FO 371/1988/12716, minute by Nicolson, n.d., on Buchanan to Grey, 23 Mar. 1914; also F. Kiessling, *Gegen den "grossen Krieg"?: Entspannung in den internationalen Beziehungen, 1911–14* (Munich: Oldenbourg, 2002), pp.244–5.
102. FO 371/1348/34756, India Office to Foreign Office, 15 Aug. 1912.
103. De Bunsen Papers, Bodleian Library, Oxford, box 15, Nicolson to De Bunsen, 16 Feb. and 30 Mar. 1914. See also the important piece by Neilson, 'My Beloved Russians', pp.521–54.
104. FO 371/2056/30091, minute by Crowe, 4 Jul. 1914, on Findlay to Grey, 3 Jul. 1914; FO 371/2092/15312, minutes by Oliphant and Crowe, 7 and 8 Apr. 1914, on Buchanan to Grey, 3 Apr. 1914; Benckendorff to Sazonov, 20 May/2 Jun. 1914, *Un Livre Noir: diplomatie d'avant guerre d'apres les documents des archives russes* (Paris: Librairie du Travail, 1922), Vol.2, pp.324–6; M. Rauh, 'Die britisch-russische Marinekonvention von 1914 und der Ausbruch des ersten Weltkrieges', *Militärgeschichtliche Mitteilungen*, 41/2 (1987), pp.37–62.
105. FO 371/1642/11813, minute by Crowe, 17 Mar. 1913. As a trial-balloon, however, Crowe and Nicolson drafted the outline of an Anglo-German agreement. See FO 800/243 (Crowe Papers), 'Suggestions for an Anglo-German Agreement', n.d. [c. Mar. 1912].
106. FO 800/241 (Spring-Rice Papers), Grey to Spring-Rice, 22 Dec. 1905 and 19 Feb. 1906; see also K. Neilson, '"Control the Whirlwind": Sir Edward Grey as Foreign Secretary, 1906–1916', in Otte (ed.), *The Makers of British Foreign Policy*, pp.129–30.
107. Memorandum by Hardinge, 'On the Possibility of War', ? Apr. 1909, G.P. Gooch and H.W.V. Temperley (eds), *British Documents on the Origins of the War, 1898–1914* (London: HMSO, 1927–38), Vol.5, Appendix 3; for the background see Neilson, *Last Tsar*, p.307.
108. FO 371/605/16587, minute by Mallet, n.d., on Buchanan to Grey, 26 Apr. 1909; and FO 800/342 (Nicolson Papers), Hardinge to Nicolson, 25 May 1909.

109. FO 800/162 (Bertie Papers), Mallet to Bertie, 13 Apr. 1905. For Bülow's reaction see
     S.L. Mayer, 'Anglo-German Rivalry at the Algeciras Conference', in P. Gifford and W.R.
     Louis (eds), *Britain and Germany in Africa: Imperial Rivalry and Colonial Rule* (New
     Haven, CT: Yale University Press, 1967), pp.225–6.
110. Churchill Archives Centre, Churchill College, Cambridge, Spring-Rice Papers, CASR I/1/2,
     Bertie to Spring-Rice, 26 Dec. 1902; Bertie Papers, Add. Mss 63015, Cranborne to Bertie,
     12 Apr. 1903.
111. FO 371/82/20308, minute by Hardinge, n.d., on Egerton to Grey, 9 Jun. 1906.
112. Minute by Hardinge, 23 Feb. 1906, on memorandum Grey, 20 Feb. 1906, in G.P. Gooch and
     H.W.V. Temperley (eds), *British Documents on the Origins of the War, 1898–1914*
     (London: HMSO, 1927–38), Vol.3, no.299. On this point see T.G. Otte, '"Almost a Law of
     Nature"? Sir Edward Grey, the Foreign Office and the Balance of Power in Europe,
     1905–1912', in Goldstein and McKercher (eds), *Power and Stability*, pp.87–8.
113. Memorandum by Crowe, 1 Jan. 1907, in G.P. Gooch and H.W.V. Temperley (eds), *British
     Documents on the Origins of the War, 1898–1914* (London: HMSO, 1927–38), Vol.3,
     Appendix A, p.417.
114. FO 371/82/20308, minute by Hardinge, n.d. on Egerton to Grey, 9 Jun. 1906.
115. FO 371/683/11613, minute by Hardinge, n.d., on Rodd to Grey, 22 Mar. 1909.
116. Rodd Papers, box 14, Rodd to Grey, 4 Sep. 1911.
117. FO 371/2117/4556, minutes by Crowe and Clerk, 2 Feb. 1914, on Mallet to Grey, 1 Feb.
     1914; FO 371/2118/10324, minute by Crowe, 11 Mar. 1914, on Mallet to Grey, 4 Mar. 1914.
118. Rodd Papers, box 14, Rodd to Grey, 16 Oct. 1911.
119. Nevertheless, Italy continued to act in concert with Vienna and Berlin when it suited her, as
     in the case of the creation of an independent Albania, much to the displeasure of Clerk and
     Crowe. See FO 371/1893/10250, minutes by Clerk and Crowe, 9 Mar. 1914, on Elliot to
     Grey, 8 Mar. 1914.
120. FO 371/399/27154, minutes by Campbell and Grey, 5 Aug. 1908, on Cartwright to Grey,
     1 Aug. 1908.
121. FO 371/599/5138, minute by Spicer, 8 Feb. 1909, on Cartwright to Grey, 5 Feb. 1909.
122. FO 800/193A and B (Lowther Papers), Hardinge to Lowther, 1 Dec. 1908, and reply, 3 Feb.
     1909. Count Aloys von Aehrenthal, (1854–1912), Austrian Minister for Foreign Affairs.
123. FO 371/1899/6901, minute by Nicolson, n.d., on de Bunsen to Grey, 13 Feb. 1914; Paget
     Papers, British Library, Add. Mss 51253, Paget to Nicolson, 7 Oct. 1912; also F.R. Bridge,
     'British Official Opinion and the Hapsburg Monarchy, 1900–1914', in McKercher and
     Moss (eds), *Shadow and Substance*, pp.108–9.
124. Steiner, *Foreign Office*, p.213. For the general background see D. Cannadine, *The Decline
     and Fall of the British Aristocracy* (New Haven, CT: Yale University Press, 1990),
     pp.35–54.
125. N. Ferguson, *The Pity of War* (London: Penguin, 1999), especially chapter 3.
126. Memorandum by Hardinge, 'On the Possibility of War', Apr. 1909, in G.P. Gooch and
     H.W.V. Temperley (eds), *British Documents on the Origins of the War, 1898–1914*
     (London: HMSO, 1927–38), Vol.5, Appendix III.
127. It is interesting to note that a whole range of Bismarckiana were published in English around
     1900. See C. Lowe, *Prince Bismarck* (London: Allen, 1895); M. Busch, *Bismarck: Some
     Secret Pages of his History* (London: Clark, 1898); J.W. Headlam, *Bismarck* (London:
     Putnam, 1899); also FO 371/1374/14421, minute by Crowe, 6 Apr. 1912.
128. Grey to Nicolson, 24 Feb. 1909, and Goschen to Grey, 18 Feb. 1909, in G.P. Gooch and
     H.W.V. Temperley (eds), *British Documents on the Origins of the War, 1898–1914*
     (London: HMSO, 1927–38), Vol.5, Nos 573 and 583.
129. T.G. Otte, '"The Winston of Germany": The British Foreign Policy Elite and the Last
     German Emperor', *Canadian Journal of History*, 36/4 (2001), pp.501–2; Howard (ed.),
     Diary of Sir Edward Goschen, pp.23, 60–61.

Preparing for Office: Lord Curzon as Acting Foreign Secretary, January–October 1919

GAYNOR JOHNSON

Lord Curzon's period as Foreign Secretary, between October 1919 and November 1923, has enjoyed something of a revival of interest among historians in recent years.[1] This was partly sparked by David Gilmour's general biography of Curzon and by the trend towards revisionist and post-revisionist assessments of the careers of British foreign secretaries of the inter-war period.[2] These studies have gone some way to reversing the negative reputation that Curzon's career at the Foreign Office earned as a result of earlier biographies and has given him due credit for some of his achievements. But they do not go far enough. Curzon remains in the shadow of Lloyd George when decisions about the conduct of British foreign policy are considered. This is particularly true of Curzon's period as Acting Foreign Secretary, which, hitherto, has received only passing, incomplete attention. This essay will argue that to appreciate the significance of Curzon's achievements as Foreign Secretary after October 1919, it is necessary to examine the ten-month period preceding that date – when he was Acting Foreign Secretary during A.J. Balfour's absence at the Paris Peace Conference. At this time, as Harold Nicolson, one of his principal allies in the Foreign Office was later to observe, Curzon established himself in a strong position to direct and influence the course of British foreign policy.[3] It would be misleading, however, to suggest that Curzon's period as Acting Foreign Secretary was devoid of controversy or did not result in his actions being justifiably criticised on occasions. Although this discussion will emphasise Curzon's achievements and place less emphasis on his shortcomings, its aim is to suggest that a more balanced assessment of his career at the Foreign Office is necessary. Curzon was an able and intelligent man who had a great deal of experience of foreign and imperial affairs. He was therefore one of the most suited to the role of Foreign Secretary of his generation and his period in office coincided with some notable diplomatic successes.

The period between January and October 1919 is also of interest because Britain effectively had two foreign secretaries – operating simultaneously but not always in tandem.[4] Curzon was in charge of the day-to-day operation of the Foreign Office, while Balfour, the Foreign Secretary, retained overall responsibility for foreign policy. A major part of this essay will focus on the impact that this division of responsibility had on the formulation of British foreign policy. It is an extension of an earlier assessment of Curzon's relationship with Lloyd George after October 1919 that questioned whether the Foreign Office's role as the driving force behind British diplomatic strategy after the First World War suffered a decline.[5] Central to that analysis was the contention that between October 1919 and the collapse of the Lloyd George coalition in the autumn of 1922, Curzon directed foreign policy with the Prime Minister in a harmonious partnership based on mutual respect. This interpretation questioned almost seventy years of scholarship on the subject. Harry Bennett's attempt to rehabilitate Curzon's reputation as Foreign Secretary is something of an exception but he nevertheless says very little about his relationship with Lloyd George.[6] The interaction between Foreign Secretary and Prime Minister was crucial in an era when foreign policy dominated the political landscape and reveals much about Britain's role in international affairs. This essay extends the debate backwards in time to the period when Curzon began to mount his challenge to become Foreign Secretary during the Paris Peace Conference. It suggests that, during Balfour's absence in Paris, deadlock was prevented by Curzon's decisiveness and that he used this period to establish his credentials as Foreign Secretary and lay the foundations for an essentially harmonious relationship with Lloyd George. These points will be illustrated through three inter-related issues: Curzon's personal impact on the Foreign Office and his relationship with his colleagues in the War Cabinet; the measures that he took to assert his position as an authority on foreign policy; and through an analysis of his involvement in policy formulation in the Middle East and in Russia – the two principal areas of political unrest remaining in the world at the time.

It has long been claimed that during the First World War, the Foreign Office became marginalised in determining British foreign policy by the War Cabinet and the Prime Minister's Office.[7] After the Armistice, it was necessary for the Foreign Office to examine its methods of operation to enable it to respond to the challenges of post-war diplomacy.[8] This would have been a demanding task even during a period of diplomatic stability, let alone during an era of unprecedented change and upheaval in international diplomacy.[9] While Balfour's prolonged absence in Paris necessitated the appointment of an assistant, this was the worst time for there to be a division of the work of Foreign Secretary. It was also widely believed within the Foreign Office that the loss of status endured during the war stemmed from Balfour's excessively compliant attitude towards Lloyd George.[10] The Prime Minister's personal involvement in diplomacy and the complexities of making peace also made it unlikely that this decline would be easily reversed. This has led some historians, such as Alan Sharp, to chart a steady deterioration in Foreign Office influence to October 1922, when the Lloyd George coalition fell from office.[11] Sharp's work describes a Foreign Office that was dismayed and disillusioned. He does not discuss Curzon's period as Acting Foreign Secretary, but if these months are examined, Sharp's view appears to be excessively pessimistic. Curzon's replacement of Lord Robert Cecil, who had held the post since the closing months of the war, can be seen as a conscious effort to rebuild Foreign Office morale and influence.[12] Curzon had a knowledge of foreign affairs that was at least equal to that of Balfour. What was more he proved to be an efficient and effective Foreign Office chief.[13]

Curzon's credentials for the post were formidable. He had been Under-Secretary of State at the Foreign Office under Salisbury and the youngest ever Viceroy of India. His familiarity with the workings of the Foreign Office allowed him to establish himself quickly. He believed that he would soon be asked to help the British delegation in Paris and to participate in its work. When Lloyd George requested that he attend a number of sessions of the peace conference in August 1919 to offer advice on Middle Eastern issues, Curzon told his wife that he had 'long predicted' such a summons. Furthermore, he had been authorised to conclude '*any settlement that* [he, Curzon] *might like to effect*'.[14] Lloyd George was also to demonstrate the same respect for Curzon's skills as an international statesman after he became Foreign Secretary in October 1919, when European diplomacy was dominated by conferences.[15]

Curzon's role in concluding what eventually became the Treaty of Sèvres is well known and demonstrates his cosmopolitan approach to foreign affairs.[16] But his involvement in peace-making with the Ottoman Empire also gave him the opportunity to demonstrate his own credentials as an international statesman in discussions about an area of the world that was diplomatically connected to but sufficiently remote from the European settlement being masterminded by Lloyd George. Thus to claim that Curzon had no interest in European affairs is to miss the point.[17] The two men built up their own spheres of influence within the conduct of British foreign policy that were mutually compatible. At the same time, the connection between the peace settlement in Europe and that in Asia Minor – establishing a new role for the Great Powers in international diplomacy and dealing with residual nationalism in the Central Powers – gave a legitimacy to Curzon passing comment on the European settlement. It is hardly remarkable that a Foreign Secretary should be permitted to comment on and influence foreign policy, but within the context of Curzon's relations with Lloyd George, it is important to note that Curzon retained that right. Lloyd George respected Curzon and his opinions after the latter formally took over from Balfour at the Foreign Office.[18] It is therefore reasonable to conclude that while he was absorbed by the peace negotiations, Lloyd George was willing to trust the judgement of a man he freely admitted possessed a greater knowledge of foreign affairs than he did himself. Curzon's involvement in the Turkish question after October 1919 demonstrates his strength of purpose and skill as an international statesman. The high point of his career was the successful negotiation of the Treaty of Lausanne in July 1923. The difficulties posed by the Turkish rejection of the Treaty of Sèvres and the subsequent need to re-negotiate the peace settlement in that region was a much greater test of nerve and ability than anything faced by Lloyd George between 1919 and 1922.

Initially, Lloyd George had been anxious that the post of Acting Foreign Secretary should not exist after the resignation of Cecil in January 1919. It was Balfour who insisted that the post be filled, and it was he who instructed Cecil to find a successor.[19] This indicates that at the start of the Paris Peace Conference, Balfour did have some influence over Lloyd George. But the fact that Curzon's appointment went ahead also provides grounds for questioning whether Lloyd George intended to marginalise the Foreign Office (and Curzon) at this time. He could have overruled Balfour but he did not. If Lloyd George's wish had been granted, the work of the Foreign Office would have been severely hampered through Balfour's prolonged absence in Paris. Lloyd George would thus have found it easier to assert his personal authority on the conduct of British foreign policy. It is tempting to explain Curzon's appointment simply in terms of practical necessity – that Balfour persuaded Lloyd George that he could not run the Foreign Office and direct foreign policy without assistance while absent from London for an indefinite period. But again, this takes no account of Lloyd George's respect for Curzon's knowledge of foreign affairs, which was so great that at the time of his appointment as Prime Minister in 1916, he stated that he intended to do all he could to secure Curzon's appointment to the Cabinet.[20] When Curzon took over from Balfour as Foreign Secretary, this harmonious relationship continued. There were some differences of opinion, but they were mostly of limited significance.

Curzon believed that it was Balfour who posed the biggest impediment to increasing Foreign Office influence on events in Paris during the peace conference. Reflecting on his time as Acting Foreign Secretary, he later wrote:

It was during that period that the fatal ascendancy and interference of L[loyd] G[eorge] in Foreign Affairs was allowed to establish itself so firmly that they could only be ultimately uprooted by L[loyd] G[eorge]'s disappearance; and the chief culprit was undoubtedly Balfour. From an early stage, he – a former Prime Minister and the Foreign Minister of the British Empire – allowed himself to be displaced in Paris and pushed aside.[21]

Curzon condemned what he termed Balfour's 'passion for surrender' and his casual, '"What did it matter?"' attitude to his responsibilities.[22] Later, Curzon observed that Balfour 'did not know, was not told, and was as a rule too careless to inquire, what was going on'. He believed that the characteristics that made Balfour 'a failure, even a danger' as Foreign Secretary were 'intellectual indolence', 'no depth of feeling' and 'no profound convictions'.[23] He complained that Balfour was incompetent and took too long to reply to letters.[24] Curzon's critics would claim that he believed that he possessed a knowledge of foreign affairs superior to that of most of his contemporaries, and not just Balfour. As the government minister in charge of foreign affairs, Curzon believed that Balfour and Lloyd George disregarded his advice at their peril. The consequences of doing so were too terrible to contemplate. On one occasion in August 1919, when complaining that he had not been consulted about a discussion of the Middle Eastern settlement, Curzon told his wife: 'Now that things in Paris are in an inextricable mess, the PM says that nothing will induce him to go back (... AJB wants to clear out. So I am left, as usual, to clear up the mess'.[25]

Yet when Curzon entered the Foreign Office in January 1919, he entered a government department that revered and admired Balfour personally and which had little desire to listen to criticism of his *modus operandi*. As one Foreign Office official put it, in place of the 'slim nonchalance' of Balfour, Curzon 'sat like impatience on a monument ready to pounce on our frailties'.[26] However others, such as Cecil, reluctantly acknowledged that the 'chaos' in the Foreign Office caused by Balfour's lackadaisical attitude was 'indescribable'.[27] As Cecil was Acting Foreign Secretary at the time of the comment, he clearly felt unable to impose some semblance of order himself. It is unlikely that Cecil would have approached Curzon if he had believed that he lacked the ability to bring about a swift and effective transformation of the situation. As it was, Cecil's faith was not misplaced. Although Curzon proved to be an exacting taskmaster and occasionally lacked tact and personal warmth, most Foreign Office officials respected him and readily adapted to his regime. The Permanent Under-Secretary, Sir Charles Hardinge, a member of the British delegation in Paris and a man seldom given to complimenting Curzon, admired his ability to send pertinent advice on how to present the British case in Paris. Complaining that Balfour had not done enough to secure a strong Foreign Office involvement in the activities of the British delegation, Hardinge was confident that Curzon would provide effective support in London.[28] Some did complain about Curzon's vigorous regime – and these complaints are often quoted – but most rose to the challenge and appreciated the advantages of a firmer style of leadership than had existed under Balfour. When Curzon's appointment as Foreign Secretary was finally confirmed in October 1919, several Foreign Office officials reflected positively on the previous ten months. Clement Jones, who had been a member of the British delegation to the peace conference, noted with approval that 'an immense change has come into the whole spirit of the place' since Curzon's appointment.[29] Others within the government also thought that the omens were good. Lord Crawford, the Chancellor of the Duchy of Lancaster, noted that: 'The more I see of G[eorge] C[urzon] the more I am amazed at his versatility and his self-confidence'.[30] Furthermore, the Diplomatic Service responded well to Curzon's approach to the conduct of diplomacy. Major Baird, head of the military mission to Bulgaria, commented that British diplomats had found it refreshing to serve Curzon since January because he 'not only took decisions, but controlled our Foreign policy'.[31]

Curzon's abilities were appreciated by officials in other departments. Sir Norman Warren Fisher, Permanent Under-Secretary at the Treasury, told Curzon that 'more, I think, may be done by one man just now as Secretary of Foreign Affairs than as Prime Minister'.[32] His forceful personality ensured that in Curzon, the Foreign Office possessed a loyal and able defender of traditional practices in the face of Lloyd George's apparent enthusiasm for a more open style of diplomacy. Hardinge and others also suspected that Balfour's willingness to defer to the Prime Minister at the peace conference implied an acceptance of a style of diplomacy that had done much to diminish the role of the Foreign Office in the conduct of foreign policy. It was therefore partly a fear of hostility and rejection that led Balfour to announce, on his departure from Paris, that he would not be returning to the Foreign Office, rather than mere mental and physical fatigue.[33] This also partly explains why senior Foreign Office officials embraced Curzon's appointment as Foreign Secretary in October 1919. His credentials as a champion of the 'old diplomacy' were, by this time, clear and untainted by close association with the activities of Lloyd George.

A number of the British delegation at the peace conference shared Curzon's concerns about Balfour's willingness to defer to the Prime Minister.[34] Even Lord Derby, the British Ambassador in Paris, who was a close friend of the Foreign Secretary, agreed that Curzon was right to be concerned about the 'policy of drift' which appeared to surround Balfour's involvement in the work of the British delegation in Paris.[35] Yet although he had misgivings about Balfour's effectiveness, Curzon had little desire to prompt his early return from Paris. He was secure in the knowledge that Lloyd George was unlikely to sanction the appointment of a new Foreign Secretary during a major international conference if such a step could be avoided. Despite his wish to retire, Balfour would probably be prevailed upon to remain in office until the end of the peace conference. This was likely to be a period of months rather than weeks and would give Curzon an opportunity to consolidate his own position in London and help to establish himself as Balfour's logical successor. Consequently, Curzon questioned Balfour's professionalism and knowledge of foreign affairs but never called for his resignation. But he was not prepared to tolerate this situation indefinitely. By September 1919, when the main work of the peace conference was drawing to a close, Curzon was ready to take over from Balfour. He told his wife that he was 'heartily sick of this indeterminate position, possessing full powers in one set of things, but powerless in others; pursuing a definite policy here which may be thrown over any day in Paris. Few can realise the unsatisfactory and almost humiliating position of being at the same time Secretary of State and yet only a substitute'.[36]

The frustration stemmed partly from the lack of anything beyond the most vague definition of their respective responsibilities. It was to Curzon that the consequences of this situation were most apparent. In August 1919, he complained that: 'A.J.B. is in Paris pursuing one policy. I am here pursuing another. No one knows what ought to be done, and meanwhile, of course, nothing is done, and we go on getting deeper and deeper into the mire'.[37] The conduct of foreign policy became more bureaucratic and slower paced as the approval of both Curzon and Balfour was often sought before action was taken.[38] The lack of clarity gave rise to a number of misunderstandings and examples of egotism, such as Hardinge's decision to describe himself as Superintending Ambassador at the peace conference until Curzon and Sir Eyre Crowe, Foreign Office Permanent Under-Secretary and Lloyd George's replacement in Paris after July 1919, insisted that he abandon the title.[39] Curzon believed that the uncertainty could be partly resolved if there was more efficient communication between the Foreign Office in London and the British delegation in Paris.[40] He applied pressure on Balfour to increase the flow of information about the discussions of the 'Big Four'. Balfour's response was to place Robert Vansittart, soon to be appointed Curzon's private secretary, in charge of 'speedy communication' – a man of legendary efficiency but often unsympathetic to Curzon and therefore unmoved by his requests for information.[41] Thus the deadlock continued. Given these circumstances, it was inevitable that Curzon's work and that of the British delegation at the peace conference was fraught with difficulties and frustrations. Nevertheless, Derby reported that senior Foreign Office officials were convinced that it was Curzon who deserved the credit for preventing a total breakdown in the conduct of foreign policy. He wrote: 'Tyrrell tells me it is absolute chaos between the Majestic and the Foreign Office. They are all very pleased with George Curzon who they say is wonderfully good at giving decisions and at backing his people up'.[42] In July 1919, Balfour himself conceded that 'thanks to [Curzon's] skill and wisdom, I do not think serious difficulties have arisen'.[43]

Despite his efforts, Curzon was unable to prevent all of the damage and confusion caused by the poor communication between London and the British delegation in Paris. The misunderstandings that inevitably resulted sometimes threatened to undermine important aspects of British foreign policy strategy. In February 1919, one such breakdown placed a strain on the Entente Cordiale. Curzon had become aware that a new draft Anglo-French agreement on the Middle East had been drawn up without his knowledge as a result of informal discussions between the French Prime Minister, Clemenceau, and Lloyd George.[44] The agreement involved the cession of Mosul and Palestine to Britain and a redrafting of the Sykes-Picot agreement of 1916.[45] Disapproving of this course of action, Curzon protested that he had first heard of the proposed agreement only when Sir Edwin Montagu, the Secretary of State for India, had 'brought over to England a copy of it in his own pocket'. He also complained that the failure to send him the text had resulted in him discussing the Eastern question with Cambon, the French ambassador to London, while being 'in complete ignorance of what was passing at the other end'.[46] When Winston Churchill, the Secretary of State for War, also voiced his objections, Balfour claimed that he was unable to respond because the relevant documents were in London and that consequently the matter could only be dealt with by Curzon.[47] Clemenceau interpreted the confusion as a British ploy to undermine French policy in the Middle East and for this he blamed Curzon, noting:

> Lord Curzon is a very charming man and one of great stature, but he is anti-French. My constant policy has been to preserve the union between France, Great Britain and the United States. To that end I have made greater concessions than I would have believed possible before the Conference. I am happy to have made them. Now you tell me that France cannot have a place in Asia Minor . . . what do you think it will do to the French public?[48]

Curzon was thus unreasonably held responsible for what Antony Lentin sees as the French government's inconsistent attitude towards the Anglo-French agreement.[49] Nevertheless, in the fullness of time, the negotiation of the agreement helped to forge a closer relationship between Curzon and Lloyd

George and reconciled important differences between them about the importance of the Entente Cordiale to British foreign policy.[50]

As the Paris Peace Conference progressed, Curzon's brief increased rather than decreased. He was given extra responsibilities on an *ad hoc* basis, usually because Balfour did not have time to deal with the matters himself. But to a person of Curzon's method of working – and his memoranda reveal that his *modus operandi* and thought processes were considered and methodical – the sudden imposition of additional responsibility placed a severe burden on him. Never in good health, requests to take on extra duties were used by Curzon to gain psychological advantage over his Cabinet colleagues. It is from the summer of 1919 that the first of Curzon's famous pencil notes written from his sick bed appears, emphasising his stoic devotion to duty despite physical discomfort, but nevertheless directing policy in a clear and decisive manner.[51] One of the most important of these additional responsibilities was inclusion in discussions about the selection of ambassadors and other diplomatic staff.[52] This not only gave Curzon a role in shaping the operation of British diplomacy in the early years of peace, but also provides the historian with a means of examining his general attitude to the conduct of British foreign policy. Curzon's approach was forthright and assertive.[53] When Balfour favoured the dispatch of his Private Secretary, Ian Malcolm, as consul in Washington to diffuse diplomatic tension over war debts, Curzon immediately favoured the appointment of a diplomat with full ambassadorial authority.[54] Looking beyond the tensions in Paris concerning American involvement in enforcing the Treaty of Versailles with Germany, Curzon realised that as the United States had emerged from the war as the world's dominant economic power, the appointment of a diplomat with full treaty signing powers was essential. His conservative instincts led him initially to consider only candidates from the aristocracy and the Diplomatic Service. These included the Speaker of the House of Commons, Lord Finlay, the Marquess of Crewe, the Marquess of Salisbury and the Duke of Devonshire.[55] But as it became clear during 1921 that British war debts threatened the stability of this important relationship, Curzon sanctioned the appointment of a financial expert, Sir Auckland Geddes, as ambassador to Washington. The selection of Geddes, who was not a member of the Diplomatic Service, represented a significant departure by Curzon, indicating that he was not as bound by convention as has been suggested.[56] To Curzon, the use of experts to advise on foreign policy, be they diplomats or employed in other capacities, was merely a means to an end. They were people whose knowledge he did not necessarily understand, but he recognised that there was an advantage to be gained through their use. As Vansittart put it, 'Curzon annexed their work as the Germans annexed Shakespeare'.[57]

Curzon's approach to Britain's diplomatic presence in the world was more adventurous than that of Balfour. In particular, he favoured a considerable extension of the number of British embassies and legations in countries on the periphery of Europe.[58] Jason Tomes has pointed out that Balfour was daunted by the complexity of the diplomatic consequences of the war.[59] By contrast, Curzon was more used to large-scale diplomacy as a result of his experience as Viceroy of India, a role that required an ability to formulate policies that affected hundreds of millions of people. It was also this organisational ability that led Curzon to form a committee with himself as chairman to consider the appointment of ambassadors. His first act was to select diplomats to fill a number of the key embassies in Europe and the Far East: Esme Howard for Madrid, Louis Mallet for Rome, Sir Henry Villiers for Brussels and Sir Charles Eliot for Tokyo – all long-established posts.[60] The question of who was to fill the more prestigious embassies in Berlin and Washington was deferred until the peace treaty with Germany had been concluded and it was clear what role the United States would play in post-war political and economic reconstruction. Nevertheless, the appointments to important European capitals as well as a commitment to the crucial relationship with Japan illustrates an adherence to tradition as all were experienced members of the Diplomatic Service who would provide continuity during a period of unprecedented change.

Between January and October 1919, Curzon further consolidated his position at the Foreign Office by integrating himself into the work of the War Cabinet by establishing a reputation as the government's principal expert on foreign affairs. Lloyd George's prolonged absence in Paris occasionally resulted in Curzon presiding over Cabinet meetings – a responsibility that he greatly enjoyed. He insisted that the views of the War Cabinet be taken into account before major policy decisions were taken in Paris. When rumours reached London that the British delegation proposed to surrender Cyprus as part of the negotiations with the French, Curzon voiced the hostility of their Cabinet colleagues to Lloyd George, writing: 'I associate myself with this attitude; and suggest that a policy which is strongly opposed by ... important members of War Cabinet, will require very powerful justification before it is pursued against their combined advice'.[61] Balfour denied that such a strategy would ever be pursued.[62] However, Curzon pointed out that the reason why concerns had been expressed was because a communication had been sent 'from an official in Paris that none of the Foreign Office delegates there were aware either of the paper that I had written or of the views of ... other specialists on the subject'.[63] Balfour's carefully worded reply is worthy of consideration.

> I feel sure that the Prime Minister, whatever his views, would never think of taking action without speaking not only to me, but to his Cabinet. I do not share to the full the views which now prevail ... But whoever is right and whoever is wrong, the matter is far too important in

my opinion, to be decided by the casual inspiration of any single member of the Government, however important.[64]

Balfour's reference to the importance of individuals not taking unilateral action, while referring to Lloyd George, could also be viewed as a veiled criticism of Curzon's forthright attitude on the subject.[65]

Events in Paris were by no means Curzon's sole preoccupation. The few surveys of this part of his career that exist claim that during his period as Acting Foreign Secretary he enjoyed some diplomatic successes, the high point being the conclusion of the Anglo-Persian Treaty of August 1919.[66] The correspondence between Curzon and Montagu – not always the most harmonious relationship – reveals the extent to which the treaty was Curzon's work.[67] The negotiations, which had been taking place since the middle of 1918, came to fruition at a time when it was politic for Curzon to reaffirm his abilities in diplomatic negotiations and so confirm his ability to run the Foreign Office once Balfour resigned. Curzon was thus annoyed when his personal hand in the conclusion of the treaty was ignored because of *The Times'* continuing preoccupation with events in Paris.[68] He wrote: 'The papers give a very good reception to my Persian Treaty, which I have been negotiating for the past year, and which is a great triumph, as I have done it all alone. But not a single paper so much as mentions my name or has the dimmest perception that, had I not been at the Foreign Office, it would never have been [signed] at all'.[69] Lionel Mosley, not the most complimentary of Curzon's biographers, emphasises that though much heralded, the Anglo-Persian Treaty collapsed after only a year. Consequently, we should think twice about claiming that Curzon had much skill in international diplomacy.[70] More recently, Houshang Sabahi has argued that Curzon misunderstood Persian motives for signing the treaty – that he failed to understand that the Persians regarded it as a first stage in gaining wider influence in Europe, while the British government simply intended it to help safeguard the Indian frontier from a threat from an unstable Russia.[71] If these arguments are to be accepted, then both Hardinge, who, as a former Viceroy of India, had as much experience of politics in that region as Curzon, and the British Minister in Tehran, Sir Percy Cox, were also equally misled by the Persians. What is more, by 1920, it was clear that the threat to Indian territorial integrity had passed as the Bolsheviks were now concentrating their efforts on fighting the Allies in the west of Russia. The agreement had thus outlived its usefulness.

There are further reasons to question Sabahi's contention that Curzon was unaware that the Persian government were seeking allies in Western Europe. As early as March 1919, Curzon had received representations from the Persian ambassador to London complaining that a delegation from his country, headed by Mushaver ul Mamalek, had been refused a meeting with Balfour in Paris.

Curzon instructed Cox to advise that henceforward all enquiries about British policy towards Persia should be addressed to London and not to Paris.[72] By mid April, Curzon was engaged in negotiations with the Persian government without the knowledge of Mamalek, who continued to seek out Balfour and Hardinge but without success. Concerned that his initiative would be undermined should they be granted an interview, Curzon pressed for the suspension of Mamalek's activities in Paris.[73] What is more, Hardinge's cautious response enhanced Curzon's role in developing British policy towards Persia. Hardinge had written that:

> The best solution would be for Sir P. Cox to obtain instructions from the Persian government to Mushaver to proceed to London and there to await instructions. This would obviate the possibility of the Persian case coming before the Conference. I venture to suggest this course as by far the simplest method of procedure.[74]

The significance of such a suggestion was not lost on Mallet, who asked Hardinge whether it meant that questions concerning British policy towards Persia were 'really to be left to the Foreign Office to answer'. Hardinge endeavoured to reassure him that surrendering such an important area of policy to Curzon did not represent a reduction in the status of the British delegation in Paris.[75] Despite the ruffled feathers of the British delegation, from that point onwards Mamalek and the government he represented regarded Curzon as the champion of their cause.[76]

Curzon's desire to be seen as the voice of reason and authority in foreign affairs was also evident in his devotion to the activities of the Eastern Committee after its establishment in 1918. The unstable and complex situation in the Middle East occupied much of Curzon's time between January and October 1919. Curzon's chairmanship of the Eastern Committee is often cited as an example of his abrasive relationship with his Cabinet colleagues. He is often portrayed as being overbearing and autocratic and criticised for failing to listen to advice. Curzon was capable of extraordinary displays of temper and did not always treat his colleagues and subordinates with the respect they deserved. But he was not alone in behaving this way and his actions were often more justifiable than most because few possessed his level of expertise in foreign policy. He therefore had a strong case for insisting that his voice be heard and that his advice be acted upon. Curzon was also single-mindedly ambitious in a way that many contemporaries thought unseemly for a gentleman, but which today would be regarded as a strength rather than a weakness in his character. Consequently, when Curzon's involvement in the work of the Eastern and Russian committees is considered, it reveals much about the strategies that he used to promote himself as Balfour's successor.

His role as Acting Foreign Secretary meant that he was perfectly placed to use his chairmanship of the Eastern Committee for this purpose. In this respect, Sabahi's contention that Curzon's chairmanship of the Eastern Committee weakened rather than strengthened Foreign Office control over this important area of foreign policy misses the point.[77]

Curzon's handling of the Eastern Question as a whole has also been criticised by John Fisher, who claims that he refused to listen to advice and adopt a 'modern' approach to the conduct of diplomacy in this region.[78] What is not clear, however, is that given the political and economic constraints of the time, what alternative strategy could have been adopted. Both Curzon and Lloyd George were not only aware of the importance of settling events in Europe but of the need to maintain a strong presence in the Near East and Asia until the problems in this region could be given greater diplomatic priority by the Allies. The strategic importance of this region to Britain both in terms of involvement in European diplomacy and imperial affairs required the committee to have a strong and assertive leader. Under Curzon's chairmanship, the Eastern Committee became highly influential. Churchill, never a friend of Curzon, once complained that 'Curzon's Eastern Committee habitually consults the Chief of the Imperial General Staff and gives him direct orders which he executes. In these circumstances I consider that I have hitherto been an observer rather than a responsible actor'.[79] This was not merely professional spite. Curzon saw a direct connection between his role as chairman and the general operation of the Foreign Office. A year before he became Acting Foreign Secretary, Curzon had viewed his chairmanship of the Eastern Committee as an opportunity to demonstrate his expertise in Middle Eastern affairs to his colleagues and to lay to rest any ghosts that remained surrounding his controversial resignation as Viceroy of India.[80] He also realised that he was now an influential part of the government. He wrote: 'Inasmuch as the greater part of the work of the Committee is performed by the Foreign Office, the War Cabinet will not be able to work effectively unless [he, Curzon was] brought into intimate relations with that office, and as the different branches of the Committee's work are dealt with in different departments of the Foreign Office, it seems desirable that the Secretary should be in close touch with the Foreign Office officials who have hitherto been performing the work'.[81] Sensing a threat to his own position as Foreign Secretary, Balfour challenged Curzon's vaunting ambition. He asked that the British presence in the Middle East, which had proved expensive both in military and administrative costs, should be reviewed.[82] He accused Curzon of failing to place the cost of administering the region high enough on the agenda of the Eastern Committee.[83] Anticipating the possible establishment of British mandates in Mesopotamia, Syria and Palestine, Balfour urged Curzon to examine the long-term implications of such a policy to Britain rather than concentrating on Britain's right to obtain such territories.[84]

Balfour's criticism of Curzon's activities was part of a wider source of tension. As he became marginalised by Lloyd George in Paris, Balfour resented the freedom of action that Curzon was permitted in determining British policy in the Middle East. This was particularly evident when Curzon discussed the extension of British diplomatic influence abroad. Balfour thought that he was being dangerously impetuous.[85] The tension was fuelled during the early months of the Paris Peace Conference when Curzon used his knowledge of Middle Eastern politics to apply pressure on Balfour to make policy statements on the diplomatic consequences of the collapse of the Ottoman Empire. Curzon thought it expedient to support the claims of Syrian refugees against the Turkish government because it was proposed to put some Turkish territory under a League mandate.[86] Balfour believed that the Turks should be expelled from Constantinople and that the city and the Straits should be administered by the League of Nations.[87] Curzon was unconvinced that such a policy would work.[88] But his warning fell on deaf ears.

By June 1919, Curzon had moved beyond protesting to Balfour about the lack of direction in British policy. He wrote a memorandum, the contents of which were to reflect his entire approach to Graeco-Turkish relations for the remainder of his period at the Foreign Office. He expressed concern that these advances had been made in the full knowledge of the delegations at the peace conference. This was despite the 'open disregard of the principle, laid down in the early days of the Paris Peace Conference, that its ultimate decisions should not be prejudiced by premature and aggressive action in respect of the occupation of territory by any of the interested States or Powers'. Consequently, Curzon predicted, the areas of the Middle East which remained under Turkish control would descend into chaos. His final sentence offered a telling comment on how he contrasted himself with Balfour: 'I venture to submit this representation, not as a protest, which I cannot but feel will be useless, but with a view to ascertaining whether it is in contemplation to place any limit to the extension of these advances, and whether there is any ground for regarding them as provisional in character and duration'.[89]

John Fisher has done much to reinforce the idea of Curzon's independence of mind during his period as Acting Foreign Secretary on general issues of diplomatic strategy. As indicated above, Curzon passionately believed that there was a need to establish a strong British presence in Palestine. He was particularly perturbed by the ability of Zionists to jeopardise the British position in the region. The Zionist question also brought Curzon into direct conflict with Balfour, who had passionately defended the Zionist cause two years earlier.[90] In January 1919, Curzon accused Balfour of being too accommodating in his dealings with Chaim Weizmann, the leader of the Zionist movement. This prompted Balfour to try to scotch the rumour that Weizmann intended to 'put forward a claim for the Jewish Government of Palestine'.[91] Curzon, however, was not convinced, and with good cause. By 1919, Jews outnumbered Arabs by 9 to 1 and there were moves afoot to make Hebrew the official language of the Jewish population. The different attitudes of Balfour and Curzon to the Palestine question became the subject of several letters of protest from Weizmann directed at junior officials at the Foreign Office.[92] Claiming that the root of British 'indecision' lay in the impetuousness of men who lacked a knowledge of the Palestine question, Weizmann berated such individuals for 'showing signs of impatience with the Jews'.[93] In reply, Curzon wrote a lengthy minute recounting how he had stood alone against the rest of the Cabinet in pointing out the dangers of Zionism and that his fears had now proved to be well founded.[94] Now, however, the die was cast and the British government had little choice but to 'march up with a self-imposed cross' upon its shoulders.[95] Despite Curzon's comments, Balfour hesitated to approve the establishment of a commission to investigate the situation. As the political climate in Palestine deteriorated, Montagu began to express public doubts about the soundness of Balfour's judgement.[96] In June, in an attempt to break the deadlock, Herbert Samuel, a leading Jewish Liberal, proposed that the British commitment to Palestine be specifically restricted to the Balfour Declaration.[97] The intensity of Curzon's opposition to Zionism reflected his growing confidence at the helm of the Foreign Office. Two months after the Samuel proposal, Curzon told Balfour:

> Personally, I am so convinced that Palestine will be a rankling thorn in the flesh of whoever is charged with its Mandate that I would withdraw from this responsibility while we can...The difficulty of drawing a boundary between Syria and Palestine and of administering these two countries by separate European Powers is becoming more manifest every day; while the task of reconciling Zionist aspirations with Arab deserts in Palestine is one that the experience of the last six months has made all our administrators unwilling to undertake.[98]

By September, it was clear that Curzon's judgement of the situation in Palestine had proved accurate. Weizmann had entered into direct negotiations with Faisal and, in return for the latter's support, had offered financial assistance.[99] Curzon's dislike of Weizmann intensified when the latter offered advice on how to conduct British policy in Palestine.[100]

Having failed to secure Curzon's support, Weizmann appealed directly to Balfour because much could 'be done by one who is sympathetic and so much can be prevented by one who is indifferent'.[101] Although it was evident that his assessment of the situation in Palestine was misguided, Balfour nevertheless clung to his position. Realising his own vulnerability, he mounted his attack on Curzon's handling of the situation indirectly.[102] The extent to which he was intimidated by Curzon's argument is also evident in this letter. Despite knowing that Curzon's views were out of step with government policy on Palestine, Balfour clearly believed that he had little control over Curzon's actions. He wrote: 'I am, as you know, not the Acting Secretary for Foreign Affairs, and am not therefore at the moment in a position to take any steps in the matter, if steps there are which ought to be taken'.[103] These are extraordinary words from one who had been the architect of British policy in Palestine. While Curzon's vociferous anti-Zionism did not bring about a change in British policy towards Palestine, it did do much to highlight the flaws in Balfour's political judgement that went far beyond a scepticism born out of concerns about his haphazard approach to being Foreign Secretary.

The second politically unstable region that occupied Curzon's attentions during the Paris Peace Conference was Russia. The Civil War had been raging for more than a year and it remained unclear how the Allies should respond to the crisis. Nevertheless, Bolshevism remained an unknown quantity and consequently a potential danger to the stability of Europe. The discussions of British policy towards the newly emerging Soviet regime provide a further insight into the dynamics of Curzon's relations with his colleagues in the War Cabinet and his approach to the conduct of foreign policy. On 13 January 1919, he wrote to Lloyd George urging that the Bolsheviks should be crushed because of the possibility of their inciting revolutionary activity in Germany. The French delegation at the peace conference took a similar view.[104] In February, while on a brief visit to London, Lloyd George came under pressure from Churchill and Curzon not to allow the request of Chicherin, the Soviet Minister for Foreign Affairs, to attend the forthcoming Prinkipo conference.[105] Throughout the spring, Curzon came under pressure to make a clearer statement on British policy towards Russia than Balfour and Lloyd George had made. By June, Curzon's patience with Churchill was wearing thin. A request by Churchill that instructions should be sent to General Milne in the Caucasus, telling him to adopt a more uncompromising attitude towards the Bolsheviks, prompted a withering reply from Curzon.[106] It is tempting to see the contrasting attitude taken by Curzon towards the Russian question between February and June 1919 as evidence of inconsistency in his thought processes. But this would be misguided. By the summer of 1919, Curzon had come to believe that a heavy-handed approach to the Bolsheviks during the Civil War might prove to be counterproductive. It might be viewed as proof that the democratic powers were indeed bullies and that the Russians had made the right decision to reject such a system of government. This, in turn, could lead to an increase rather than decrease in Bolshevik fervour. What is more, Curzon would have relished the opportunity to put Churchill in his place. But this analysis of Curzon's change of heart over intervention in the Russian Civil War has a wider significance. It is often claimed that Curzon's attitude towards Russian affairs was completely at odds with that of Lloyd George – that the former adopted a hard-line approach to dealing with the new Soviet regime, while the latter took a more liberal attitude.[107] Curzon's statements about Russia during his period as Acting Foreign Secretary suggests that there was much less polarity of opinion between the two men. While there were to be some areas of disagreement between them concerning the negotiation of the Anglo-Russian Trade agreement of 1921, their shared indignation at the way in which the Russians helped to undermine the Genoa Conference did much to reinforce their relationship during the difficult six months that led to the collapse of the Lloyd George government in the autumn of 1922.[108]

Reflecting on Curzon's career at the Foreign Office, Lord Crawford wrote: 'As a brain I put him as high as any living politician of my acquaintance – above Balfour, Ll[oyd] G[eorge], Asquith – but somehow he doesn't "cut ice" as the Americans say'.[109] There was more than an element of truth in the first part of the statement, as even Curzon's sternest critics never failed to be impressed by his intellectual talent and prodigious memory. The second half of Crawford's description is much more controversial. While impatience and shortness of temper may make adverse comparisons with the more suave politicians of his generation inevitable, Curzon's impact on the operation of the Foreign Office and the conduct of British foreign policy was significant. The force of his personality and intellectual *gravitas* also enabled him to carve out a role within the War Cabinet as the leading authority on foreign policy and world affairs. This role he developed more fully after October 1919 in many of the areas of foreign policy discussed above, and in continental European affairs.

Curzon's period as Acting Foreign Secretary demonstrates that he was a popular Foreign Office chief and that those with whom he worked most closely responded well to his firm leadership. During this period, he established a good working relationship with Lloyd George that enabled both men to establish complementary rather than rival areas of involvement in the conduct of foreign policy. Curzon was able to demonstrate his own credentials as an international statesman through the conclusion of the Anglo-Persian treaty and the negotiation of the Treaty of Sèvres. He was vociferous in his insistence that the War Cabinet be consulted by the British delegation at the peace conference before all major statements of policy were made. Curzon effectively and convincingly fought off challenges to his authority at the Foreign Office from within the Cabinet and was looked to for leadership in the discussion of foreign policy by senior members of the British delegation at the peace conference. These factors collectively challenge the view that, after the First World War, the Foreign Office had suffered a loss of influence that was so great that it was not possible for officials to resist Lloyd George's idiosyncratic attitude to the conduct of post-war diplomacy. Curzon possessed greater mental energy and insight than Balfour and had a much greater talent for system and organisation than Lloyd George. Between January and October 1919 he established his credentials as Foreign Secretary with such authority that, under his stewardship, the Foreign Office was able to adopt an integral role in shaping British foreign policy during the early years of peace.

NOTES

All references to Foreign Office (FO) documents relate to materials held at the National Archives, London (formerly the Public Record Office) unless otherwise stated.

1. G.H. Bennett, *British Foreign Policy during the Curzon Period* (London: Macmillan, 1995); A. Sharp, 'Lord Curzon and British Policy Towards the Franco-Belgian Occupation of the Ruhr in 1923', *Diplomacy and Statecraft*, 8/2 (1997), pp.83–96; J. Fisher, *Curzon and British Imperialism in the Middle East, 1916–1919* (London: Frank Cass, 1999); J. Fisher, '"On the Glacis of India": Lord Curzon and British Policy in the Caucasus, 1919', *Diplomacy and Statecraft*, 8/2 (1997), pp.50–82; I. Rose, *Conservatism and Foreign Policy during the Lloyd George Coalition, 1918–1922* (London: Frank Cass, 1999).
2. D. Gilmour, *Curzon* (London: John Murray, 1994).
3. H. Nicolson, *Curzon: The Last Phase* (London: Constable, 1934).
4. This situation is not discussed at length in E. Goldstein, *Winning the Peace: British Diplomatic Strategy, Peace Planning, and the Paris Peace Conference, 1916–1920* (Oxford: Clarendon Press, 1991), or Z.S. Steiner and M.L. Dockrill, 'The Foreign Office and the Paris Peace Conference of 1919', *International History Review*, 2/2 (1980), pp.56–70.
5. G. Johnson, 'Curzon, Lloyd George and the Control of British Foreign Policy, 1919–1922: A Reassessment', *Diplomacy and Statecraft*, 11/3 (2000), pp.49–71.
6. Bennett, *British Foreign Policy*, p.76.
7. R. Warman, 'The Erosion of Foreign Office Influence in the Making of Foreign Policy, 1916–1918', *The Historical Journal*, 15/1 (1972), pp.133–59.
8. Goldstein, *Winning the Peace*, pp.9–90.
9. E. Maisel, *The Foreign Office and Foreign Policy, 1919–1926* (Brighton: Sussex University Press, 1994), p.206.
10. For example see Lord D'Abernon papers, British Library, Additional Manuscripts (BL Add Mss), 48954, D'Abernon's diary entry, 18 Dec. 1921.
11. A. Sharp, 'The Foreign Office in Eclipse, 1919–1922', *History*, 61/2 (1976), pp.198–218.
12. Lloyd George Papers, House of Lords Record Office, F/12/1/7, Harmsworth to Lloyd George, 4 Feb. 1919.
13. Derby Papers, Liverpool Record Office, 920 DER (17)/28/1/3, diary, 7 Jan. 1919.
14. Curzon to Lady Curzon, 20 Aug. 1919, in Earl of Ronaldshay, *The Life of Lord Curzon* Vol. III (London: Ernest Benn, 1928), p.204. Curzon's emphasis.
15. Johnson, 'Curzon, Lloyd George', p.54.
16. It is given a fuller treatment in Gilmour, *Curzon*, pp.528–48.
17. Nicolson, *Last Phase*, p.193.
18. See in general Johnson, 'Curzon, Lloyd George'.
19. Lloyd George Papers, F/12/1/5, Balfour to Curzon, 22 Jan. 1919.

20. Lord Riddell, *Lord Riddell's War Diary, 1914–1918* (London: Hodder and Stoughton, 1933), p.229.
21. In L. Mosley, *Curzon: The End of an Epoch* (London: Longman, 1961), p.205.
22. Ibid., p.165. The date is not given, although the context makes it clear that the observations were made in 1919.
23. Curzon Papers, Oriental and India Office Library, Mss Eur F 112/319, Curzon 'Notes for my biographer', Nov. 1922.
24. In Mosley, *Curzon*, p.204.
25. Ibid., p.203.
26. R. Vansittart, *The Mist Procession* (London: Hutchinson, 1958), p.232.
27. Quoted in J. Barnes and D. Nicholson, (eds.), *The Leo Amery Diaries: Volume I, 1896–1929* (London: Hutchinson, 1980), p.249 (2 Jan. 1919).
28. Lloyd George Papers, F3/3/35a, Hardinge to Balfour, 10 Oct. 1918.
29. Clement Jones to Curzon, ? Oct. 1919, in Ronaldshay, *Curzon*, Vol. III, p.207.
30. J. Vincent (ed.), *The Crawford Papers* (Manchester: Manchester University Press, 1984), p.400.
31. Major Baird to Curzon, 26 Oct. 1919, in Ronaldshay, *Curzon*, Vol. III, p.205.
32. Warren Fisher to Curzon, 30 Oct. 1919, in Ronaldshay, *Curzon*, Vol. III, p.205. See also Maisel, *The Foreign Office*, p.206.
33. Derby Papers, 920 DER(17)/28/1/3, diary, 2 Apr. 1919.
34. Lord Riddell, *Lord Riddell's Intimate Diary of the Peace Conference and After, 1918–1923* (London: Hodder & Stoughton, 1933), p.24.
35. Derby Papers, 920 DER (17)/28/1/, diary, 25 Mar. 1919.
36. Curzon to Lady Curzon, 9 Sep. 1919, in Ronaldshay, *Curzon*, Vol. III, p.204.
37. Curzon to Lady Curzon, 19 Aug. 1919, in ibid., p.203.
38. Nicolson, *Last Phase*, p.71.
39. Derby Papers, 920 DER(17)/28/1/3, diary, 9 Mar. 1919.
40. Lloyd George Papers, F/12/1/13, Curzon to Davies, 28 Feb. 1919.
41. FO 608/375/3/5/14985, Balfour to Curzon, 1 May 1919.
42. Derby Papers, 920 DER (17)/28/1/3, diary, 19 Apr. 1919. The Majestic was the name of the hotel at which the British delegation was based.
43. Balfour Papers, British Library, BL Add Mss 49734, Balfour to Curzon, 1 Jul. 1919.
44. Cecil Papers, British Library, BL Add Mss 51131, diary of the Paris Peace Conference, 25 Feb. 1919.
45. See Fisher, *Curzon and British Imperialism*, pp.302–4; M. Hughes, *Allenby and British Strategy in the Middle East, 1917–1919* (London: Frank Cass, 1999), pp.113–29.
46. Curzon to Hardinge, ? Feb. 1919 (FO 800/153) quoted in H. Elcock, *Portrait of a Decision: The Council of Four and the Treaty of Versailles* (London, 1972), p.114.
47. Churchill to Lloyd George, 2 Mar. 1919, in M. Gilbert, *Winston S. Churchill, Volume IV (Companion, Part I: Documents, January 1917–June 1919* (London: Heinemann, 1977), p.561.
48. P.J. Mantoux, *The Deliberations of the Council of Four*(trans.) (Princeton: Princeton University Press, 1992), Vol. I, pp.138–9.
49. A. Lentin, '"*Une aberration inexplicable*": Clemenceau and the Abortive Anglo-French Guarantee of 1919', *Diplomacy and Statecraft*, 8/2 (1997), pp.31–49.
50. In general see Johnson, 'Curzon, Lloyd George'.
51. The first of these is in Balfour Papers, BL Add Mss 49734, Curzon to Balfour, 9 Aug. 1919.
52. Balfour Papers, BL Add Mss 49734, Balfour to Curzon, 9 Jun. 1919.
53. Lloyd George Papers, F/12/1/21, Curzon to Lloyd George, 7 Jul. 1919,.
54. Balfour Papers, BL Add Mss 49734, Curzon to Balfour, 6 Jul. 1919; Curzon Papers, Mss Eur F 112/208A, Balfour to Curzon, 15 Jun. 1919
55. Balfour Papers, BL Add Mss 49734, Curzon to Balfour, 2 Jul. 1919.
56. In general see Johnson, 'Curzon, Lloyd George'.
57. Vansittart, *Mist Procession*, p.44.
58. Balfour Papers, BL Add Mss 49734, Balfour to Curzon, 7 Jul. 1919.

59. J. Tomes, *Balfour and Foreign Policy: The International Thought of a Conservative Statesman* (Cambridge: Cambridge University Press, 1997), p.277.
60. Balfour Papers, BL Add Mss 49734, Curzon to Balfour, 20 Jul. 1919.
61. Ibid., Curzon to Balfour, 18 Jan. 1919.
62. Ibid., Balfour to Curzon, 21 Jan. 1919.
63. Ibid., Curzon to Balfour, 22 Jan. 1919.
64. Ibid., Balfour to Curzon, 25 Jun. 1919.
65. Balfour made his views known in Curzon Papers, Mss Eur F 112/208A, Balfour to Curzon, 23 Mar. 1919.
66. Ronaldshay, *Curzon*, Vol. III, pp.218–9.
67. Ibid., p.216; H. Sabahi, *British Policy in Persia, 1918–1925* (London: Frank Cass, 1990), pp.17–22.
68. Balfour Papers, BL Add Mss 49734, Curzon to Balfour, 23 May 1919.
69. Curzon to Lady Curzon, 17 Aug. 1919, in Ronaldshay, *Curzon*, pp.214–6.
70. Mosley, *Curzon*, p.203.
71. Sabahi, *British Policy in Persia*, pp.2–8.
72. FO 608/98//375/1/7/4468, Curzon to Cox, 12 Mar. 1919.
73. FO 608/98/375/1/7/10359, Curzon's views reported by Hankey, 3 May 1919.
74. FO 608/98/375/1/7/8172, minute by Hardinge, 24 Apr. 1919.
75. FO 608/98/375/1/7/2335, minute by Hardinge, 20 Feb. 1919 on memorandum by Mushaver ul Mamalek, 15 Feb. 1919.
76. FO 608/101/375/3/5/15571, Moore to Oliphant, 12 May 1919; FO 608/101/375/3/5/15201, Curzon to Balfour, 11 Jul. 1919.
77. Sabahi, *British Policy in Persia*, p.2.
78. Fisher, *Curzon and British Imperialism*, pp.2–4.
79. Churchill to Lloyd George, 2 Mar. 1919, in Gilbert, *Churchill, Vol. IV: Companion/ Documents*, p.560.
80. Balfour Papers, BL Add Mss 49734, War Cabinet, Eastern Committee, memorandum by Curzon, G.T. 3905, 13 Mar. 1918.
81. Ibid.
82. The text of the letter has not survived, although Curzon's response makes its substance clear. Balfour Papers, BL Add Mss 49734, Curzon to Balfour, 20 Aug. 1919.
83. Ibid.
84. FO 800/199, Balfour to Curzon, 16 Dec. 1918.
85. Balfour Papers, BL Add Mss 49734, Balfour to Curzon, 22 Jul. 1919.
86. FO 608/110/385/1/7/1949, Curzon to Balfour, 11 Feb. 1919.
87. FO 608/110/385/1/8/5380, Crowe to Balfour, 26 Mar. 1919.
88. Note, 15 Mar. 1919, in Ronaldshay, *Curzon*, Vol.III, p.264.
89. Curzon to Balfour, 20 Jun. 1919, Ibid., pp.267–8.
90. Fisher, *Curzon and British Imperialism*, p.213.
91. FO 800/215, Balfour to Curzon, 20 Jan. 1919.
92. Minute by Kidston, 27 Feb. 1919, in Fisher, *Curzon and British Imperialism*, p.215.
93. Ibid.
94. Minute by Curzon, 28 Feb. 1919, in Gilmour, *Curzon*, p 258
95. Ibid.
96. FO 800/215, Montagu to Balfour, 2 Feb. 1919.
97. Samuel to the Foreign Office, 5 Jun. 1919, in Fisher, *Curzon and British Imperialism*, p.220.
98. Balfour Papers, BL Add Mss 49734, Curzon to Balfour, 20 Aug. 1919.
99. Fisher, *Curzon and British Imperialism*, p.221.
100. Balfour Papers, BL Add Mss 49734, Curzon to Balfour, 9 Aug. 1919.
101. Scottish Record Office (SRO), Whittingehame, Balfour Papers (private), 5, Weizmann to Balfour, 25 Sep. 1919.
102. SRO Balfour Papers, 5, Balfour to Rothschild, 29 Sep. 1919.
103. Ibid.
104. Elcock, *Portrait of a Decision*, p.64.

105. Ibid., p.92. See also War Cabinet Minutes, 13 Feb. 1919, in Gilbert, *Churchill, Vol.IV: Companion/Documents*, pp.525–7.
106. Ibid., p.681, Curzon to Churchill, 10 Jun. 1919.
107. Maisel, *The Foreign Office*, pp.66–7.
108. In general see Johnson, 'Curzon, Lloyd George'.
109. Vincent, *Crawford Papers*, p.400.

Adapting to a New World? British Foreign Policy in the 1920s

ALAN SHARP

At the end of the Great War, the British Foreign Office faced a brave new world with some trepidation. It did not anticipate the outbreak of major hostilities in the near or medium future but this was indeed a world from which the captains and the kings had departed, where the great European empires of 1914 were no more and where new and threatening regimes and ideologies were emerging. As the Paris Peace Conference moved into its less frenetic stages after the signature of the German settlement, the old familiar balance of power had gone. Russia was in chaos though the Bolsheviks were gradually gaining control, the Austro-Hungarian empire had imploded and vanished, the Ottomans were, apparently impotently, awaiting their fate. Germany was defeated and menaced by internal revolution from both left and right. Several new, or revived, states such as Poland and Czechoslovakia now filled the vacuum left by the sequential collapse of traditional authority in eastern and central Europe. The United States had made what was perceived to be a vital intervention in the war and had played a major role in drawing up a peace settlement from which it was, apparently, about to withdraw from enforcing. Not the least of the legacies of the American President, Woodrow Wilson, was the League of Nations which, taken at face value, was about to transform the conduct and course of international relations. Japan was confirmed as a major regional power with an increasing world role, though its experience of the peace conference had not been totally satisfactory. Italy, in a world of fewer powers, perhaps seemed larger and stronger than it was. After 1922 and the rise of Mussolini, Italy arguably joined a growing group of states whose conduct of foreign affairs was influenced, perhaps dominated, by considerations of ideology.[1] At the centre of Britain's post-war world remained France, both an ally and a rival, a paradox reflected in the complexity of Anglo-French relations across a wide series of issues.[2]

The Foreign Office did, with reluctance, come to recognise that, much as Britain might wish to revert to its imperial role, it could not rapidly or easily cast aside its European obligations. Harold Nicolson, then working in the Central Department of the Office, reminded the Committee of Imperial Defence in July 1920 that

> For the last century the policy of His Majesty's Government has been inductive, intuitive and quite deliberately opportunist, but through it all has run the dominant impulse of the defence of India ... (the events of the last twenty years have shown that we cannot be free to carry out our main objects, which are Indian and Colonial, unless we are safe in Europe, and it will be many years yet before we can free ourselves of responsibility for Europe). If this dominating impulse is not to be maintained, the whole perspective of Imperial responsibility will be altered, and the whole basis of our Foreign and Colonial policy will have to be revised.[3]

Britain's European responsibilities had a long-term air about them and it is arguable that it was not until the Locarno agreements of 1925 that these were defined with an acceptable ambiguity.[4] There were also clear signs that particularly the white Dominions, and indeed the Empire as a whole, had a new perspective on their relationship with Britain after the raising of national consciousness by the First World War experiences of Gallipoli (1915), Pozières (1916), Delville Wood (1916) and Vimy Ridge (1917). It was, for example, politic, if not constitutionally necessary, to allow each of the Dominions to consult its own parliament before depositing British ratification of the Treaty of Versailles in October 1919. These were emerging nations whose future European support could not automatically be guaranteed and whose own security concerns led them to expect help from Britain in their own regions.

The Foreign Office was thus faced with reassessing and reconfiguring its world view and adjusting to new realities. As if this was not already a formidable task the Office also faced strong competition within Whitehall for its place as the controlling foreign affairs agency in Britain.[5] It was subjected to greater public scrutiny in its conduct of foreign policy and it was expected to introduce radical internal reforms. It accomplished the latter with greater success than the former. This surprised many, given the reputation and commanding appearance of George Curzon who first deputised in London whilst Arthur Balfour, the Foreign Secretary was in Paris from January 1919 and then, on 24 October 1919, assumed formal control of the Foreign Office, a post he held until January 1924.

In its farewell edition R.W. Seton-Watson's radical weekly *The New Europe* wrote: 'We are in the hands of a Prime Minister who has usurped the functions of the Foreign Secretary ... The Foreign Office seems incapable of asserting its right to control policy, and has irresponsible competitors, not only in the Garden Suburb of Downing Street, but in the War Office, the Admiralty and the India Office'.[6] Curzon did not fail for want of effort in his attempts to reverse this situation, but, as a typical note to a Cabinet colleague in April 1921 reveals, the result was neither a foregone conclusion nor readily and decisively accomplished. After a long catalogue detailing War Office interference in Foreign Office affairs, he stated, 'The Foreign Office is by its constitution, and must be in practice, the sole exponent of the Foreign Policy of this country, and, now the War has receded into the background, and more normal conditions prevail, it is forced to insist upon the resumption of its prerogative'.[7] The widespread perception within and beyond the Foreign Office was that he had not succeeded, and contemporary insiders and observers in significant numbers believed he had not reasserted sufficiently the position of the department or the Foreign Secretary, particularly in the era of Lloyd George's premiership. Curzon blamed his predecessors, especially Arthur Balfour, but even those like his colleague, the Earl of Crawford, thought very highly of Curzon's ability, versatility and self-confidence but concluded that 'somehow he doesn't "cut ice" as the Americans would say. His influence is far smaller than his profound knowledge and experience would justify'.[8] Both Curzon and his colleagues believed that contemporary perceptions of how the Foreign Office should operate influenced their ability to control and deliver Britain's foreign policy and this certainly affected institutional self-confidence. As Curzon graphically put it, 'I have observed lately that whenever a particularly ticklish question comes up the FO instead of advising says "This is a Cabinet question" – and looks the other way. But when I get to the Cabinet the boot's on the other leg – and the Cabinet say "What is the view and advice of the FO?!"'.[9]

It may be that, as his more sympathetic critics suggest, Curzon's achievements have been underrated.[10] This judgement by historians with their perspective and distance from events is certainly defensible but they are battling against a weight of contemporary opinion that suggests that perceptions at the time were very different. Edgar D'Abernon, Edward Derby, Austen Chamberlain, Charles Hardinge, Eyre Crowe, James Headlam-Morley – ambassadors, ministers, officials, friendly and less friendly critics alike – all testified to their belief that the Foreign Office under Curzon was not in proper control of British foreign policy.[11] He was certainly one of the more impressive British foreign secretaries of the inter-war period but he never

believed that he enjoyed adequate support from any of the three prime
ministers he served. Arthur Balfour's opinion was that 'it's the rarest thing
when the Prime Minister and the Foreign Minister don't clash' but Curzon's
relationship with Lloyd George in particular was notorious and lived on in the
institutional memory.[12]

The Foreign Office was also under pressure to reform itself and to
implement the recommendations of the 1914 McDonnell Royal Commission
on the Civil Service, postponed by the intervention of the war.[13] The Foreign
Office was supposed to come more into line with the rest of the civil service,
particularly in terms of recruitment. It was not happy. It would concede that
the property qualification and the prior approval of the Foreign Secretary to
any candidature should be abandoned but it wanted to maintain selection for a
number of reasons. Sir Maurice de Bunsen, the pre-war Ambassador to Madrid
and Vienna, stated in 1918 that 'The type of man required by the Foreign (or
"Imperial") Service is the man who by previous education, personality and the
growing experience gained in his career should be fitted to understand and
interpret foreign governments and foreign peoples... In other words a
specialist ...' and certainly not a mere civil service administrator.[14] The
Foreign Office needed to select its diplomats with an eye to social
compatibility because in 'the conditions of close relationship in which men
necessarily work in an Embassy they form and must form something like a
family party, not because diplomats are different from other people but
because it is the case with all colonies in a foreign country'. It had to be a
separate service because its officials 'ought to learn many things and imbibe
many ideas which it is probably needless for a clerk in the Home Office to
learn, and they should move among men of influence in the Government and
in the country'.[15] Less elegantly the diplomatic secretary, Theo Russell,
expressed his alarm that men without a public school background might be
accepted and, even worse, that they might be 'Jews, coloured men and infidels
who are British subjects'.[16] This was not an auspicious omen for the
development of a diplomatic service more in tune with a democratic age.
Sir Ronald Graham and Curzon succinctly summarised the Office view of a
merger with the Home Civil Service. The former minuted: 'I regard the
scheme with some misgiving'. Curzon added: 'So does everybody'.[17] The
Foreign Office did not object to the more generous Treasury pay scales
achieved after Curzon's intervention in 1919, and it did create an
amalgamated Foreign Office and diplomatic and consular service, though
the comprehensive joint seniority list was soon curtailed and the service did
not achieve compulsory interchangeability of home and foreign service until
the Eden reforms of 1943.[18] Red tape reappeared in 1922 when the white war-
time economy tape was exhausted, but Foreign Office officials had responded
to the post-war challenge, handling three times the 1913–14 volume of papers

by 1921 and employing three times as many staff – and in rather cramped conditions until 1925.[19]

Wilson's policy in Paris had pinned great hopes on the League of Nations as an effective alliance for peace. If taken seriously the demands of the Covenant, which governed the conduct of member states, would revolutionise international relations and diplomacy, and it is clear that there was a constituency within Britain that expected the government to take the Covenant seriously. The Foreign Office had, however, grave reservations about the League, partly because it did not control this new aspect to Britain's foreign policy which was the responsibility of one of its potentially most dangerous internal rivals, the Cabinet Office, and partly because its senior members in particular did not think it would work. There were officials like James Headlam-Morley, historical advisor to the Foreign Office, who believed the League should be made more central to the post-Versailles world and who sought, for example in the government of areas under League jurisdiction such as Danzig or the Saar, and in the continuing monitoring and protection of minorities, to give the League a defined and positive role. When, however, that inveterate League supporter, Lord Robert Cecil, encouraged the government to refer to the League the question of the French occupation of a number of German towns in the wake of the abortive Kapp *putsch* in March 1920, his arguments were fobbed off, despite the Foreign Office's internal admission that his case was strong. Such matters were for the allied governments to settle, not the League.[20] Yet, as Ruth Henig has argued, it was too big an electoral risk to ignore the League. Consequently, successive British governments 'were driven to express fulsome support for the League in public while expressing deep cynicism and pessimism about its capacity to act in private'.[21] The debacle over the Italian invasion of Abyssinia in 1935 exposed the fatal consequences of such a schizophrenic policy for any hope of success for a strategy based either on collective security or on the balance of power.

The Foreign Office had mixed feelings too about the attempts of those within and on the fringes of the British establishment, some of whom had been at the Paris Peace Conference, to open the field of foreign policy to greater scrutiny and thus fulfil one of the League's underpinning requirements – an informed public opinion. Eyre Crowe, Foreign Office Permanent Under-Secretary at this time, was in favour of admitting historians to the departmental archives. Curzon was more jealous of the privacy of the 'official arcana' and there were wider misgivings about the development of the Institute for the Study of International Relations, forerunner of the Royal Institute for International Affairs (Chatham House). Members of the Foreign Office were not banned from joining the Institute, though Charles Hardinge, Crowe's predecessor as Permanent Under-Secretary, believed they would not care to go even if invited. However, some such as Foreign Office minister Eustace Percy did join. Crowe was convinced that this had come about because 'he belong[ed] to that class of intensely virtuous men which takes a certain pleasure in fouling its own nest'. Curzon was scathing: 'The Thing is developing on exactly the lines which I expected and I regard it as I have done throughout with unconcealed suspicion. I cannot see what is to be gained from our people meeting with our avowed and most envenomed critics'.[22] There was some cooperation between members of the service and Chatham House with Headlam-Morley admitting authors of chapters in the Institute's first major publication, *A History of the Peace Conference of Paris*, into the archives to allow them to refresh their memories of the Paris negotiations. Nonetheless Wilsonian hopes of increased public scrutiny and informed critical appraisal of foreign policy were not universally welcomed by the Foreign Office.

A central problem remained the redefinition of Britain's role and objectives in an unfamiliar post-war world. Curzon's liverish reaction to the honouring of old enemies could be seen as reflecting the frustrations and uncertainties of Britain's new world position. He deprecated the current fashion for flattering Britain's foes with portraits of George Washington in Number 10 Downing Street and celebrations of the canonisation of Joan of Arc. The United States and France may have just fought alongside Britain in a successful war against Germany but they were rivals just the same, whilst Germany was perceived to have a key role in the new world despite being a defeated enemy. But how was Britain to achieve its objectives of remaining friendly with the United States and France and yet prevent them from trespassing too closely on its naval supremacy and imperial positions? Both states did at least have the virtue of still being governed by the same sort of people as before the war and it might be possible, in their case at least, to posit a certain continuity of attitude and ambition, both of which might make it easier to deal with them. No such familiarity surrounded the new governments of much of Europe and in particular those of the two major pariahs of the post-war world, Germany and the Soviet Union.

Of the two, Germany seemed easier to read, though Headlam-Morley's plea that it was in Britain's interest to cultivate the new liberal and socialist Germany was not entirely in tune with the implied preference of many senior officials for the old, familiar, monarchist Germany – even if it had been that regime they most blamed for the traumas of the war, or whose influence they saw as exposing the new Germany to the temptations of revisionism.[23] The question of how different the new Germany was from the old was partly obscured by continuities of personnel in the German Ministry for Foreign Affairs and the German state in general, but it was clear that the revolution in Germany was not nearly as profound as that in Russia. Nonetheless it was a new Germany, and Britain needed to establish a working relationship with it, partly to re-establish trade links, partly to create an effective barrier to Bolshevism and partly (though less readily admitted in public) to act as a counter to a France perceived to be over-dominant on the continent.

British policy towards Germany in the early post-war years veered between exasperation at its failure to execute the terms of the treaty and suspicions that some of the treaty clauses were impractical, if not actually wrong, and worse still, that Britain might be at fault; as Sydney Waterlow of the Foreign Office Central Department pointed out in a memorandum written shortly after the German and Russian governments had signed a treaty of mutual assistance at Rapallo in the spring of 1922, 'We are as much, or even more responsible than France for imposing on Germany a reparation burden now generally admitted to be far beyond her capacity to pay'. Curzon had many reservations about Waterlow's first draft of this memorandum but he did not demur from this judgement.[24] In Berlin, Britain had a new type of ambassador, Edgar D'Abernon, who was very sympathetic to the German point of view and about whom historians have generally been complimentary. D'Abernon believed that he had the ear of successive German governments and that his advice was eagerly received in Whitehall. He may well have seen himself as the 'great man' Churchill had advised Lloyd George to send to Berlin 'to help consolidate the anti-Spartacist – anti-Ludendorff elements with a strong left centre block',[25] but his reputation has taken a severe jolt recently at the hands of Gaynor Johnson and Stephanie Salzmann, neither of whom see him as effective or efficient an envoy as he perceived himself to be.[26]

Salzmann is even more critical of the British Minister in Moscow, Robert Hodgson, whom she accuses of still living in the Tsarist era, with no appreciation of the role played by ideology in Soviet policy: 'He was neither familiar with Marxism, nor could he imagine that a country would base its policies on values other than power politics'.[27] The implication here is that power politics was the sole basis of British policy, and this is a theme to which we must return. There is no doubt, however, that both during the inter-war period and then in the era of the Cold War, diplomats faced a severe challenge in trying to read the motivations and intentions of states with unconventional ideologies (if indeed they were states in the conventional sense at all). The Soviet Union was the first of these; fascist Italy and Nazi Germany would soon follow. Philip Kerr, Lloyd George's private secretary recognised the problem when he advised the Prime Minister in September 1920 that 'Peace is at present impossible with the Soviet Government because their principal object still lies in world revolution and not Russian prosperity'.[28] Lloyd George tended to be more sympathetic to Russia than his Conservative allies (and certainly than his Liberal colleague, Winston Churchill, whom Austen Chamberlain accused of being 'more Tory than the Tory ministers'[29]) and, indeed, than the Foreign Office itself. His policy was to try to engage the Soviets in dialogue, to wean them from extremes and to kill Bolshevism with kindness. The great Genoa Conference at Easter 1922 was to accomplish a whole raft of things: to create business opportunities for Germany and others in the Soviet Union; to boost European prosperity so that Bolshevism would be eroded; Germany could then pay its reparation debts; France would feel more secure; and, *sotto voce*, Britain could escape from the leading role in Europe which it had reluctantly assumed during and after the war. The policy failed; the pariahs of Europe concluded the Treaty of Rapallo; and Lloyd George was under increasing Conservative grassroots pressure until the demise of the coalition government in October 1922.

As far as the United States was concerned, the truth was starkly presented to the government by the General Staff in October 1919: 'It must be admitted that, financially we cannot afford to make the preparations which would be essential were we to contemplate the possibility of war with America. And, indeed, were we to enter upon a competition in naval matters with the United States we should have fought Germany for nothing'.[30] Britain needed, therefore, to maintain good relations with the United States which might not be easy, given their sharp ideological differences over imperialism, emotional issues like Ireland, practical rivalries over oil supplies and the continuing problem of inter-allied debts, which Britain and France wished to link to reparations but the United States did not.[31] Sir Auckland Geddes managed to combine many of these issues in his second letter to Curzon from his new post as Ambassador to Washington, declaring, rather puzzlingly, that 'The Irish question equals sentimental Irish Nationalism plus Bolshevism plus Germanism plus Oil and from the financial point of view the greatest of these is Oil'.[32]

Geddes' linkage of apparently disparate threats, each with potential terrorist connections, does have a contemporary relevance. C.J Phillips, in the Foreign Office, did point out than Sinn Fein and Bolshevism were 'almost diametrically opposed to each other', but he added that 'Sinn Fein has made desperate struggles recently, and with considerable success, to seize the control of the Bolshevik Movement in Ireland, recognising it as amongst its most deadly enemies'.[33] There was often a perception within the Office, and the British establishment more generally, that there were links between Bolshevism and groups and individuals who opposed British rule, and that frequently Moscow was manipulating and coordinating worldwide attacks on the empire. This was sometimes linked to suspicion of Jews. In November 1918 Crowe wrote:

> It is as well to remember – with regard to our pro-Zionist policy and our general sympathy for Jewish communities – that the heart and soul of all

revolutionary and terroristic movements have invariably been the Jews, the Bolsheviks and the Turkish Committee of Union and Progress being the most notorious examples. There is also every indication that the extreme socialists in Germany are led and organised entirely by Jews. We are facing a powerful international organisation and it is well to bear this constantly in mind.[34]

Balfour was scornful: 'I should like to hear more of this international Jewish conspiracy which seems equally interested in accumulating money in the west and cutting throats in the east and which sometimes takes the form of a centralised military and imperialistic despotism (as in Turkey); sometimes of a chaotic welter of proletariat rule (as in the Soviet Union)'.[35] His scepticism was not always shared by colleagues facing an unfamiliar world.

The United States had an important role to play in Britain's considerations of its future options in the Far East. Sir John Tilley, the Assistant Under-Secretary at the Foreign Office responsible for this area, summed up, in December 1919, the difficulty facing Britain. 'Owing to Japan and the United States being apparently irreconcilable, it is very difficult for us to work a policy in the Far East conjointly with both of them, whilst it is essential for us, owing to our naval weakness in the Pacific, to have a friendly Japan'.[36] Ian Nish's view was that the Anglo-Japanese alliance had probably outlived its utility and needed to be replaced by arrangements more compatible with the international climate of the 1920s. He argued that the United States, even though acting for selfish interests, probably did both Britain and Japan a favour by forcing them to consider with greater urgency the future of their pact. Nonetheless, reinforced particularly by Canadian urgings, the need to conciliate the United States was influential in the ending of the only modern alliance with which Britain had entered the First World War.[37]

If war with the United States was unthinkable, apparently war with France was not, or at least British decision-makers frightened themselves by discussing the possible effects of such a war, whilst at the same time declaring that it would be 'a world calamity which seems almost unthinkable: but where national security is concerned even the unthinkable must be faced'.[38] Balfour invited the Committee of Imperial Defence to contemplate the French dropping at least 84 tons of bombs on London on a daily basis even though he admitted that such an attack was 'hardly conceivable'.[39] Yet much of Britain's foreign policy was inseparably entwined with its relationship with France, and was the cause of much debate and heart-searching amongst contemporaries. In a perceptive and thoughtful appraisal of Britain's position in early 1921, Crowe wrote:

> It is to be feared that failing some general settlement of the German question which will satisfy French public opinion, we may drift into

a serious quarrel, if not a definite breach, with France. Such a contingency cannot be contemplated without grave anxiety. England has not been fortunate enough to gain, or retain, the effective goodwill of any of the European Powers: her relations with America are far from satisfactory; Anglo-American tension reacts upon our position both in South America and in the Far East; and in the Near and Middle East we are seriously threatened with the dangers arising from the influence of Bolshevik – or Russian – hostility.[40]

It was not a very rosy world view. Crowe's suggestion was that 'If we could at this juncture reconstitute, or if possible fortify, the solidarity of the entente with France, the whole situation would be materially changed to our advantage'.[41]

Here lay the great dilemma of post-war international affairs for Britain – should there be an alliance with France in the hope of providing France with the stability and confidence to offer generous treatment to Germany, or would such an alliance only encourage French intransigence, secure in the knowledge of British support? For the French, of course, this alliance had already been promised during the peace negotiations (or at least that is what seemed to have happened until Lloyd George put the rabbit back in the hat) but the British thought the French wanted to bargain separately over every issue.[42] There were many variations on the theme of the durability and nature of the alliance, and there were various episodes and negotiations when it seemed a deal was in sight but it was never clinched, despite general agreement that such a pact would go far to securing peace in Europe for the foreseeable future. Both the British and French governments believed, or claimed to believe, that the alliance was worth more to the other and hence each wanted to sell its support for the best price. On the whole the British did not want to be engaged to defend Eastern Europe – where the French believed the German assault on the settlement would begin – and the French did not want to cave in on every imperial dispute with Britain. In the end there was no pact, just a reluctant recognition that each needed the other in a rather sad partnership where each did just enough to thwart the main aims of the other. It is in the failure to make this relationship work effectively that many of Britain's post-war difficulties lie because somewhere in almost every other problem the lack of a firm Anglo-French consensus made any solution more elusive.

The debate about an entente with France was never conducted entirely on the grounds of power politics, important though these were. The protagonists raised moral and ethical considerations as well as issues of *Realpolitik* and this was not unique to this discussion. Britain did have an ideology. Underlying British policy at the Paris Peace Conference and after was the defence of liberal values and the hope that these would spread. This was partly for reasons of self-interest, but also because it is clear that many British officials, such as Headlam-Morley, did firmly believe that these values held universal virtue and that their application would make the world a better place. In common with many of the junior officials at the Foreign Office, Harold Nicolson had gone to Paris a convinced Wilsonian and returned disillusioned with the President but retaining faith in many of the ideals he felt had been betrayed in the peace settlement – self-determination, liberal civic nationalism, the virtues of the League and a sense of international justice. It is true that these ideas were often expressed conveying a self-satisfied air amongst British decision-makers. There is often, within their comments, an unspoken assumption that British policy was altruistic and benign. This complacent view that it was right for them to hold what they had and that what was good for Britain was automatically good for others does sometimes jar – the problem with foreign affairs was that the foreigners could not grasp this.

'*Pax Britannica*', according to Philip Kerr, 'includes three things, law, order and democracy'.[43] He was anxious that these benefits should be spread within the Empire, but for many in the Foreign Office, whenever they had the time to think about such matters, these were certainly ideas that deserved a wider currency. Some of the Foreign Office's attitudes made its officials rather paradoxical advocates of democratisation, if not liberalism, but, like President Wilson, they believed in such values not least because making the world safe for democracy would make the world a safer place. Despite British short-term optimism about the improbability of major wars in Europe, anything was welcome which enhanced the prospect of continuing peace for a nation of shopkeepers that did not want to repeat its recent martial experiences.

NOTES

All references to Cabinet (CAB), Foreign Office (FO) or War Office (WO) documents relate to materials held at the National Archives, London (formerly the Public Record Office) unless otherwise stated.

1. In general see A. Cassels, *Mussolini's Early Diplomacy* (Princeton: Princeton University Press, 1970); C.S. Maier, *Recasting Bourgeois Europe: Stabilization in France, Germany, and Italy in the Decade after World War I* (Princeton: Princeton University Press, 1975.

2. See P.M.H. Bell, *France and Britain 1900–1940: Entente and Estrangement* (London: Longman, 1996).

3. CAB 4/7, CID Paper 251-B by Nicolson, 10 Jul. 1920.

4. See D. Johnson, 'Austen Chamberlain and the Locarno Agreements', *University of Birmingham Historical Journal* 8/1 (1961), pp.62–81; J. Jacobson, *Locarno Diplomacy: Germany and the West, 1925–1929* (Princeton: Princeton University Press, 1972); F. Magee, '"Limited Liability"? Britain and the Treaty of Locarno', *Twentieth Century British History*, 6/3 (1995), pp.1–22; R.S. Grayson, *Austen Chamberlain and the Commitment to Europe: British Foreign Policy, 1924–1929* (London: Frank Cass, 1997); G. Johnson, 'Lord D'Abernon, Austen Chamberlain and the Origins of the Treaty of Locarno', *Electronic Journal of International History* 1/1 (2000: www.history.ac.uk/ejournal/art2.html)

5. P. Hennessy, *Whitehall* (London: Secker and Warburg, 1989), pp.398–407, 542–3.
6. *The New Europe*, 17/11, 28 Oct. 1920.
7. FO 800/149, Curzon to Worthington-Evans, 28 Apr. 1921.
8. J. Vincent (ed.), *The Crawford Papers: The Journals of David Lindsay 1871–1940* (Manchester University Press, Manchester, 1984), p.400, diary entry, 17 Feb. 1919. As Lindsay suggested, part of Curzon's problem lay in his sometimes unrealistic ventures, such as trying to have Big Ben quietened at night because it disturbed his Carlton House Terrace sleep. See in general the essay in this collection by Gaynor Johnson, on Lord Curzon as Acting Foreign Secretary, January–October 1919.
9. FO 371/4288/162305/32842/18, minute by Curzon, 18 Dec. 1919.
10. See G.H. Bennett, *British Foreign Policy during the Curzon Period, 1919–1924* (Basingstoke: Macmillan, 1995); G.H. Bennett, 'Lloyd George, Curzon and the Control of British Foreign Policy 1919–1922', *Australian Journal of Politics and History*, 45/4 (1999), pp.467–82; D. Gilmour, *Curzon* (London: John Murray, 1995); G. Johnson, 'Curzon, Lloyd George and the Control of British Foreign Policy, 1919–1922: A Reassessment', *Diplomacy and Statecraft*, 11/3 (2000), pp.49–71.
11. See A.J. Sharp, 'The Foreign Office in Eclipse, 1919–1922' *History*, 61/2 (1976), pp.198–218.
12. B.E.C. Dugdale, *Arthur James Balfour: Volume 2* (London: Hutchinson, 1936), p.215.
13. See Z. Steiner, *The Foreign Office and Foreign Policy, 1898–1914* (Cambridge: Cambridge University Press, 1969).
14. FO 366/780, de Bunsen memorandum, 10 Mar. 1918.
15. Ibid., draft memorandum, 16 Mar. 1918.
16. Ibid., Note by Russell, 14 Jun. 1918.
17. FO 366/788, minutes by Graham and Curzon, 14 Jul. 1919.
18. On the post-war reforms see C. Larner, 'The Amalgamation of the Diplomatic Service with the Foreign Office' *Journal of Contemporary History*, 7/2 (1972), pp.107–26; M. Dockrill and Z. Steiner, 'The Foreign Office Reforms, 1919–1921' *The Historical Journal* 17/1 (1974), pp.131–56.
19. See FO 366/799. In 1913–14, the Foreign Office handled 58,790 papers, and in 1921, 146,846; respectively it employed 132 and 482 people. In 1925 the Office expanded its building by an extra storey.
20. Cecil wrote to Curzon, Balfour and Lloyd George on 12 Apr. 1920 arguing that the German troop movements could be construed as contraventions of Articles 42 and 43 of the Treaty constituting a threat of war and hence the League should be summoned. Waterlow commented 'Either we must sooner or later find an occasion to promote recourse to this machinery, or we must reconcile ourselves to the Covenant becoming a dead letter'. See FO 371/3783/191340/4232/18.
21. R. Henig, 'Britain France and the League of Nations in the 1920s' in A. Sharp and G. Stone (eds), *Anglo-French Relations in the Twentieth Century: Rivalry and Cooperation* (London: Routledge, 2000), pp.139–57, p.140.
22. FO 371/4383, minutes by Hardinge, n.d., and Curzon, 18 Dec. 1919; Curzon Papers, India Office Library, Mss Eur F112/223, Crowe to Curzon 14 May 1922. See also chapters by D. Lavin and M. Dockrill on the founding of Chatham House and Foreign Office reactions in A. Bosco and C. Navari (eds), *Chatham House and British Foreign Policy 1919–1945: The Royal Institute of International Affairs in the Inter-War Period* (London: Lothian Foundation Press, 1994).
23. Headlam-Morley feared the allies might arouse suspicion that they were 'turning to the idea of a monarchical reaction in order to preserve society. It is not to the extreme Right, to the nobles and to the Church that we can depend for this. We must win the confidence of the Liberal and Socialist Left'. See FO 608/9/41/1/1, minute, 24 Jan. 1919. Crowe stated, 'It is implied that if and when conditions in Germany have again become more normal and she has resumed her place in the council of nations, militarism and nationalist feeling will disappear. I do not read the situation this way'. See FO/371/4757/C11056/113/18, 13 Nov. 1920.

24. W.N. Medlicott, D. Dakin and M.E. Lambert (eds), *Documents on British Foreign Policy*, First Series, Vol. 20 (London: HMSO, 1976), pp.31–46, 35, memorandum, 'British Central European Policy in its relation to Genoa', 9 May 1922. For Curzon's comments on the original draft of 29 Apr. 1922 see FO 371/7569/C6200/6200/18.
25. Lloyd George Papers, House of Lords Record Office, F/9/2/20, Churchill to Lloyd George, 24 Mar. 1920.
26. G. Johnson, *The Berlin Embassy of Lord D'Abernon, 1920–1926* (Basingstoke: Palgrave Macmillan, 2002); S.C. Salzmann, *Great Britain, Germany and the Soviet Union: Rapallo and After, 1922–1934* (Woodbridge: Royal Historical Society, 2003).
27. Salzmann, *Rapallo and After*, p.23.
28. Lloyd George Papers, F/90/1/18, Kerr to Lloyd George, 2 Sep. 1920.
29. Lloyd George Papers, F/7/5/20, Chamberlain to Lloyd George, 21 Mar. 1922.
30. WO 943, memorandum by General Staff, Oct. 1919.
31. See Bennett, *British Foreign Policy*, pp.160–75; B.J.C. McKercher (ed.), *Anglo-American Relations in the 1920s: The Struggle for Supremacy* (Basingstoke: Macmillan, 1991).
32. Curzon Papers, Mss Eur F112/206, Geddes to Curzon, 21 May 1920.
33. Ibid., minute by Phillips, 1 Jun. 1921.
34. FO 371/4369/PID547/547, minute by Crowe, 18 Nov. 1918.
35. FO 371/4369/PID547/547, minute by Balfour, n.d.
36. Quoted by I. Nish, *Alliance in Decline: A Study in Anglo-Japanese Relations 1908–1923* (London: Athlone Press, 1972) p.277.
37. Ibid., pp.392–7.
38. CAB 16/47, CID Paper 108A by Balfour, 'The Air Menace', 29 May 1922.
39. CAB 16/46, CID Sub-Committee meeting, 15 Nov. 1923.
40. Curzon Papers, Mss EUR F112/242, memorandum by Crowe on the Anglo-French Pact, 12 Feb. 1921.
41. Ibid.
42. See A. Lentin, '"*Une aberration inexplicable*": Clemenceau and the Abortive Anglo-French Guarantee of 1919' *Diplomacy and Statecraft*, 8/2 (1997), pp.31–49.
43. Lloyd George Papers, F/90/1/18, Kerr to Lloyd George, 2 Sep. 1920.

The Foreign Office, 1930–39: Strategy, Permanent Interests and National Security

B.J.C. McKERCHER

For eight years – from January 1930 until December 1937 – the Foreign Office dominated the making and execution of British foreign policy. Led by the Permanent Under-Secretary (PUS), Sir Robert Vansittart, the professional diplomats provided the strategic basis of British external policy that endeavoured to ensure the security of the home islands and for the effective protection of the Empire. Basing policy on maintaining balances of power in those regions vital to British interests, using the military and financial resources of the state to underpin that policy, and relying on the practices of what was then called 'old diplomacy', the pre-1914 tradition of pursuing British foreign policy dominated Foreign Office advice to its political masters. For the last two years of the decade, however, when Neville Chamberlain, the Prime Minister after May 1937, moved to control foreign and defence policy, the reduction of Foreign Office influence in policy-making witnessed the advent of a different diplomatic strategy that endangered both British and Imperial interests and the security of the state.

However, for the first four years after the First World War, Downing Street succeeded in taking the conduct of British foreign policy away from the Foreign Office. Antipathetic to the Foreign Office because he thought it a bastion of upper-class privilege and incompetence, and convinced of his own diplomatic brilliance, David Lloyd George and a clutch of his private secretaries used a series of multilateral conferences to defend narrow British interests.[1] Avoiding active British involvement in Europe's security, the Prime Minister produced ineffective diplomatic strategies that weakened British influence in European affairs.[2] After Lloyd George fell from office in October 1922, the Foreign Office once again emerged as the guiding force behind British foreign policy because of sympathetic Prime Ministers and influential Foreign Secretaries.[3] In this regard, the influence of Sir Eyre Crowe, PUS 1920–25, proved critical in re-establishing professional control of foreign policy-making.[4] Crowe's two successors, Sir William Tyrrell and Sir Ronald Lindsay, followed in his footsteps. With his appointment in January 1930, Vansittart continued this process.

Hence, the Foreign Office that existed for most of the 1930s was a reflection of Vansittart's approach to the conduct of British external relations. His diplomatic apprenticeship was also shaped by Sir Francis Bertie, Ambassador at Paris, and by Sir Charles Hardinge, a former Viceroy of India, and PUS 1906–10 and 1916–20.[5] Foremost in this context was Vansittart's acceptance that the most effective strategy for the protection of Britain's external position lay in the pursuit of balance of power diplomacy.[6] And this pursuit was not just restricted to Europe; it had equal efficacy in other regions of the globe where British interests in the form of prestige, markets, strategic outposts, and lines of communication required protection (in the Mediterranean, the Middle East, and South and East Asia). In the view of Vansittart and his mentors, effective British foreign policy devolved from supporting diplomatic initiatives with the power of the state – strong armed forces, the economic sinews provided by the City of London, the country's industrial capacity, and the political influence that every British government could bring to bear on friendly, neutral, and adversarial powers. In his diplomatic apprenticeship, Vansittart was not only exposed to the important European situation, he served in Persia and in Egypt, as well as on international commissions dealing with Imperial issues, thereby supplementing his knowledge in the intricacies of continental Great Power politics with those relating to the Empire. When the Great War broke out, he was one of a group of younger British diplomats who believed that Britain had been forced into a war of survival against militaristic Germany.[7] The First World War was therefore designed as much to protect British interests in Europe and the wider world against the Central Powers as it was to re-establish the balances of power in Europe and those other regions of the globe vital to Britain's position as the world's foremost Great Power.

After the war, Vansittart was appointed as private secretary to George Curzon, Foreign Secretary after October 1919. In this central position, which he held until February 1924, Vansittart came both to understand the myriad of foreign policy problems confronting Britain and to apprehend the administrative and bureaucratic pressures of making and executing diplomatic initiatives. While appreciative of the constitutional prerogative of the elected politicians to determine the shape of and have responsibility for Britain's foreign policy, he shared the distrust of Crowe, Tyrrell and others for what they saw as the interference of amateurs in policy making, and the apparent ignoring of professional advice.[8] In this regard, Lloyd George's campaign to control foreign policy from Downing Street, and his appointment of political cronies to important embassies abroad, like the Marquess of Crewe at Paris and Lord D'Abernon at Berlin, found disfavour with Vansittart.

The consistency of his views with those of senior figures within the Foreign Office also led to rapid promotion. In February 1924, he was appointed head of the American Department – an important position given the rising importance of the United States in international affairs. Vansittart helped contain growing difficulties in Anglo-American relations over the naval question.[9] By 1928, Vansittart had been transferred to the Premier's private office to advise on foreign policy issues. There, he played a central role in the resolution of Anglo-American differences in the run-up to the London Naval Conference of 1930, winning the support and friendship of the two prime ministers he served, Stanley Baldwin and James Ramsay MacDonald.[10] He was renowned for a calm and detached approach to problem solving, and, by the end of the decade had become the leading candidate for the post of Permanent Under-Secretary.

By the time Vansittart became PUS, Lloyd George's experiment in foreign policy-making had been undone. During his period as PUS from 1920 to 1925, Crowe had worked to ensure that 'our long suffering Service is recaptured from the outsiders'.[11] This involved promoting capable professional diplomats like Vansittart to important Foreign Office posts and placing professional diplomats in important embassies. By the end of the 1920s, the Foreign Office and Diplomatic Service were once again in professional hands. This process had also been assisted by two Foreign Secretaries – Curzon and Austen Chamberlain – who resisted outside interference. Of the prime ministers of the later 1920s, MacDonald was particularly important. The reputation of MacDonald, who served as his own Foreign Secretary in the short-lived minority first Labour government in 1924, had been damaged by the Zinoviev letter scandal, containing an apparent call for revolution in Britain by Bolshevik Russian authorities. Thereafter, when Labour Party luminaries proposed means to ensure party control over the Foreign Office, MacDonald resisted because he did not think professional diplomats were responsible for the Zinoviev letter. MacDonald's faith in the professionalism of the Foreign Office was reflected in his decision to appoint Vansittart as PUS in December 1929. As MacDonald told Vansittart privately at this time: 'The F.O. needs the most efficient guidance it can get. The amateurs must be controlled. You may not have an easy time but you will have very important work'.[12]

To appreciate Vansittart's influence as PUS is to understand that MacDonald and Baldwin rotated as Prime Minister until May 1937. Thus, from January 1930 to December 1937, when Neville Chamberlain replaced

Vansittart with Sir Alexander Cadogan, the Foreign Office was dominated by a permanent official with lengthy diplomatic experience, with more than a grounding in European questions, with a wide strategic vision, and, until his last months as PUS, with political support from Downing Street. In early 1934, when the Foreign Secretary, Sir John Simon, was criticised by the Cabinet for his lack of diplomatic skill, Vansittart privately discussed replacing Simon with MacDonald – a most unusual circumstance.[13] Furthermore, Vansittart used his position to ensure that diplomats who shared his vision, and supported him, held key ambassadorial posts abroad and headed the Foreign Office administration at home. Some of his choices were not successful – the egregious Nevile Henderson's appointment as Ambassador to Berlin is a case in point.[14] Later in his tenure as PUS, political pressures from Anthony Eden, the Foreign Secretary after December 1935, saw the promotion of Vansittart's eventual successor, Cadogan, within the Foreign Office bureaucracy. But more successful appointments of ambassadors whose views were consistent with Vansittart's own included Sir George Clerk (Ambassador at Ankara, 1926–33, and at Paris, 1934–37); Sir Robert Clive (Ambassador at Tokyo, 1931–34); Sir Robert Craigie (Ambassador at Tokyo, 1937–41); Sir Eric Drummond (Ambassador at Rome, 1933–39); Sir Ronald Graham (Ambassador at Rome, 1921–33); Sir Francis Lindley (Ambassador at Tokyo, 1931–34); Sir Ronald Lindsay (Ambassador at Washington, 1930–39); Sir Percy Loraine (Ambassador at Ankara, 1933–39); Sir Eric Phipps (Ambassador at Berlin, 1933–37, and Paris, 1937–39)[15] and Sir Horace Rumbold (Ambassador at Berlin, 1928–33).[16] A similar pattern was mirrored in appointments to lesser posts. For example, Sir Joseph Addison (Ambassador at Prague, 1930–36); Sir Archibald Clark-Kerr (Minister at Stockholm, 1931–35); Sir Esmond Ovey (Ambassador at Brussels, 1934–37) and Sir Walford Selby (Minister at Vienna, 1933–37); Laurence Collier (Head of the Northern Department); Lancelot Oliphant (Assistant Under-Secretary); Owen O'Malley (Head of the Southern Department); Orme Sargent (Head of the Central Department) and Ralph Wigram (Head of the Central Department).

These men constituted the heart of professionalism in British foreign policy; a professionalism that looked back to the period before the Great War for its origins. As a generation of experts in foreign policy, which has been characterised as 'Edwardian',[17] its self-appointed singularity flowed from the relative homogeneity of the class and educational background of 'professional' diplomats; and this attitude was re-enforced by the belief that these men were members of the most socially exclusive and prestigious department of state in Whitehall. As a Royal Commission on the Civil Service observed in 1914, the Foreign Office and Diplomatic Service were populated by 'the type of man who is fit for this international career called diplomacy'.[18] The continuity of beliefs amongst pre- and post-war Edwardians can be seen in their memoirs, of which those of Vansittart are typical.[19] They laud professional expertise; they disparage what they perceive were the ill-conceived ideas of Lloyd George and Neville Chamberlain that endangered Britain's security because they ignored diplomatic realities like maintaining the balances of power;[20] they had little use for public opinion groups such as the Union for Democratic Control or the League of Nations Union that appeared to advocate subordinating British interests to a wider international morality; and their argument that foreign policy is successful only if buttressed by the combined economic and armed strength of the state. There was an unquestioning assumption that the will to pursue a hard-line, including armed force against menacing powers, was essential for effective diplomacy. The strategic objective always entailed deterring threatening powers but, if necessary, such powers had to know that Britain would fight rather than back down.

Foreign Office influence in policy-making in the period from January 1930 until late 1937 can be seen in the intra-governmental debates over diplomatic strategy and the means to secure British interests in the rapidly changing milieu of the 1930s caused by the advent of three challenges to international stability: Japan's effort to restructure the Far Eastern balance of power that began with the Manchurian crisis in September 1931; growing German strength after the Nazi seizure of power in January 1933; and the nettled Italian question after October 1935 when, because of the Abyssinian crisis, Anglo-Italian relations soured. The origins of the crises that confronted the British in the 1930s lay with the onset of the Great Depression in the winter of 1929–30 that, beginning with the crash of the American stock market, undermined international trade and produced severe economic dislocation within all powers great and small. The capitalist system of the 1920s was a delicate and interlocking structure in which any disruption spread quickly to all its parts. Supply and demand largely determined international prices for most basic raw materials, food, and industrialised goods; and regional divisions of labour developed whereby large areas prospered by producing specific materials and goods for sale abroad. Credit financed much of this production: an arrangement based on mutual confidence: lenders and investors would get their funds back; debtors would pay; and producers of food, raw materials, and industrial products would be able to sell at fair prices. Through this process, sellers could purchase from primary and secondary producers, debts could be honoured, and new investment could be undertaken. To ensure smooth financial transactions, there was a stable medium of exchange. Gold underpinned the major currencies, particularly sterling and the dollar. Although London and New York banking houses contested for advantage, this competition occurred within defined rules and was overseen to a degree by cooperation between the Bank of England and the Federal Reserve Bank of New York.

Spreading outwards from the United States, the crisis passed from finance
to industry. Wall Street's weakness constrained the export of American capital
so that American creditors began calling in their loans. As these loans were to
be paid in dollars, and as European and other debtors confronted higher
American tariffs that made acquiring dollars difficult, the confidence that had
marked the 1920s eroded. Other powers constructed tariff walls to protect their
economies. International commodity prices declined further; debts negotiated
before 1929 were paid with difficulty, if at all; and unemployment emerged
everywhere. Tied to regular liabilities, like capital investment, were special
ones incurred in the 1920s: inter-Allied war debt and German reparations
payments. In full swing by mid-1930, the general international economic and
financial malaise continued for the rest of the decade.

In the Far East, the Japanese reaction to the international economic crisis was
to seize Manchuria, the most industrialised province of China with a population
of 60 million.[21] This Sino-Japanese struggle lasted until May 1933 when the
Chinese Nationalist government was forced to sign a peace treaty acknowledging
the sovereignty of a new state, Manchukuo, nominally independent but controlled
by Japan and Japanese domination over provinces in the north-east. Working
through the League of Nations, Britain and the other powers tried to resolve the
crisis by an investigation and recommendations to ensure peace. Although
League criticism of Japanese actions was relatively mild, the Japanese
government announced in February 1933 that it would leave the League; this
action had added implications for the balance of power in East Asia as the
League-sponsored World Disarmament Conference was meeting concurrently.[22]
Japan would probably not be bound by its results, a situation made more piquant
by opposition in Japan from powerful quarters towards the naval arms limitation
agreement that had been concluded at Washington in 1921–22 and extended in
1930 at London.[23] The Imperial Japanese Navy had been fixed at a building ratio
inferior to both that of the Royal Navy and the United States Navy – 5:5:3 – and it
seemed possible that when the London naval treaty was to be renewed in 1935,
Japan would oppose continued limitations on its naval strength. Clearly, the
balance of power in East Asia and the western Pacific, with Britain's substantial
investment in the China market at its heart, was in a state of flux.

In Germany, although having risen to prominence by criticising the Treaty
of Versailles, Hitler pursued a careful and cautious foreign policy until the
autumn of 1933.[24] However, in mid-October 1933, he announced that
Germany was leaving both the League and the Disarmament Conference.
Whilst he made no comments about German rearmament, little doubt existed
that his government would follow such a course as soon as it was able. For the
British, substantial potential threats to their security and interests in East Asia
and on the continent of Europe could not be ignored; they required a measured
and effective diplomatic response.

Since the British government signed the Treaty of Locarno in 1925, British foreign policy had been pursued on the basis of international arms limitation. Despite international opposition, the successive governments of Baldwin and MacDonald worked to reduce the British armed forces to the minimum essential for national and imperial defence. In this process, British foreign policy was designed to allow those various governments to maintain the balances of power in those parts of the globe essential for the preservation of British interests. In the late 1920s, Tyrrell and Lindsay provided the diplomatic material to allow Austen Chamberlain, Baldwin's Foreign Secretary, to play the 'honest broker' in Franco-German relations and find a workable *modus vivendi* with Japan in China.[25] Their efforts were continued by Vansittart and the Foreign Office after 1930. In the planning for the Disarmament Conference after 1930, Foreign Office advice tendered to the Cabinet had the same tenor. As the Foreign Office Central Department on Vansittart's prompting asserted: 'Both [Britain and France] have been satiated by the Peace Settlement: neither is striving to obtain anything more. Both only want to keep and develop what they have got. Both, in fact, are seeking peace and security'.[26] Of course, efforts to maintain the balance between France and Germany were crucial.[27] But it involved more than just working with Paris and Berlin. Thus, when Franco-Italian difficulties emerged over the naval balance in the Mediterranean in September 1930, Vansittart and Craigie persuaded Henderson to inform Paris and Rome that he would 'do anything which either the Italian or French Government felt I could do by way of helping them to reach a satisfactory settlement'.[28] After twisted diplomacy in which Vansittart and Craigie took the lead on the British side, a Franco-Italian compromise that played a major part in preparing a draft treaty for the Disarmament Conference was effected through the medium of the Foreign Office.[29]

But despite the possibility that the Disarmament Conference would see arms limitation accepted by all the powers, limitation balanced by the security of their varied interests, Japan's forward policies in China indicated to Vansittart and others in London that the 'Ten Year Rule' review of British defence spending was inadequate to protect the British position in East Asia. In March 1932, the Chiefs of Staff Committee (COS), comprised of the Chief of the Imperial General Staff, the First Sea Lord, and the Chief of the Air Staff, recommended to the Committee of Imperial Defence (CID) that the 'Rule' be cancelled.[30] Vansittart agreed, although he had been critical of this policy since becoming PUS. Because even building programmes falling within the 'Ten Year Rule' and accepted by the Cabinet were being delayed for reasons of retrenchment, he contended consistently that weakened British armed forces were enervating British diplomatic strength. Unless British foreign policy could be backed by a minimum of armed strength, its effectiveness would be limited. The Cabinet accepted the COS-Foreign Office arguments on

23 March 1932, but it did not put a new policy in its place and warned the fighting services that rearmament was not yet possible. Its reasoning centred on the parlous nature of the British economy and that the Disarmament Conference was less than two months old and might produce an agreement.[31]

Over the next year, coextensive with a lack of progress at the Disarmament Conference, the failure of multilateral efforts to confront the worsening international economic situation,[32] and the rise of Nazi Germany, the international situation darkened for the British. Of principal concern was Japan's announcement about leaving the League and the Nationalist government in China suing for peace – security in that vital sphere created by the Washington Treaty of 1922 was fast disappearing. In April–May 1933, the Foreign and Colonial Offices and other departments of state concerned with defence policy supported unabated COS concern about the deterioration of the armed forces at a moment when the requirements for Imperial Defence and the treaty obligations that Britain had assumed since 1919 had not diminished.[33] These issues were the focus of the 1933 Annual Review, circulated on 12 October 1933. 'No guiding principle has yet been established to replace the Ten Year Rule' the COS stated. 'We ask the Committee of Imperial Defence whether they confirm generally our appreciation of the situation as set forth above, and whether they can give any further guidance to our Government Departments responsible for Imperial Defence'.[34] Hitler's decision two days later to take Germany out of both the League and the Disarmament Conference emphasised the need to re-evaluate foreign and defence policy.

Tied to the international situation, this assessment led the National Government to create an *ad hoc* advisory body, the Defence Requirements Sub-Committee (DRC), of the CID.[35] Chaired by Sir Maurice Hankey, the secretary to both the CID and Cabinet, its members were Vansittart, Sir Norman Warren Fisher, the Permanent Secretary to the Treasury, and the Chiefs of Staff: Field Marshal Sir Archibald Montgomery-Massingberd, Admiral Sir Ernle Chatfield, and Air Marshal Sir Edward Ellington. The work of the DRC is well known.[36] Meeting twelve times between 14 November 1933 and 26 February 1934, its members advocated more than £70 million extra spending on the three armed services by 1939.[37] Most significant in the DRC deliberations was the determination of Germany as Britain's 'ultimate potential enemy' and the placing of Japan secondary in importance.[38]

Determining the size and disposition of military forces is always a sub-set of national strategy. In this regard, Vansittart proved formidable within the DRC in deciding Britain's strategic response to the changing international milieu in the Far East and Europe; and the efforts that he made in the advisory body continued in the five months after, when its recommendations were weighed by the Cabinet and came under attack by Neville Chamberlain, who emerged as the principal critic of balance of power strategy. The initial mandate of the DRC was that the Japanese and German threats, plus Indian defence, were to be considered within a modified Ten Year Rule that did not anticipate war with the United States, France and Italy.[39] In this context, based on the COS 1933 Annual Review, Japan was the first in the order of threat. However, the German withdrawal from the League and from the Disarmament Conference after that Review was circulated saw an amended mandate: to consider the effect of British armament policy on German strategies on this issue and to review Britain's general security requirements.[40] In other words, the DRC was now to consider which of the two powers was the chief threat to British security.

The Foreign Office and Treasury were the leading departments of state in inter-war Whitehall. In the DRC, therefore, despite differences over the American question, especially fuelled by Treasury criticism of United States' armaments policy, Vansittart and Warren Fisher formed a bureaucratic alliance that placed Germany first in the order of British threats, and produced a strategy designed to allow Britain to maintain the balance of power in Europe. This occurred in contradistinction to Chatfield, the dominant personality in the COS, who saw Japan as Britain's principal antagonist.[41] Warren Fisher advanced arguments about the need to ameliorate Anglo-Japanese differences, which would limit heavy naval spending, but his focus rested on strengthening the deterrent value of improved defences at Singapore and battleship modernisation. Strengthening Britain's position in the Far East would foster Tokyo's appreciation that it could not imperil British interests with impunity.[42] Despite the anti-American tone of his arguments, which Vansittart did not share, Warren Fisher found himself agreeing to Vansittart's prescription about the need to have British strategy focus primarily on the continent. In fact, it was Warren Fisher who first used the term 'ultimate potential enemy' to refer to Germany.[43]

Since Hitler's rise to the Chancellorship, Vansittart had become increasingly concerned with Germany's potential to disrupt the European balance.[44] This in no way suggests that Vansittart was an implacable anti-German, a charge that has been levelled at him retrospectively.[45] His principal consideration centred on deciding what were British interests, which power threatened them, and how to offer protection. He had been highly critical of Germany before 1914 and worked assiduously during the war to bring about its defeat. After 1918, in Vansittart's estimation, new threats to British interests emerged: France, because of its desire to dominate on the continent and thus upset the balance; and the United States, through the desire of successive American administrations to achieve naval parity with the Royal Navy. With the advent of the Nazi regime in Berlin, Germany re-emerged in his calculations as a renewed threat that had to be neutered.[46]

It was his assessment of the strategic dilemma confronting Britain by late 1933 that laid the basis for DRC recommendations to the Cabinet. As he put it: 'The order of priorities which put Japan first pre-supposed that Japan would attack us after we had got into difficulties elsewhere. "Elsewhere" therefore came first, not second; and elsewhere could only mean Europe, and Europe could only mean Germany'.[47] Resolute and persuasive in advancing his strategic vision, he won Warren Fisher's agreement that Germany remained Britain's principal concern and that British defence inadequacies had to be remedied with this in mind. This vision lay at the core of the DRC 'Report': the balances of power in Europe and the Far East were linked; the Royal Navy had to be effective in western Pacific waters; the RAF needed building up for home defence and operational support abroad; and an army expeditionary force was needed to ensure Britain's willingness for a continental commitment. This was an ironic situation. As Lieutenant-Colonel Henry Pownall, secretary to the DRC, commented: 'It is curious how, all through, the Chiefs of Staff have been the moderating influence in the Committee. The civilians, whose presumable line was to keep down impossible service demands, have continually been the alarmist party, demanding quicker and heavier rearmament, whatever the price.'[48]

In the DRC Report, defence deficiencies were to be remedied by 1939 when Germany might be ready for war.[49] Expeditionary ground troops – a Field Force – for the continent were to be given priority at £25 million of the army's £39,990,980 allocation, and some 35 per cent of entire DRC proposed spending.[50] This resulted from Vansittart's contention that Germany not Japan constituted the principal threat to British security and global interests: weakness in Europe would imperil British security and, as a result, its ability to protect its widespread interests. Even before the DRC reported, he counselled Simon and MacDonald that 'Germany will attract friends to her camp if she is allowed to grow, while we remain weak'.[51] But he did not negate Japan's adversarial potential. In December 1933, he told the DRC that Foreign Office minutes on the COS Annual Review 'agreed with the priority which had been given'. But, he stressed, his view differed, arguing that Japan would avoid confronting Britain unless Britain faced a crisis 'elsewhere'.[52]

Through its ministerial disarmament committee – DC(M) – which considered arms limitation, rearmament, and ancillary defence policy issues, the Cabinet began consideration of the DRC Report on 3 May 1934. Vansittart and Hankey had anticipated that opposition to the Field Force would emerge in the DCM.[53] They were correct. In the nearly three months that the DC(M) deliberated, before it reported on 31 July,[54] Vansittart and Neville Chamberlain became locked in a dispute over British strategy. As the PUS was not a member of Cabinet, he used his pen and his connections with Baldwin and MacDonald, as well as pressure on Simon, to put his case for British involvement in the European balance.[55] Ironically, Vansittart and Chamberlain shared the view that Germany was the 'ultimate potential enemy'. But whereas Vansittart took the position that active involvement on the continent via a foreign policy built around the commitment of the Field Force could bring security, Chamberlain argued that any threat to British interests posed by Germany could be removed without despatching ground forces. Chamberlain believed in the deterrent value of a strengthened RAF. Building up the RAF would be less expensive; and the Field Force was not a deterrent.[56]

In the Report that emanated from the DC(M), Chamberlain won approval for reduced defence spending: £55.4 million by 1939 instead of £71.32 million. In this revised allocation, the RAF would receive £22.4 million, the Royal Navy £13 million, and the Army £20 million. However, the Army's total included £12,004,000 for the Field Force, 60 per cent of the Army total and 21.66 per cent of the entire allocation.[57] Chamberlain won his argument for a deterrent RAF; but in an important compromise, Vansittart prevailed in the need for the Field Force. The first Foreign Office paper received by the DC(M) as it considered the DRC Report was Vansittart's advocacy of active involvement in the European balance.[58] He explained that German actions in July 1914 came from the Kaiser's government not knowing whether Britain would go to war if the continental equilibrium was threatened. As he had earlier contended, Japan would not move unless Britain encountered trouble elsewhere. Elsewhere could only mean Germany. Not looking solely at Europe, he believed that other powers, even the United States, might be useful in British policy. Consequently, eschewing regional understandings with other powers or pursuing policies that suggested British diplomacy lacked force would not protect Britain's global interests: 'The Foreign Office has long endeavoured to make bricks without straw'. In this process, Vansittart's position gained support from Baldwin and MacDonald, and ministers such as Lord Hailsham, Secretary of State for War.[59] It was these men who grasped that Britain must not be isolated from the politics that affected its position in Europe and beyond – the explicit thrust of Chamberlain's entreaties.

Over the next three and a half years, even after Italy was added to the list of potential enemies, it was this conception that lay at the basis of British external policy in Europe and the wider world. The handling of the Japanese and German questions from mid-1934 to mid-1937 was primarily concerned with making judgements about British strength, military capacity, and in relation to the threat posed by those countries. Yet, at the heart of British strategy in this pivotal period lay the balance of power. Two case studies are exemplary. The first centres on Japanese diplomatic probing in the summer of 1934 to win support from Britain and the United States, the other main powers within the Washington treaty system, for the post-Manchurian crisis status quo in China. In early July, Hirota Kōki, the Japanese foreign minister, suggested to Clive 'that Japan would be only too ready to conclude non-aggression pacts with America and Britain'.[60] An Anglo-Japanese rapprochement seemed possible.

Reaching Chamberlain in early August – he was acting Prime Minister as both MacDonald and Baldwin were vacationing – the Chancellor immediately sought Foreign Office views. Vansittart asked the American and Far Eastern departments to assess the inter-locking issues of naval limitation and the non-aggression proposal. Their reactions differed. Orde, the Far Eastern Department head, thought that the Japanese Foreign Ministry might sincerely want to ameliorate Anglo-Japanese differences, but with the 1935 naval conference in the offing, Hirota, a civilian, would have difficulty in getting naval authorities to accept limitation within the existing ratios.[61] Moreover, an Anglo-Japanese non-aggression pact would antagonise the Americans, Chinese, and other powers with colonies in the Far East. The American Department, through Craigie, suggested that conceding 'equality of status' over naval arms would better protect British interests than a pointless search for Anglo-American common ground.[62] If 'non-aggression' could be adequately defined, with Britain retaining the right of self defence, he could accept the Japanese proposal. Orde looked to balance all the powers in the region; Craigie saw a new balance built around an Anglo-Japanese condominium.

Siding with Orde, Vansittart posited that 'equality of status' would allow Japan to 'estimate [its] needs at a figure which will entirely alter the status quo', whilst a bilateral non-aggression pact would provide the Japanese with 'a free hand in China'; the latter would undermine Britain's good relations with those other powers with Far Eastern interests.[63] Such a course, therefore, would undercut Britain's ability to influence East Asian affairs. Although Vansittart advised Simon to dampen Cabinet support for a non-aggression pact, Chamberlain forced the issue. Prior to receiving Clive's despatch, he penned a paper on 'The Naval Conference and Our Relations with Japan'. Arguing that it was possible that Britain could shortly be confronted by a hostile Germany as well as an unfriendly Japan, he proposed: appeasing Japan over naval arms; concluding an Anglo-Japanese non-aggression pact; doing nothing respecting the Americans beyond keeping Washington informed of what was transpiring; taking a soft line in naval negotiations with Paris to keep the Germans in line; and conducting a public education campaign in Britain to explain why the government was meeting British defence deficiencies.[64] Hirota's proposal steeled Chamberlain about the virtue of his bargaining strategy. He sent his draft to Baldwin, Simon, and two other senior ministers in early September.[65]

This led to an exchange between Chamberlain and Simon who, strengthened by Vansittart, prevented an immediate approach to the Cabinet.[66] Simon maintained that accepting Hirota's démarche would threaten the East Asian balance by kindling mistrust amongst other powers with interests in the Far East. Giving the Japanese increased security might encourage them to pursue a forward policy in East Asia. Simon suggested a joint Treasury-Foreign Office submission to Cabinet on 16 October, a week before preliminary talks began for the next naval conference.[67] Whilst Chamberlain's arguments from his August draft remained, Foreign Office misgivings about Tokyo receiving 'a free hand' were emphasised. As the Manchurian crisis of 1931–32 had shown, the risk existed that the Japanese might not honour the guarantee.[68] By this time, Clive reported that Hirota saw a non-aggression agreement as substituting for the naval treaty should the latter prove impossible to extend.[69] In this light, the Cabinet delayed formal discussions with the Japanese. When Japan refused to join in another extension of the Washington naval treaty in January 1936, the possibility of an Anglo-Japanese non-aggression pact had disappeared.

Over the next three years, as Simon was succeeded by Sir Samuel Hoare in June 1935 and Hoare by Eden in December 1935, the Foreign Office worked to maintain the Far Eastern balance of power. As difficult as it was given domestic isolationist sentiment, the United States had importance in this balance through the naval question: the Foreign Office saw only renewed naval animosities arising from failure to renew the Washington treaty. Vansittart and his closest advisors also saw Bolshevik Russia as increasingly important in British strategic calculations in both Europe and the Far East. If handled properly and assuming that Moscow's desire for 'collective security' after Germany's withdrawal from the League was genuine, the Russian lever could be used by Britain in dealing with both Japan and Germany.[70] As early as January 1934, when Russo-Japanese tensions were high, Vansittart sought opinions from Collier, head of the Northern Department, and Orde about this matter.[71] The worst eventuality would be a Russo-Japanese rapprochement. Indeed, the lack of such an understanding later in the year probably led to Hirota's proposal. The best outcome would be a stalemated war, in which both sides would be weakened. The middle course offered the most expedient strategic result: continued Russo-Japanese antagonism short of armed conflict. For the rest of his tenure as PUS, Vansittart worked to keep the Japanese and Russians from ameliorating their differences.[72] Avoiding specific commitments towards either power, whilst seeking to entrench British strategic and economic interests, marked British policy in this vital region. Moreover, in Vansittart's strategic conception, finding common East Asian ground when possible with the Russians had the double merit in Europe of having another power to balance Nazi Germany. To a degree, working with France in East Asia could also provide strategic capital in limiting German resurgence – again, showing the connection between the Far Eastern and European balances. The end of Vansittart's efforts in the Far East came after July 1937, when the Japanese Army moved south in China out of its northern strongholds.[73] But he was no longer PUS when Chamberlain's government looked for new means to protect British interests in East Asia.

The second case study concerns the German question. In May 1934, in the aftermath of the DRC deliberations, the Foreign Office examined British security policy. Three tactical approaches to maintain the balance flowed to Vansittart. Allen Leeper, the head of the Western Department, contended that the collapse of the Disarmament Conference would probably see a Franco-Russian rapprochement designed to contain Germany, on one hand, and, because Mussolini would never allow himself to be aligned with communists, the emergence of an Italo-German alliance, on the other. As Anglo-German interests differed, Britain would have to combine with France and Russia, the result being the 'restoration of the old system of the Triple Alliance and the Triple Entente'.[74] Craigie, now an Assistant Under-Secretary at the Foreign Office, wished Britain to retain a free hand by not joining either camp. All Britain needed to do was proclaim unilaterally that it would oppose any attack on the Low Countries, the destination of the Field Force.[75] Wigram in the Central Department believed that British policy backed by armed strength would give Germany pause, would doubtless disincline Italy from aligning with Germany, and would show Paris that in the long run, French containment of Germany would be best achieved by working with London.[76] Vansittart believed that the Central Department's vision offered the most effective means to maintain the balance. Using arguments made to the DC(M) about making 'bricks without straw', he observed that during the period of disarmament, French security concerns had not been allayed by Britain so as to accept limited German rearmament.[77] Britain lacked the military capacity. With the Field Force, the situation had now changed.[78]

Accordingly, when Hitler announced full German rearmament in March 1935, Vansittart played a central role in forging a common Anglo-Franco-Italian front against Nazi Germany. At the Stresa conference 11–14 April, MacDonald and Simon conferred with Flandin, the French Premier, and with Mussolini. Avowing the need for Central European and Danubian security pacts, the three leaders issued a resolution censuring Hitler's unilateral repudiation of the disarmament provisions of Versailles – which secured unanimous support from the League Council.[79] Hugh Wilson, the American observer at the League, reported that Vansittart had 'played the decisive role' in bringing the three anti-revisionist Powers together.[80] Certainly within the British government, Vansittart led in convincing Simon and the Cabinet about finding common ground with the French; he cleared the way with Paris and Rome; and he did so for balance of power reasons.[81] A recent critic of Vansittart has argued that he exaggerated British weakness by 'ignoring Germany's unpreparedness for major war in 1934–5'.[82] Not only does this belie Vansittart's views, it overlooks the domestic milieu from which British foreign policy sprang. The National Government had suffered several recent by-election defeats, British peace advocates were promoting the so-called Peace Ballot, and the National Government had to face the electorate within the year. Voters would not countenance forward action against Germany.

However, aligning with France and Italy, whose military strength combined with that of Britain could deter Germany, was not only palatable to domestic opinion, it conformed to the successful traditions of British diplomacy touching the continental balance that had long informed policy. It was at this moment, moreover, in terms of the global balance, that Vansittart was moving towards the idea that Russia might be useful in helping to contain both Germany in Europe and Japan in the Far East.[83]

But international politics are always evolving. In the year after May 1935, good Italian relations with France and Britain ruptured, partly as a result of the conclusion of the Franco-Russian security pact in May 1935 and, the next month, the conclusion of the Anglo-German naval agreement.[84] However, more significant was Mussolini's decision to expand the Italian empire in East Africa through the conquest of Abyssinia. In October 1935, Italian forces invaded Abyssinia, and there then developed a major crisis that, when the war ended in May 1936, saw Italy estranged from its Stresa partners. In May 1935, as Italo-Abyssinian relations worsened, the Foreign Office produced a strategy that guided British policy for the next several months: Britain should seek a settlement between Mussolini and Haile Selassie, the Abyssinian emperor, whilst safeguarding firm Anglo-Italian ties.[85] When the crisis erupted, Hoare, the new Foreign Secretary, and Vansittart understood that bloodshed in East Africa could adversely affect the European, Mediterranean, and Far Eastern balances of power. Vansittart even considered purchasing Italian goodwill by ceding British Somaliland to Rome.[86] After the Italian attack, British policy was simple: prevent Mussolini's ambitions from thwarting Britain's ability to influence the balances of power in Europe and the Far East. But whilst the goal was uncomplicated, achieving it was not. When League economic sanctions failed to provide a peaceful solution because of American reluctance to support an oil embargo, Vansittart played a pivotal role in hammering out an Anglo-French bargain that would have given Italy seven-eighths of Abyssinia and provided a rump state for Haile Selassie. Concluded in early December 1935, this agreement, the Hoare-Laval pact, named after the British and French Foreign Ministers, was leaked to the press in Paris before other powers and the League were appraised of its contents.[87] Public revulsion about the supposed immorality of the pact drove Hoare and Laval from office. Eden, Hoare's replacement at the Foreign Office, possessed a pathological hatred of Mussolini that prevented any repair to the Anglo-Italian relationship.[88] This meant that after final Italian victory in Abyssinia in May 1936, the material to reconstruct Stresa had disappeared. It also meant that one of the guiding precepts of the DRC in 1934 had vanished: Italy was now added to the list of potential British adversaries.

In that troubled year, Vansittart took the lead in Britain in trying to pursue an effective balance against Germany – an effort rendered more difficult by

Hitler's decision in March 1936 to remilitarise the Rhineland in violation of Versailles.[89] Importantly, the strategy determined in 1934 was not watered down. The DRC had been reconstituted in 1935 as the crisis in East Africa mounted. It reported twice: to argue that defence deficiencies still had to be remedied by 1939; and to recommend that the cost was now £417.5 million.[90] Through a new ministerial committee of the CID, the Defence Policy and Requirements Sub-committee (DPR), the Cabinet modified the DRC allocation: to spend £394.5 million (£241 million by 1 January 1939 and £153.5 million by 1 January 1941).[91] The Field Force remained in place, and the RAF and Royal Navy were to be further augmented. In the DRC, though still certain about the German threat, Vansittart did not reason in purely European terms.[92] '[I am] sure the tendency in the next few years would be for Germany and Japan to draw closer together', he observed, 'and Japan would take advantage of the complications in Europe to erode our position in the Far East'.[93] By October, with the Abyssinian crisis unfolding, his assessment remained unchanged.[94] Supported by Warren Fisher, the potency of a united Foreign Office-Treasury front in the bureaucratic debate over foreign and defence policy remained firm. Germany and Japan, in that order of priority, remained the chief menaces to international stability and, hence, British security. And, now, Mussolini seemed ready to use Italy's Abyssinian conquest as a steppingstone for further aggrandisement in the Mediterranean. Surmising that Italy might later help Hitler realise his Central and Eastern European aspirations, especially in Austria, Vansittart decried COS suggestions that London allow Berlin freedom in these regions; German strengthening would damage British interests. Although Anglo-German cooperation remained possible on particular matters – the naval agreement was a case in point – an adventurous Hitler had to be deterred. Coupled with an entente with France, strengthened British armed forces would do much to effect this strategy. Yet Far Eastern issues could not be detached from European and Mediterranean considerations. Vansittart continued to support the tactic of 'friendliness towards Japan' supported by a regional military presence to obviate Japanese covetousness towards British markets, colonies, and the two South Pacific dominions. And Britain should not ignore Geneva in these calculations. Support for League collective security, however, should only occur if sanctions provided legal cover to protect British strategic or economic interests.

In 1936–37, the Foreign Office endeavoured to produce policy to maintain the balances of power in Europe, the Mediterranean and the Far East. In cleaving to the assertion about 'elsewhere' coming 'first, not second', Vansittart and his Foreign Office colleagues looked to build continental stability in both its western and eastern reaches. This brought the PUS and diplomats like Sargent and Wigram into conflict with Eden and, through him, elements of the Cabinet over the means to achieve that stability. In a general sense, the Foreign Secretary and his senior advisors shared a common desire: finding means to work with Germany to achieve a settlement. But where Eden looked for an actual Anglo-German rapprochement, Vansittart held that a permanent Anglo-German settlement remained 'unobtainable'.[95] Vansittart, Sargent and Wigram looked to ameliorate differences to buy time so that British rearmament could be completed before an inevitable breakdown in cooperation between London and Berlin. When that happened, British policy needed to be underwritten by military strength necessary to restrain Germany: the currency to win continental powers to help maintain the balance. In determining the finer details of strategy, further divisions emerged. Eden argued that British policy should concentrate only on Western Europe, that Hitler's ambitions lay in the east, and that Eastern Europe was not a British responsibility.[96] Part of the Foreign Secretary's conception of achieving stability lay with his strong support of the League, part on a desire to restrict British commitments, and another on an antipathy towards working with the Soviet Union.[97] Vansittart took the view that stability and real security could only be attained by finding a means to balance what occurred in the Anglo-French relationship, on one hand, with that between Britain and the Eastern European states, including Russia, on the other.[98]

In December 1936, Vansittart prepared another 'Old Adam' memorandum for the Cabinet.[99] Surveying the international horizon, he argued that international politics was now being distinguished by the emergence of competing blocs of powers. When civil war erupted in Spain, Germany and Italy had cooperated in supporting the right-wing Nationalist rebels. Furthermore, Germany and Japan had signed the Anti-Comintern Pact in late November. Apart from giving Tokyo an ostensible anti-Russian ally, which could weaken impediments to further Japanese expansion in China, this agreement brought the Japanese question 'into the orbit of European affairs at a particularly delicate and dangerous phase'. In these considerations, Hitler remained the essential issue. With Germany rearming both 'spiritually' and 'materially', peace in Europe would hinge on a man 'obsessed with the idea of expansion'. A crisis in Europe, where Italy would probably not support the Anglo-French Powers, would have grave implications for the Far East. As Vansittart told the Cabinet, the only way to protect British interests, to maintain the balances vital to British security, lay in increased rearmament. Strengthened armed forces would deter German ambitions, which were not restricted solely to Eastern Europe. And what was true in the German case was equally so concerning Japan and Italy. Returning to the Stresa paradigm, Vansittart argued that the balance of power on the continent could be improved in British favour if Italy could be detached from Germany. 'Elsewhere' could be made more secure.

Over the next year, Vansittart sought to provide British foreign policy with bricks of straw to sustain the balances of power in Europe, the Far East,

and the Mediterranean. But both the PUS and his department of state had
critics within the government. Chamberlain was singularly strident, especially
after his attempt to improve Anglo-Japanese relations failed as much from
Foreign Office effectiveness in policy-making as from the actions of Tokyo.[100]
Following the Hoare-Laval debacle, Chamberlain found more Cabinet allies.[101]
Then, Eden's appointment as Foreign Secretary saw an incremental division
between him and his chief advisor that, in December 1936, saw pressure to
have Vansittart replace Sir George Clerk at Paris. Only Baldwin's intervention
saved Vansittart.[102] Once Chamberlain became Prime Minister in May 1937,
however, Vansittart's days were numbered. In early December 1937, with
Baldwin retired and MacDonald dying suddenly in November, Chamberlain
moved. Anxious to avoid war – the implicit result of the failure of the balance
of power – and considering that neither the League nor multilateral
conferences achieved anything, Chamberlain and a new group of leaders
believed that bilateral settlements with British adversaries could better
preserve international peace.[103]

This echoed Chamberlain's contentions about Anglo-Japanese conciliation
in 1934; and, once Vansittart was removed, it formed the basis of the variant of
appeasement diplomacy practised by his government until March 1939.[104] In
this process, after a defence review in late 1937–early 1938, Chamberlain's
Cabinet cancelled the Field Force and increased funds for the RAF.[105] A new
strategic approach to British foreign policy was now being followed. After
Eden's resignation in February 1938 over a dispute with Chamberlain about
how to handle the Italians, Downing Street controlled foreign policy. Ignoring
Realpolitik, British policy began hunting for elusive compromises and, by
September 1939, it led to Britain's weakening in the Far East, the
Mediterranean and continental Europe. None of this is to say that the Second
World War would have been prevented if Foreign Office professionals rather
than amateurs led by Chamberlain had continued to dominate policy-making.
Given what Vansittart and others saw as Hitler's obsession with 'the idea of
expansion', that war was Hitler's war. But it is to say that the course of events
would not have been worse. The professionals working with Vansittart
understood the reality of power and worked in a tradition with doctrines that
had long produced effective diplomatic strategy. They saw the world as it was,
not as it should be. British strength had limits. The generation of British
diplomats that achieved maturity before the Great War understood that Britain
had to work with powers that shared its interests. Such cooperation permitted
the maintenance of the balances of power in the world vital to British security.
But as Chamberlain showed after mid-1937, and as Lloyd George showed
before late 1922, 'old diplomacy' worked only if there was political will to
utilise it. In the 1930s, only Vansittart and the Foreign Office produced
realistic policies able to protect British interests.

NOTES

All references to Cabinet (CAB) or Foreign Office (FO) documents relate to materials held at the National Archives, London (formerly the Public Record Office) unless otherwise stated.

1. C. Finke, *The Genoa Conference: European Diplomacy, 1921–1922* (Chapel Hill: University of North Carolina Press, 1984); S. Salzmann, *Great Britain, Germany, and the Soviet Union: Rapallo and After, 1922–1934* (London: Royal Historical Society, 2003), Chapter I; A.J. Sharp, 'The Foreign Office in Eclipse 1919–22', *History*, 61/2 (1976), pp.198–218; R. Warman, 'The Erosion of Foreign Office Influence in the Making of Foreign Policy, 1916–1918', *The Historical Journal*, 15/1 (1972), pp.133–59. See also K.O. Morgan 'Lloyd George's Premiership: A Study in "Prime Ministerial Government"', *The Historical Journal*, 13/1 (1970), pp.130–57.

2. See G.H. Bennett, 'Lloyd George, Curzon and the Control of British Foreign Policy 1919–22', *Australian Journal of Politics and History*, 45/3 (1999), pp.467–82; G. Johnson, 'Curzon, Lloyd George and the Control of British Foreign Policy, 1919–22: A Reassessment', *Diplomacy and Statecraft*, 11/3 (2000), pp.49–71.

3. See G.H. Bennett, *British Foreign Policy During the Curzon Period, 1919–24* (Basingstoke: Macmillan, 1995); D. Marquand, *Ramsay MacDonald* (London: Jonathan Cape, 1977), pp.329–56; B.J.C. McKercher, 'Austen Chamberlain and the Continental Balance of Power: Strategy, Stability, and the League of Nations, 1924–29', in E. Goldstein and B.J.C. McKercher, (eds), *Power and Stability: British Foreign Policy, 1865–1965* (London: Frank Cass, 2003), pp.207–36.

4. E. Maisel, *The Foreign Office and Foreign Policy 1919–1926* (Brighton: Sussex University Press, 1994), pp.48–54; B.J.C. McKercher, 'Old Diplomacy and New: The Foreign Office in the Interwar Period', in M.L. Dockrill and B.J.C. McKercher (eds), *Diplomacy and World Power: Studies in British Foreign Policy, 1890–1951* (Cambridge: Cambridge University Press, 1996), pp.79–114. See also S. Crowe and E.T. Corp, *Our Ablest Public Servant: Sir Eyre Crowe, GCB, GCMG, KCB, KCMG, 1864–1925* (Braunton: Merlin, 1993), Chapter 17.

5. See B.J.C. McKercher, 'The Last Old Diplomat: Sir Robert Vansittart and the Verities of British Foreign Policy, 1903–1930', *Diplomacy and Statecraft*, 6/1 (1995), pp.1–38; N. Rose, *Vansittart: Portrait of a Diplomat* (London: Heinemann, 1977), pp.17–60.

6. This derived from Crowe's influence. See R. Vansittart, *The Mist Procession*, (London: Hutchinson, 1958).

7. Vansittart, *Mist Procession*, pp.130–31; G. Campbell, *Of True Experience* (New York: Hutchinson, 1947); H. Knatchbull-Hugessen, *Diplomat in Peace and War* (London: John Murray, 1949); M.D. Peterson, *Both Sides of the Curtain; An Autobiography* (London: Constable, 1950).

8. R. Vansittart, 'The Decline of Diplomacy', *Foreign Affairs*, 28/4 (1950), p.186.

9. B.J.C. McKercher, 'A British View of American Foreign Policy: The Settlement of Blockade Claims, 1924–1927', *International History Review*, 3/1 (1981), pp.358–84.

10. B.J.C. McKercher, 'From Enmity to Cooperation: the Second Baldwin Government and the Improvement of Anglo-American Relations, November 1928–June 1929', *Albion*, 24/1 (1992), pp.64–87.

11. An observation made when he secured Sir Esme Howard the Washington embassy in 1924. See Howard Papers, Cumbria Record Office, DHW 9/39, Crowe to Howard, 9 Jan. 1924.

12. Vansittart Papers, Churchill Archives Centre, Churchill College, Cambridge, VNST II 6/9, MacDonald to Vansittart, 26 Dec. 1929.

13. MacDonald Papers (UK National Archives), 30/69/1767, Vansittart to MacDonald, n.d. (probably Jan. 1934).

14. See P. Neville, 'The Appointment of Sir Neville Henderson, 1937: Design or Blunder?', *Journal of Contemporary History*, 33/2 (1998), pp.609–19.

15. See J. Herman, *The Paris Embassy of Sir Eric Phipps: Anglo-French Relations and the Foreign Office, 1937–1939* (Brighton: Sussex University Press, 1998).

16. See M. Gilbert, *Sir Horace Rumbold: Portrait of a Diplomat, 1869–1941* (London: Heinemann, 1973).

17. In contradistinction to the earlier 'Victorians', who believed that Britain should have a 'free hand' to maintain the balances of power in Europe and the wider world and, thus, avoid formal alliances and agreements with other powers, the 'Edwardians' held that international circumstances had changed by the late 1890s so as to make a completely independent foreign policy impractical and dangerous. See the first essay in this collection, Zara Steiner, 'The Foreign and Commonwealth Office: Resistance and Adaptation to Changing Times'.

18. *Fifth Report of the Royal Commission on the Civil Service, 1914*, quoted in Z.S. Steiner, *The Foreign Office and Foreign Policy, 1898–1914* (Cambridge: Cambridge University Press, 1969), p.19. Also Z.S. Steiner, 'Elitism and Foreign Policy: The Foreign Office Before the Great War', in B.J.C. McKercher and D.J. Moss, (eds), *Shadow and Substance in British Foreign Policy, 1895–1939: Memorial Essays Honouring C.J. Lowe* (Edmonton: University of Alberta Press, 1984), pp.19–55.

19. Vansittart, *Mist Procession*.

20. This was not retrospective criticism. See Hardinge's disdain for 'amateur diplomacy and illicit bargains' in Hardinge Papers, Cambridge University Library, Vol.32, Hardinge to Rodd, 26 May 1917.

21. See J.B. Crowley, *Japan's Quest for Autonomy: National Security and Foreign Policy, 1930–1938* (Princeton: Princeton University Press, 1966), pp.82–183; I.H. Nish, *Japan's Struggle With Internationalism: Japan, China, and the League of Nations, 1931–3* (London: Kegan and Paul, 1993), pp.23–43.

22. C. Kitching, *Britain and the Problem of International Disarmament, 1919–1934* (London: Routledge, 1999); B.J.C. McKercher, 'Of Horns and Teeth: The Preparatory Commission and the World Disarmament Conference, 1926–1934', in B.J.C. McKercher, (ed.), *Arms Limitation and Disarmament, 1899–1939: Restraints on War* (Westport, CT: Praeger, 1992), pp.173–201.

23. C. Hall, *Britain, America and Arms Control, 1921–37* (Basingstoke: Macmillan, 1987), pp.88–115; S.W. Roskill, *Naval Policy Between the Wars, Volume II: The Period Of Reluctant Rearmament* (London: Collins, 1976), pp.37–70.

24. For an example of German policy at the Disarmament Conference see Neurath to Nadolny, *Documents on German Foreign Policy*, Series C, Vol. I, pp.42–4.

25. FO 800/258 (Chamberlain Papers), Chamberlain to Crewe, 2 Apr. 1925. See also P.G. Edwards, 'The Austen Chamberlain–Mussolini Meetings', *The Historical Journal*, 14/2 (1972), pp.153–64; B.J.C. McKercher, 'A Sane and Sensible Diplomacy: Austen Chamberlain, Japan, and the Naval Balance of Power in the Pacific Ocean, 1924–1929', *Canadian Journal of History*, 21/1 (1986), pp.187–213.

26. FO 371/14261/2283/1, Vansittart minute to Henderson, n.d., enclosing Sargent memorandum, 18 Mar. 1930.

27. See FO 800/281(Henderson Papers), Tyrrell to Henderson, 1 and 24 Feb. 1930; FO 371/14259/1463/1, minute by Vansittart, 21 Feb. 1930; CAB 27/476, CP(32)4, 'The United Kingdom and Europe', 1 Jan. 1932.

28. E. L. Woodward and R. Butler, *Documents on British Foreign Policy* (Second Series, Volume 1, London: HMSO, 1946), pp.400–02, Henderson despatches to Tyrrell and Graham, both 1 Oct. 1930.

29. For typical examples see ibid., pp.422–8, Vansittart to Tyrrell, 4 Nov. 1930, Tyrrell to Henderson, 6 Nov. 1930, Henderson to Graham, 7 Nov. 1930, Graham to Henderson, 7 Nov. 1930.

30. CAB 4/21, CID 1082-B, Chiefs of Staff Annual Review of Defence Policy, 11 Mar. 1932. See also CAB 53/22, COS 294 (DC), report by the Deputies of the Chiefs of Staff Sub-Committee on the Situation in the Far East, 22 Feb. 1932.

31. CAB 23/70, CC(32)19, 23 Mar. 1932.

32. The ultimate failure was the World Economic Conference, held in London in June–July 1933.

33. CAB 53/23, COS papers on Imperial Defence Policy [COS 306], 24 Apr. 1933, and COS papers on Imperial Defence Policy [COS 307], 20 May 1933, enclosing Foreign Office

memorandum on the Foreign Policy of His Majesty's Government in the United Kingdom, 19 May 1933.

34. CAB 4/22, CID 1113-B, COS Annual Review for 1933, 12 Oct. 1933.
35. CAB 2/6, CID Meeting 261, 9 Nov. 1933; CAB 23/77, CC(33)62, 15 Nov. 1933.
36. Most recently B.J.C. McKercher, 'From Disarmament to Rearmament: British Civil–Military Relations and Policy-Making, 1933–1934', *Defence Studies*, 1/2 (2002), pp.21–48; C. Morrisey and M.A. Ramsay, '"Giving a Lead in the Right Direction": Sir Robert Vansittart and the Defence Requirements Sub-Committee', *Diplomacy and Statecraft*, 6/3 (1995), pp.39–60. See also K. Neilson, 'The Defence Requirements Sub-Committee, British Strategic Foreign Policy, Neville Chamberlain, and the Path to Appeasement', *English Historical Review*, 118/3 (2003), pp.651–84.
37. CAB 16/109, DRC Report, 28 Feb. 1934, Table A(1), Deficiencies over a Five-Year Programme.
38. Ibid.
39. CAB 16/109, DRC 1, Note on 'Defence Requirements Sub-Committee: Composition and Terms of Reference', 10 Nov. 1933.
40. CAB 16/109, DRC 4, Hankey to DRC members, 23 Nov. 1933.
41. CAB 16/109, DRC meeting 3, 4 Dec. 1933.
42. CAB 16/109, DRC 9, Warren Fisher note, 12 Jan. 1934.
43. Ibid.
44. See for example Vansittart Papers, VNST I 2/2, Vansittart memorandum, 26 Feb. 1933; E.L. Woodward and R. Butler, *Documents on British Foreign Policy* (Second Series, Volume 5, London: HMSO, 1956), pp.421–8, Vansittart memorandum 'German Rearmament', 14 Jul. 1933.
45. For example, Rose, *Vansittart*, pp.13–14, 41.
46. McKercher, 'Last Old Diplomat'; M. Roi, *Alternative to Appeasement: Sir Robert Vansittart and Alliance Diplomacy, 1934–1937* (Westport, CT: Praeger, 1997), Chapter 1.
47. CAB 16/109, DRC Meeting 3, 4 Dec. 1933.
48. B. Bond (ed.),*Chief of Staff: The Diaries of Lieutenant-General Sir Henry Pownall*, Vol. I (London: Leo Cooper, 1972), p. 38, diary entry, 28 Feb. 1934.
49. CAB 16/109, DRC Meeting 1, 14 Nov. 1933.
50. The total for the RAF was £10,265,000, and the Royal Navy £21,067,600.
51. Vansittart Papers, VNST I 2/14, Vansittart to Simon, 10 Feb. 1934.
52. CAB 16/109, DRC Meeting 3, 4 Dec. 1933. He later circulated these views in 'Situation in the Far East 1933–34'. See CAB 16/109, DRC 20.
53. CAB 21/434, Hankey to Vansittart, 8 Mar. 1934.
54. CAB 16/110, DC(M)(32) Meetings 41–55, and its Report, 31 Jul. 1934.
55. See CAB 24/248, CP(34)104, Vansittart memorandum, 'The Future of Germany', 7 Apr. 1934; CAB 21/388, Vansittart to Simon, 14 May 1934; CAB 27/510, DC(M)(32) 118, Simon memorandum, 14 Jun. 1934; CAB 27/511, DC(M)(32)119, Simon memorandum, 14 Jun. 1934. See also MacDonald and Baldwin's comments in CAB 16/110, DC(M)(32) meeting 50, 25 Jun. 1934.
56. CAB 16/109, DC(M) Meeting 51, 26 Jun. 1934.
57. CAB 16/110, DC(M) Report, 31 Jul. 1934.
58. CAB 27/510, DC(M)(32) 117, minute by Vansittart, 2 Jun. 1934.
59. For example, Hailsham's comments in CAB 27/510, DC(M)(32) meeting 50, 25 Jun. 1934.
60. Clive to Simon, 5 Jul.1934, *British Documents on Foreign Affairs*, Part II, Series E, Vol.13, pp.229–31.
61. FO 371/17599/7695/1938, minute by Orde, 28 Aug. 1934.
62. FO 371/17599/7695/1938, minute by Craigie, 23 Aug. 1934.
63. FO/371/17599/7695/1938, minute by Vansittart, 25 Aug. 1934, and Vansittart minute to Simon, 29 Aug. 1934.
64. Neville Chamberlain Papers, University of Birmingham Library, NC/8/19/1, Chamberlain memorandum, 'The Naval Conference and Our Relations with Japan', n.d. [but early Aug. 1934].

65. Ibid., Chamberlain minutes (2), both n.d.
66. FO 800/291, Chamberlain to Simon, 10 Sep. 1934, and Simon to MacDonald, 3 Oct. 1934; Simon Papers, Bodleian Library, Oxford, SP79, Simon to Chamberlain, 7 Sep. 1934.
67. CAB/24/250, CP(34)223, Simon-Chamberlain memorandum, 16 Oct. 1934.
68. The suggestion that Simon yielded to Chamberlain on this matter made by D. Dutton, *Simon: A Political Biography* (London: Aurum, 1992), pp.192–3, is misplaced. See Orde memorandum, 4 Sep. 1934, *Documents on British Foreign Policy*, Second Series, Vol. XIII, pp.31–4; FO 371/18184/5846/591, minutes by Craigie and Vansittart, 2 Oct. 1934; FO 371/18184/5859/591, minutes by Allen and Randall, 3 Oct. 1934; FO/371/18184/6192/591, minutes by Craigie and Wellesley, 5 Oct. 1934.
69. FO 371/18184/5846/591, Clive to Simon, 29 Sep.1934.
70. See J. Haslam, *The Soviet Union and the Struggle for Collective Security in Europe 1933–1939* (London: Macmillan, 1984), pp.15–26, 41–42; J. Hochman, *The Soviet Union and the Failure of Collective Security 1934–1938* (Ithaca, NY: Cornell University Press, 1984).
71. FO 371/18297/140/2, minute by Vansittart, 13 Jan. 1934.
72. FO 371/17707/4205/29, minute by Vansittart 2 Jul. 1934; FO 371/17707/4391/29, minute by Vansittart, 11 Jul. 1934; CAB 24/260, CP(36)42, memorandum, 'Britain, France, and Germany', 3 Feb. 1936. See also S. Bourette-Knowles, 'The Global Micawber: Sir Robert Vansittart, the Treasury and the Global Balance of Power 1933–1935', *Diplomacy and Statecraft*, 6/1 (1995), pp.91–121.
73. See B. Lee, *Britain and the Sino-Japanese War 1937–1939: A Study in the Dilemmas of British Decline* (Stanford: Stanford University Press, 1973), pp.23–49.
74. FO 371/18527/5693/1, minute by Leeper, 23 May 1934.
75. FO 371/18527/5693/1, minute by Craigie, 24 May 1934.
76. FO 371/18527/5693/1, minute by Wigram, 24 May 1934.
77. FO 371/18526/5206/1, minute by Vansittart, 1 Jun. 1934.
78. FO 371/18524/4153/1, minute by Vansittart, 2 May 1934.
79. Simon to Baldwin, 18 Apr. 1935, *Documents on British Foreign Policy*, Second Series, Vol. 12, pp.927–28.
80. See A.L. Goldman, 'Sir Robert Vansittart's Search for Italian Cooperation against Hitler, 1933–1936', *Journal of Contemporary History*, 9/2 (1974), pp.93–130.
81. FO 371/18830/2214/55, minute by Vansittart, 19 Mar. 1935; FO 371/19106/1139/1, minute by Vansittart, 29 Mar. 1935; FO 371/18833/2656/55, minute by Vansittart 1 Apr. 1935.
82. N. Rostow, *Anglo-French Relations, 1934–1936* (London: Macmillan, 1984), p.81.
83. Bourette-Knowles, 'The Global Micawber'; M. Roi, 'From the Stresa Front to the Triple Entente: Sir Robert Vansittart, the Abyssinian Crisis, and the Containment of Germany', *Diplomacy and Statecraft*, 6/3 (1995), pp.61–90.
84. See R.A. Best, 'The Anglo-German Naval Agreement of 1935: An Aspect of Appeasement', *Naval War College Review*, 34/2 (1981), pp.68–85; E. Haraszti, *Treaty-Breakers or "Realpolitiker"? The Anglo-German Naval Agreement of 1935* (Boppard am Rhein: Boldt, 1974); D.C. Watt, 'The Anglo-German Naval Agreement of 1935: An Interim Judgement', *Journal of Modern History*, 28/1 (1956), pp.155–76.
85. CAB 24/55, CP(35)98, Simon memorandum, 11 May 1935; CAB 23/81, CC(35)27, 15 May 1935, and CC(35)28, 17 May 1935.
86. Goldman, 'Vansittart's Search', p.114.
87. See R.A.C. Parker, 'Great Britain, France and the Ethiopian Crisis', *English Historical Review*, 89/1 (1974), pp.293–332; J.C. Robertson, 'The Hoare–Laval Plan', *Journal of Contemporary History*, 10/3 (1975), pp.433–65.
88. For instance, Eden's comments in CAB 23/83, CC(36)8, 14 Feb. 1936.
89. J.T. Emmerson, *The Rhineland Crisis, 7 March 1936: A Study in Multilateral Diplomacy* (London: Temple Smith, 1977).
90. See CAB 16/112, Pownall memorandum, 9 Jul. 1935, DRC meetings 13–14, Interim Report (DRC 25), 24 Jul. 1935, DRC meetings 15–26 (3 Oct.–14 Nov. 1935), DRC Third Report (DRC 37), 21 Nov. 1935.

91. CAB 24/259, DPR(DR) Report, CP(36)26, 12 Feb. 1936. These funds would be added to the totals projected in a 1935 White Paper on defence spending. The 1936 budget was already established at £124 million. Cmd. 5114.

92. I. Colvin, *Vansittart in Office* (London: Gollancz, 1965).

93. CAB 16/112, DRC Meeting 14, 19 Jul. 1935.

94. CAB 16/112, DRC Meetings, 15–18, 20, 22–24. FO 800/295, Vansittart to Hoare, 19 Aug. 1935, uses the 'bricks without straw' metaphor.

95. See FO 371/19905/3677/4 minute by Wigram, 16 May 1936; FO 371/19906/3879/4, minutes by Sargent and Vansittart. Also FO 371/19906/3879/4, minute by Eden, 3 Jun. 1936.

96. See CAB 23/85, CC(36)50, Eden's comments, 6 Jul. 1936.

97. On the League see A. Eden, *Foreign Affairs* 17/4 (1939), pp.54–61; on Russia, see Phipps Papers, Churchill Archives Centre, Churchill College, Cambridge, PHPP/II/1/16, Eden to Phipps, 28 Feb. 1936.

98. FO 371/19898/2487/4, minute by Vansittart, 15 Apr. 1936.

99. FO 371/20354/6289/6289, 'The World Situation and British Rearmament', 16 Dec. 1936.

100. Chamberlain Papers (Birmingham), NC/18/1/942, 18/1/1020, 18/1/1028, Chamberlain to Hilda Chamberlain, 15 Dec. 1935, 12 Sep. 1937, and 14 Nov. 1937; NC/7/11/29/19, Warren Fisher to Chamberlain, 15 Sep. 1936.

101. See CAB/23/90B, CC(35)56.

102. Vansittart Papers, VNST II, 1/5, Baldwin to Vansittart, 7 Jan. 1937.

103. Chamberlain Papers (Birmingham), NC 7/11/29/16, Eden to Chamberlain, 9 Nov. 1936; NC/7/11/30/74, Hoare to Chamberlain, 17 Mar. 1937.

104. See D.C. Watt, *How War Came: The Immediate Origins of the Second World War, 1938–1939* (London: Heinemann, 1989).

105. CAB 24/273, CP(37)316, Inskip 'Interim Report on Defence Expenditure in Future Years', 15 Dec. 1937; CAB 24/274, CP(38)24, Inskip 'Report on Defence Expenditure in Future Years', 8 Feb. 1938; CAB 23/92, CC5(38)9, 16 Feb. 1938.

The Foreign Office and Britain's Ambassadors to Berlin, 1933–39

PETER NEVILLE

Between 1933 and 1939, one of the most testing postings for British diplomats was in Berlin.[1] During this period, three men represented Britain as ambassador: Sir Horace Rumbold, Sir Eric Phipps and Sir Nevile Henderson. They had to deal with a devious and unscrupulous totalitarian regime and report their impressions of Nazi Germany back to the Foreign Office in London. Only those with a similar experience of dealing with a totalitarian regime can perhaps fully understand the strain these men were placed under.[2] The permanent officials in London with whom the ambassadors had to deal often lacked this sort of coalface experience (this was certainly true of Sir Robert Vansittart, the Permanent Under-Secretary 1930–37, and Orme Sargent, an Assistant Under-Secretary 1938–46). Had they done so, they might have been more understanding about the problems that Rumbold, Phipps and Henderson encountered in Berlin.

Britain's first ambassador in Berlin in the Nazi period was Sir Horace Rumbold who was entering the last phase of his posting in January 1933 (he had been in Berlin since 1928). Rumbold was the son of a diplomat who was posted to Berlin at the end of a long and distinguished career which had sent him to Cairo, Teheran, Vienna, Munich, Tokyo (where Nevile Henderson served under him), Berlin, Constantinople, Berne and Warsaw. As Minister in Warsaw, Rumbold had formed a low opinion of the Poles, but in Constantinople he inspired Henderson's admiration for the way in which he handled the Chanak crisis of 1922. He wrote to his subordinate on 2 January 1923 about how situations arose 'from which one would think that there was no escape except a conflict, and yet in the end a formula has been found which averts the impending catastrophe'.[3] In Constantinople, Rumbold was robust but emollient, but soon recognised that emollience was unlikely to work in Berlin. He watched the rise of the Nazis with growing alarm and pinpointed the withdrawal of French troops from the Rhineland in 1930 as a key turning point. 'The snowball of "revisionism"', Rumbold reported back to London

> continues to roll down the electoral slopes, and as it rolls, it is gathering speed and size. It may now indeed be said that the first electoral campaign which has taken place in Germany without the shadow of the Rhineland occupation [Hitler won 107 seats in the Reichstag] has brought out into the open, through one party or another, all that Germany hopes for and intends to strive for in the field of external affairs.[4]

As time passed, Rumbold's detestation of the Nazis grew. He had reported on the death agonies of the Weimar Republic and had little doubt where the appearance of Hitler as German Chancellor would lead. In March 1933, he told the Foreign Office that Nazism had succeeded in 'bringing to the surface the worst traits of the German character, that is, a mean spirit of revenge, a tendency to brutality and a noisy and irresponsible jingoism'.[5] Hitler himself, Rumbold thought, was 'an uncommonly clever and audacious demagogue'.[6]

On 26 April 1933, Rumbold impressed Vansittart with what became known in the Foreign Office as his *Mein Kampf* despatch in which he analysed the contents of Hitler's book. Indeed, Vansittart was so impressed that he had the 5,000-word telegram circulated to the Prime Minister Ramsay MacDonald, Baldwin, Neville Chamberlain (then Chancellor of the Exchequer) and other Cabinet members. Rumbold concluded that it would be misleading to expect any improvement in Nazi behaviour (by then real democracy in Germany had already been destroyed), 'or a serious modification of the views of the Chancellor and his entourage'.[7] In his final despatch prior to retirement in August 1933, Rumbold rammed the message home. Hitler, Göring and Goebbels were, according to Rumbold, 'notoriously pathological cases' and the Nazi leadership as a whole made up, he warned, of 'fantastic hooligans and eccentrics'. Reverting to typical English understatement, and Rumbold was the most English of ambassadors, he concluded that 'the persons directing the policy of the Hitler Government are not normal'.[8] Vansittart agreed. Many years later, he was to write that if Sir Horace had been five years younger and not coming up to his retirement from the Diplomatic Service, 'given time, he might have frightened the Cabinet'.[9] Rumbold himself was pleased to have avoided social contact with the Nazi leaders. In 1940, one of his successors in Berlin, Nevile Henderson, sent him

a copy of his *Failure of a Mission* which traced the history of his own time in
Berlin. But Rumbold retorted:

> you have described much in your book as 'the failure of a mission' but
> for two reasons nobody could have succeeded at Berlin. These reasons
> are a) the nature of the character of the beast with which any
> representative would have to deal and b) the fatuous belief of
> Chamberlain and presumably of his Government that in 1937 it was
> possible to achieve anything by a policy of appeasement of Germany.
> Hitler is an evil man and his regime and philosophy are evil. You cannot
> compromise with evil.[10]

Rumbold had completely rejected the assumptions on which the MacDonald-
Baldwin-Chamberlain appeasement policy was based, that concessions and
patience could lead to an accommodation with Germany.

But while he was in Berlin, Rumbold seems to have avoided the tensions with
the Foreign Office which were to characterise Henderson's period in Berlin four
years later. This was not because he feared querying his instructions, for he had
angered the Cabinet when High Commissioner in Constantinople in 1922 by his
unwillingness to deliver an ultimatum to Turkish leader, Mustafa Kemal, and this
irritation was written into the Cabinet minutes at the time.[11] The reason was rather
that, in 1933, Rumbold's line in Berlin was generally approved at the Foreign
Office. On 10 May, the President of the Saar Commission, Geoffrey Knox, wrote
to Rumbold about his *Mein Kampf* despatch: 'I am ending a flying visit to
London, where I have had the undiluted joy of reading your recent despatch on
Nazi policy. The Office are enthusiastic about it'.[12] Indeed the admiration for the
Mein Kampf despatch was to continue for years to come even outside the Foreign
Office. At the time of the German *Anschluss* with Austria in 1938, the Cabinet
Secretary, Sir Maurice Hankey, retrieved a copy of the despatch from a Foreign
Office pigeonhole, and sent it to Sir Horace Wilson, Neville Chamberlain's Chief
Diplomatic Adviser, with an accompanying note: 'I think you would find it worth
your while, as I did, to glance through the attached prophetic despatch by
Rumbold of five years ago. It shows in the light of after events, how closely Hitler
had adhered to *Mein Kampf* and perhaps provides some guide to the future'.[13]

At the time of his retirement though, Rumbold received a typically bland letter
of thanks from the then Foreign Secretary, Sir John Simon, which referred to his
despatches being of 'great and permanent value to His Majesty's Government in
determining their policy towards Germany'.[14] The Cabinet would not in fact be
swayed by what was perceived as Rumbold's alarmist analysis. But when
Rumbold died in 1941, the historian and ex-diplomat Harold Nicolson wrote that
the former ambassador represented 'a standard of integrity, intelligence and fair-
mindedness which was higher than that of most people'.[15] Vansittart thought that
Rumbold's warnings in 1933 were better than anything obtained later, and

a refutation of former Foreign Secretary Lord Curzon's view that Rumbold was 'not alert enough for Berlin'.[16]

The irony, in the light of the Cabinet's attitude to Rumbold's despatches, was that his replacement, Sir Eric Phipps, was in his own distinctive way just as robustly critical of the Nazis as Rumbold had been. Phipps was Vansittart's brother-in-law, and the Permanent Under-Secretary had no real complaints to make about Phipps' despatches from Berlin in the period 1935–37. Later, when Phipps had been transferred to Paris, tensions increased and Sir Eric was to complain in 1940 about 'constant stabs in the back from my relative at the FO'.[17]

Phipps was a seasoned diplomat who had been Minister in Vienna (1928–33) before coming to Berlin (Vansittart was to be much less happy with his successor there, Sir Walford Selby, whose despatches he subjected to caustic criticism).[18] But before Phipps took up his post, there was an internal debate within the Foreign Office that demonstrated that the Vansittart view of German policy was starting to be challenged. The then head of the Southern Department, Owen O'Malley, put forward the idea that instructions should be given to Phipps, later to be published, which would then clarify the attitude of the British government towards the Nazi regime. O'Malley, a future Minister to Mexico and Portugal, supported the idea of 'a friendly and intimate attitude' towards Germany which would recognise the legitimacy of German grievances, and loosen ties with France so allowing Britain to play the role of mediator between Paris and Berlin.[19]

Vansittart sharply disagreed with O'Malley's conception of the direction Anglo-German relations should take. Instead he believed that Phipps should do 'all he could to cultivate good personal relations with the powers that be in Germany ... but that, in adopting this attitude, his friendship should be tempered by firmness and frankness ... he should leave the German government under no illusion of the effects caused in this country by their methods'.[20] In the event, no instructions were issued to Phipps, but O'Malley continued to lobby for a different approach to Anglo-German relations (in 1937 he would write a supportive letter to Henderson just after he had arrived in Germany telling him that 'for the last ten years he had doubted the wisdom of Foreign Office policy towards Germany').[21]

On arrival in Berlin, Phipps tried to act on Vansittart's advice. He hoped also that Hitler might 'possibly respond to some rather theatrical appeal to his emotions'.[22] He was soon disillusioned. A natural Francophile who had lobbied for the Paris Embassy, Phipps hated Berlin and set himself to portray the Nazi regime in as negative a light as possible.[23] Hitler thought 'Sir Phipps [sic] was a thug', and Phipps made a memorable quip when Göring (heavily involved in massacring the Brownshirt leadership on 30 June 1934) was late for a banquet at the British Embassy, and excused himself by

saying he had been out shooting. 'Animals, *this time*, I hope,' said Phipps.[24]
Such an attitude won Phipps few admirers in Berlin. The aide to the German
Foreign Minister, Joachim von Ribbentrop, Reinhard Spitzy, subsequently
described Phipps as being 'from the very beginning inspired by a hatred of the
Nazis, if not for the German people in general'.[25] This was an exaggeration,
but by 1934 Phipps was clearly of the same school as Rumbold where the
Nazis were concerned.

This did not mean that differences of nuance could not be found between
Phipps and the permanent officials in London. In 1935, for example, Phipps
sided with the politicians Sir John Simon and Anthony Eden about whether
their visit to Berlin should go ahead in the light of Hitler's blatant
infringement of the military clauses of Versailles by announcing peacetime
conscription. Vansittart was unenthusiastic telling Phipps about the need to
treat the Germans firmly: 'I hope therefore I may count on you Eric, to put
all your weight into the maintenance of the only line which can be of any
avail ... and that this firm line, will be maintained unflinchingly by you *all*'.[26]
But more typical was the accord when Phipps warned that when the Popular
Front came to power in France in 1936, Hitler would be even more unwilling
to agree to talks about the revision of the Treaty of Locarno because he wanted
a bilateral Anglo-German agreement which would not involve France. The
Deputy Under-Secretary at the Foreign Office, Sir Orme Sargent, arguably a
greater critic of government policy towards Germany than 'Van', concurred
with Phipps' view. Sargent believed that 'as soon as we recognise that the
isolation of France is the one and only thing he is working for, all his
manoeuvres become clear'.[27]

Perspectives on the Nazi leadership were an important aspect of the
ambassador's role, but it is surprising to find that Phipps, in the light of his
comments about him above, saw Göring as a potentially more useful point of
contact and a more moderate influence. In November 1936, nearly two and a
half years after the infamous murder of the leadership of the SA during the
'Night of the Long Knives', Phipps was telling the Foreign Office that he had
developed 'very helpful points of contact with General Göring, who is an old
army officer with few Nazi proclivities in his saner moments'.[28] This analysis,
which was much favoured by his successor Henderson, would not have found
favour with Vansittart and Sargent but one can sympathise with Phipps'
predicament in trying to find signs of moderate attitudes amongst the group of
oddballs and fanatics surrounding Hitler. What does surprise, perhaps, is that
so late in his period in Berlin (he left in April 1937), Phipps still registered
hopes where Göring was concerned. His relationship with Hitler had by then
hopelessly broken down, as Prime Minister Baldwin's Private Secretary,
Thomas Jones, noted in his diary on 15 January 1937: 'Phipps, our
ambassador,' he wrote, 'has no telephone line to Hitler who despises him'.[29]

A whispering campaign against Phipps was already underway in 1936 which prompted Vansittart to write to Jones on 31 March to deny suggestions that Phipps was too anti-Nazi to remain in Berlin; Anthony Eden, who had replaced Sir Samuel Hoare as Foreign Secretary in December 1935, assured Baldwin that such rumours were ill-founded,[30] but Jones told his master in May 1936 that 'if it is our policy to get alongside Germany, the sooner Phipps is transferred the better'.[31] Jones had already advised Baldwin that Phipps should be replaced by 'a man of the D'Abernon or Willingdon type, unhampered by a professional diplomatic tradition, able of course to speak German, and enter with sympathetic interest into Hitler's aspirations'.[32]

Phipps was well connected, more so than Henderson. He was a close friend of the Cabinet Secretary Sir Maurice Hankey, and also of the Permanent Under-Secretary at the Treasury, Sir Warren Fisher (whom Selby had accused of interfering with appointments to the Diplomatic Service).[33] He also corresponded with Orme Sargent in private but none of this could save him from his critic, and in 1937 he was duly moved on to Paris. By then he had become deeply disillusioned about the prospects of reaching any sort of accommodation with the Nazis. Soon after coming to Paris as ambassador in April 1937, Phipps confided in his American counterpart, William Bullitt, that Hitler was 'a fanatic who would be satisfied with nothing less than the domination of Europe'. He therefore could not 'see the faintest possibility of coming to any kind of agreement with Hitler' as the 'only thing that would impress the Germans today was military force'.[34] This bleak conclusion exactly mirrored what Rumbold had been saying four years earlier, and provided ammunition for the Vansittartites in the Foreign Office who cautioned against putting too much faith in German assurances.[35]

When Nevile Henderson heard that Phipps was being sent to Berlin in 1933, he wrote from his own Legation in Belgrade saying: 'I shan't congratulate you, because I think you are going to the wrong capital. You should be going to Brussels where you would be much closer to your spiritual home'.[36] In the small incestuous world of the Diplomatic Service, still in those days a distinct entity from the Foreign Office itself, the two men knew and cordially disliked one another. Henderson told Hugh Dalton, the Labour politician and former Under-Secretary of State at the Foreign Office 1929–31 that, in his view, under Phipps 'there was no British embassy at all, only a branch of the Quai d'Orsay'.[37] Henderson believed, he told Dalton, that Phipps was 'a most unsuitable appointment'.[38]

No one could accuse Sir Nevile of being too pro-French. But his appointment was controversial because in 1935, after a lengthy and successful spell as Minister in Belgrade, he had seemingly been put out to grass in Buenos Aires. The irony was, in the light of what followed, that it was Vansittart who had recommended Henderson's appointment. Eden had never

met Henderson before his departure for Berlin, but 'Van' admired the way
he had dealt with the authoritarian King Alexander in Yugoslavia. Austen
Chamberlain had been another of Henderson's admirers when he was serving
in Constantinople and Cairo in the 1920s.[39]

Henderson was disappointed by his transfer to Buenos Aires in 1935
(at first the Foreign Office had wanted to send him from Belgrade to Lisbon),
particularly as Vansittart had written to him in February 1935 congratulating
him on his work in Belgrade and telling him that it was 'time to have some of
your life in the sun and in the First Eleven'.[40] Henderson's mentor at the
Foreign Office, Laurence Oliphant, also wrote to say that he hoped to see him
'in one of the very biggest posts'.[41] At this stage of his career, relations
between Henderson and Vansittart were cordial and Henderson visited 'Van'
in his home at Park Street. This intimacy (Vansittart was writing to Henderson
in 1935 'as a friend'), made the falling-out which followed when Henderson
was posted to Berlin even more dramatic. For Vansittart had not forgotten his
friend and secured this major posting for him. Later he tried to disparage
Henderson's qualities by writing that his success in Belgrade was due to his
'skill in shooting', but the real reason for his appointment was that he
was perceived to be a man who could get on with authoritarian rulers.
Rumbold and Phipps had been, in Donald Watt's word, 'toughies', and failed
to get on terms with the Nazi leadership. Now it was time to try a more
emollient approach.[42]

Henderson had a messianic view of his new role in Berlin. In his memoir of
his time there, he wrote of how he had been 'specially selected by Providence
for the definite mission of, as I trusted, helping to preserve the peace of the
world'.[43] Rumbold and Phipps had a more prosaic vision of the ambassador's
role in Berlin. So, too, did Vansittart and the Foreign Office. But Henderson
appears to have been encouraged in this elevated view of his posting by a
mysterious interview he claimed to have had with Neville Chamberlain (still
then Chancellor of the Exchequer) prior to his departure to Berlin in April
1937. No documentary evidence has ever been found to prove that such an
interview did take place, but Henderson subsequently attached great
importance to it, claiming that the Prime Minister-in-waiting had 'outlined
to me his general policy on Germany ... and I think I may honestly say that to
the last and bitter end I followed the general line which he set me'.[44]
The editors of the post-war *Documents on British Foreign Policy* series noted
that 'Henderson worked out for himself' the line he would follow in Berlin.
They found nothing in Henderson's *Failure of a Mission* about a Foreign
Office briefing before he went off to Berlin, or anything which indicated what
the Foreign Office thought about the current condition of Anglo-German
relations.[45] This seems on the face of it to underline the fact that Henderson
regarded himself primarily as the agent of the Prime Minister rather than of

the Foreign Office. Evidence to support this analysis was provided by T.P. Conwell Evans, an English Professor who taught at the University of Königsberg, and had links with the Berlin embassy. Conwell Evans claimed that Henderson had told him that the line he followed in Berlin was 'based on instructions constantly received from Downing Street and not on the view of the Permanent Head of the Foreign Office'.[46] This certainly rings true, and was at the root of the acrimonious relationship between Henderson and the Foreign Office in London. A battle royal ensued in particular with Henderson's old friend and ally, Vansittart, when Henderson availed himself of Chamberlain's alleged suggestion that 'a calculated indiscretion was sometimes a very useful form of diplomacy'.[47]

If Rumbold is best remembered for his *Mein Kampf* despatch and Phipps for his 'bison' telegram of June 1934 (in which he sent up Göring's interest in hunting), Henderson was most noted (or notorious) for his despatch of 10 May 1937 on the parameters of British foreign policy. The memorandum is thirteen pages long and is covered with angry interjections by Vansittart. A few examples suffice to show how the two men were at fundamental odds about the conduct of Anglo-German relations. When Henderson wrote that the French should renounce their relationship with the Little Entente powers, Czechoslovakia, Rumania and Yugoslavia, Vansittart wrote 'this is full acceptance of German doctrine'. And when Henderson said that Austrians would wish to be 'reunited with Germany', Vansittart detected the perverse influence of Lord Lothian, who had two personal interviews with Hitler in 1937.[48] Vansittart himself described Lothian as 'a very amiably inaccurate amateur' who proposed 'to be quite precise, the conquest of Austria and Czechoslovakia and the reconquest of Memel and Danzig'.[49] The Foreign Office was jealous of its status and resented the interference of outsiders, hence its annoyance when Chamberlain selected Sir Horace Wilson from the home Civil Service as his chief diplomatic adviser.

Vansittart went on to damn Henderson's despatch as 'ill-thought out and above all contrary to the policy of HMG ... So crude a piece of work that it was not worthy of circulation'.[50] He vehemently rejected Henderson's suggestion that Britain should have no objection in principle to 'German economic and even political predominance in Eastern Europe' and ignored Henderson's caveat about the difficulties involved in the Anglo-German relationship which the ambassador recognised as being 'extraordinarily formidable. Quite apart from Germany itself, the Nazi regime, her traditional mentality, and her inevitable urge towards unity and expansion is not in the interests – for obvious reasons – either of Italy or of Russia to witness its consummation.[51]

The problems which arose when Henderson arrived in Berlin in 1937 offer an excellent example of the potential pitfalls which may arise in

the relationship between an ambassador and a Foreign Ministry. Henderson
got into trouble again on 14 July when he wrote to Maxwell Garnett of the
League of Nations Union about a pamphlet the latter had written about
the effectiveness of the League. Henderson told Garnett that he had no faith
in the League, and asserted his conviction that an Austro-German *Anschluss*
was inevitable providing it was 'desired by the peoples themselves'.[52] With
a degree of naivety Henderson sent a copy of his letter to Garnett back to the
Foreign Office, and his superiors lined up to castigate him. William Strang of
the Central Department minuted that in his view it was a mistake for
'HM Ambassadors to air their views like this, especially when their views are
unorthodox'. Orme Sargent minuted his agreement. In his opinion,
Henderson's letter was both 'uncalled for and regrettable'. Unsurprisingly,
the biggest broadside came from Vansittart himself. He wrote of Henderson
that it seemed 'incredible that he should have sent us a copy of a letter like this
without realising what he has done ... In 35 years' experience I cannot recall
such a series of incidents created by an Ambassador – and in so short a while.
He is exceeding his functions and exceeding them light-heartedly'.[53] Sir
Nevile was being categorised as a loose cannon in the Diplomatic Service just
three months after his arrival in Berlin.

     Yet Henderson did have his supporters in the Foreign Office. Owen
O'Malley, who had just been appointed Minister to Mexico, wrote to him on
9 June 1937 about his anxieties over the handling of Anglo-German relations
by the Foreign Office. While conceding that his 'masters' might be right and
he himself wrong, O'Malley accused them of shunting him off to Mexico to
get him out of the way. He went on to assure Henderson that 'those who think
like me will watch your work in Berlin with the deepest sympathy and
solicitude. We shall not think that because you try to make friends with the
Germans that you have illusions about them, and we shall not expect you to
work miracles'. While Henderson was bound to run into difficulties because of
his emollient approach in Berlin, O'Malley told him that he personally was
'friends with some of the highest authorities outside the Foreign Office whom
you saw before leaving for Berlin [we can only speculate about who O'Malley
was referring to], and I was glad to find there was a weighty body of opinions
ready to support you'.[54] Disappointingly, O'Malley makes no reference to
Henderson in his memoirs in which he seemed to have carried respect for the
Official Secrets Act to extremes, although he did complain that 'of all the
'background' despatches I ever wrote from abroad to the Foreign Office, I do
not suppose that more than a dozen were read by anyone above the ranks of an
Assistant Under-Secretary'.[55] No doubt his fellow diplomats would have
endorsed such complaints. Focused as they were on 'high policy', the
permanent officials could ignore what hard-pressed diplomats regarded as
perceptive day-to-day commentary. But Germany was such a pressing issue in

the 1930s that officials in the Central Department at lower levels did get an opportunity to contribute to the debate about policy-making.

Another supporter of Henderson in the Foreign Office was R.H. Hadow, a former First Secretary in the Prague Legation who was to become a First Secretary in the Northern Department. During the 1938 Czech crisis, Hadow wrote to Henderson saying that 'All that you have said will of course come true; but here the clique who would not allow of any right on the German side are still doing what they can to bring on the day of reckoning'.[56] Hadow thought the Office too pro-French (a common complaint) and sent Henderson a copy of a memorandum he had written on the prospects of an Anglo-French alliance with the USSR (which he opposed). This was taking a considerable risk as Hadow had no authority to send such a document to Henderson and he asked him to treat it as '*nul et non avenu*'.[57]

Even at the highest levels of the Foreign Office, Henderson's performance in Berlin was not universally condemned. He was glad when Vansittart was removed as Permanent Under-Secretary at the end of 1937, telling Lord Halifax, whom he had got to know when he visited Germany in November 1937, that he would feel 'happier with Alec Cadogan as Head of the Office'.[58] Initially Cadogan, a fellow Etonian, seemed equally happy with Henderson's work. When Henderson was called back to London to report in January 1938, Cadogan noted in his diary, 'Nevile Henderson dined. I think he's very good'.[59] It is only right to record that with the passage of time, Cadogan changed his opinion although he became as frustrated with Vansittart, demoted to the position of Chief Diplomatic Adviser, as he did with Henderson.[60] Nevertheless Cadogan was more in tune with Chamberlain's thinking, although he did briefly revolt against the government line over the Godesberg terms in September 1938.

An area of concern to both the Foreign Office and the Berlin embassy was security. The weakest link in the embassies and legations in the 1930s was Rome, where the ambassador Sir Eric Drummond (later Lord Perth) was unaware that the contents of his safe was regularly being pilfered by Secondo Constanti, a chancery servant in the pay of the Italian intelligence services. The Foreign Office knew that something was wrong for in 1936 Eden wrote a memorandum complaining of 'serious breaches of information obtained by Her Majesty's Ambassador at Berlin, Sir Eric Phipps, which threatened [according to Phipps] to prejudice his own position and the sources of his information'. Count Ciano, the Italian Foreign Minister, was able to give Hitler a copy of one of Phipps' telegrams denouncing the Nazi government as dangerous adventurers. This would, of course, have reinforced Hitler's low opinion of Phipps, although he was impressed by the Italian intelligence coup.[61]

Only in 1937 did Sir Eric Drummond accept that there was something amiss when his wife's diamond necklace was stolen from a locked red box in his own personal apartment next to the embassy chancery. But because the Foreign Office did not have a security department as such, Drummond approached Major Vivian, the Deputy Head of the Secret Intelligence Service for help. Vivian visited Rome in February 1937 and was appalled by the security slackness in the embassy. It was logical therefore for Vivian to move on to inspect the security in the Berlin embassy, which he duly did in July 1937, and was equally appalled by what he found there. He noted that during Henderson's two-month summer leave, the German porter had the run of the place and that the ambassador's official residence had no proper guard. Vivian told the Foreign Office: 'This means, in fact, that the Gestapo could if so minded introduce nightly and for a practically unlimited period each night any number of lock-smiths and experts in safe-breaking, thereby having continuous access to current papers, telegrams and prints without leaving any trace'. Vivian said that there was no concrete evidence that the German porter had liaised with Gestapo agents 'but in view of the situation in Berlin and the German mentality' it would be madness to ignore the real possibility that he was in the pay of the Gestapo.[62] Henderson himself was also notoriously indiscreet on the telephone and it has been unkindly remarked that the Germans did 'not need a key to British ciphers. They only needed to lure Sir Nevile to the telephone'.[63] Henderson himself was sceptical about the usefulness of SIS and was rebuked by Cadogan for his agnosticism in February 1939 (there had been a number of 'scare stories' about possible German attacks in the winter of 1938–39). It was the task of SIS, Cadogan reminded Henderson, 'to report rumours or items of information themselves: they exercise a certain amount of discrimination themselves, but naturally do not take the responsibility of too much selection ... Moreover, it is true to say that the recent scares have not originated with SIS agents in Germany'. Cadogan became increasingly exasperated by the activities of Vansittart's own unofficial intelligence network which ran in parallel with the SIS (the relationship between 'Van' and Chamberlain was so bad that by September 1938 he was being followed by MI5 agents).[64]

Henderson's own role as a reporter of events in Germany was circumscribed by the fact that Hitler disliked him, as he had disliked Eric Phipps. Part of the problem was Henderson's extremely poor relationship with von Ribbentrop, who replaced the more conservative and less fanatically Nazi Constantine Freiherr von Neurath in January 1938. Ribbentrop's aide, Spitzy, describes how von Ribbentrop went out of his way to discredit Henderson: 'For instance, he pointed to Sir Nevile's friendship with the Rothschilds ... and he even asserted that Henderson turned up improperly dressed for discussions in the Chancellery. How on earth could anybody take seriously a man who wore a blue pin-stripe suit with a claret pullover and a red carnation?'[65]

Hitler sneered at Henderson as 'the man with the carnation', a representative of Britain's decayed and effete upper class, and was disinclined to see him except on rare occasions. Henderson blamed von Ribbentrop for this, accurately telling the Foreign Office that von Ribbentrop was 'eaten up with conceit and, if he can make himself out in his new position to be the author of better relations with Great Britain, he may sincerely work to that end'.[66] As it turned out, von Ribbentrop became bitterly anti-British and Henderson circumvented him by trying to build up a relationship with the more conservative and sympathetic State Secretary, Ernst von Weizsäcker. Von Ribbentrop rapidly became Henderson's *bête noire* in the Nazi leadership, showing that, contrary to his post-war reputation, Sir Nevile did get it right sometimes. It is hard in this context to understand the accusation by an historian of the relationship between the Foreign Office and the German opposition that Weizsäcker was very upset by Henderson's performance in Berlin and 'to have repeatedly referred to Sir Nevile Henderson's tactically and psychologically wrong attitude towards Ribbentrop'.[67] Von Ribbentrop was impossible to deal with, and Henderson's opinion of him was shared in the Foreign Office and by all those diplomats who had the misfortune to have dealings with him.

By contrast, Donald Watt refers to a remarkable 'transnational linkage ... between Sir Nevile Henderson, the British ambassador, his French and Italian colleagues, André François-Poncet and Bernardo Attolico, and the State Secretary in the German Foreign Ministry Ernest von Weizsäcker where ... the four men kept each other informed and worked to thwart von Ribbentrop and the war party'.[68] Weizsäcker, who was an unreconstructed German nationalist, was certainly more devious than Henderson and his colleagues realised, but the British ambassador needed to work at this relationship when he was, as Phipps had been, plagued by von Ribbentrop's meddling and pernicious influence. This was one area where the home-based permanent officials lacked sufficient understanding about the travails of an ambassador's life, or indeed, the pressures on all the diplomats in the Berlin Embassy. Sir George Ogilvie-Forbes, the Counsellor at the Embassy, and no great admirer of Henderson (who preferred to work with the First Secretary, Ivone Kirkpatrick), complained to his boss that 'one cannot get any peace and quiet'.[69]

Criticism has been levied at the Foreign Office and its ambassadors in Berlin, especially Henderson, for not being sufficiently receptive towards the anti-Nazi opposition.[70] This did not amount to much in the early days when the Communist and Social Democratic Parties had been driven underground, but Rumbold did keep in touch with conservative anti-Nazis like former Chancellor Bruning, whom he admired. Even then such conservatives and centrists showed an alarming capacity for political misjudgement. Thus as late as June 1933, Rumbold was amazed to be told by Bruning that he would 'support Hitler if the latter pursued a moderate policy'.[71] Certainly while Hitler successfully dismantled Versailles and introduced a massive rearmament programme between 1935 and 1937, there seemed very little disposition in either the German right-wing establishment (ex-Vice-Chancellor von Papen was comfortably in place as Minister in Vienna) or the Armed Forces to challenge the Führer's increasingly radical policies. Matters changed in 1938 when for the first time Hitler put Germany into a situation which threatened a general war over the Czech Sudetenland in September.

The ambassador in Berlin was obviously a key link between the German opposition and the Foreign Office in 1938. But Henderson, unlike Vansittart, who had links with men like Theo Kordt, a counsellor in the Wilhelmstrasse, and Karl Gordeler, the conservative ex-Mayor of Leipzig, played down the significance of such figures. He has been accused of failing to convey adequately the strength of opposition warnings about the nearness of war, or the likelihood of British intervention if Hitler did indeed, as he was threatening to do, invade Czechoslovakia. Henderson, however, had important links of his own with the German opposition and their testimony does not sustain this accusation. On 14 September, for example, just after Hitler had made a belligerent anti-Czech speech at the 1938 Nuremberg Rally, Henderson had an interview with Ulrich von Hassell, the former German Ambassador in Rome, who was thoroughly disillusioned with the Nazis.[72] According to von Hassell, Henderson told him that if Germany resorted to force over the Sudetenland, 'the English will march with France'. Henderson also blamed von Ribbentrop for the worsening of Anglo-German relations and in von Hassell's presence telephoned Göring to explain the British attitude.[73] Spitzy, who may perhaps be a slightly more dubious source because of his association with von Ribbentrop, although he did turn against him, claims that Henderson 'was clear and outspoken with his continuous warnings'.[74] Absurdly on the other side, von Ribbentrop continued to believe that Henderson was pro-Czech (very few people in either the Foreign Office or the Diplomatic Service had much sympathy for the Czechs, including successive Ministers in Prague, Addison and Newton).[75]

Henderson was certainly right in his assessment of the German opposition which, in 1938, although it had won over army generals like Ludwig Beck, seemed reliant on primary Anglo-French action against Hitler before it would risk anything itself.[76] Vansittart apart, and he was sidelined in 1938–39, the Foreign Office was also disinclined to take the German oppositionists seriously. Indeed by 1938, a note of real impatience was evident amongst officials in London. On 18 August, Vansittart met with the German oppositionist von Kleist in London (he also saw Churchill and Chamberlain) who pressed the need for outside assistance for the Opposition. The Central

Department was unimpressed by von Kleist's pleas. Rather it favoured putting pressure on the Czechs to make concessions to Germany. Ivo Mallet minuted that 'it would be rash, I think, to imagine that we should bring the regime down'.[77] His colleagues Sargent and Cresswell (the latter was the Foreign Office expert on the thorny issue of Anglo-German front-line air strengths) agreed that it would be wiser to rely on the efforts of Chamberlain's mediator Lord Runciman who had been sent to the Sudetenland earlier in the month. But it is significant that Chamberlain, so often deemed to have been under Henderson's malign influence, did not take his advice. When von Kleist came to London on 16 August, Henderson telegraphed that 'it would be unwise' for Cabinet members to see him.[78] Nevertheless, Chamberlain did see von Kleist three days later, although he told the Foreign Secretary, Lord Halifax, that 'I think we must discount a good deal of what he says'.[79]

Seven months later when independent Czechoslovakia had disappeared and Britain had guaranteed Polish independence, Orme Sargent had become distinctly hostile to the German opposition, in tones which his ambassador would have approved. On 15 April 1939, Sargent minuted: 'Last year we were reportedly told that moderate opinion was disappointed and discouraged because HMG was not standing up to Hitler. Now that HMG are standing up to Hitler, we hear this same moderate opinion is disgusted with us and can't understand why HMG are standing up to Hitler'.[80] By the time war broke out in September 1939, Vansittart, too, had become disillusioned with the German opposition.

Both the Foreign Office and its Berlin ambassadors were also concerned about the attitude of the British press towards Germany, and some reporters such as Norman Ebbutt of *The Times* and Ian Colvin of *The News Chronicle* had good contacts inside the country (though Foreign Officials like Cadogan found Colvin excitable and not totally reliable).[81] Phipps was unsympathetic when British journalists like Ebbutt were expelled from Germany (although the pro-appeasement editor of *The Times*, Geoffrey Dawson, watered down Ebbutt's reports or excluded them altogether to avoid upsetting Nazi sensitivities). Phipps believed that 'both tact and intelligence are essential to journalists in Germany, although he admitted that these were qualities which commanded a high salary which many newspapers could not afford'.[82] There was close liaison between Rex Leeper, who became Head of the Foreign Office News Department, and favoured journalists such as Robert Dell of *The Manchester Guardian*, who were briefed by the News Department. When Simon and Eden visited Berlin in 1935, Dell admitted to a colleague that Leeper often showed him Phipps' reports as guidance.[83]

Henderson was much concerned about the negative tone of much British reporting on Germany, and was infuriated when the news of Lord Halifax's visit to Germany in November 1937 was prematurely leaked by

The Evening Standard. It speculated about whether Hitler would get a free hand in Central and Eastern Europe if he agreed to withdraw Germany's claim for colonies. Henderson cabled London in a furious mood denouncing what he called 'an almost incredible attempt to poison the atmosphere ... which even the history of western journalism has seldom hitherto approached'.[84] In this instance, Henderson's venting of spleen was caused in part by the well-justified suspicion that the source of the leak was none other than his own Permanent Under Secretary, Vansittart, who was on close personal terms with Frederick Voigt, the Central Europe correspondent of *The Manchester Guardian*. The offending *Evening Standard* article was actually written by its diplomatic correspondent Poliakoff whom Henderson claimed had received 'first information of the visit from the FO, [and] he is continuing to receive information from the same persons for the same purpose'.[85] Voigt himself certainly thought that Vansittart was the source of the leak in an attempt to get the visit cancelled as a result of unfavourable publicity (Hitler himself was furious as he wanted to keep details of the visit secret). Predictably, Vansittart denied that the Foreign Office could have been the source of the leak, but it is interesting to note that his own long-serving and faithful Private Secretary, Clifford Norton, shared Henderson's attitude to the British press. He wrote to Henderson in July 1937 deploring its tendency to be 'unnecessarily provocative and sensational'.[86] Sir Nevile himself continued to be very sensitive about press reportage. He constantly told the Foreign Office that the German government would assume that hostile coverage had the approval of Whitehall, and continued to harbour suspicions about the Foreign Office News Department, headed as it was by Rex Leeper, one of Vansittart's acolytes. Even Phipps, as has been noted, was not uncritical of the behaviour of British pressmen inside Germany, although he did not suffer from Henderson's paranoia about domestic press coverage. Neither was Henderson able to build up the sort of relationship of trust which Horace Rumbold had with Norman Ebbutt, *The Times'* correspondent in Germany. Ebbutt's deputy in Berlin, Douglas Reed, wrote that Rumbold was the source of Ebbutt's prediction in 1933 that Nazism's advent 'meant war in about five years'.[87]

When he came to summarise his experience in Berlin, Henderson wrote: 'I had gone to Berlin without illusion. It was my duty to understand them and their view point. I talked frankly, and listened freely and was listened to freely. I went to bless and ended up cursing'.[88] This was typical of Henderson's rather melodramatic style, but by the end he had come to realise that he was, like Rumbold and Phipps, dealing with a gangster regime. His predecessors had soon realised (after an initial burst of optimism in Phipps' case) that Hitler was a dangerously irrational and ruthless dictator and had given the Foreign Office a realistic portrayal of the whole Nazi leadership. Henderson, too, ultimately came to understand Hitler's personality telling Halifax, for example, at the time of the Nuremberg Rally in 1938 that the Führer might already 'have crossed the border-line of insanity'.[89] His error was to put too much faith in alleged 'moderates' like Göring to whom he devoted a whole chapter of *Failure of a Mission*. But he was not alone in this. The Foreign Office had plenty of other sources of information (although the Berlin embassy was a key one) yet as late as 19 January 1939 Gladwyn Jebb, who was the Private Secretary to both Vansittart and Cadogan, could write in the following terms: 'The extremist leaders are advocating a course which is likely to lead to a general war and ... this is opposed not only by important people in the Army, the industrial world, and so on, but even the moderates in the ranks of the party itself'.[90] This showed a failure to understand that Hitler directed policy, and was not restrained by 'moderates', least of all by Göring. Significantly, too, Jebb's comments were written during Henderson's sick leave during the winter of 1938-39 when the Berlin Embassy was being run by Ogilvie-Forbes who was supposedly more robust in his dealings with the Nazis, yet apparently failed to shift Foreign Office thinking in this respect.[91]

One of the strangest aspects of the relationship between the Foreign Office and the Berlin embassy in the years 1933-39 was the Office's failure to recall Henderson when he had been diagnosed with cancer in 1938. The obvious point to have done this would have been on, or after, 15 March 1939 when Hitler's occupation of Bohemia and Moravia exploded Henderson's hopes for an accommodation with Nazi Germany. But Halifax and Cadogan huffed and puffed about this issue for months, as the pages of the latter's diary show, before in the end doing nothing.[92] Conversely, the Foreign Office refused to extend Rumbold's period of service in Berlin, yet allowed Phipps, who was two years over the normal retirement age in 1937 to continue for another two years in the Diplomatic Service (the hand of Sir Maurice Hankey has been detected here) in his new Paris posting.[93]

The treatment of Henderson in particular shows a bizarre failure by the officials in London (and indeed Lord Halifax), to appreciate the strains to which ambassadors in totalitarian states are subjected. The health issue involved here is but one example of the inconsistencies with which British ambassadors to Berlin had to deal in their relationship with the Foreign Office. Yet the Office itself was mired in difficulty when it came to dealing with Hitler, as Lord Halifax complained: 'I am ... all the time groping like a blind man trying to find his way across a bog, with everybody shouting from the banks different information as to where the quagmire is'.[94] The ambassadors in Berlin had tried both toughness and emollience to ease the task of successive Foreign Secretaries, but neither approach could succeed given the rabid nature of Hitler's ambitions.

NOTES

All references to Cabinet (CAB) or Foreign Office (FO) documents relate to materials held at the National Archives, London (formerly the Public Record Office) unless otherwise stated.

1.　These difficulties are well analysed in M. Hughes, 'The Virtues of Specialisation: British and American Diplomats Reporting on Russia 1921–39', *Diplomacy and Statecraft*, 11/2, (2000), pp.79–104.

2.　An example being the late Sir Frank Roberts who showed more sympathy for the problems faced by Henderson in particular than many have done. See his *Dealing with Dictators: The Destruction and Revival of Europe* (London: Weidenfeld & Nicolson, 1991), ch.26. Roberts served as British Minister in Moscow in the late 1940s.

3.　FO 800/254 (Henderson Papers), Rumbold to Henderson, 2 Jan. 1923.

4.　Rumbold to Henderson, 29 Aug. 1930, *Documents on British Foreign Policy*, Second Series, Vol. 1.

5.　Rumbold to Simon, 14 Mar. 1933, *Documents on British Foreign Policy*, Second Series, Vol. 6.

6.　Ibid.

7.　Rumbold to Simon, 26 Apr. 1933, *Documents on British Foreign Policy*, Second Series, Vol. 5.

8.　Rumbold to Simon, 30 Jun. 1933, *Documents on British Foreign Policy*, Second Series, Vol. 5.

9.　Lord Vansittart, *The Mist Procession* (London: Hutchinson, 1958), p.476.

10.　FO 800/254, Rumbold to Henderson, 15 Apr. 1940.

11.　M. Gilbert, *Sir Horace Rumbold: Portrait of a Diplomat* (London: Heinemann, 1973), p.269.

12.　Ibid., p.379, footnote 1.

13.　CAB 21/540.

14.　FO 370/16681, Undated memorandum by Simon.

15.　Cited in Gilbert, *Rumbold*, p.454.

16.　Vansittart, *Mist Procession*, p.274.

17.　Phipps Papers, Churchill Archives Centre, Churchill College, Cambridge, PHPP II 2/19, Phipps to Hankey, 29 Dec. 1940.

18.　Phipps entered the Diplomatic Service in 1899, and served variously in Constantinople, Rome, Paris, Madrid and Brussels; First Secretary 1912 and Counsellor 1920. In 1911, he married Frances Ward, the younger sister of Sarita Vansittart. Selby reciprocated Vansittart's hostility in his memoir *Diplomatic Twilight 1930–1940* (London: John Murray, 1953) in which he accused his former superior of allowing the Treasury undue influence in the Foreign Office, and being in favour of the *Anschluss*. Vansittart strongly rejected such charges.

19.　N. Rose, *Vansittart: Portrait of a Diplomat* (London: Heinemann, 1977), p.119. O'Malley entered the Foreign Office in 1911 and was also Minister to Hungary 1939–41 and Ambassador to Poland 1942–45.

20.　Rose, ibid., p.119.

21.　FO 800/268, O'Malley to Henderson, 9 Jun. 1937.

22.　M. Gilbert and R. Gott, *The Appeasers* (London: Weidenfeld & Nicolson, 1963), p.49.

23.　D. Cameron Watt, 'Chamberlain's Ambassadors', in M. Dockrill and B.J.C. McKercher (eds), *Diplomacy and World Power: Studies in British Foreign Policy 1890–1950* (Cambridge: Cambridge University Press 1996), p.154.

24.　Gilbert and Gott, *Appeasers*, p.49.

25.　R. Spitzy, *How We Squandered the Reich* (Norwich: Michael Russell, 1997), p.243.

26.　Phipps Papers, PHPP I 2/17, Vansittart to Phipps, 22 Mar. 1935.

27.　Phipps Papers, PHPP I 1/16, Phipps to Eden, 26 May 1936; FO 371/19906/C3879/4/18, minute by Sargent, 28 May 1936.

28.　Phipps Papers, PHPP I 1/16, Phipps to Foreign Office, 4 Nov. 1936.

29.　T. Jones, *A Diary With Letters 1931–40* (Oxford: Oxford University Press, 1954), p.304.

30. Baldwin Papers, Cambridge University Library, Vol. 124, Vansittart to Cleverley, 31 Mar. 1936 and Eden to Baldwin, 27 Dec. 1936.
31. Jones, *Diary With Letters*, 22 May 1936.
32. *Ibid.* Lord D'Abernon was British ambassador in Berlin from 1920 to 1926. See G. Johnson, *The Berlin Embassy of Lord D'Abernon, 1920–26* (Basingstoke: Palgrave Macmillan, 2002). Willingdon was a former British Viceroy in India.
33. Watt, 'Chamberlain's Ambassadors', p.154.
34. *Foreign Relations of the United States, 1937*, Vol. 1 (Washington DC: US Government Printing Office, 1954), pp.84–5, Bullitt to Hull, 30 Apr. 1937. Much more material about Phipps will be available with the forthcoming publication of G. Johnson (ed.), *Our Man in Berlin: The Diary of Sir Eric Phipps, 1933–1937* (London: Brassey, 2004). I am grateful to Dr Johnson for supplying me with a copy of her paper, 'The Berlin Diary of Sir E. Phipps', presented at the 2003 British International History Group Conference at Nottingham University.
35. Vansittart's closest supporters included Orme Sargent, Laurence Collier, Rex and Allen Leeper, and Ralph Wigram, who died tragically young in December 1936.
36. P. Schwartz, *This Man Ribbentrop: his Life and Times* (New York: Messner, 1943), pp.188–9.
37. H. Dalton, *The Fateful Years 1931–45*, (London: Muller, 1957), p.105.
38. Ibid.
39. Henderson entered the Diplomatic Service in 1905 and served variously in St. Petersburg, Nish, Rome, Paris, Constantinople and Cairo. He was Minister in Belgrade 1929–35 and Buenos Aires 1935–37. Unlike Phipps and Rumbold, he never married.
40. FO 800/268, Vansittart to Henderson, 13 Feb. 1935.
41. FO 800/268, Oliphant to Henderson, 18 Apr. 1935.
42. Vansittart, *Mist Procession*, p.360; D.C. Watt, *How War Came* (London: Heinemann, 1989), p.72. For a more detailed analysis of the reasons behind Henderson's appointment see P. Neville, 'The Appointment of Sir Nevile Henderson, 1937: Design or Blunder', *Journal of Contemporary History*, 4/33 (1998), pp.609–19.
43. Sir N. Henderson, *Failure of A Mission* (London: Hodder & Stoughton, 1940), p.13. Henderson wrote a second posthumous memoir, *Water Under the Bridges* (London: Hodder & Stoughton, 1945), about the whole career in the Diplomatic Service.
44. Henderson, *Failure of a Mission*, p.20.
45. Eden to Henderson, 30 Apr. 1937, *Documents on British Foreign Policy*, Second Series, Vol. 18, p.692.
46. T.P. Conwell Evans, *None So Blind: a Study of the Crisis Years, 1930–1939* (London: Harrison, 1947, printed and distributed privately), p.72. It is right to add here that the editors of the *Documents on British Foreign Policy* series found no evidence in the Foreign Office archives or in Neville Chamberlain's papers held at the University of Birmingham to support Henderson's claims.
47. Henderson, *Failure of a Mission*, p.17.
48. Henderson to Sargent, 20 July 1937, *Documents on British Foreign Policy*, Second Series, Vol. 19, pp.98–105 and FO 371/20736/7232; Lothian, the former Philip Kerr, had been a member of the British delegation at the Paris Peace Conference in 1919 and worked closely with Lloyd George. Initially a convinced appeaser, Lothian made a complete *volte face* before the war. He was British ambassador to Washington 1939–40.
49. *Documents on British Foreign Policy*, Second Series, Vol. 18, No. 480, p.727, n.9.
50. FO 371/20736/7232, undated minute by Vansittart.
51. Ibid.
52. FO 371/20736/5377/270/18, Henderson to Maxwell Garnett, 14 Jul. 1937.
53. FO 371/20736/5377, minutes by Strang, 27 Jul. 1937, Sargent 29 Jul. 1937, and Vansittart 30 July 1937.
54. FO 800/268, O'Malley to Henderson, 9 Jun. 1937.
55. Sir O. O'Malley, *The Phantom Caravan* (London: John Murray, 1954), p.20
56. FO 800/268, Hadow to Henderson, 11 May 1938.

57. Ibid.
58. Hickleton Papers, Borthwick Institute, University of York, A4/410/3, Henderson to Halifax, 10 Jan. 1938.
59. D. Dilks (ed.), *The Diaries of Sir Alexander Cadogan* (London: Cassell, 1971), p.43, entry for 30 Jan. 1938.
60. For references to such frustrations see P. Neville, 'Rival Foreign Office Perceptions of Germany 1936–9', *Diplomacy and Statecraft*, 13/3 (2002), pp.137–52.
61. D. Dilks, 'Appeasement and Intelligence', in D. Dilks (ed.), *Retreat from Power: Studies in British Foreign Policy of the Twentieth Century*, Vol. 1 (Basingstoke: Macmillan, 1981), pp.151–4.
62. FO 850/2/Y832, Major V. Vivian, 'Security Measures at HM Embassy, Rome', 22 Jul.1937.
63. D. Cameron Watt, 'Introduction' to D. Irving, *Breach of Security: the German Secret Intelligence File in Events Leading to the Second World War* (London: Kimber, 1968), p.32
64. FO 800/294 (Cadogan Papers), Cadogan to Henderson, 26 Feb. 1939; N. Rose, *Vansittart: Study of a Diplomat* (London: Heinemann, 1978), p.45)
65. Spitzy, *How We Squandered the Reich*, p.68.
66. FO 800/269, Henderson to King George VI, 2 Oct. 1938.
67. P. Meehan, *The Unnecessary War: Whitehall and the German Resistance to Hitler*, (London: Sinclair-Stevenson, 1992), p.24.
68. D. Cameron Watt, 'Diplomacy and Diplomats' in R. Boyce and J. Maiolo (eds), *The Origins of World War Two: The Debate Continues* (Basingstoke: Palgrave Macmillan, 2003), p.334.
69. Ogilvie-Forbes Papers, University of Aberdeen, 2740/39, Ogilvie-Forbes to Henderson, 7 Dec. 1938. Ogilvie-Forbes had served in Mexico 1927–30, the Vatican 1930–32, Baghdad 1932–35 and Madrid 1935–37 before going to Berlin. For detail on his earlier career, see T. Buchanan, 'Edge of Darkness: British Front-Line Diplomacy in the Spanish Civil War, 1936–7', *Contemporary European History*, 12/3 (2003), pp.19–30, and for information on his tense relationship with Henderson, see P. Neville, *Appeasing Hitler: The Diplomacy of Sir Nevile Henderson 1937–9* (Basingstoke: Palgrave Macmillan, 2000), pp.125–30.
70. Notably in Meehan, *The Unnecessary War*; see especially ch. 2, fn. 67.
71. Gilbert, *Rumbold*, p.383.
72. Von Hassell served with Henderson in Belgrade. He was executed in the wake of the failed attempt on Hitler's life in 1944.
73. U. von Hassell, *The Von Hassell Diaries: The Story of the Forces against Hitler inside Germany* (New York: Hamish Hamilton, 1946), pp.2–3.
74. Spitzy to the author, 31 Dec. 1997.
75. Spitzy, *How We Squandered the Reich*, p.242.
76. For further material on Henderson's dealings with German oppositionists via his military attaché, Mason MacFarlane, see Neville, *Appeasing Hitler*, pp.90–91.
77. Meehan, *The Unnecessary War*, p.154.
78. Henderson to Halifax, 16 Aug. 1938, *Documents on British Foreign Policy*, Third Series, Vol. 2, Appendix 4, p.683 (document referred to in the Appendix only).
79. Ibid., p.686, Chamberlain to Halifax, 19 Aug. 1938.
80. FO 371/22958/C4897/13/18, minute by Sargent, 15 Apr. 1939.
81. FO 800/37/294, Cadogan to Ogilvie-Forbes, 18 Apr. 1939.
82. FO 371/2076/1242, Report by A. Rumbold, 10 Feb. 1937.
83. *Manchester Guardian* Archive, John Rylands University Library of Manchester, MGA 13, Dell to Crozier, 2 Mar. 1935; for more detail on the relationship between the Foreign Office News Department and journalists see R. Cockett, *The Twilight of Truth: Chamberlain, Appeasement and the Manipulation of the Press* (London: Weidenfeld, 1990), pp.16–23.
84. FO 371/20763/ 7799, Henderson to the Foreign Office, 14 Nov. 1937.
85. Hickleton Papers, A441032, Henderson to the Foreign Office, 15 Nov. 1937.
86. Neville, *Appeasing Hitler*, pp.40–43 and p.185, fn. 84.
87. Gilbert, *Rumbold*, p.382.
88. FO 800/270, draft for 'The Man who Shouted at Hitler' by William Hillman.

89. Henderson to Halifax, 12 Sep. 1938, *Documents on British Foreign Policy*, Third Series, Vol. 2.
90. CAB 27/627, FP(36), memorandum by Jebb, 'Summary of Information From Secret Sources', 19 Jan. 1936. Jebb (by then Lord Gladwyn) was caustic about Henderson in his post-war memoir conveniently forgetting his own pre-war pro-appeasement views. See *Memoirs of Lord Gladwyn* (London: Weidenfeld & Nicolson, 1972), pp.23, 106.
91. This view is put by B. Strang, 'Two Unequal Tempers: Sir George Ogilvie-Forbes, Sir Nevile Henderson and British Foreign Policy', *Diplomacy and Statecraft*, 5/1 (1994), pp.107–37; for a riposte see Neville, *Appeasing Hitler*, pp.124–9.
92. Neville, ibid., pp.141–4.
93. Watt, 'Chamberlain's Ambassadors', p.160; for a detailed study of Phipps' Embassy in Paris, see J. Herman, *The Paris Embassy of Sir Eric Phipps 1937–9* (Brighton: University of Sussex Press, 1999).
94. FO 800/314 (Halifax Papers), Halifax to Henderson, 6 Sep. 1938.

Splendid Isolation to Finest Hour:
Britain as a Global Power, 1900–1950

JOHN CHARMLEY

The title of this essay would match its content better were the title to be reversed and read: 'Finest Hour to Splendid Isolation'. The need to understand the origins of the two world wars dominated the study of British foreign policy in the first half of the twentieth century, shaping a narrative in which the themes of triumph and decline coexist without any sense of unease. Simultaneously the story is one of two great victories, followed by a period of precipitous decline. Paul Kennedy, writing in the early 1980s, thought that 'since Britain did occupy for so long a period such a pre-eminent role in world affairs, it is important to emphasise how swiftly and how completely that position has vanished'.[1] Twenty years on, no one would write quite in this vein, but historians have not yet adjusted themselves away from the obsession with what has been called (in an ugly neologism) 'declinology'. If the grand narrative no longer ends where it did, there may also be a case for arguing that it may not begin there either. In four books dealing with aspects of British diplomacy after 1874, the author of this essay has endeavoured to argue the need for a different perspective on the subject;[2] clamant arguments over the virtues, or otherwise, of Winston Churchill have sometimes obscured the deeper argument pursued. This essay takes the opportunity to suggest how British foreign policy in the first half of the twentieth century might look if the triumphal lenses are laid aside.

European diplomacy from the creation of the *Kaiserreich* to the outbreak
of the Great War was first studied in order to understand how the first event led
to the second. Works by the giants of diplomatic history, W.L. Langer, Luigi
Albertini, Bernadotte Schmitt and A.J.P. Taylor, pioneered the way, followed
in a later generation by magisterial studies by James Joll, Paul Kennedy, Zara
Steiner, Samuel Williamson, Dominic Lieven, Richard Bosworth, John Keiger
and Volker Berghahn.[3] Unconsciously a teleology emerged and all roads led
to 1914. The fact that understanding the outbreak of the Great War failed to
prevent a Second World War confirmed the centrality of the Anglo-German
antagonism as an organising theme of the meta-narrative of twentieth century
British foreign policy. A.J.P. Taylor (again), Donald Watt, Sidney Aster,
Martin Gilbert and others all tried to explain how the second cataclysm had
occurred.[4] All of this scholarly activity created the framework within which
we came to understand the history of British foreign policy in the last century.
The picture itself was painted in its boldest colours by one of the most
influential historians of the twentieth century – Winston Churchill. His clear,
broad brush strokes revealed a Britain passing from the isolationism of
Salisbury through a continental commitment by Grey to the triumph of the
First World War; but this was followed by a retreat from commitment, the
disaster of appeasement and a new German attempt at world domination. This
story was already familiar from the documentary record, most notably Eyre
Crowe's famous memorandum of 1 January 1907, reproduced in Gooch and
Temperley's third volume of *British Documents on the Origins of the War.*[5]
This placed recent British policy into a longer tradition, arguing that since the
days of the Elizabeth I, Britain had tried to maintain the balance of power in
Europe by opposing the attempts of any single power to dominate the
continent. Churchill's narrative fitted easily within this wider picture, the
effect of which was to enable him to argue that the appeasers of the 1930s had
(in a favourite phrase) fallen below the level of events; they were outside the
grand tradition of British foreign policy. Thanks to Churchill, what Lord
Robert Cecil, third Marquess of Salisbury, had written in 1864 was as true a
century later: 'We have been brought up to believe that England's voice is of
weight in the councils of the world. Our national pride has been fed by
histories of the glorious deeds of our fathers, when single-handed they defied
the conqueror to whom every other European nation had been compelled to
humble itself'.[6] It was, of course, difficult to deny by then that decline had set
in, and in the hysteria surrounding Churchill's death there was a sense that in
burying him the British were saying farewell not just to their greatest son, but
to their greatness itself. The view that the period from 1900 to 1940 saw a
passage from 'Splendid Isolation' to 'Finest Hour' seemed set in stone, its
heroes and villains in plain view: Sir Edward Grey (Foreign Secretary
1905–16), Herbert Asquith (Prime Minister 1908–16) and Winston Churchill

(especially as First Lord of the Admiralty 1911–15 and Prime Minister 1940–45 and 1951–55), on one side, and Neville Chamberlain (Prime Minister, 1937–40), Sir Samuel Hoare (Foreign Secretary 1935) and Lord Halifax (Foreign Secretary 1938–40) on the other. Far from diminishing the power of this picture, events after 1945 were influenced by it, reinforcing it in the process. It was, Churchill argued, as necessary to stand up to Stalin as it had been to oppose Hitler. This version of the lessons of appeasement has come down to the present day, when President George W. Bush and Prime Minister Blair are both happy to cite Churchill as an authority for pre-emptive action in Iraq. Thus does history influence the present, and is in turn influenced by it.

Attempts have been made to show that far from appeasement running counter to the tradition of British foreign policy, it occupied a central place within it;[7] but they have had little effect on popular perceptions that it was a doomed policy, bred by folly out of ignorance. Against this ignoble payment of Danegeld is set the golden tradition of maintaining the balance of power and British prestige: Elizabeth I, Queen Anne and the Duke of Marlborough, the Duke of Wellington at Waterloo, the apparently badly led British troops during the First World War, 'Monty' at Alamein, Churchill on 'their Finest Hour', and, latterly, Thatcher and Blair; others, like George Canning (Foreign Secretary 1807–09 and 1822–27), Viscount Palmerston (Foreign Secretary 1830–34, 1835–41 and 1846–51) and Harold Macmillan (Foreign Secretary, 1955), can be added according to taste. But if the ingredients are rearranged and cooked in a different way, the dish comes out differently. Writing in 1938 to a friend, R.A. Butler, then Under-Secretary to Halifax at the Foreign Office, contested the view that the British Empire had ever had a 'simple traditional policy': her interests and 'the world itself, are too complicated to enable us to follow any one high road'.[8] He divined, correctly, that Churchill and his ilk had been 'reared in Edwardian politics' and were so imbued with former Foreign Office Permanent Under-Secretary Sir Eyre Crowe's view of British foreign policy that they 'failed to appreciate the facts of life'.[9] This cut to the heart of the matter.

Churchill had come of age in a political world convulsed by a very public argument between Lord Salisbury and Joseph Chamberlain about the direction of British foreign policy, which came to a head in May 1898; at the centre of the debate was the policy of 'splendid isolation'. Speaking at the Albert Hall on 4 May 1898, Salisbury, recently returned from illness, asserted his position by declaring that: 'We know that we shall maintain against all comers that which we possess, and we know, in spite of the jargon about isolation, that we are amply competent to do so'.[10] From his Birmingham stronghold, Chamberlain riposted on 13 May by alleging that the 'policy of strict isolation' was now a liability to a Britain which, faced by a hostile world, 'must not reject the idea of an alliance with those Powers whose interests most nearly approximate to our own'.[11] This illustrated the fault line between the 'Victorians' and the 'Edwardians', terms of art rather than science, but ones which neatly sum up the difference between those, like Salisbury, who were nurtured on the optimistic mid-Victorian assumptions about British power, and Chamberlain and others who were more obsessed by the insecurities of the late-Victorian world.[12] The difference was not as generational as the names suggest: after all Chamberlain was only six years younger than Salisbury; it was as much temperamental as anything else. But in this debate at the end of the Victorian era, Salisbury, like the policy that became shackled to his name – 'isolation' – was a symbol of inaction and decay, and there was no doubt where the young Churchill stood in the argument. For him Salisbury united 'the brain of a statesman to the delicate susceptibilities of a mule'.[13] As far back as the 1930s, Salisbury's daughter and biographer, Lady Gwendolyn Cecil, had strenuously denied that her father had ever had a policy of 'isolation';[14] a view reinforced by C.H.D. Howard's unjustly neglected *Splendid Isolation*.[15] It was a target hung on him by those like Chamberlain who were dissatisfied by what they took to be Salisbury's complacency about the international situation. Chamberlain, characteristically, had a good point but did not know what to do with it.

The good point was that things were not as they had been when the Conservatives had left office in 1892. Then there had been no 'jargon' about isolation, because there was nothing from which Britain could be isolated; this was not so in 1895 when Salisbury returned to office. In the intervening years the Franco-Russian alliance had been forged, and Rosebery's Liberal government had discovered the dangers of being isolated from both alliance systems when Russia, France and Germany had intervened in China in 1895 to force the Japanese to disgorge their gains from the Sino-Japanese war.[16] The events of the following few years, in particular the German reaction to the Jameson Raid (1896) and the squabble with the United States over Venezuela, had reinforced the impression that Britain was isolated, leading those of a nervous disposition to conclude that this situation was dangerous.[17] In fact, Salisbury, who had first come to office as Prime Minister in 1885 when Britain had really been isolated, thanks to Gladstone's diplomacy, knew all about its dangers and had steered British policy as close to Bismarck's Triple Alliance as he could. This had been the safest line in the later Bismarckian era. The great Chancellor knew that a satiated Germany could only lose from further changes in the balance of power, and he wished things to remain as they were; France, which had disrupted that balance in the 1850s and 1860s, and had a motive to do so again, was nicely quarantined. All of this suited Salisbury, not least because it also helped neutralise the power from whom Britain had most to fear, Imperial Russia. However, this comforting option was no longer available by 1895. The German Kaiser, William II, was a far from conservative figure, and Salisbury was no more inclined towards him than he was to the equally unpredictable French and Russians; in this situation, isolation was not a policy of choice, it was a necessary fact of life. Much though he deplored change in domestic politics, in foreign policy it held out the hope that the unsatisfactory nature of international relations would not last; until that time came, it was best to sit tight and rely on Britain's navy. Chamberlain, ever the advocate of action, and unable to abide its opposite, came to the simplistic conclusion that Britain needed an alliance, and argued for one. Salisbury's stubborn rearguard action against such folly inevitably led to his being dubbed an isolationist.[18]

In the debate about 'isolation' that dominated Cabinet politics in 1898, Salisbury became, perforce, a proponent of isolation, not because it represented his policy or preferences, but because in the discourse of the day it was the alternative position to the one adopted by those who opposed him. In so far as it represented the view that Britain had nothing to gain from joining the Triple Alliance, 'isolation' did duty as a label, but hardly as a description. No power with global reach could be truly isolated diplomatically; indeed it was for that very reason that Salisbury preferred to steer clear of the post-Bismarckian alliance systems: France and Russia were imperial rivals, whilst it was inconceivable that Germany, however friendly, would risk a two-front war in Europe for the sake of British quarrels in India or the Far East. Salisbury's logic was as unassailable as it proved unconvincing to his colleagues. Between 1897 and 1900 it seemed as though Britain's position was under assault from every side, and that as a result she would lose out in any scramble for China; Salisbury's Olympian answer that Britain would look after her own seemed to men of Chamberlain's stamp simply further evidence that the old man was no longer fit to run British foreign policy. In the autumn of 1900 Salisbury left the Foreign Office, handing over to Lansdowne. But replacing Salisbury proved easier than finding an alternative diplomatic strategy.

If Salisbury's policy had not been one of isolation, Britain could hardly have been moving from it in the years following his retirement from the Foreign Office. If we move from the teleology imposed by having to map the road to 1914, it might be that British policy was inspired by motives other than preparing for Armageddon. We lack a modern account of Lansdowne's foreign policy; he has generally been treated either as the antechamber to Grey or the departure lounge to Salisbury.[19] These views tend to see him presiding over a change of direction in British policy. As early as 1911 Grey was putting forward the view that the Anglo-French Entente Cordiale of 1904 had been a turning point in British diplomacy.[20] This is a prime example of the unconscious influence of the teleology of 1914. It is certainly true that Lansdowne did not share Salisbury's reluctance to enter into definite diplomatic commitments, but there is no sign at all that in negotiating the Entente with France he was motivated by fear of Germany. What Lansdowne shared with Salisbury was what might be called an 'Indian perspective' on British policy.[21] Salisbury, as a former Secretary of State for India, and Lansdowne as a past Viceroy, both regarded Russia as the primary danger to British interests. Both men tried to negotiate with Russia to remove causes of friction, but neither had any great success. Lansdowne was not wedded to any one way of averting the Russian threat. If St. Petersburg would not come to an accommodation over the Far East, then other ways must be found of providing security for Britain's interests there: he tried the Germans, but they seemed to blow hot and cold; he tried the Japanese, and they seemed willing to talk. There was nothing doctrinaire in Lansdowne's attitude towards the Anglo-Japanese alliance of January 1902. For all the talk in parts of the press of the end of isolation, there is no sign that Lansdowne regarded his actions as marking a caesura in British diplomatic history; perhaps further study will reveal Lansdowne as something of a technician, more concerned with solving the problem than anything else. It may be that just as in the seventeenth century, Cromwell was so obsessed with Britain's old enemy Spain that he failed to see the rise of a new one in the form of France, so Salisbury and Lansdowne thought in terms of the traditional rivalry with Russia rather than the coming German menace.

To take this view of Lansdowne, and to accept Salisbury as not being a proponent of something called 'splendid isolation', creates a problem with the usual perspectives on Grey. He liked to claim continuity with Lansdowne, seeing the Entente with Russia as completing the work begun with its French counterpart. There is not much in this if we accept the correctives to the traditional version of events offered above. Grey was clearly motivated by fear of Germany: 'An *entente* between, Russia, France and ourselves', he wrote as early as 20 February 1906, 'would be absolutely secure. If it is necessary to check Germany it could then be done'.[22] For all his claims not to have believed in the balance of power, Grey behaved in practice as though he did.[23] In October 1905 he declared that the 'spirit' of the Entente mattered more than the exact terms;[24] this was the opposite of the view taken by Lansdowne, who thought that the terms mattered a great deal. Perhaps, however, Grey's protests about not pursuing a policy of the balance of power were correct; it may be that he was so marked by his time as Under-Secretary of State at the Foreign Office under Rosebery and Kimberley in the 1890s that like other 'Edwardians', he believed that the worse thing that could befall Britain was to fall back into isolation.

Ironically, if one is looking for a 'Finest Hour', it may well have come just before Grey came to the Foreign Office. The threat that Russia had posed to British interests from the Straits to the South China Sea, and which had dominated so much of British policy making under Salisbury and Lansdowne, was lifted in 1905. When Salisbury and Balfour had protested against the alliance with Japan at the turn of 1901–02, they had argued that it might have unintended consequences; they had been right.[25] The Japanese had wanted the alliance for two reasons: one was obvious – they wanted an ally if France should join Russia's side against her; but they also wanted protection against being robbed of the gains of a successful war as they had been after the treaty of Shimonoseki in 1895. Back then Japan had been isolated against a European 'Triplice'; with Britain's help this would not happen again, and so Japan was now free to deal with Russia. Violence is, rumour to the contrary, sometimes the answer: what the patient diplomacy of Salisbury and Lansdowne had failed to achieve was brought about by the Russo-Japanese war of 1905. With Russia's defeat and political destabilisation, Britain had no need to fear her, and from the Bosphorus through the Northwest frontier to the Yellow River, all was quiet. The great loser from the events of 1905 (the Russians apart) was Kaiser William II and his *Weltpolitik*. Since his accession he had assumed that the most likely outcome of any diplomatic crisis would be either an Anglo-French or an Anglo-Russian war, a circumstance that would bring his English cousins knocking on his door urgently and respectfully seeking entry into his alliance system; now that would not happen. It was part of the process of trying to answer the question of what to do about such an unexpected turn of events that brought about the Moroccan crisis of 1905.

From this unfamiliar angle the Anglo-German antagonism assumes the form of the cloud on the horizon, no bigger than a man's hand, whilst the problem of Russia looms large in every imagination. The end of France's sulk over Egypt gave to Salisbury's successors a freedom of manoeuvre unknown to him. The Marquess had been right in supposing that only time and circumstance would bring any relief from the alarums and excursions of the mid-1890s; and as for the dangers of 'isolation', when, even at the height of the Boer War, had Britain really felt them? However, the problem with change, as Salisbury knew only too well, was that it was constant.

Although we often say 'look to the future', it is always blank, so we usually approach it looking backwards, which is perhaps one reason why we so often stumble on our way to it; so it was with British diplomacy in the decade after the Entente Cordiale. There is much sense in John Morley's comment that 'one great spring of mischief in these high politics is to suppose that the situation of today will be the situation of tomorrow'.[26] Grey failed to adapt his assumptions to the situation created by Russia's defeat. He had been impressed by the difference which the 1904 Entente had made to Britain's position, and mistaking effect for cause, sought one with Russia; what had eased Britain's position was the defeat of the Russians, not the entente. This did not mean, as his opponents were later to allege, that Grey was either anti-German or influenced by Foreign Office officials who were. He always professed his willingness to come to diplomatic arrangements with Berlin; but equally often, it proved impossible to do so because of fears of alienating Paris, or, after 1907, St. Petersburg. At the same time, the clumsiness with which German foreign policy was conducted gave credence to the growing view that Berlin's aims were akin to those of Napoleon's France or the Spain of Philip II. Those who had lived through the late nineteenth century as participants in its diplomacy such as Lord Sanderson took another view: to them it seemed more likely that clumsiness rather than conspiracy lay at the root of German foreign policy;[27] they were not in the majority.

Grey's diplomacy created a gulf between perception and reality, not least for the Foreign Secretary himself. Rhetorically Britain was as 'isolated' as ever she had been under the late great Marquess. It was true that the Kaiser complained frequently after 1907 that Britain had thrown itself into the balance alongside Germany's enemies, but Grey always protested that this was not the case; as late as the end of July 1914 he was still to be heard talking about Britain's 'free hand'. Yet alongside that existed something occasionally called the 'Triple Entente', complete with capital letters, which the Colonial Secretary, Lewis Harcourt, rightly complained about; such a thing, he pointed out to Grey in 1914, had been authorised neither by the Cabinet nor yet by Parliament.[28] There were Staff talks with the French, although most of the Cabinet did not find out about them until 1911, nearly six years after they had been initiated; but there was nothing comparable with the Russians, at least until the summer of 1914 when there were Naval talks. However, diplomatically, Britain was always to be found aligned with Russia and France, as the Bosnian crisis of 1908 and the Second Moroccan crisis of 1911 showed. In retrospect there had been a significant shift. For Salisbury and Lansdowne the view from Delhi and the imperial perspective this gave to British diplomacy was ultimately more important than the balance of power in Europe; for Grey the opposite was true. Yet the habits of the past lingered into a future where they were no longer so appropriate. The innate conservatism of British foreign policy abhors diplomatic revolutions, so it was only at the end of July 1914 that the reality of the present bridged the gap between Grey's rhetoric and the requirements of Britain's position.

Grey thought that the alternatives open to him were so weighted that they narrowed to one: war alongside France and Russia against Germany and Austria-Hungary. He thought this because to do otherwise would be to leave Britain isolated. Not for him the robust response of Salisbury, who had asked when we had felt that danger 'practically'.[29] Grey assumed there was a danger and acted to avert it. Asking whether he would have done differently had he known what would follow is pointless; those involved in the decision for war in 1914 would all have done differently had they been able to see the future.

But since they were not, they would all have done the same thing for the same reason they did it in reality; they felt they had no choice. This was the major consequence of the replacement of Russia by Germany as Britain's main rival. The ramifications of this development dominated British foreign policy until the mid-1940s, at which point Russia resumed her old position.

Only a counterfactual hypothesis would enable an answer to be given to Grey's presumption that the only thing worse for Britain than involvement in the Great War would have been non-involvement; the results of Grey's preference were clear enough. For a while, at least, the experience of the Great War acted as a purgative or catharsis, if one wishes to be grandiloquent about it. Just as in the period between the Congress of Vienna (1815) and the Crimean War (1854–56) the British had grown so used to the notion of their own power that they actively wished to intervene in a Continental War, only to regret it afterwards, so too between the Congress of Berlin and the Great War had the British taken to the policy of Disraeli of 'prestige' and imperialism; the War shook that faith.

It had been Disraeli who, back in 1878, had hooked Britain's star to the politics of 'prestige'. As the fifteenth earl of Derby, his Foreign Secretary, noted at the time to Salisbury, the Prime Minister 'believes thoroughly in prestige – as all foreigners do', but his ideas were 'not mine, nor yours'.[30] In this last assumption Derby had been right and wrong simultaneously. Salisbury did not believe in Disraeli's ideas, but he was willing to back them as a means to the end of succeeding him. The history of Conservative foreign policy in the mid- to late-nineteenth century has been written as though Disraeli was central to it, giving the impression that his jingoism was normative, which makes Derby appear an oddity. Recent research is beginning to challenge this assumption, and to mount the argument that there was another tradition in nineteenth century Conservative foreign policy in which it was Derby, and not Disraeli, who was normative.[31] Be that as it may, it is hard to sustain the argument that Salisbury's diplomacy had much in common with Beaconsfieldism, despite the fact that he was happy enough to throw Derby over in 1878 in order to succeed him at the Foreign Office. Indeed it could be argued that the assault on 'isolation' at the turn of the century was simply Salisbury being hoist by his own petard, with Chamberlain raising the jingo spirit Beaconsfield had conjured up in 1878. The Great War undoubtedly diluted this non-jingo Conservative line of thought, although Lansdowne's plea for a negotiated peace in 1917 may well be an echo of it, but the period after 1922 offered a more congenial environment in which it might flourish – especially after the excesses of Lloyd George.

In the absence of a sustained study of this alternative brand of Conservative foreign policy, it is only possible here to note some of its features: it was non-interventionist in practice and non-belligerent in tone; its proponents believed in diplomacy rather than bluff, and they preferred to work with the Concert of Europe rather than to defy it: Viscount Castlereagh (Foreign Secretary 1812–22) and Lord Aberdeen (Foreign Secretary 1828–30 and 1841–46) would have recognised it; Canning and Palmerston would have sniffed at it, as did their spiritual descendant, Winston Churchill. What united Churchill and the others was their belief in the Disraelian policy of 'prestige'. This was not quite as senseless as Derby liked to imply. His belief that it was better to eat a little humble pie than to pay out a fortune on a war had something to commend it at the time, and seems even more commendable after the experiences of the twentieth century, but there are times when prestige can save money. A belief in the reality of power can be a powerful diplomatic instrument in itself. Such diplomacy involves a willingness to bluff, and it is worth noting that Neville Chamberlain found Harold Temperley's version of George Canning a good guide in warning that 'you should never menace unless you are in a position to carry out your threats'.[32] It was an invariable mark of this non-jingo Conservatism that it considered means as well as ends.

The history of the struggle between these contending strands of Conservatism awaits its chronicler, but throughout the inter-war years its traces can be read. There is the Unionist Lord Carson's bitter maiden speech in the Lords, when he asked how anyone could expect a country that could not hold on to territory across St. George's Channel to hold onto India or Egypt.[33] It runs like a thread through the Baldwin government of 1924–29 when Churchill and Leo Amery thought that the Prime Minister and Austen Chamberlain at the Foreign Office were insufficiently robust in their assertion of British power. Most of all it was visible in the bitter debates over Samuel Hoare's India Bill in 1935, where Churchill and the Tory Right accused Baldwin and Ramsay MacDonald of betraying British interests in the sub-continent. When they criticised Baldwin, the Viceroy of India Lord Irwin, Sir John Simon (Foreign Secretary 1931–35) and Hoare for their appeasement of Egyptian and Indian nationalism, they missed the point. Formal Empire, which was expensive, was only a stage in the imperial story, and not necessarily a very interesting or profitable one. As early as 1922 the *patron* of latter-day imperialism, the Colonial Secretary Lord Milner, had shown himself more flexible than those who called his name in aid when he recommended that Britain should regularise her position in Egypt through a treaty with the Egyptians. Such a treaty would have effectively delegated Home Rule to Egypt at the same time as preserving Britain's control over her real interests – the Suez Canal and Egyptian foreign policy; the Montagu reforms in India moved in a similar direction, as did the Irwin declaration and Hoare's India bill.[34]

Like much of Salisbury's diplomacy, this line of policy was easily criticised by the jingo element, not least by that *über*-jingo, Churchill. It involved much making of inessential concessions and an attitude of conciliation when nothing vital was at stake; at the same time it meant not shouting that this was what you were doing. From that point of view men like Churchill and Lord Lloyd, the High Commissioner for Egypt, were useful camouflage; they allowed the government to point out to the nationalists that there were limits beyond which they could not be expected to go. The tactics that were developed to deal with nationalist fanatics in the Empire could be equally well deployed to deal with the same species outside of the Empire, such as Hitler.

This version of events exonerates no one for misreading Hitler. But the Churchillian version, that an earlier Grand Alliance would have solved all problems, is easier to argue than it is to sustain. When Chamberlain investigated the idea in early 1938 he concluded that 'there is almost everything to be said for it until you come to examine its practicability. From that moment its attraction vanishes'.[35] America was neither politically nor militarily ready for intervening in Europe; her politicians were still passing neutrality legislation, whilst her army was small and poorly equipped. The argument, favoured by some now, and by Churchill then, that the Soviet Union was a putative member of the Grand Alliance could be sustained only by adopting Anglo-Saxon attitudes.[36] From London, Moscow might have seemed part of the solution; from Prague, Warsaw and all points south-east, she seemed more like part of the problem. Powers who survived by balancing off between the Soviets and the Nazis were not easily to be dissuaded from that practice, particularly by a Great Power lacking the ability to attack Germany. For all the ink spilt over Munich 1938, two brute facts remain: one was that Czechoslovakia was a sovereign state that chose dismemberment rather than fighting to preserve its territorial integrity; the other was that there was little, if anything, Britain could have done to prevent this eventuality. To accept the argument that Czechoslovakia could only fight with backing from other powers is to tacitly acknowledge that despite her army and air force she lacked the first requisite of a sovereign state – the ability to protect itself. Even had the British been willing to align with the Soviets in 1938, it is difficult to see what the Soviets could have done to help the Czechs, since the Poles would not have let the Red Army pass through their territory, not least because of a well-founded fear that it might have been difficult to persuade them to leave. It was all very well for the believers in 'prestige' to argue for intervention in a war in central Europe; they did not have the responsibilities of power.

Indeed, the possibility opens up that the real criticism of Neville Chamberlain is not that he appeased too much and for too long, but that he abandoned non-intervention too speedily and over the wrong issue. If there really was nothing to be done to help the Czechs, why did Chamberlain get involved at all? The answer to that lies in his own belief in that version of British diplomatic history that saw the country as the regulator on the balance of power; historians, like many well-intentioned folk, do more harm than they always realise. Such is the intractability of the British belief in this version of their history that nothing seems to shake it; not even the fact that when it was put to the test in 1939, Britain was totally unable to prevent Hitler from over-running Europe. The often-employed argument that Britain had to go to war to prevent herself being attacked has a perverse charm about it. Hitler was moving eastwards in 1939, and he attacked Britain because it had declared war on him. It is true that he might have attacked Britain later, but later might never have come, and it is folly to take risks today to guard against what might not happen tomorrow.

But this is to fall too easily into the conclusion that appeasement was a great and total failure; at least until the summer of 1940 there would seem to be some grounds for questioning this. Appeasement was not simply about averting war with Germany, it was an attempt to avoid something that had not happened since the mid-1890s, namely the eruption of simultaneous crises across the global reach of British power. In Rosebery's day the concatenation of crises in the Balkans, in Siam and in China had been too much for Britain's diplomatic resources. This was not a sign of Liberal incompetence as Unionists liked to claim, but rather the inevitable consequence of running an Empire on the cheap with the assumption that crises would occur in a manner that allowed resources to be moved around. Such concerns lay behind the quiet diplomatic revolution of the Lansdowne era, where Japanese ships would help pull British chestnuts from Far Eastern fires, leaving the Home Fleet free to deal with those nearer the Channel coast. One of Neville Chamberlain's many misfortunes was that he came to power at a time when crises threatened in Western Europe, the Mediterranean and the Far East; it was his task to prevent what a later generation would call 'imperial overstretch'. Those, like Churchill, who argued that the answer was to be strong everywhere, were bound to win jingo plaudits, but they could never explain how their policy would be paid for; being in the comfort of opposition, they were never called on to do so. It was Neville Chamberlain who brought at least some sense of order into determining Britain's priorities; he it was who sought to bring Britain's liabilities and resources into some sort of alignment. Since his achievement was not showy, and since it involved neither the creation of a Grand Alliance nor the avoidance of war with Germany, it is easily overlooked; so, of course, it has been.[37]

Chamberlain failed in his primary objective – the avoidance of war – but then, given what we know about Hitler, it is hard to see how that could ever have been attained; but in his secondary objectives he enjoyed a measure of success. It was important that Britain should not face three geographically dispersed challenges simultaneously; nor did she, until 1941–42: Japan was successfully appeased; and whilst it was impossible to recover the ground with Italy lost by the Abyssinian crisis (1935–36) and the fiasco over sanctions, at least the Italians did not enter the war with Germany in 1939. Moreover, Chamberlain successfully identified Britain's most likely enemy, Germany, and by ignoring Churchill in 1937 (when he wanted priority given to medium-range bombers) and in 1939 (when he wanted a continental-sized army to take priority over radar), he created the conditions in which Churchill would be able to win the Battle of Britain. What Chamberlain did not plan for was what no Prime Minister can – namely the eventuality that his country's armed forces will prove, in the audit of war, inferior to those of another country. Those who would argue that a different priority in rearmament could have prevented the defeat of 1940 need to explain which French or British General would have been capable of defeating the Germans in battle in 1940. No diplomacy can provide against a catastrophic military defeat – as the Austrian Chancellor, Metternich, discovered in 1806.

Still, whatever defence may be made of Chamberlain, nothing will erase the fact that he failed. It was true that there were those, including himself and Butler, who would have liked to have found a way of coming to terms with Germany after September 1939, but they would have found it difficult to have rallied the British people to that cause. Churchill's successful evocation of the triumphalist notion of Britain's ability to win the war whilst losing most of the early battles, showed how close to the surface lay the instincts of an imperial people, to whom the notion of defeat was unthinkable. The sublime prose and oratory of Churchill should not, however, blind us to the fact that it is the summer of 1940 which comes closest to being the time when Britain was truly in 'splendid isolation'. Chamberlain and Churchill's hopes in the French proved vain; Churchill's frantic appeals to the Americans produced little in the way of aid and nothing in the way of active assistance against Germany; the Nazi-Soviet pact, cemented, like the old Holy Alliance, by the partition of Poland, promised nothing but hostility from the East; only the Empire stood by the Mother Country. All of this offered a chance of avoiding defeat; none of it provided a hope of victory. That was provided by Hitler's *hubris*. In attacking the Soviet Union and then declaring war on the United States, the German dictator did something Churchill had signally failed to do – provide Britain with allies.

The appearance of allies, welcome as it was, ended the one advantage that isolation brought by making it necessary to think about the future. Churchill, one senses, was at his happiest when Britain was isolated and there were no allies to pamper and no complex plans about the future to consider; he was fond of commending to the Foreign Secretary, Anthony Eden, Mrs. Glass' recipe for jugged hare: 'first catch your hare'.[38] But as Eden argued, the British Empire could not wait until the end of the war to decide what it had been fighting for. Although the dominant theme of British policy after 1945 was to be the American connection, it should be noted that other options were canvassed.

The American alliance was, above all, Churchill's conception; indeed he was not averse to floating the idea of a currency and legal union when he thought they might get an audience.[39] Eden, who has not been given the credit that he is due for his constructive thinking during the war, told his colleagues in 1942 that the absence of any 'guiding principle' for British foreign policy was 'a grave weakness'; unlike Churchill he did not think that an optimistic reliance on America would do as a substitute for a policy.[40] What Eden wanted was to create a latter-day 'Triple Entente', with British policy in Europe resting on the twin pillars of cooperation with the Soviet Union and France. This meant cultivating Stalin whilst nurturing de Gaulle, neither task being particularly easy, although Churchill was usually willing to devote more time to the former than to the latter; beyond that was the option of taking the lead in helping to create a European union of some sort. This idea, occasionally floated by some members of the various allied governments-in-exile in London, was really launched by Churchill's old friend and ambassador to de Gaulle, Duff Cooper, who in May 1944 argued that the 'leadership of Europe' awaited Britain, if she cared to take it on.[41] Churchill was unwilling to link himself with what he thought was (and would remain) a weak and exhausted Europe, whilst Eden feared that the Soviets would interpret such a move as being directed against them, so nothing came of it.

By passing quickly over the years 1945-47 it is easy to miss how contingent Churchill's triumph was. President Roosevelt was more interested in a future partnership with Stalin under the aegis of the United Nations than he was in one with the fading glories of British imperialism, and Truman showed no greater interest until he became worried about the direction being taken by the Soviet Union. The Foreign Secretary, Ernest Bevin, was more convinced than the Premier, Clement Attlee, that Britain should (and could) maintain its role as a global power, and he took it for granted that the cost would be worth it. From that angle American support after 1947 came as a Godsend – and certainly allowed the triumphalist version of British foreign policy in the twentieth century to be written. But there was, as there remains, a cost in all of this. Even an old Balliol man like Harold Macmillan should have realised the implications of his statement that 'we are Greeks in the new Roman Empire'; if he did not, subsequent Prime Ministers have done so. But the real cost lay elsewhere. Despite the fact that twice in the century Britain had decided that Europe was important enough to die for, Bevin and Attlee, and following them Churchill and Eden, all decided that it was not important enough for Britain to reconstruct. The myth of 'Finest Hour' led ineluctably to an isolation which, by the 1960s, was far from 'splendid'; but that is to trespass more closely on the heels of contemporary history than is wise.

Certainly, even in the twenty-first century, the legacy of the crosscurrents surveyed briefly here can be traced clearly. The Churchillian, grand heroic, version of events points firmly in the direction of the Atlanticist orientation that continues to dominate British foreign policy; from its perspective the American alliance is the foundation upon which Britain can continue to punch above her weight in international affairs. The heirs to the Disraelian politics of prestige can rest content that the Union flag will continue to fly alongside the Stars and Stripes. But, however dominant, they do not quite hold the field alone. It may be fanciful, but perhaps the lineaments of that Conservative tradition which lost out to Disraeli and then to Churchill, still lingers in those sections of the party attached to the idea of a closer union with Europe.

NOTES

All references to Cabinet (CAB), Prime Minister's Office (PREM) or Foreign Office (FO) documents relate to materials held at the National Archives, London (formerly the Public Record Office) unless otherwise stated.

1. P. Kennedy, *The Realities Behind Diplomacy: Background Influences on British External Policy, 1865–1980* (London: Fontana, 1981), p.384.
2. In order as follows: J. Charmley, *Chamberlain and the Lost Peace* (London: Hodder & Stoughton, 1989); *Churchill: the End of Glory – A Political Biography* (London: Hodder & Stoughton, 1993); *Churchill's Grand Alliance: The Anglo-American Special Relationship 1940–1957* (London: Hodder & Stoughton, 1996); *Splendid Isolation? Britain and the Balance of Power 1874–1914* (London: Sceptre, 1999).
3. W.L. Langer, *European Alliance and Alignments, 1871–1890* (New York: Knopf, 1931); W.L. Langer, *The Diplomacy of Imperialism, 1890–1902* (New York: Knopf, 1935); B.E. Schmitt, *The Coming of the War, 1914* (London: Scribner, 1930); L. Albertini, *The Origins of the War of 1914* (London: Oxford University Press, 1952); V. Berghahn, *Germany and the Approach of War in 1914* (New York: St Martin's Press, 1973); R. Bosworth, *Italy and the approach of the First World War* (Basingstoke: Macmillan, 1983); J. Joll, *The Origins of the First World War* (London: Longman, 1984); J.F.V. Keiger, *France and the Origins of the First World War* (Basingstoke: Macmillan, 1983); P.M. Kennedy, *The Rise of the Anglo-German Antagonism, 1860–1914* (London: Ashfield, 1981); D.C.B. Lieven, *Russia and the Origins of the First World War* (Basingstoke: Macmillan, 1983); Z.S. Steiner, *Britain and the Origins of the First World War* (Basingstoke: Macmillan, 1977); S.R. Williamson, *Austria-Hungary and the Origins of the First World War* (Basingstoke: Macmillan, 1991).
4. A.J.P. Taylor, *The Origins of the Second World War* (London: Hamish Hamilton, 1961); M. Gilbert, *The Roots of Appeasement* (London: Weidenfeld & Nicolson, 1966); S. Aster, *1939: The Making of the Second World War* (London: Deutsch, 1973); D.C. Watt, *How War Came: The Immediate Origins of the Second World War, 1938–1939* (London: Heinemann, 1989).
5. G.P. Gooch and H. Temperley (eds), *British Documents on the Origins of the War 1898–1914* (London: HMSO, 1928), Vol. 3, Appendix A, pp.397–420.
6. Lord Salisbury, *Essays: Foreign Politics* (London: John Murray, 1905), p.151.
7. P.W. Schroeder, 'Munich and the British Tradition', *The Historical Journal,* 19/1 (1976), pp.223–43; P.M. Kennedy, 'The Tradition of Appeasement in British Foreign Policy 1864–1939', *British Journal of International Studies,* 2/3 (1980), pp.195–215.

8. R.A. Butler Papers, Trinity College, Cambridge, RAB/G/9/13, Butler to Ian Black, 21 Apr. 1938.
9. Brabourne Papers, British Library, India Office Records, Mss EUR.F/97/22B, Butler to Lord Brabourne, 12 Oct. 1938. See also the first two essays of the present collection: Zara Steiner, 'The Foreign and Commonwealth Office: Resistance and Adaptation to Changing Times', and T.G. Otte, 'Old Diplomacy: Reflections on the Foreign Office before 1914'.
10. *The Times*, 5 May 1898.
11. *The Times*, 14 May 1898.
12. K. Neilson, *Britain and the Last Tsar: British Policy and Russia, 1894-1917* (Oxford: Clarendon Press, 1995), p.48.
13. R.S. Churchill, *Winston S. Churchill*, Vol. 1 (London: Heinemann, 1966), p.315.
14. Lady G. Cecil, *The Life of Robert, Third Marquess of Salisbury*, Vol. 4 (London: Hodder & Stoughton, 1932), p.85.
15. C.H.D. Howard, *Splendid Isolation: A Study of Ideas Concerning Britain's International Position and Foreign Policy during the Later Years of the Third Marquis of Salisbury* (London: Macmillan, 1967), especially Ch. 8.
16. G. Martel, *Imperial Diplomacy: Rosebery and the Failure of Foreign Policy* (London: Mansell, 1986), Chapter 4.
17. J.A.S. Grenville, *Salisbury and Foreign Policy: The End of the Nineteenth Century* (London: Athlone Press, 1964), pp.24-97.
18. Charmley, *Splendid Isolation?*, chapters 13 and 14 for this argument in detail.
19. Grenville, *Salisbury and Foreign Policy* is an excellent study, but it was published forty years ago and without access to Lansdowne's private papers. It is symptomatic of the state of modern history in our universities that despite a plethora of doctoral dissertations, no one had tackled this topic.
20. Extract from the minutes of the Committee of Imperial Defence, 26 May 1911, in Gooch and Temperley (eds), *British Documents on the Origins of the War*, Vol. 6, pp.782-4.
21. See especially K. Wilson, *The Policy of the Entente: Essays on the Determinants of British Foreign Policy 1904-1914* (Cambridge: Cambridge University Press, 1985), who is good on this.
22. Memorandum by Sir Edward Grey, 20 Feb. 1906, in Gooch and Temperley (eds), *British Documents on the Origins of the War*, Vol. 3, p.267.
23. Viscount Grey of Falloden, *Twenty Five Years, 1892-1916*, Vol. 1 (London: Hodder & Stoughton, 1925), pp.xxiv-xxv.
24. G.M. Trevelyan, *Grey of Falloden* (London: Longman, 1937), p.108.
25. Charmley, *Splendid Isolation?*, pp.301-3 for the detail
26. Lord Morley, *Recollections*, Vol. 2 (London: Macmillan, 1923), p.205.
27. Gooch and Temperley (eds), *British Documents on the Origins of the War*, Vol. 3 Appendix B, pp.420-33.
28. FO 800/91 (Grey Papers), Harcourt to Grey, 14 Jan. 1914.
29. Lansdowne to Herbert, 7 Feb. 1903, in Gooch and Temperley (eds), *British Documents on the Origins of the War*, Vol. 2, pp.68-9.
30. Cecil, *Third Marquis of Salisbury*, Vol. 2, p.171.
31. Three PhD theses being written at the University of East Anglia all help establish this position: G. Hicks, 'Derby, Malmesbury and Conservative Foreign Policy 1852-1959' (2003); B. Grosvenor, 'The Fifteenth Earl of Derby and the Great Eastern Crisis'; and C. Armstrong, 'Disraeli, Salisbury and Conservative Foreign Policy 1878-1880'.
32. K. Feiling, *The Life of Neville Chamberlain* (London: Macmillan, 1946), p.360.
33. Hansard, *House of Lords Debates*, 5th Series, Vol. 47, 14 Dec. 1921.
34. Charmley, *Churchill: the End of Glory*, pp.249-98, for the evidence on which this and the previous paragraph is based.
35. Neville Chamberlain Papers, Birmingham University Library, NC/18/1/1042, Neville Chamberlain to Hilda Chamberlain, 20 Mar. 1938.
36. R.A.C. Parker, *Chamberlain and Appeasement: British Policy and the Coming of the Second World War* (London: Macmillan, 1993), Ch. 15.

37. Charmley, *Churchill: the End of Glory*, chapters 31 and 32 for much of this.
38. PREM 4/100/7, Churchill minute M.461/42 to Eden, 18 Oct. 1942.
39. J. Charmley, 'Churchill and the American Alliance', *Transactions of the Royal Historical Society*, Sixth Series, 11 (2001), especially pp.362–3.
40. PREM 4/100/7, WP(42)516, Eden's 'Four Power Plan', 8 Nov. 1942.
41. J. Charmley, *Duff Cooper* (London: Macmillan, 1986), pp.186–7.

Managing the Americans: Anthony Eden, Harold Macmillan and the Pursuit of 'Power-by-Proxy' in the 1950s

KEVIN RUANE AND JAMES ELLISON

When it comes to post-1941 British foreign policy there is perhaps no more well-worn subject than Anglo-American relations and, more particularly, the 'special relationship', a term which, as here, 'can hardly appear in public unless wrapped in inverted commas and accompanied by a question mark'.[1] Although this study will add in its own way to the already large corpus of work on the Anglo-American alliance, the aim is to provide a fresh perspective by examining how successive Conservative governments in the 1950s set out to manage relations with the United States in ways that would advance the aims of British foreign policy. During this period there were three important reviews of Britain's foreign policy and, by extension, of official thinking on the Anglo-American relationship. The first, in June 1952, was submitted to the Cabinet by Foreign Secretary Anthony Eden as a purely Foreign Office treatment.[2] The second, in June 1956, was an inter-departmental Whitehall review solicited by Eden as Prime Minister.[3] The third, in June 1958, was instigated by the Foreign Office and endorsed by Eden's successor in Number 10, Harold Macmillan.[4] Eden's 1952 paper, entitled 'British Overseas Obligations', is noteworthy for codifying an approach to Anglo-American relations that David Reynolds has called 'power-by-proxy'.[5]

The idea of using American power 'for purposes which we regard as good', as the Foreign Office put it in 1944, had been a feature of British foreign policy during the life of the 1945–51 Labour administrations.[6] The transfer to the United States in 1947 of primary responsibility for funding the anti-communist forces in Greece, and the securing of an American commitment to West European security in 1949, can be read as successes for power-by-proxy as practised by Ernest Bevin at the Foreign Office. Nevertheless, in general, power-by-proxy remained an ill-defined and sporadically pursued objective under Labour. In 1952, however, with the Conservatives back in office and Britain in the grip of a balance of payments crisis, Eden elevated power-by-proxy from an aspiration to a necessity. It became, in short, a strategy, one designed to help Britain sustain its world position at a time of economic enervation. To date, there has been no serious attempt to compare and contrast the 1952 review with its 1956 and 1958 successors in order to establish either pattern or discontinuity in the way that the Conservative governments viewed both Britain's place in the world and the form and function of the Anglo-American partnership. This study aims to correct this omission. To begin with, the focus will be on Eden since power-by-proxy was initially driven forward by his critical view of US foreign policy. Macmillan will provide the focus in the second part of the discussion, along with a comparison of the way in which Eden and Macmillan both sought to manage transatlantic relations.

In the early 1950s Britain found itself in the grip of a serious economic crisis. The principal causal factor was the massive rearmament programme agreed to by the Labour government following the outbreak of the Korean war in June 1950. Initially costed at £3,600 million over three years, in January 1951 the programme was increased to £4,700 million. The subsequent diversion of resources from the productive economy saw a balance of payments surplus of £307 million in 1950 turned into a deficit of £369 million by 1951.[7] In 1952, Treasury calls for major cut-backs in defence expenditure to help ease the situation provided the economic backdrop to the Chiefs of Staff's celebrated 'Review of Defence Policy and Global Strategy'.[8] Approved by the Cabinet's Defence Committee in June, the Service Chiefs' recommendations regarding an independent British nuclear capability were partly based on the cost-effectiveness of nuclear over conventional defence.[9] The Global Strategy paper has since become one of the most discussed documents by historians of post-war British foreign and defence policy and has all but eclipsed Anthony Eden's parallel review of 'British Overseas Obligations'. Yet when the two papers are viewed in tandem – as they were meant to be – they represent a co-ordinated politico-military attempt to square the circle of how to maintain a world role and national security with diminishing resources. Moreover, in terms of the present discussion, Eden's Cabinet memorandum of 18 June 1952 marks the formal enunciation of power-by-proxy.

Eden began his review by stating the economic imperative. 'The essence of a sound foreign policy is to ensure that a country's strength is equal to its obligations', but it was now 'becoming clear that rigorous maintenance of the presently-accepted policies of Her Majesty's Government at home and abroad is placing a burden on the country's economy which it is beyond the resources of the country to meet'. Eden went on to catalogue a wide range of existing and costly obligations arising out of Britain's geographical position (the defence of Western Europe through NATO), those related to Britain's imperial heritage (Egypt and the Middle East, Malaya and Southeast Asia), and those that were a consequence of Britain's international position (membership of and commitments relating to bodies like the United Nations). Ultimately, Eden conceded that there were few ways to effect meaningful reductions in overseas obligations without simultaneously damaging 'the world position of the United Kingdom and sacrificing the vital advantages which flow from it'. Prestige was paramount. The 'effects of a failure of will and relaxation of grip in our overseas commitments are incalculable', he warned, but 'once the prestige of a country has started to slide there is no knowing where it will stop'. The only solution Eden could come up with was to spread the burden of two major obligations for which Britain currently bore primary responsibility. 'Our present policy is in fact directed towards the construction of international defence organisations for the Middle East and South-East Asia in which the United States and other Commonwealth countries would participate', he pointed out. 'Our aim should be to persuade the United States to assume the real burdens in such organisations, while retaining for ourselves as much political control – and hence prestige and world influence – as we can'. Eden ended his presentation with a word or two on methodology. A policy of this kind 'will only be successful with the United States in so far as we are able to demonstrate that we are making the maximum possible effort ourselves, and the more gradually and inconspicuously we can transfer the real burdens from our own to American shoulders, the less damage we shall do to our position and influence in the world'.[10] This, then, was the theory. The real test of Eden's strategy would be in putting it into effect in the two parts of the world he singled out for special attention.

Turning first to Southeast Asia, Eden quickly discovered that the US government, particularly the Pentagon and the Joint Chiefs of Staff, had no desire to surrender its military freedom of manoeuvre in the area through membership of any formal collective defence grouping and much preferred to continue to rely on the loose ANZUS arrangement supplemented with bilateral defence agreements with local states.[11] This remained the American position until March 1954 when the Vietminh assault on the French garrison at Dienbienphu in north-west Vietnam wrought a significant change in Washington's attitude. Fearful that a Vietminh victory would lead to the communisation of the rest of Indochina and Southeast Asia generally, the Eisenhower administration issued a public call for 'united action' to help preserve the French position. The British government initially welcomed the American conversion to multilateralism but on further reflection Churchill and his ministers felt they had no choice but to oppose US plans. The problem was that while London favoured a *defence* organisation, the American scheme seemed predicated on *offensive* military action in Vietnam. As Eden explained to the Cabinet on 7 April, US or US-led intervention would give Communist China, the Vietminh's principal backer, 'every excuse for invoking the Sino-Soviet treaty, and might lead to a world war'.[12] Rejecting all military solutions to the crisis, the British set out to broker a political settlement at the Geneva Conference on Asian Cold War problems, which was due to open on 26 April. Denied British support – the key to wider allied and Congressional endorsement of its war plans – the Eisenhower administration was obliged to await the outcome at Geneva. There, on 21 July, after two months of negotiations in which Eden took the leading role, an agreement was reached that brought the eight-year Franco-Vietminh war to an end: Vietnam was partitioned (the Vietminh to the north, France and its supporters to the south) pending nationwide elections and reunification in 1956. Publicly, the US government distanced itself from the settlement insofar as it surrendered territory to the communist-led Vietminh, but privately it was relieved that the southern half of the trigger-domino of Southeast Asia had been preserved for the time being at least.[13]

In the wake of Geneva, the Eisenhower administration, aggrieved at the earlier British refusal to back 'united action', took steps to line up allies in advance of any future crisis. The result was the Manila Treaty of September 1954, which paved the way for the formation of the Southeast Asia Treaty Organisation (SEATO) in February 1955.[14] On the face of it, SEATO could be said to mark the successful culmination of Eden's efforts to create a collective defence organisation. In truth, though, it was far removed from the Asian NATO he had envisioned in 'British Overseas Obligations'. The United States vetoed the NATO model – 'an elaborate organisation with forces earmarked for the area and complex staff and command structures' – and settled instead on a looser planning body akin to ANZUS.[15] Two years earlier, Eden would have found this SEATO 'zoo of paper tigers' disappointing, but by 1954–55 he seemed able to live with it: when, in June 1954, the British ambassador in Washington, Roger Makins, expressed his fear that the Americans might be losing interest in regional defence, Eden's response was a pithy 'I don't mind!'[16] The full involvement of the United States in area security still had advantages, but to Eden the disadvantages had become telling. The close relationship with important neutral Asian states like India that Britain valued was increasingly jeopardised by America's aggressive and militantly anti-Chinese policy and by the related assumption that Britain, through its association with the US, endorsed that policy.[17] The 1954 Indochina crisis had also shown that there was something to be said for Britain retaining an independent position, one that offered freedom to criticise and if need be distance itself from America. However much Washington may have disapproved of Eden's diplomatic crusade at Geneva, it clearly found favour with the so-called 'Colombo Powers' of India, Indonesia, Burma, Ceylon and Pakistan.[18] Moreover, US adventurism (as the British saw it) had been curbed in 1954 in spite of the absence of a formal defence grouping. In this connection, there is evidence that by the high summer of 1954 the British had privately concluded that the disadvantages of a defence organisation might actually outweigh the advantages, and that the Foreign Office only went along with SEATO because it was the 'price of American acquiescence in the Geneva settlement, thus avoiding unilateral American intervention and the risk of war'.[19] Robert Scott, British Minister in Washington in 1954 and responsible for Asian affairs, later confirmed that SEATO had been a 'sop' to Washington – it was 'part of the price of getting the Americans ... to Geneva'.[20] For Eden, the 'price' was worth paying. As he wrote in the midst of the Geneva Conference: 'It is still even money we may reach an armistice. I am more than ever convinced of dangers of 3rd world war if we don't'.[21]

But what does all this say of power-by-proxy? It suggests that Eden was beginning to have second thoughts. The dark economic clouds of 1952 – the original backdrop to the strategy – were less glowering by 1954–55 and Eden was commensurately less inclined to allow British foreign policy to be constrained by economic imperatives.[22] It should also be remembered that when SEATO was launched in 1955 Eden was still basking in the glory of his *annus mirabilis*. The year 1954 had been the most successful of his career as a diplomatist, the high points being his key role in bringing peace to Indochina and in resolving the vexed question of West German rearmament.[23] In both cases, Eden believed American policy was ill-conceived, and in successfully promoting his own alternatives – a political rather than military solution in Indochina, and an intergovernmental rather than federal way forward on German rearmament – his negotiating triumphs were simultaneously victories for British diplomacy over American diplomacy.[24] In other words, in 1954 Eden appeared to be wielding power without recourse to, and even in defiance of, the American proxy.

In the Middle East, too, Eden's preference for operating independently of the United States was increasingly apparent by 1955. To begin with, though, in line with the recommendations of 'British Overseas Obligations', he had worked for the construction of a Middle East Defence Organisation (MEDO) that would shift the primary financial and material burden of regional defence from British to allied – in particular American – shoulders. MEDO, however, failed to materialise. Egypt, the pied-piper of Arab nationalism, proved implacably opposed to participation in an organisation bearing a British imprimatur and where Cairo led, the bulk of Arab opinion tended to follow.[25] Then, in July 1953, the Eisenhower administration, influenced by Arab opposition, put forward a rival scheme and in the process delivered the *coup de grace* to MEDO. Focusing on the Northern Tier or 'roof' of the Middle East, the US government encouraged defence cooperation between countries like Turkey, Iraq, Syria, Pakistan and Iran which, largely by dint of geography, had an obvious interest in uniting to block Soviet expansionism. In favouring the Northern Tier, Dulles placed MEDO 'on the shelf': as a British colonial construct the scheme was anathema to Arab opinion, and the Secretary of State recommended that the United States distance itself from British policy in the region lest it be tarred by the imperialist brush. In furtherance of this aim, in 1953–54 the US government entered into bilateral military aid agreements with a number of key Middle East states.[26] The concomitant demise of MEDO left the British without a vehicle for effecting power-by-proxy. Although the increased American interest in regional security was welcomed by London, Eden had always anticipated that US power would be projected into the Middle East via a multilateral mechanism. Instead, by early 1954 he was faced with a largely independent American policy which, if allowed to continue unchecked, could erode rather than buttress British influence. For instance, following the start of direct US military assistance to Iraq, the Foreign Office could be found fretting lest 'the Iraqis and others may get the idea that we are leaving it to the Americans to make the running in that part of the world'.[27]

The British were presented with an opportunity to regain some control over defence arrangements when, in February 1955, Turkey and Iraq signed a mutual defence treaty. The Iraqi leader, Nuri Sa'id, invited Britain and America, as well as other Middle East states, to adhere to the treaty and so convert it into a wider defence grouping. Britain accepted Nuri's offer and in April 1955 joined Turkey and Iraq in what became known as the Baghdad Pact.[28] When Pakistan and Iran also joined later in 1955, the Northern Tier seemed close to realisation. There was, however, one notable absentee from the membership list: the United States. In July, the Eisenhower administration ended speculation about its position by ruling out adherence in the immediate future and by suggesting that US military aid to individual pact members should be 'clear and tangible evidence' of its continuing interest in the Northern Tier.[29] Harold Macmillan, the new British Foreign Secretary, begged to differ. The Americans, he complained, having started the Northern Tier, simply 'ran out' on their own scheme.[30] It was also the case that American aloofness rendered the Baghdad Pact an imperfect successor to MEDO as a means of effecting power-by-proxy.

Leaving aside Macmillan's criticism, membership of the Baghdad Pact posed genuine problems for the United States, not least its potential for complicating on-going efforts to resolve the Arab-Israeli dispute. The Eisenhower administration regarded Egypt as the most influential Arab country and, as such, the key to winning general Arab approval for any settlement with Israel. But when Cairo adopted a policy of outright hostility towards the Baghdad Pact – ostensibly because Nuri's insistence on a defence connection with the West threatened to undermine Arab autonomy, but also for reasons related to the Iraqi-Egyptian contest for leadership of the Arab world – US policymakers reasoned that American adherence would be an affront to the Egyptian leader, Colonel Gamal Abdel Nasser, who might withdraw his backing for regional peace proposals. Moreover, US membership of the Baghdad Pact would probably lead to Israeli calls for a reciprocal security guarantee which, if given, would involve America in entangling alliances with both sides in the Arab-Israeli conflict. Yet if the United States joined the Baghdad Pact without giving Israel the security assurances it sought, then the Tel Aviv government was likely to be less accommodating to its Arab neighbours.[31] All in all, from an American standpoint, there was much to recommend non-membership.

Eden, however, displayed little sympathy for US difficulties. The Americans 'cannot expect to command respect in the Middle East unless they pursue a consistent policy based on their convictions', he complained in March 1955. Washington's 'enthusiastic support' of the Northern Tier and of the Turkish-Iraqi pact in particular was 'too recent in men's minds to enable them to execute a *volte-face* with safety or dignity'. The British were no less interested in brokering an Arab-Israeli settlement, and in fact worked closely with the United States in 1955 to this end, but Eden considered the US emphasis on Egyptian good offices to be excessive. It was above all 'most unwise to try to help Nasser at the cost of weakening our support for the Turco-Iraqi Pact'.[32] Eden was unaware that American aloofness was also partly based on a refusal to play the role allotted them in his script for power-by-proxy. In May 1955, Under-Secretary of State Herbert Hoover Jr. warned the National Security Council (NSC) about 'transparent British designs' by which they sought 'to assure themselves of command responsibility' in the Middle East whilst expecting 'the United States to foot the bill required to place the area in some posture of defense', a judgement shared by Secretary Dulles and Admiral Arthur W. Radford, chairman of the Joint Chiefs of Staff.[33] For his part, President Eisenhower was adamant that 'every effort' be made to get the British to 'dig further into their own resources to help in the defense of the area'.[34]

While Eden was bitter about the US decision to stand outside the Baghdad Pact, his disappointment was probably rather easier to bear than he later admitted in his memoirs for the same reason that he felt able to accept the limited liability attendant upon US membership of SEATO.[35] In October 1955 he told the Cabinet that, in the Middle East, 'We should not allow ourselves to be restricted overmuch by reluctance to act without full American concurrence and support. We should frame our policy in the light of our interests in the area and get the Americans to support it to the extent we could induce them to do so'.[36] Still buoyed by the memory of his *annus mirabilis* and with economic indicators pointing – albeit tentatively – in the right direction, Eden had little compunction in arguing against his own strategy. Evidently the lesson he drew from working with the Americans in the Middle East 1952–55 was that there was much to recommend working without them. Interestingly, Dulles shared Eden's sentiment, albeit in reverse: the United States should be prepared to 'cooperate with the British', he told the NSC in November 1955, but 'we could not let the British make our policy for us in this area, or follow the British line blindly'.[37]

What caused Eden to draw back from power-by-proxy in the Middle East just as he had retreated from the strategy in Southeast Asia? One answer is suggested by his well-known mistrust of the United States and his view of America as a rival as well as an ally. In this regard, the Eden of 1955 differed little from the Eden of 1945 when, in a diary entry, he wrote vis-à-vis the Americans that 'we couldn't allow them to dictate our foreign policy and if they were wrong we would have to show independence'.[38] Furthermore, as David Dutton has shown, the 1956 Suez crisis 'exacerbated an anti-American strand in Eden's make-up, but it by no means created it'.[39] From this viewpoint, power-by-proxy was, for Eden, a strategy of despair, one born of economic necessity not free choice in 1952. Reliance on the United States, even Machiavellian manipulation of the United States, went against the grain of his latent anti-Americanism and it comes as no surprise to find him retreating from his own strategy once the economic crisis of the early 1950s had begun to ease. Moreover, Eden's experience of trying to work with the Americans in the 1952–55 period was hardly a positive one. 'They like to give orders, and if they are not at once obeyed they become huffy', he complained in 1954. That was 'their conception of an alliance – of Dulles' anyway'.[40] It was Eden's sense that the disadvantages of alliance with the United States in both the Middle East and Southeast Asia had become as great as the advantages that allowed him to accept with some equanimity the failure to construct formal and fully-functioning defence organisations in both parts of the world. Finally, Eden's diplomatic *annus mirabilis* clearly caused him to question the necessity of power-by-proxy. In 1954, Britain – and Eden – appeared to be wielding power without the need for artificial props. The word 'appeared' requires emphasis because there is much to recommend the argument that Eden's apparent 'mastery of the international scene distorted his view of Britain's, and his own, ability to direct events' and led him to 'indulge in self-deception about the country's inherent strength and its capacity to pursue a course independent of the United States'.[41] Two years on, Suez would add some perspective. In retrospect, Eden might have done better to remain loyal to power-by-proxy, even to the extent of occasionally following the US lead in the greater interest of harmonious Anglo-American relations. But that was not his style. Whether power-by-proxy was the right strategy for Britain in the early and mid-1950s can be debated, but what seems unmistakably clear is that Eden, with his jaundiced view of American foreign policy and his tendency to strike out in an independent direction given half a chance, was the wrong man to front the strategy.

In January 1957, Eden resigned as Prime Minister, brought down by the Suez crisis and ill health. The details of the crisis are sufficiently well known as to require no recapitulation at this point. Suffice to say that it fell to Eden's successor, Harold Macmillan, to repair the damage that Suez had done to Anglo-American relations. The question that Macmillan wrestled with was how far Britain could or should act independently of the United States in world affairs. The Eisenhower administration, in successfully applying financial and political pressures on the Eden government to abandon military action against Egypt in 1956, had delivered a stark warning to future British governments about the risks of over-independence. As for Eden, he may have come to regret his *annus mirabilis* both in terms of the illusion of independence it engendered in his mind and the price he paid in 1956 for the diplomatic victories he won in 1954 at the expense of US preferences. A few days after his resignation, Eden conceded that he had been 'wrong in underestimating the American – or rather the Ike-Dulles – hostility' to his Egyptian policy.[42] Ten years on, in 1966, he privately accepted that Dulles perhaps 'never forgave me' for failing to support 'united action' in Vietnam in 1954 and that this 'sentiment multiplied his unhelpfulness all through the Suez Crisis'.[43] In some ways, then, Eden's 'Suezide' can be directly related to his earlier quest for independence from America.[44] Macmillan, heeding Eden's fate, quickly determined that 'Britain should not pursue her independent ambitions to the point where they brought her into an open confrontation with America'.[45] Even so, this operating premise still allowed plenty of scope for the pursuit of independence below the threshold of confrontation. The first essential was to rebuild Anglo-American relations, but this goal, once achieved, would open up the possibility of relaunching power-by-proxy. Moreover, if Eden's innate mistrust of the United States was a reason for the failure of the strategy under his leadership, Macmillan's marked pro-Americanism seemed to hold out improved prospects for its success. Macmillan stands high in the ranks of those post-war Prime Ministers who have prioritised connections with the United States above all other nations. Even without the imperative of post-Suez reconstruction, Macmillan's instinct would still have been to work closely with the Americans.

As will be seen, Macmillan took part in two important reviews of British foreign policy – descendents of Eden's 1952 paper – in June 1956 and June 1958. These reaffirmed Britain's search for international power via its relationship with the United States. Moreover, because 'Macmillan was determined to be anybody-but-Anthony', he would prove better than Eden at working the Americans.[46] Also, at least in 1957–58, the Americans would be readier than ever before to strengthen their bonds with the British. Notwithstanding the collision over Suez, US leaders acknowledged that Britain remained their foremost ally. The concerns raised by the launch of Sputnik in October 1957 further reinforced this conviction. In theory, therefore, the conditions for Britain to pursue power-by-proxy were in place in the first years of Macmillan's premiership. Yet in practice the strategy proved to have significant limitations and by 1960 Macmillan would begin to think of reconstructing his foreign policy to strengthen its foundations by building a new Anglo-European relationship alongside the transatlantic one. Although neither as extensive nor final as Eden's disillusionment with the Anglo-American partnership in 1956, Macmillan's was personally the more disquieting after its great post-Suez revival. The interdependence achieved in 1957–58 fitted with the continued significance placed on the Anglo-American relationship for Britain's international status in the policy review papers of 1956 and 1958. But thereafter, the limited endurance of this new closeness and wider changes in Britain's international relations, principally with Europe and the Commonwealth, led to re-evaluations. Power-by-proxy was not abandoned, but the means by which it was to be achieved were altered. And it is here that the coalescence of Anglo-American and Anglo-European affairs in 1960–61 is most significant.

There are two important dissimilarities between Eden's June 1952 paper on 'British Overseas Obligations' and the policy review papers of June 1956 and June 1958.[47] First, while the Foreign Office was the sole author in 1952, the latter papers were products of interdepartmental Whitehall collaboration. Although the Foreign Office played a dominant role in their creation (the 1958 paper was inspired by its intervention), other key departments concerned with Britain's overseas affairs were involved. Second, by design, the papers dealt explicitly with Britain's economic predicament and policies to a greater degree than the 1952 paper. Despite these differences the three papers shared points of substance. They had the same objective: to examine Britain's overseas commitments in light of its economic debility with the aim of decreasing burdens. They also reached the same fundamental conclusions – that further large-scale reductions in Britain's overseas commitments were impossible lest they undermine British international prestige, and that Anglo-American relations were paramount in the search for a solution to Britain's chronic economic problems. What a comparison between the three papers shows is that the strategy of power-by-proxy was maintained over the 1950s, reflecting the continuation of British foreign policy tenets established in the late 1940s. That is not to say that tactics remained the same. Indeed, the 1952 paper's clear targets of burden sharing and shifting via defence cooperation in the Middle East and Southeast Asia were supplemented and advanced upon in the 1956 and 1958 papers. Yet in essence, the idea that cooperation with the United States could alleviate Britain's economic position and in the long-term save British resources was sustained.

The June 1956 policy review on 'The Future of the United Kingdom in World Affairs' was initiated by Eden for purposes reminiscent of 1952: to consider Britain's overseas obligations in light of its economic weakness.[48] It was the emphasis on both internal and external commitments which set the report apart from the 1952 paper.[49] Britain's economic predicament since 1945 – its reliance on '£3,000 million of help from abroad', the 'constant anxiety about our balance of payments and the gold reserves which even now are lower than at the end of the war', and the inadequacy of home investment – had to be alleviated. The report thus argued that the government needed to establish where Britain's essential interests lay, achieve a sound economy through home investment and the build-up of reserves, and 'to an extent that we have shed external burdens or commitments, shed them in an orderly way and seek wherever necessary to ensure that other friendly countries assume them'. The basis of what Alan Milward has called Britain's national strategy for post-war renewal was not the focus of criticism.[50] Sterling's value as an international currency was described as 'a matter of life or death to us as a country' as it lay at the heart of the search for a one-world system through economic bargains with the United States which would be uniquely advantageous to Britain's place at the head of the Sterling Area and the Commonwealth. The weakness was not the strategy but the demands placed on it by Britain's overstretch. Hence the report focused on areas where pressure could be relieved and it was here that the Anglo-American relationship was expected to play its part.

There was the proposition that the United States and Canada might be persuaded to lift the heavy burden of North American loans by giving Britain relief on interest payments, but this was a half-hearted hope as previous attempts to achieve a waiver from the United States had not been fruitful. More positive suggestions were made in relation to Britain's political and military objectives, with particular reference to the successful decrease in commitments initiated by Eden's 1952 paper (the Suez Canal base and the British garrisons in Austria and Trieste). In 1956, the proposed reductions would be found mainly in defence, and principally in relation to collaboration with the United States. The costs of Britain's nuclear strategy might be reduced through Anglo-American cooperation but the biggest economies would come from the adoption of a new NATO trip-wire strategy which would enable Britain to reduce its forces stationed in Europe. In both of these areas, prior consultation and agreement with the United States was considered vital. Cut-backs in British expenditure elsewhere in the world were not expected to be as great. In the Middle East, while reluctantly accepting US non-membership of the Baghdad Pact, Britain would encourage states 'to look to the United States for the provision of any equipment and to the United States and ourselves for training facilities'. It could also plan to trim down its conventional force commitment and instead develop non-military means of extending its influence. Limited economic assistance was not ruled out, and, ironically given events that were soon to develop, the report urged that 'We should continue our efforts to improve the harmony of American policy and our own'. In East Asia, non-military cooperation with the Americans was also recommended, as was the shifting of defence burdens to Australia and New Zealand.

The June 1956 paper was discussed and accepted by a Cabinet Committee chaired by Eden which called for further studies to produce policies for implementation.[51] The Prime Minister's approval of the review as it stood demonstrated that while he had become frustrated with the poor return from working with the United States on the politico-military level, especially in Southeast Asia and the Middle East, he remained fully alive to the necessity of Anglo-American cooperation for economic purposes. Yet, within a few months, Eden disregarded this economic imperative when, in his opinion, the preservation of British interests required forceful and independent action over Suez. In the process he pushed Anglo-American relations to the point of rupture and the ensuing crisis proved to be the nadir of his attempt to wield power *without* recourse to the US proxy.

The 1956 policy review was one of the lesser known casualties of Suez. However, a year on, it was revived on the initiative of the Foreign Office. On 9 October, the Permanent Under-Secretary, Sir Frederick Hoyer Millar, urged the Cabinet Secretary, Sir Norman Brook, to engage Whitehall in the renewal of the policy review of 1956 'to resolve a major problem which has been worrying the Foreign Office a good deal lately', namely 'the chronic and ... enduring "international poverty" of the United Kingdom and its effect on our foreign policy generally'.[52] The consequent June 1958 policy review on 'The Position of the United Kingdom in World Affairs' had the same intent as its 1956 antecedent and brought it up to date.[53] The intervening painful experience of the Suez crisis was clear in the report.[54] Written in a tone comprised of resignation and resilience, it began by noting Britain's reduced status (albeit in comparison with 'the heyday of our Imperial power') but also its ability still to 'exercise a substantial influence in world affairs' especially given its position in Europe and the Commonwealth. The post-Suez dependence on the United States was, however, immediately stated: 'We must now bring that influence to bear, in support of the superior material strength of the United States'. Suez had not affected the aims of the national strategy outlined in the 1956 report, except that it had increased Britain's reliance on the United States in their attainment: 'To achieve them maximum Anglo-American co-operation is indispensable'. Officials also added that Britain's Commonwealth association was 'equally vital' but, as their report went on to show, it was the Anglo-American alliance which could offer the greatest degree of economic and political power.

Unlike Eden's 1952 paper and the 1956 policy review, the 1958 report presented very limited expectations of reducing Britain's global responsibilities. Of the 'Principal Existing Political Commitments', only Anglo-American co-operation offered possible savings. Written at the time when the Macmillan government was heartened by the success of the October 1957 Washington conference, the report stated that 'Anglo-American "interdependence" should in the long-term save us resources through the sharing of burdens which we could not carry alone'. There was, however, a price to be paid: 'If ... we are to retain our influence in the Alliance, we shall have to make our contribution towards the execution of agreed policies'. The greatest contrast between the 1958 report and its predecessors was the enervating economic legacy of the disaster of Suez. Britain's chronic balance of payments problems had been intensified by the addition of IMF and Export-Import Bank debts to existing North American loans, the growing costs of long-term overseas investment, prospective withdrawals of sterling holdings and weakness in Britain's gold and dollar reserves. These demands made it all the more difficult, but all the more necessary, to achieve an 'adequate current balance of payments surplus', otherwise Britain would 'fall short of [its] political objectives oversea[s]'. At the same time, the report warned that 'unless we can intensify our effort in the foreign policy field when we are building up our reserves (and making military reductions which must involve us in some loss of prestige), we run the risk of weakening our position in world affairs, with a significant loss of confidence which will make it harder to increase the strength of sterling'.

The report sustained the view of 1956 that the switch from military to civil expenditure in support of Britain's foreign policy would bring savings but its assessment of large-scale economies was that all that could be done was being done. No further reduction of troops in Germany than that already planned was feasible and neither could the nuclear deterrent be abandoned. In a trenchant restatement of Britain's national strategy, the report concluded by rejecting the alternative to it: a down-sized role as a European power. But that still left the central dilemma of how to match resources with obligations. The report's answer was that ministers would have to consider adjustments in civil expenditure; savings 'on the home front' would help to solve the problem of Britain's world position. Here the connection between domestic and foreign policies was exceptionally taut. Any further overstretch overseas could cause it to snap. Despite this predicament, the strategy which was the focus of the 1956 and 1958 policy reviews was not questioned. When Macmillan chaired the ministerial meeting on the 1958 report, there was no debate about the fundamentals.[55] Clearly, the fortitude of Britain's position was questionable, but ministers did not question it. They were firm adherents of Britain's national strategy. Post-war predilections explain this but so does timing. It must be noted that despite the bleakness of the 1958 policy review report, it was submitted during the revival of Britain's relationship with the United States, its efforts to secure new trading relations with Western Europe and its attempt to strengthen sterling. If all went well, these developments could stabilise Britain's overseas position. That was especially true of the Anglo-American relationship through which the Macmillan government hoped to reduce costs and shift burdens. And in 1957–58, the potential of this seemed strong. Power-by-proxy might be achieved as the Eisenhower administration sought to assist its first ally's post-Suez recovery, resurrect nuclear collaboration and present a Declaration of Common Purpose to the world which involved a new strategy for NATO.

Anthony Eden, through his approach to Anglo-American relations, pitching them into their infamous lowest point, bequeathed to Harold Macmillan a fertile soil from which to tend the re-growth of the relationship. Macmillan's personal style, his experience of working with Americans during the Second World War and his actions throughout the Suez crisis, matched productively with the realisation of the Eisenhower administration that the United States needed Britain.[56] Such were the circumstances which ensured the rapid revival of Anglo-American ties at Bermuda in March 1957 and Washington in October.[57] Within a year of the Suez crisis, the relationship had been restored and the United States had agreed to exclusive nuclear collaboration with the United Kingdom – the 'great prize', as Macmillan put it[58] – and to a new trip-wire strategy in NATO which enabled Britain to seek reductions in forces stationed in Germany. In these areas of cost-cutting at least, power was achieved via the proxy and the expectations set out in the 1956 policy review report had been met. On a more general level, less quantifiable returns were also produced, specifically in the overall improvement of relations. Publicly, the Declaration of Common Purpose published on 25 October 1957 after the Washington conference spoke of the unity and intent of the free nations but it was clearly an Anglo-American initiative.[59] Privately, there was the establishment of new machinery for bilateral co-operation in the form of a number of secret working groups to coordinate planning and policy in defined areas.[60] Whilst the British did not achieve American agreement to the term they preferred to describe this new arrangement – 'inter-dependence' – they felt that they had 'now succeeded in regaining the special relationship with the United States which we had formerly enjoyed', as Selwyn Lloyd put it to Cabinet.[61]

As Macmillan and his Cabinet colleagues examined the 1958 policy review report, they could have wished for no greater confirmation of the revived Anglo-American relationship recommended by it than the private comment of John Foster Dulles to a meeting of US ambassadors in July 1958: 'Dulles ... said that relations between the United States and the United Kingdom were now as intimate as it was possible for relations between two Powers to be'.[62] In the pursuit of Britain's national strategy and power-by-proxy, this was a vital pre-requisite. Yet for the strategy to work, power would have to be realised and Britain's economic problems alleviated. In contrast to Eden, Macmillan was committed to doing all he could via the Anglo-American relationship for the good of Britain, but after the first flush of the reconciliation of 1957 had passed, much rested on the development of interdependence through the Working Groups and on wider Anglo-American co-operation in matters of shared interest and activity. In these areas, limitations and disappointments began the process of re-evaluation which would lead Macmillan to reconsider the primacy of the Anglo-American relationship in British economic and foreign policies.

By April 1958, the Foreign Office had reached significant conclusions about the expected dividends from the new era of Anglo-American interdependence embodied in the Working Group machinery. The report to Cabinet highlighted diplomatic problems, especially in relation to potential European concerns 'that we are tiptoeing out of Europe' but it also noted that interdependence could not 'produce great savings in money'.[63] Predating a similar comment in the June 1958 policy review report, the Foreign Office warned that 'While we hope in the long term that the concept of interdependence will bring us certain economies through the sharing of burdens which are too heavy for us to carry alone, it will necessarily involve us in making contributions towards the execution of agreed policies if we are to maintain any substantial influence over the Americans and our other friends in areas where we have important interests'. With this in mind, Anglo-American relations were still thought to be Britain's best option in foreign relations: 'interdependence ... is perhaps the only policy to hold out hopes of the stability and security without which we cannot prosper'. The proxy would not necessarily produce power in the short term, but it might in the long term. It was thus a great disappointment to the British government that interdependence did not supply the expected returns. By 1959, whilst some positive results had been achieved in consultation, the limitations of the Working Group machinery became clear.[64]

This would have not been so disastrous for the strategy of power-by-proxy had evidence of Anglo-American co-operation outside of the Working Groups been overwhelming, but this was not the case. In key regions of the world differences ensued. Macmillan's attempt to enlist US support in reducing Nasser's influence in the Middle East, including attaining American membership of the Baghdad Pact, were not fruitful. Collaboration over Syria after August 1957 did not bring the desired US support for Anglo-American action against Egypt and in favour of Iraq, and despite planning in the Washington Working Groups, the lack of active co-operation over the Lebanon and Jordan in 1958 served to reveal longstanding tensions between London and Washington over the Middle East.[65] In Europe, the Americans cautiously supported British attempts to decrease burdens as outlined in the 1956 and 1958 policy review reports. They agreed to the reduction of British troops in Germany and encouraged a financial solution to the support costs associated with the British Army of the Rhine.[66] But in the more significant area of European policy, European economic integration, the British realized that they were out of step with the United States. Britain's attempt to accommodate the European Economic Community (EEC) via a European Free Trade Area and thus reduce its discriminatory impact on British trade received no wholehearted support from the US.[67] The threat to Britain's trade from the EEC was always a significant concern to the British government. As the 1958 policy review report stated, 'A high level of exports will be vital' to an adequate balance-of-payments surplus and the stability of sterling. It was the growing status of the EEC, and the response of the United States to it, which above all jeopardised power-by-proxy.

Britain's national strategy, based on the primacy of Anglo-American relations and the creation of a one-world system which would enable it to sustain sterling's international stature and the economic benefits of the Commonwealth, whilst adjusting to changes in the organisation of European trade, was a bespoke policy for British interests. However, as Alan Milward has written, 'by the close of 1958 the national strategy on which Britain had agreed by 1950 was in serious trouble'.[68] The long-term stability of the British economy was endangered by a European economic association which discriminated against British exports, threatened to outstrip Britain economically and politically, and, significantly, had the full support of the United States. In October 1959, the Foreign Office put it bluntly in its warning that the European Community 'could completely out-class the U.K. in terms of military and economic importance'.[69] This realisation, together with continued American pressure on the Macmillan government to move beyond further discriminatory trade arrangements like the European Free Trade Association (EFTA) began the process of policy development which brought the first application for membership of the EEC in July 1961. The application has been described as an attempt by the Macmillan government to meet American pressure and thus strengthen Anglo-American relations against the power of the EEC: 'At least for Macmillan, the EEC application was in the first instance an instrument of British transatlantic policy'.[70] There is a contrary view which suggests that Macmillan's motive to seek EEC membership was not to fortify the Anglo-American relationship but 'to build an alternative power-base for Britain as leader of Europe. This would provide a hedge against the unreliability of British influence over the United States'.[71] It is this interpretation which is most convincing when the fate of power-by-proxy is considered.

By 1960, Anglo-American relations had seemingly lost much of the closeness that Macmillan had worked so hard to achieve over the previous three years. The turning point was the Paris summit of May 1960 and Eisenhower's refusal, in the wake of the U-2 fiasco, to save the talks and with them the prospects for détente in Europe. Later, Macmillan attested that this 'was the most tragic moment of my life'.[72] Thereafter he questioned the strategy of pre-eminent reliance on the Anglo-American relationship as the keystone of British foreign policy.[73] Power had not been achieved via the proxy and Britain's economy remained unstable: balance-of-payments problems persisted; convertibility with the dollar in December 1958 had not seen a resurgence of sterling, and Britain's trade relations were undergoing transformation as the EEC established itself and Commonwealth trade patterns altered. When over Christmas and the New Year of 1960–61 Harold Macmillan wrote his own kind of policy review to match those of 1956 and 1958, his 'Grand Design', this predicament was clear. 'Britain – with all her experience – has neither the economic nor military power to take the leading role. We are harassed with countless problems – the narrow knife-edge on which our economy is balanced; the difficult task of changing Empire into Commonwealth . . .; the uncertainty about our relations to the new economic, and perhaps political, State which is being created by the Six countries of continental Western Europe; and the uncertainty of American policies towards us – treated now as just another country, now as an ally in a special and unique category'.[74] In these circumstances, power-by-proxy based alone on Anglo-American relations could not bring Britain the necessary economic stability to achieve its desired world position. With the first EEC application, power-by-proxy was transformed. A new proxy, Europe, would henceforward act as insurance against the vicissitudes and limitations of the Anglo-American relationship.

As previously seen, just a few days after his resignation, Eden admitted to Norman Brook that 'I was wrong ... in underestimating the American – or rather the Ike-Dulles – hostility' to his policy in Egypt. Eden's underestimation derived in part from his several triumphs over Dulles and US diplomacy in 1954 and from the related assumption that British policy preferences in areas like the Middle East would, in the final analysis, be respected in Washington. But he also blamed the perfidy of his *bête noire*, Dulles. 'I suppose that they always wanted us out of the Middle East, or at least Dulles did. I was warned of this years ago when the Republicans came in, but I did not believe it'.[75] In May 1958, he admitted to a further misjudgement over Suez. 'I think it rather hard to say we bungled', he wrote to his friend, Arthur Mann, 'except, I suppose, in failing to estimate that the Americans would take the lead against us. Perhaps also we did not allow enough for our financial weakness and for the consequent ability of the United States to compel us and the French to throw our negotiating cards away after the cease-fire'.[76] The irony, of course, was that the 1952 and 1956 policy reviews, both of which involved Eden, were brutally frank in their assessment of Britain's economic weakness and of the need to render the nation's foreign policy affordable. However, as seen, it was the erroneous politico-diplomatic lessons drawn by Eden from his *annus mirabilis* that led him to discount the possibility of the United States 'taking the lead' against Britain over Suez and temporarily to ignore the economic realities of national life in 1956.

Following his resignation, Eden kept a close eye on the progress of the Macmillan government and the state of Anglo-American relations. He was none too pleased by what he saw. In December 1957, he complained that Britain 'seems content to tag along as [the] 49[th] state' of the United States, 'tho[ugh] this American gov[ernmen]t cannot run the other 48'.[77] A year later, he remained unhappy that 'we let Americans do just as they like ... Of this I am sure. American policy will ruin us. Nobody cares'.[78] Eden was wrong. Macmillan cared. It was just that it took the pro-American Macmillan longer than Eden to face up to the difficulties inherent in working with the United States. When he did it was a matter of some regret given that the necessity of Anglo-American co-operation after the Suez crisis had corresponded with his natural inclination towards the primacy of relations with the United States. As Macmillan's 1960–61 'Grand Design' made clear, he was 'an unrepentant believer in "interdependence"'.[79] It was this which separated him from Eden, but, in time, Macmillan came to share Eden's scepticism of reliance on the Americans. Ultimately, both leaders concluded, for different reasons, that the American proxy was not the solution to Britain's long-term economic and foreign policy problems and that the Anglo-American relationship could not alone be relied upon to uphold Britain's world position.

NOTES

All references to Cabinet (CAB), Prime Minister's Office (PREM) or Foreign Office (FO) documents relate to materials held at the National Archives, London (formerly the Public Record Office) unless otherwise stated.

1. N. Ashton, *Kennedy, Macmillan and the Cold War: the Irony of Interdependence* (Basingstoke: Palgrave Macmillan, 2002), p.6.
2. CAB 129/53, C(52)202, 18 Jun. 1952.
3. CAB 134/1315, PR(56)3, 1 Jun. 1956.
4. CAB 130/139, GEN.624/10, 9 Jun. 1958.
5. D. Reynolds, *Britannia Overruled: British Policy and World Power in the 20th Century* (Harlow: Longman, 1991), pp.177−8.
6. Ibid.
7. P. Hennessy, *Never Again: Britain, 1945−1951* (London: Vintage, 1993), p.415.
8. The cost of retaining Britain's worldwide interests in 1951−52 was put at £140.6 million in foreign currencies spent on forces overseas and £100.9 million in foreign currencies for purchases either for British defence production or for the British armed forces. The total − £241.5 million − accounted for almost two-thirds of the 1951−52 balance of payments deficit. C. Barnett, *The Verdict of Peace: Britain Between Her Yesterday and the Future* (London: Pan, 2002), p.83.
9. J. Baylis and A. Macmillan, 'The British Global Strategy Paper of 1952', *Journal of Strategic Studies*, 16/2 (1993), p.204.
10. CAB 129/53, C(52)202, 18 Jun. 1952. Among the few historians who give consideration to Eden's paper are A. Adamthwaite, 'The Foreign Office and Policy-making', in J. W. Young, (ed.), *The Foreign Policy of Churchill's Peacetime Administration, 1951−1955* (Leicester: Leicester University Press, 1988), pp.8−11, and Barnett, *Verdict of Peace*, pp.79−92. Both argue that Eden's approach was not radical enough and that he should have jettisoned certain major commitments.
11. See K. Ruane, 'Containing America: Aspects of British Foreign Policy and the Cold War in South-East Asia, 1951−54', *Diplomacy and Statecraft*, 7/1 (1996), pp.143−62; G. C. Herring, 'Franco-American Conflict in Indochina, 1950−1954', in L. S. Kaplan, D. Artaud and M. R. Rubin, (eds), *Dien Bien Phu and the Crisis of Franco-American Relations, 1954−1955* (Wilmington: Scholarly Resources, 1990), pp.33−4.
12. CAB 127/27, CC(54) 26th meeting, 7 Apr. 1954.
13. See Ruane, 'Containing America', p.143.
14. SEATO comprised Britain, the United States, France, Australia, New Zealand, the Philippines, Pakistan and Thailand.
15. FO 371/111874/283G, Washington tel. 1645, 29 Jul. 1954.
16. FO 800/842/82, Makins letter to Eden, 21 Jun. 1954. The 'zoo' description comes from J. Cable, *The Geneva Conference of 1954 on Indochina* (Basingstoke: Macmillan, 1986), p.139.
17. FO 371/111852/5, MacDonald letter and enclosure, 7 Aug. 1954.
18. See PREM 11/646, messages to Eden from Nehru and Mohammed Ali, 21 Jul. 1954.
19. FO 371/111883/504, Cable minute, 20 Aug. 1954.
20. Sir Robert Scott Papers, National Library of Scotland, Edinburgh, ACC.8181/18, Box 2, transcript of Scott-Seldon interview, 1980, p.20.
21. Lord Avon Papers, University of Birmingham, AP20/45/49, 22 May 1954.
22. K. O. Morgan, *The People's Peace: British History, 1945−1989* (Oxford: Oxford University Press, 1990), p.119; Barnett, *Verdict of Peace*, p.105.
23. See R. Rhodes James, *Anthony Eden* (London: Weidenfeld & Nicolson, 1986), pp.389−90.
24. On German rearmament see K. Ruane, *The Rise and Fall of the European Defence Community: Anglo-American Relations and the Crisis of European Defence, 1950−55* (London: Macmillan, 2000).

25. See in general D. R. Devereux, 'Britain and the Failure of Collective Defence in the Middle East, 1948–53', in A. Deighton, (ed.), *Britain and the First Cold War* (Basingstoke: Macmillan, 1990), pp.237–51.

26. *Foreign Relations of the United States 1952–54* [hereafter *FRUS*], Vol. IX (Washington: Government Printing Office, 1986), pp 395–6, 406–7; W. Scott Lucas, *Divided We Stand: Britain, the US and the Suez crisis* (London: Hodder & Stoughton, 1991), pp.26–7, 30.

27. CAB 129/68, C(54)81, 31 May 1954.

28. See CAB 129/74, C(55)70, 14 Mar. 1955.

29. *FRUS 1955–1957*, Vol. XII (Washington: Government Printing Office, 1993), p.141.

30. P. Catterall (ed.), *The Macmillan Diaries, 1950–1957* (Basingstoke: Macmillan, 2003) p.449, entry for 14 Jul. 1955. Macmillan was appointed Foreign Secretary when Eden succeeded Churchill as Prime Minister in April 1955.

31. *FRUS 1955–1957*, Vol. XII, pp.38–9, 43, 47–8, 82, 89. In general see N. Ashton, 'The Hijacking of a Pact; the Formation of the Baghdad Pact and Anglo-American Tensions in the Middle East, 1955–58', *Review of International Studies*, 19/2 (1993), pp.123–37.

32. FO 371/121282/48, Eden tel. 1349 to Washington, 31 Mar. 1955.

33. *FRUS 1955–1957*, Vol. XII, pp.54, 84–5, 165; also *FRUS 1955–1957*, Vol. XV (Washington: Government Printing Office, 1989), pp.506–7.

34. *FRUS 1955–1957*, Vol. XII, p.132.

35. See A. Eden, *Full Circle* (London: Cassell, 1960), pp.335–6.

36. CAB 128/29, CM(55) 34th meeting, 4 Oct. 1955.

37. *FRUS 1955–1957*, Vol. XII, p.202.

38. Cited in D. Dutton, *Anthony Eden: A Life and Reputation* (London: Arnold, 1997), p.174.

39. Dutton, *Eden*, p.143.

40. Avon Papers, AP20/17/118A, 16 May 1954.

41. S. Greenwood, *Britain and the Cold War 1945–91* (Basingstoke: Macmillan, 2000), p.135; also Dutton, *Eden*, p.358; Cable, *Geneva Conference*, p.143.

42. Lord Normanbrook Papers, Bodleian Library, Oxford, MS.Eng.lett.c273, fol.66, Eden letter to Brook, 16 Jan. 1957.

43. Avon Papers, AP23/14/34A, Eden letter to Harold Caccia, 9 Sep. 1966.

44. The term 'Suezide' is taken from David Reynolds in 'Eden the Diplomatist: Suezide of a Statesman?', *History,* 74 (1989), pp.64–84.

45. N. Ashton, '"A Rear Guard Action": Harold Macmillan and the Making of British Foreign Policy, 1957–63' in T.G. Otte, (ed.), *The Makers of British Foreign Policy: From Pitt to Thatcher* (Basingstoke: Palgrave, 2002), p.242 and pp.238–260.

46. P. Hennessy, *The Prime Minister: The Office and its Holders since 1945* (London: Penguin, 2001), p.258.

47. CAB 134/1315, PR(56)3, 1 Jun. 1956 and CAB 130/139, GEN.624/10, 9 Jun. 1958.

48. CAB 134/1315, PR(56)1, 4 Jun. 1956.

49. CAB 134/1315, PR(56)3, 1 Jun. 1956.

50. A. S. Milward, *The UK and the European Community, Volume I: The Rise and Fall of a National Strategy 1945–1963* (London: Frank Cass, 2002). Chapter 1 establishes his argument.

51. CAB 134/1315, PR(56)1st meeting, 6 Jun. 1956.

52. CAB 21/4717, Hoyer Millar to Brook, 9 Oct. 1957; Brook to Macmillan, 25 Nov. 1957.

53. CAB 130/139, GEN.624/1st meeting, 6 Dec. 1957.

54. CAB 130/139, GEN.624/10, 9 Jun. 1958.

55. CAB 130/153, GEN.659/1st meeting, 7 Jul. 1958.

56. PREM 11/2189, Caccia to Selwyn Lloyd, 1 Jan. 1957, and *FRUS 1955–1957*, Vol. XXVII (Washington: Government Printing Office, 1992), pp.693–4.

57. M. Dockrill, 'Restoring the "Special Relationship": The Bermuda and Washington Conferences, 1957', in D. Richardson and G. Stone (eds), *Decisions and Diplomacy: Essays in Twentieth-Century International History* (London: Routledge, 1995), pp.205–23.

58. Macmillan Papers, Bodleian Library, Oxford, MS Macmillan dep.d.30*, diary, 24 Oct. 1957.

59. H. Macmillan, *Riding the Storm 1956–1959* (London: Macmillan, 1971), pp.756–9.

60. FO 371/132330/3G, SC(58)8, 27 Jan. 1958. Also M. Jones, 'Anglo-American Relations after Suez: the Rise and Decline of the Working Group Experiment and the French Challenge to NATO, 1957–59', *Diplomacy and Statecraft*, 14/1 (2003), pp.49–79.
61. CAB 128/31, CC(57) 76th meeting, 28 October 1957; CAB 129/90, C(57)271, 15 Nov. 1957.
62. FO 371/132330/27, Steel to Hoyer Millar, 4 Jul. 1958.
63. CAB 129/92, C(58)77, 10 Apr. 1958.
64. CAB 130/137, GEN.617/4, 10 March 1959; CAB 130/137, GEN.617/4th meeting, 12 Mar. 1959. Also in general, Jones, 'Anglo-American Relations after Suez'.
65. See N. Ashton, *Eisenhower, Macmillan and the Problem of Nasser: Anglo-American Relations and Arab Nationalism, 1955–59* (Basingstoke: Macmillan, 1996).
66. S. Dockrill, 'Retreat from the Continent? Britain's Motives for Troop Reductions in West Germany, 1955–1958', *Journal of Strategic Studies*, 20/3 (1997), pp.45–70.
67. J. Ellison, *Threatening Europe: Britain and the Creation of the European Community, 1955–1958* (Basingstoke: Macmillan, 2000), pp.39–40, 220.
68. Milward, *National Strategy*, p.309.
69. PREM 11/2985, SC(59)40, 27 Oct. 1959.
70. W. Kaiser, *Using Europe, Abusing the Europeans: Britain and European Integration, 1945–63* (Basingstoke: Macmillan, 1996), chapter 5, especially pp.130–5.
71. Ashton, *Kennedy, Macmillan and the Cold War*, p.132.
72. A. Horne, *Macmillan, 1957–1986* (London: Macmillan, 1989), p.231.
73. See for example Ashton, '"Rearguard Action"', pp.249–50.
74. PREM 11/3325, Macmillan memorandum, 29 Dec. 1960–3 Jan. 1961. It is probable that this was intended to read: 'treated now as just another country, *not* as an ally in a special and unique category'.
75. Normanbrook Papers, MS.Eng.lett.c.273, fol.66, Eden letter to Brook, 16 Jan. 1957.
76. Arthur Mann Papers, Bodleian Library, Oxford, MS.Eng.c.3278, fols 113–15, Eden letter to Mann, 5 May 1958.
77. Mann Papers, MS.Eng.c.3278, fol. 108, Eden letter to Mann, 31 Dec. 1957.
78. Mann Papers, MS.Eng.c.3278, fol. 123, Eden letter to Mann, 15 Dec. 1958.
79. Horne, *Macmillan 1957–1986*, p.284.

From Carbon Paper to E-mail: Changes in Methods in the Foreign Office, 1950–2000

SIR ALAN CAMPBELL

The interplay of character and personality has always played a part in international affairs, but until very recent years personal contact between ministers of different countries has been comparatively rare. It is only since the 1960s and 1970s that meetings or telephone conversations between Prime Ministers and Foreign Ministers, especially of course European Union ministers, have been so frequent as to be a major factor in the conduct of foreign policy, supplementing or even sometimes supplanting the normal processes of diplomacy. Usually this extra personal factor is beneficial though it cannot be relied upon in all circumstances and can sometimes have a negative effect. What is certain is that it is now an established feature of international intercourse. It is no longer possible, as it was to some extent even fifty years ago, for a British Prime Minister or Foreign Secretary to avoid being personally involved in face-to-face meetings with foreign opposite numbers. Whether they like it or not they are condemned to meet each other or speak to each other frequently. This is a theme that will be returned to later.

Of course, during these last fifty years, many other things have changed. Britain's position in the world has changed, and the changes in British society especially in the status of women have amounted virtually to a revolution. Naturally the Foreign Office has reflected all this. But this contribution will be predominantly limited to discussing changes of method. These new methods, including the development of personal diplomacy, all emanate from and are made possible by the extraordinary progress during this period of all forms of communication.

What are the methods by which the Foreign Office seeks to provide the Foreign Secretary with the information and advice which enable him to determine the course of British foreign policy and to carry out that policy at home and abroad?

First, it is useful to say something about the building in which the business of the Foreign Office is carried out. In appearance the outside of the Foreign Office building is much as it was when I first went to work in it in 1950, except that it was then blackened by a century of London soot. At that time the Foreign Office occupied only the West side of the building, that is the side including the old India Office facing onto St James's Park. At the other side of the quadrangle there was the old Home Office and Commonwealth Relations Office. The rest of the Foreign Office departments had to be housed elsewhere in Whitehall or indeed further afield. The main building was in a sorry state of repair, the interior very shabby if not actually dirty, cold in winter and hot in summer, meanly lighted, some heat unevenly provided by sparse radiators and coal fires. Most of the rooms had been chopped about in various ways over the years and some of the most ornamental ones such as the Locarno Suite and the Durbar Court had been converted for utilitarian purposes. Clearly the building was no longer adequate for the transaction of Foreign Office business and it was intended to replace it as soon as funds were available. After many changes of plan over the years the decision was taken by Sir Geoffrey Howe, when he was Foreign Secretary in the 1980s, to rehabilitate and modernise all the buildings surrounding the Foreign Office quadrangle including the old Home Office and to preserve or restore the most notable architectural features. It was a bold decision which was brilliantly carried out, albeit at great expense and disruption of business while the work was in progress for some six years. But the upshot was an outstanding success. The Foreign Office is now housed in this one building except for the administrative departments which are in the Old Admiralty Building on the other side of the Horse Guards Parade. The buildings are efficient and suitable for their purpose as well as handsome in appearance. They are also within a few minutes walk of the Foreign Secretary's official residence at 1 Carlton Gardens, first occupied by Ernest Bevin in 1945 and used by most of his successors to the great advantage of public business.

The human structure of the Foreign Office remains very much as it was when I knew it. It is a pyramid under the roof of the Foreign Secretary and his Ministers. At the apex of the pyramid is the Permanent Under-Secretary (PUS), the most senior official, and at the bottom are some seventy or so departments of about a dozen people dealing with the different geographical areas or functions. In between, and under the PUS, are four or five Deputy

Under-Secretaries who constitute a sort of inner directorate; and then below them there are between 10 and 15 Assistant Under-Secretaries (or Directors as they are now called) who supervise groups of departments. Fifty years ago the grouping of these departments was sometimes arbitrary so that the burden on the Under-Secretaries was uneven. Now the organisation is more coherent and the work is more efficiently distributed. Of course the structure has to be adjusted from time to time in order to cope with changes in the international scene.

Regarding methods of communication, it is not necessary to go into detail about all of the bits of apparatus which are now in use in all places of governmental or non-governmental business – the fax, the e-mail, the improved telephone systems, the photocopying machines, the word processors and computers, the modern encrypting and decrypting processes, the increased speed and reliability of air travel. All of this eliminates or simplifies many of the tasks which used to be so very time-consuming and boring – the enciphering and deciphering of telegrams, typing and retyping of drafts, the numerous messengers carrying sealed bags or locked boxes with their trolleys thundering down the passages. Then there were metal tubular cylinders which enclosed papers to be sent all over the building by a compressed air system. They sometimes got stuck. But fifty years ago, an expert typist, operating the good old Imperial typewriter, could produce five but not more than five legible copies of a typescript using carbon paper. And then there were the roneo machines. The earlier models had to be carefully anointed with ink and then copies would be extruded by turning a handle. Many of these manual tasks are a thing of the past. Screens and keyboards have already replaced a great deal of paper. Messengers and even typists are so few as to be almost extinct. Of course the result is that everything can go much quicker than in my day. The speed of consultation within Whitehall and between the Foreign Office and embassies abroad has enormously increased.

One practical consequence of all these changes is that everything can start a good deal earlier in the day than when I worked in the Office. We did not then get to our desks before 9 or 9.30, whereas nowadays most people arrive at work at least an hour earlier. Then our lunch hour would have been at least half an hour longer than is usual nowadays. However, nowadays most people manage to get away by 6.30 or so, whereas in my day that would have been on the early side – 7.30 would have been more usual. In the 1950s, it was also not unusual to work on Saturday morning.

Another consequence of this new technology is that everybody has to find some kind of new technique or habit on first arriving in the morning. In my day there would be safes and presses to be unlocked, a mass of incoming telegrams to be scanned and sifted, several tubes or boxes containing files to be opened. Now there will be similar information to be looked at but more of it and in an entirely different form – messages of varying importance, both oral and written, incoming messages on the computer screen. Rather less physical activity perhaps but much the same slightly agitated twenty minutes or so while you sort out, so far as possible, the day's priorities.

And nowadays there are no files, or hardly any. But systems for consulting previous papers through the computer work very well, though from time to time there are hiccups. Of course, the registry system was far from perfect and indeed there were great frustrations caused by searches for missing files and so on. So maybe the present system is an improvement. But I rather wonder what the historians will make of it.

The use of the telephone has greatly increased in the last thirty years, not only at the highest level but also between officials of European Union countries who nowadays frequently telephone their opposite numbers on European Union business. As regards ministerial contact by telephone I venture to make a cautionary comment. There is no doubt about its value in the right circumstances, that is, between ministers who know each other fairly well, who are both well briefed in advance. But ministers would be wise not to overdo this method of transacting business. It can sometimes lead to misunderstanding. It can also lead to envy if too often successfully pursued. And it must be borne in mind that while many politicians get on well – or at least think they do – with their foreign opposite numbers, some of them dislike each other intensely. In such cases it may be better to avoid personal contact so far as possible.

A surviving habit of Foreign Office life which has not – or at least not yet – been eliminated is the complex pattern of office meetings of one kind or another, which are an important feature of Whitehall activity. The meeting habit developed most vigorously in the Second World War and is likely to continue for some years to come. It extends of course to other government departments and is then coordinated for the most part by the Cabinet Office. Within the Foreign Office, the system is partly organised on a regular periodical schedule and partly in response to some new turn of events. The character and frequency of *ad hoc* meetings depend to a large extent on the preferred habit of work of ministers and senior officials.

This is perhaps a convenient point to discuss the media and its impact on Foreign Office methods. Already in 1950 the Foreign Office News Department was of considerable importance and was so regarded by the Secretary of State and senior officials. In consequence the Head of the Department enjoyed immediate access to Foreign Office Ministers and to the PUS. But at that time it was the press and radio rather than the television that were of primary concern. By the end of the twentieth century, television was the most important opinion former, and the way the various commentators handled foreign affairs was naturally of great concern not only to the Foreign Office but to the Prime Minister's office. It follows of course that not only the Foreign Secretary but also the Prime Minister have now to be more fully and continuously informed and consulted about foreign affairs than in the past. Incidentally, a tiresome consequence of the great impact of television is that undue prominence is quite often given to a situation abroad which, although newsworthy, is no more than a distorted snapshot on which a minister is expected to comment, often without notice. I suspect that Bevin would have been astonished, not to say outraged, to hear that his successors should from time to time agree to be interrogated in a radio van before breakfast by a BBC reporter about something he had heard of only five minutes earlier.

A point of importance sometimes raised by historians is the level at which any given question is considered. On this point in my day officials would be encouraged to take decisions in the name of the Secretary of State if they felt competent to do so. Thus a simple enquiry which arrived in any department would be answered by a quite junior official without any need to submit the question to his superiors, the test being whether the question fell within existing policy as decided by ministers. New or more complicated or more important questions would be decided further up the hierarchy and only the most important would be referred to the PUS and the Secretary of State. This is still the system, although there has been a tendency in recent years to involve ministers at an earlier stage of discussion of any given question – not necessarily the Secretary of State himself but perhaps the Minister of State to whom the Foreign Secretary may have delegated some area of his responsibility. This leads to considerable pressure on the Private Secretaries. Their judgement of what their Minister ought or ought not to get involved in is often crucial. Although this has always been so, especially in the case of the Private Secretary at the Foreign Office and the Assistant Private Secretary at 10 Downing Street, the responsibility of these quite young officials has become even greater during the last twenty or thirty years. It is not surprising that those who survive this gruelling task have in most cases risen to the top of the service.

The Private Secretary is also involved in another important matter, that is, the timely commissioning of a brief for the Minister. (A 'brief', in Foreign Office parlance, is anything between a small book and a half sheet of paper, intended to suggest how a minister might handle a forthcoming interview or meeting.) Production of briefs also looms quite large in the work of many of the departments. By the time I became a member of the Service it was fully understood that for any conference or even bilateral meeting between Foreign Office Ministers and their foreign opposite numbers a full brief would be required, often backed up by a meeting (or meetings) beforehand when the Minister would have an opportunity to absorb the subject and question the experts about the background. Essentially this system continues to operate and the current brief is very similar to what it was fifty years ago. The actual process of production is however a good deal less laborious. We could not then consult so rapidly with our embassies abroad and we had constantly to arrange for the typing and retyping of draft opening statements or speeches with the consequent risk of errors and omissions. On the other hand, although the process of producing briefs may be less laborious, the number of briefs required may be greater than ever and more and more urgently demanded because of pressure from Parliament and the media.

Pressure on ministers comes not only from Parliament and media but from the increased speed and frequency of air flights. This can be plainly seen when we look at the diaries of Prime Ministers and Foreign Secretaries at the end of the twentieth century. Two of Margaret Thatcher's Foreign Secretaries, Sir Geoffrey Howe and Sir Douglas Hurd, both paid frequent brief visits abroad, sometimes even for less than a day if it were to a European or American destination. This extremely busy schedule of travel for Foreign Ministers has gathered pace rapidly over the last thirty years. By contrast, Bevin spent six weeks in Moscow in 1947; Selwyn Lloyd spent five weeks in Geneva in 1959. Until the 1960s, it used to be arranged that another minister, sometimes the Prime Minister, would take charge of the Foreign Office in the absence of the Foreign Secretary. However, for some years now the Foreign Secretary has remained in charge even when abroad, largely because it is possible to consult them rapidly even if they are away from their base. Clearly, the present arrangements require a good deal of self-discipline on the part of those wishing to communicate with the Foreign Secretary; otherwise the poor soul would be bothered with a lot of unnecessary consultation. The present schedule also requires a great deal of stamina on the part of the Minister.

I have been talking about methods, but one cannot entirely separate methods from the people using them, starting with the Foreign Secretary. Anthony Eden (1935–38; 1940–45), Ernest Bevin (1945–51), Alec Douglas-Home (1960–63), David Owen (1977–79), Douglas Hurd (1989–95) – how different they were from one another! And yet, if the system is to work properly, the officials of the Foreign Office must adjust themselves and their methods to suit the habit of mind of the Secretary of State. Ideally there is a sort of triangular relationship between the Foreign Secretary, their Principal Private Secretary, and the PUS and their deputies. If this is harmonious it can be a powerful factor in the adoption of a particular policy. A happy relationship between the Prime Minister and the Foreign Secretary is also of course highly desirable.

This last point – relations between the Prime Minister and the Foreign Secretary – has been over the years a question of some delicacy. At the end of the First World War, which at one time caused some friction with the Foreign Office. An even more dangerous development took place in the period just before the Second World War when Nevile Chamberlain as Prime Minister, advised by Sir Horace Wilson, took various initiatives with the Italian government which he kept secret from his own Foreign Secretary and from the Foreign Office. In the latter half of the twentieth century, there has been no repetition of any attempt by a Prime Minister to establish, as it were, their own alternative Foreign Office. What has happened is something rather different, which arises mainly because of our membership of the European Union. This not only involves the Prime Minister in very frequent meetings with his European opposite numbers but also imposes the need to coordinate British policy covering several government departments. Thus there has grown up an important new piece of bureaucratic machinery in the Cabinet Office (which is of course formally responsible to the Prime Minister). It is sometimes suggested that the Prime Minister thus trespasses on Foreign Office territory, but I do not myself think that this is so. For one thing most of the alleged trespassers are themselves Foreign Office officials temporarily seconded to the Cabinet Office, and for another thing the input into these coordinating committees is in the nature of things provided mainly by the Foreign Office itself. Essentially of course the proper working of all this depends on the good relations between the Prime Minister and the Foreign Secretary and between their respective officials.

It is also true to say that administration has assumed much greater importance over the years. The departments under the Chief Clerk, that is, the chief administrator of the Foreign Office, have grown in size and number over the century for obvious and justifiable reasons in response to the increased demands and the need to satisfy calls for economy. At the top the burdens imposed on the PUS and on the Chief Clerk are formidable. There is perhaps a tendency to over-administration amounting sometimes to petty bureaucracy at the expense of what might be called the operations departments which themselves have tended to be reduced in recent years. I realise that some aspects of administration were rather too haphazard in my day but I have the impression that the Foreign Office may not have been immune to some of the recent fashionable doctrines and bureaucratic practices. There are some nasty pieces of management jargon which seem to have found their way into the system. Performance indicators? What would Bevin have said about those? And would he have acquiesced in the frequent renaming of departments and functions? I think he might have given one of his negative growls.

In conclusion, as I have said or implied, many of the changes in the operation and role of the Foreign Office have been for the better. The Foreign Office is better housed and more logically structured than in my day. The adoption of modern means of communication (still evolving of course) has been handled with skill, and the standard of work is still of a very high order at all levels of the service. There is much greater informality of personal contacts both within the Office and with other Whitehall departments – and indeed with non-governmental bodies. All that is to the good. Yet there are of course risks and disadvantages arising from some of these modern developments and it is perhaps worth mentioning them even if they are perfectly well known to those responsible for managing the service.

First, speed of communication entails risks. Mistakes are bound to be made, though of course they can often be rectified. But sometimes they cannot and result in a cock-up. This just has to be coped with as well as possible. There is no way of avoiding risk. Ministers and officials have to play the game as best they can. Sometimes they can run with the ball and sometimes it is best to kick for touch. What is important is that they should work as a team.

Secondly, even in the middle of pressing day-to-day business it is desirable to pause and look at the long term. Of course this has always been done up to a point. Some of the ablest people in the Office have been in the Planning Department in their time. However, it is desirable for ministers and senior officials on occasion to set aside a day at Chevening or at Chequers (the official country residences of the Foreign Secretary and Prime Minister, respectively) to discuss policy over the next five years, setting aside their current preoccupations. I believe this is done nowadays but perhaps too rarely.

Thirdly, there is the question of wear and tear. Ministers travel incessantly; Under-Secretaries work very long hours. Nearly everybody suffers from the traffic-congested state of London. This is far more wearing than it was fifty years ago, especially if account is taken of the much greater domestic pressures which everybody has to cope with. Foreign Secretaries are traditionally overworked, as indeed are PUSs. Politicians seem to have special constitutions and extraordinary resilience. All the same, even for a Foreign Secretary with iron self-discipline and excellent health, politically comfortable and enjoying the full confidence of the Prime Minister, surely the limit must be five years or so. It is a killing job. Indeed I am surprised at how many Foreign Secretaries seem to have survived. As regards officials I think that a most important aspect of personnel management is to see that after a tough job there should be a change of pace and if possible a bit of fun.

Some of us, perhaps most of us, who worked in the Foreign Office thirty or forty years ago will have vivid memories of crises of various kinds and of how we all tried to cope with them – the amazing energy of some of our colleagues, the apparently unruffled calm of some of our superiors. One remembers too the loyal, but in the afternoon sometimes unsteady, frock-coated office keepers who among other duties conducted an ambassador into the PUS's room on the ground floor. Then there were the cavernous wooden cupboards outside the Northern Department on the second floor in which, so it was believed, devoted departmental ladies would secrete inconvenient files. And there was the green safe in the PUS's outer office containing correspondence about the misdemeanours of China Consuls and others in the nineteenth century. Things are very different nowadays, though I hope I have not suggested that *everything* is much better than it used to be. I think that many things *are* better. But it must be remembered that pretty high standards were expected in earlier years. Sloppy drafting would be smartly sent back to its author, whereas good work would usually be recognised and commended. Lord Curzon, a notoriously exacting chief, nevertheless commended his subordinates for their good work. This caused pleasure. By contrast e-mails nowadays are often badly written, I fear, as well as being far too numerous.

As to the alleged stuffiness of Foreign Office life fifty years ago, to a modern eye we young men of fifty years ago in our dark suits and stiff collars must seem grotesquely old-fashioned stuffed shirts, but I think that an impartial observer might have found more rigid hierarchies at that time in the business world. Still, I repeat that many things *are* better than they used to be and enough of the old public service ethos has survived to ensure that the Foreign Secretary can still rely on the Foreign Office to produce the best advice they can and to carry out his policy actively and loyally.

'Not the "General Will" but the Will of the General': The Input of the Paris Embassy to the British "Great Debate" on Europe, Summer 1960[1]

SEAN GREENWOOD

1960 was a pivotal year in Britain's progress towards European cooperation. Although the formal announcement to open negotiations with the original six signatories of the Treaty of Rome (France, West Germany, Italy, Belgium, Luxembourg and the Netherlands) was not made by Macmillan until the summer of 1961, it is likely that he had taken his own decision to attempt to join the European Economic Community (EEC) – or had, at least, more than half persuaded himself that this was the right course for Britain – by the very end of that year.

The stages of this development have been fully explored elsewhere and may be swiftly dealt with here.[2] The British resolution in 1955 to quit the deliberations of the six Western European states which had decided at the Messina Conference (1955) to expand their integrationist experiment, was founded on the familiar basis of the economic and political significance of the Commonwealth, concerns over erosion of sovereignty and also scepticism about the ability of the Six to match reality to aspiration. By the spring of 1956, agreement among the Six to form a common market suggested that this later scepticism might have been misplaced. As a result, the Board of Trade and the Treasury came up with a scheme that was designed either to destroy or to absorb the proposed common market. This was the Free Trade Area (FTA) to be made up of the Six and other Organisation for European Economic Cooperation (OEEC) states working together as an industrial trading bloc and without integrationist baggage.

Looked at from a distance of nearly fifty years, the FTA appears so obvious an attempt to conserve Britain's world role and economic position that it is hard to believe that anyone in Whitehall could have seen it being remotely attractive to the major Western European states. Among those who did was Harold Macmillan, Chancellor of the Exchequer during the gestation of the FTA and Prime Minister during its demise. More than this, Macmillan seems to have convinced himself that the FTA plan was a real innovation in British and European policy. He had entered the Treasury at the end of 1955 determined to be 'something of a reformer'. So far as European cooperation was concerned this meant that 'we might try to find a constructive alternative' to the Messina plan. Macmillan believed he had found his surrogate in the shape of the FTA – 'this great venture' as he called it.[3] Even after it became clear that the Messina powers were 'solid' in their determination to move forward, the Chancellor considered that 'they do not understand. It will be the E[uropean] D[efence] C[ommunity] story all over again'.[4]

In fact it was the FTA that was to experience a re-run of the EDC experience. Negotiations were fettered by British resistance to including agricultural produce in their own plan, by increasing solidarity between the Six and a sense amongst the latter that even if the British objective was no longer to swamp their new creation this is what their scheme would do in practice. This assortment of difficulties meant that the work of the inter-governmental committee set up to promote a free trade area was protracted over two years and its discussions in a state of acrimonious frustration by the spring of 1958. The *coup de grâce* was provided by the return to power in France of General de Gaulle in June of that year. By November 1958 the French had virtually vetoed progress towards an FTA by insisting that it should include agriculture as well as a common external tariff. Macmillan called the failure of the negotiations 'a tragic decision and the crowning folly of the twentieth century in Europe'.[5] This was the Prime Minister in hyperbolic mode, but there is no doubting the jolt this gave to the British or the bitterness they felt towards their Continental neighbours. The sense was of 'an unpleasant undercurrent' in relations and 'a feeling of division, almost of mistrust'.[6]

In the aftershock of the collapse of the talks there was brief talk of 'retaliatory action' against the Six.[7] This was soon discarded, on the ground that 'we held very few economic cards', in favour of a more limited free trade grouping so as to avoid Britain's complete detachment from Europe and to discourage other West European states from drifting into the EEC.[8] The desultory outcome, by the end of 1959, was the European Free Trade Association (EFTA). Even before it was a year old the British had arrived at the conclusion that in EFTA they had opted for a consolation prize for having lost the FTA.

By 1960 the issue was not simply one of how unsatisfactorily EFTA served British requirements but increasingly how damaging exclusion from the EEC was likely to be to these interests. On the economic front there was the notably vibrant economic performance of the Six compared to that of Britain. Politically, there was the growing anxiety that the United States would increasingly choose to work with the EEC, with the resulting marginalisation of Britain as a power of world significance. Entangled with this were concerns that the division of Western Europe into two blocs, for which of course the British were significantly responsible, would be to the advantage of the Soviet Union in the Cold War.

The landmarks in the shift in the British position towards entry into the EEC during 1960 are familiar. The cancellation of the British Blue Streak weapons system, American refusal to back EFTA as against the EEC, the failure of the Paris Summit on East–West disarmament, plus a general recognition that the Commonwealth was no longer a pedestal for London's world authority gave a nervous edge to British self-perception. These matters were examined by an inter-departmental committee chaired by the Head of the Treasury, Sir Frank Lee, which delivered its final report in April.[9] The Lee Committee advised of a strong political rationale for 'near-identification' with the EEC. It also presented the economic benefits to Britain of pursuing this avenue. In a Cabinet reshuffle announced on 27 July, Macmillan gave prominence to 'Europeanists'. On the other hand, there remained divisions within the Cabinet and opposition within sections of the Conservative Party and its supporters. There was also, even if the government did decide to go ahead, the problem of the French.

The winning arguments over British entry into the EEC so far as Macmillan was concerned were the political ones; that exclusion would mean the end of the 'special relationship', the diminution of Britain's world position and the domination of Western Europe by the EEC. His longer-term fear was of a Western Europe under the thrall of Germany 'giving them on a plate what we fought two wars to prevent'.[10] Increasingly, however, Macmillan was fixated by the attitude of the French, and, after June 1958 when he returned to power in France, especially of de Gaulle.[11] As was noted in the Foreign Office, 'the long-term main threat to Western unity lies in future of Germany. In the short term de Gaulle's policy is the main threat to unity of Western Europe'.[12] Even before the de Gaulle Presidency, Macmillan's anxieties about the French were at a high pitch and his diaries are littered with assertions on the lines that 'the French are making things very difficult'.[13] Matters seemed even worse after June 1958. By then he recognised that the FTA was 'being strangled to death by the French'. On meeting the new President shortly after he took office, Macmillan judged him to be 'just as obstinate as ever' and unmoved by a personal appeal on the need to resolve the difficulties over the Free Trade plan. 'He clearly was neither interested nor impressed', Macmillan noted.[14]

Over the next two years Macmillan had the opportunity to assess the attitude to Europe of his old political associate through a number of direct meetings. But the principal day-to-day conduit of information on de Gaulle's position on

Europe was, naturally, the Paris Embassy. In 1960 this was in the hands of Sir Gladwyn Jebb (elevated to the House of Lords later that year as Lord Gladwyn, as he will be referred to throughout this contribution) one of the most experienced diplomats of his generation. He had served in Paris since 1954, and 1960 was to be both his final year in the French capital and his last year in the Foreign Service before his retirement in September. In a speech to the French Press Association in February 1960, Gladwyn was to claim that 'I have always myself thought it a great pity that the United Kingdom was not directly associated with the European Coal and Steel Community ... and a still greater pity that she did not continue to cooperate with the Six Powers when invited to do so in the summer of 1955'. There is an element of hindsight at play here and the fact is that he was a relatively late convert to the 'European idea'.[15] Some time after this, presumably whilst going through his own papers to write his memoirs ten years later, Gladwyn came across material from late 1951 which he found surprising. These reports, he noted, were 'written at time I was attending the 1951 United Nations Assembly in Paris. Interesting as showing that I then was "anti-Federalist" and certainly against our joining the European Defence Community'.[16] Precisely when the shift came is uncertain but by the spring of 1957 Treasury officials were noting a 'sea change' in the ambassador's attitude to Britain and European cooperation.[17] This was stimulated less by Messina than by the experience of Suez in 1956. It had, in other words, a political rather than an economic underpinning. Following that 'humiliation' at the hands of the Americans he saw no future in the reconstruction of an 'Anglo-American Directorate' which would end up with Britain as either 'a sort of 49th state' or 'Airstrip One' whilst simultaneously giving encouragement to neutralist opinion on the Continent. A neutralist Western Europe would lead to a 'Yugoslav' approach to world affairs and advantage to the Soviet Union. The solution he advocated was for Britain to throw in its lot more closely with the Europeans.[18] By the start of 1960, however, his conversion was still incomplete. At this point he was advocating, not entry into the EEC, but some form of arrangement with it. That is that Britain might 'more or less join up with the Six' and 'gradually, and not, so to speak in so many words'.[19]

Gladwyn's public statements on Europe at the beginning of the year generally toed the government line; that is, 'we did not object to the Common Market and so on and so on'.[20] This reflected the drift in the British position since the shock of the FTA's demise in November 1958. Thus in February 1960 his position was that Britain had neither the intention nor the desire to break up the Common Market; the objective was to promote the economic association of the Six and the Seven; and the British people were increasingly coming to realise that they had a role to play in Europe. But 'we cannot rush things too fast' and 'in the meantime there can be no question of Great Britain joining the Common Market'.[21] Five months later this had changed, and in July 1960 he was recommending that 'we should soon make a resolute attempt to batter open the door which was so politely closed on us eighteen months ago' and that Britain should decide to join the EEC.[22] This was new and at this point Gladwyn was alone in putting forward such a potentially far-reaching proposal.

A number of factors contributed to this acceleration. If, in the early part of 1960, it was not clear in London what exactly the way forward in Europe should be there was also some nervousness of a repetition of 'another head-on collision with the French in a multilateral meeting'. The Foreign Office favoured informal bilateral talks with the French, and Gladwyn was informed that 'Ministers here take the view that contact with anyone less than the top or very nearest top, is pretty useless'. The ambassador, who hoped 'to be able to do a little real diplomacy in the background', pursued this course with his characteristic assiduity. Detecting in a Presidential address to the French nation on radio and television on the evening of 31 May the possibility that de Gaulle envisaged an eventual political and economic association of the United Kingdom with the countries of the Common Market, Gladwyn proposed to the Foreign Secretary, Selwyn Lloyd, that he should approach de Gaulle to obtain further clarification.[23]

Though he suspected that it was 'likely that [de Gaulle] will maintain his rather Sybilline attitude' this turned out not to be the case. When the two met at mid-day on Saturday 18 June 1960 the President seemed in candid frame of mind. It was, he suggested, for Britain to decide whether, on the political level, she wanted a closer association with the Continent. For his part it was necessary in the long run for the United Kingdom to somehow be a part of the European Confederation which he advocated. 'He did not think it could be said', he declared, 'that he had ever 'let England down'. It was true he had been very disagreeable sometimes and he regretted this; but never, never had he rejected the concept of the United Kingdom as France's European partner'. Gladwyn put a surprisingly cautious, even dismal, interpretation on the encounter. This was that the entry of Britain into the Common Market was a necessary condition of the formation of de Gaulle's 'European Confederation', but (and the ambassador did not disagree) that this was impossible at present. Moreover, in the President's view arrangements for association between the United Kingdom and the Six were unhelpful as they merely postponed Britain's moment of decision between Europe and the United States.[24]

Yet, as Gladwyn's reflections on this meeting matured so did his position begin to shift resulting in a conviction that 'we can after all reverse engines and join the Common Market'. He was clearly impressed by de Gaulle's fervent avowal of support for Britain's European role as well as his position that an extension of the EEC was the only way forward. Any form of Six/Seven association was a non-starter. He was also aware that the debate on British entry to the EEC had reached the ministerial level and was eager to influence this.

(In fact the Cabinet decided on 13 July, two days before Gladwyn drafted his own arguments, not to seek entry). As much as anything, he was anxious to dispel the inclination, still prevalent in Whitehall, of leaving matters to drift in the hope that changed circumstances would produce an easier solution. 'Time', he asserted, 'is definitely not on our side', for the attitude of the Six would harden after the beginning of 1961 when the Treaty of Rome would accentuate Western European division. At that point, however, there were indications that both the Germans and the Italians would accept the opening of negotiations with the British.[25] With the recent acrimonious collapse of the East–West summit in Paris plainly in his mind he argued that such a schism 'at a time when the whole position of the Western World seems to be crumbling in the face of determined communist assaults' would mean that the 'the triumph of communism must become increasingly probable'.[26]

Gladwyn saw a further reason for urgency. This was related to the central position of de Gaulle himself. Gladwyn was aware of serious opposition in France to British entry to the EEC. Apart from the animosity of particular politicians, there was hostility from French nationalists and federalists as well as most industrialists. Gladwyn was now convinced that de Gaulle did not share this antagonism and was, indeed, 'in advance of the majority of his countrymen' in his understanding of the British position. The essential point was that 'the General himself does not wish to keep us out of Europe for political reasons, which in turn must mean that he would eventually be willing to share the leadership of the Continent with the United Kingdom'. Indeed, if put forward in the right way, implying a decision to choose Europe in preference to the United States, de Gaulle could 'probably be relied upon to use his great influence to stifle any resistance to our admission that may show itself in France'. More than this, 'as a political act . . . I would expect him to be willing to give instructions to his officials to find a way of reconciling the obligations of membership of the Community with the right of free entry into the United Kingdom market of Commonwealth food-stuffs'. The worry was the uncertainty over how much longer he would remain as the Head of the French State; in Gladwyn's view, Britain's chances of entry to the EEC would be 'considerably diminished when he has vanished from the scene'. This had been of concern to the ambassador for some time now. He had noted in his Annual Review for 1959 that 'we must remember that General de Gaulle is 69 and that his three younger brothers have already predeceased him . . . It would not seem as if his enormous frame is capable of supporting, Atlas-like, the burdens of office very much longer'.[27] Then there was his still unresolved colonial problem and should 'he attempt to take the army away from Algeria before the revolution is really crushed it may well be either that he will fail in the attempt or that his regime will fall in France itself'.[28] There were also rumours, passed on to him by his old diplomatic friend René Massigli, of thwarted plots to unseat the President. 'The real test', Gladwyn considered, 'is still to come . . . [and] when it does come the General's chances are not very much better than evens'.[29] Yet it was in Britain's interest that he should remain in power, for 'any alternative French regime would either be one even more intolerably nationalist and anti-Anglo-Saxon or one which would certainly be prepared to do a deal with the Soviet Union'.[30] This raised the spectre of a dangerous 'neutralist tendency' which Gladwyn had for some time discerned in Europe and now in Britain too.[31]

Gladwyn's analysis gained support in London though in one important quarter he was to discover that he had overestimated any meeting of minds with his own. He had been impressed by pro-Common Market statements made by Selwyn Lloyd in Strasbourg at the beginning of the year which may have encouraged him to think that a more positive position was developing inside the government.[32] Now, in another statement by Selwyn Lloyd in the House of Commons of 25 July – which was essentially an explanation of why the British government could not agree to open negotiations to join the EEC – Gladwyn read into it a measure of urgency not dissimilar to that in his own embassy. This was something of a false dawn. Three Deputy Under-Secretaries met with him in the Foreign Office and put him right. The speech, he was told, 'represented in fact rather more of a holding operation' as there were 'still substantial divergencies amongst Ministers'. On the other hand, the three did agree to his suggestion that he make 'a very special approach to the General', a 'purely verbal approach [which] would be unlikely to leak' and which 'by playing on his vanity, his fears and emotions' might move matters forward. This *démarche* also had the approval of the new Lord Privy Seal, Edward Heath.[33]

In his memoirs, Gladwyn refers to this initiative as 'an unheeded swansong'.[34] This is not an accurate description. The meeting which he proposed to hold did take place and during a 'long and quite frank exchange' with de Gaulle on the afternoon of 1 September 1960 Gladwyn posited the idea of secret prenegotiation meetings with experts to 'break the ice' before official discussions might take place. It was a more low-key discussion than the two had held in June – Gladwyn recognised that the President was distracted by Algeria. He also appears, though the ambassador gave less prominence to this, to have been absorbed, following a recent Macmillan-Adenauer meeting in Bonn, by the need to tie Germany further into Europe than to bring the British in. Although Gladwyn found de Gaulle merely 'moderately impressed' by his proposal he, nevertheless, remained buoyant and had 'the definite impression that he would reflect on what I had said and that the net result would not be altogether unfavourable'. Presumably his optimism rested on the President's fervent reaffirmation that he 'would welcome us with open arms' and 'begged us to believe that he did not *want* us to be outside'.[35]

Nothing, of course, came of this. In one of his final comments on European matters before he left Paris, Gladwyn observed a sourness in de Gaulle's demeanour, which the retiring ambassador again blamed on the stresses imposed upon the President by having to deal with the nationalist revolts in Algeria. In any case, he now expected de Gaulle would continue to exclude Britain from 'his Europe' for a while to come. 'The trouble is', he noted, 'whereas he can give us something which we want, we can give him precious little that he wants'.[36] As de Gaulle's attitude seemed to firm up against British entry, Macmillan's, following the negative Cabinet decision of 13 July, returned to indecision with the Prime Minister casting around for some way of appeasing the President. Sometimes this involved cooperation on nuclear questions or support for de Gaulle's 'tripartisme', which Gladwyn approved of, provided 'we can encourage him to think that it is only by giving the PM something that the latter wants as regards Europe that he can get any high-level Three Power meetings'.[37] At other times it entailed thoughts of the Six joining EFTA as a unit. This Gladwyn was vehemently against as 'not a starter. But worse than that, if we ever put it forward seriously the French, at any rate, would simply think that it represented a new effort to torpedo the Common Market. In other words, we would be back to square one'.[38] In some ways they were. In his last speech as ambassador he pointed out that 'my Government ... has simply not as yet finally made up its mind'.[39]

Clearly, this was a disappointment to him. In 1960 he was an old-ish man in a hurry trying to shake his government from its vacillation on an issue he had come to see as one of fundamental importance and with a fleeting opportunity to pull it off. 'It is no good', he asserted to Edward Heath, 'thinking that things would just solve themselves by some kind of 'historical process' pushing us all on vaguely from behind'. He continued: 'What frightens me is that unless a real effort is soon made to achieve the politico-economic unity of Western Europe we shall *all* (and I mean without exception) go into a slow decline in comparison with the bloc of the Eastern countries. And we know in our hearts where such a process will inevitably lead. It will lead to the disruption of the Occident and to the triumph of Communism'.[40]

Gladwyn's energetic interventions in the latter part of 1960 have left him open to accusations of 'immoderate Europeanism' and 'incautious optimism' as well as an inability 'to stand back and calculate objectively the true intentions behind French declarations'.[41] Of course, he was wildly wrong, as he later freely admitted, in his belief that de Gaulle would support British entry into the EEC and that he would envisage sharing the leadership of Western Europe with Britain.[42] He was also mistaken in his view that the French leader would ever contemplate an arrangement which would accommodate British links with the Commonwealth. In this sense he was, as he had been at the time of Messina, 'a false prophet'.[43] Yet his views on the security dimension of the European question were not out of line with the Foreign Office position by this time.[44] Whereas at the start of the year this had remained attached to the notion of forming a Free Trade Area which would embrace both the Six and the Seven, the view had emerged by the spring that a more radical approach to Europe was required based upon the political advantages to the Soviet Union of dissension among the West Europeans. This explains why Gladwyn's approaches to de Gaulle in June and September had approval at the highest levels in Whitehall. It may be that he, and therefore they, might be criticised for taking de Gaulle's enthusiastic assertions of support for British entry too much at face value. Yet it would seem to be a reasonable assumption, and one of course that Macmillan himself was to make two years later, that 'the blind support [of] most Frenchmen' for General de Gaulle's 'foreign policy of *grandeur*' meant that the assertions of this 'extraordinary one-man band' whose 'hold over the country was almost absolute' could be taken to be authoritative.[45]

Whether the General's statements were entirely truthful is, of course, another matter. Again, it was reasonable of Gladwyn to expect a Head of State with whom he evidently had a 'rather special relationship' not to dissimulate on such a crucial aspect of policy.[46] Indeed, the British latched on to de Gaulle's words in part because it was not always clear to them who else would be able to enlighten them. Selwyn Lloyd complained that 'the difficulty was that one did not know who could speak with authority among the Six. One did not know, for example, whether M. Couve de Murville really spoke for President de Gaulle. It might be that Herr von Brentano sometimes was competent to speak for Dr Adenauer, particularly if he had seen him recently, but Dr Erhard often had differing views'.[47] In Paris, where the key to the question lay, this problem was magnified. As one official noted, 'there is more than one point of view in French official circles'.[48] A related problem, Sir Pierson Dixon, Gladwyn's successor in Paris, pointed out was that 'it would have been possible to produce evidence in support of almost any interpretation of General de Gaulle's attitude'.[49]

The supposition was also made, then and later by historians, that the President in 1960 fully knew his own mind about the direction Europe should take. This might have been a false assumption. On the other hand, it may simply be that the President was being duplicitous and pursuing an agreed Gaullist policy of leading the British on in order to elude criticism of being too negative until his own plan for a '*europe d'états*' – without Britain – had matured.[50] If this was so, it was only de Gaulle himself who was following this path with any consistency. Couve de Murville, the French Foreign Minister, Wormser, Director of Economic Affairs at the Quai d'Orsay, and Chauvel, the French ambassador were each consistently negative about Britain's relations with the EEC.[51] Apart from de Gaulle himself, only Jean Monnet offered the British the hope of some arrangement with the Six, but the expert view was that 'the "European" lobby has no longer much influence on French policies'.[52]

The question of 'influence' is frequently a slippery one, and it would be imprudent to suggest that Gladwyn's 'comments from the outposts' had a predominant sway on the Prime Minister's thinking. Clearly though, it was an important part of the persuasive mix which reinforced a more general acceptance of the need for change.[53] What was more, Gladwyn's new direction hit Macmillan when his faith in the Anglo-American relationship had been severely dislodged following the failed Paris summit and the manifest refusal of the Eisenhower administration to back EFTA. An examination of Macmillan's evaluation of the situation, begun in the closing days of 1960, reveals a close correlation with Gladwyn's judgment that the question was a political one. Europe, Macmillan now asserted, presented 'not primarily an economic but a political problem'; at the core of this was 'the monolithic strength of the Kremlin'; 'if a settlement is not reached in the near future, the split will get worse and will become (from the point of view of our overriding aim – the joint struggle against Communism) dangerous and perhaps fatal'; but 'it is now pretty clear that an accommodation *could* be reached'; the obstacle was de Gaulle, 'yet by a strange paradox, if de Gaulle were to disappear, an accommodation might be still more difficult'; his departure would mean the triumph of federalism and 'sooner or later, the triumph of the unilateralists and neutralists here'; if de Gaulle 'gave the word, all the Wormsers would turn at once'. He might be persuaded via concessions over 'tripartism' or the sharing of nuclear technology – though 'he would have to know that it was *we* who had got it for him'.[54]

In a constructive way, Gladwyn had arguably assisted in Macmillan's realisation that there was no halfway house for Britain in its path towards Europe. It was negotiation to join the EEC or nothing. Anything else was 'wishful thinking' and a 'continuance of the present deadlock'.[55] Less helpfully, in the long run, he had likely added to Macmillan's over-confidence on that most critical, yet uncertain hurdle: whether de Gaulle would be cooperative. If it is impossible to pin down the precise consequences of Gladwyn's input at this juncture, it is possible to note his prescience over two important aspects of Britain's meander towards Europe. In July 1961 Macmillan announced not that he would present an application to the Six but that there would be exploratory conversations to discover whether Britain could construct an application – an echo of Gladwyn's position the previous summer. In the longer term, his view that it would be best that Britain 'should clearly emphasise their acceptance of the Treaty of Rome rather than the special arrangements into which we would have to enter before that acceptance could be put into practice' was the strategy adopted by Edward Heath prior to the successful entry negotiations of 1971.[56] In conclusion, it might be said that Gladwyn, like all those on the British side who sought to divine the best and most realisable route forward for Britain and Europe was engaged upon a sharp process of re-education. It seems reasonable to suggest that the ambassador learned to reassemble the building blocks of Britain's external policy with more alacrity and conviction than most.

NOTES

All references to Cabinet (CAB), Prime Minister's Office (PREM), Lord Chancellor's Office (LCO) or Foreign Office (FO) documents relate to materials held at the National Archives, London (formerly the Public Record Office) unless otherwise stated.

1. FO 371/153916, WF1052/23, despatch from Gladwyn, 9 Sep. 1960.
2. J. Ellison, *Threatening Europe: Britain and the Creation of the European Community, 1955–58* (London: Macmillan, 2000); W. Kaiser, *Using Europe, Abusing the Europeans: Britain and European Integration, 1945–63* (Basingstoke: Macmillan, 1996); J. Tratt, *The Macmillan Government and Europe* (Basingstoke: Macmillan, 1996); G. Wilkes (ed.), *Britain's Failure to Enter the European Community, 1961–63: The Enlargement Negotiations and Crises in European, Atlantic and Commonwealth Relations* (London: Frank Cass, 1997).
3. Macmillan Papers, Bodleian Library, Oxford, MS.Macmillan dep.d.24*, d.25* and d.27*, diary entries for 24 Oct. 1955, 28 Jan. 1956, and 5 Sep. 1956. On Macmillan's desire for innovation towards Europe see also Kaiser, *Using Europe*, pp.62, 74.
4. Macmillan Papers, MS.Macmillan dep.d.25*, diary, 9 Feb. 1956.
5. FO 371/13451, record of a meeting between Macmillan and Couve de Murville, 6 Nov. 1958.
6. FO 371/150218, references in speech by Selwyn Lloyd, Jan. 1960.
7. S. Greenwood, *Britain and European Integration Since the Second World War* (Manchester: Manchester University Press, 1996), p.106.
8. Macmillan Papers, MS.Macmillan dep.d.34, diary, 12 Dec. 1958.
9. CAB 134/1852.
10. Macmillan to the Head of the Treasury, Feb. 1956, quoted in Kaiser, *Using* Europe, pp.61–2. See also Greenwood, *Britain and European Integration*, p.126.
11. See H. Young, *This Blessed Plot: Britain and Europe from Churchill to Blair* (London: Macmillan, 1998), pp.116–18; D. Gowland and A. Turner, *Reluctant Europeans: Britain and European Integration, 1945–1998* (London: Longman, 2000), p.124; Tratt, *Macmillan Government*, p.197.
12. FO 371/152095, ZP5/13/G, minute by Ramsbotham, 22 Jan. 1960.
13. Ibid., 18 Apr. 1957. See also: 3 Mar. 1957, 9 Mar. 1957, 18 Mar. 1957, 11 Jul. 1957, 4 Dec. 1957, 16 Dec. 1957, 21 Feb. 1958, 19 April 1958, 4 Jul. 1958, 26 Oct. 1958.
14. Ibid., 23 and 30 Jun. 1958.
15. FO 371/150218, M619/20.
16. Gladwyn Papers, Churchill Archives Centre, Churchill College, Cambridge, GLAD 1/1/1, undated comment written on file cover, 'Correspondence 1951'.
17. Ellison, *Threatening Europe*, p.144.
18. PREM 11/2329, despatch by Gladwyn, 14 Jan. 1958; Lord Gladwyn, *The Memoirs of Lord Gladwyn* (London: Weidenfeld & Nicolson, 1972), pp. 289, 293.
19. Gladwyn, *Memoirs*, p.305.
20. Ibid.
21. FO 371/150218, M619/20, draft of speech to the French Club of the review 'Occident', Feb. 1960.
22. FO 371/150221, M619/73, despatch from Gladwyn, 15 Jul. 1960.
23. FO 371/153898, WF1022/3, Gladwyn to Selwyn Lloyd, 6 Jun.1960.
24. FO 371/150221, M619/66.
25. FO 371/150222, M619/87; CAB 128/34, CC(60)41, 13 Jul. 1960.
26. FO 371/150221, M619/73, despatch from Gladwyn 15 Jul. 1960. This was seen by the Foreign Secretary.

27. LCO (Lord Chancellor's Office) 27/140, WF1011/1, Annual Review, 6 Jan. 1960.
28. Ibid.
29. FO 371/153894, WF 1012/3, Gladwyn to Tomkins, 26 Feb. 1960. This report was shown to Macmillan.
30. LCO 27/140, WF1011/1, Annual Review, 6 Jan. 1960.
31. FO 371/150222, M619/80; FO 371/150221, M619/73.
32. FO 371/150218, M619/20.
33. FO 371/150222, M619/80, record of a meeting between Gladwyn, Sir Evelyn Shuckburgh, Sir Paul Gore-Booth and Sir Roderick Barclay, 29 Jul. 1960. Gladwyn was not alone in finding encouragement in Lloyd's statement. Both Guy Mollet and Jean Monnet did too. See FO 371/150222, M619/80 and FO 371/150233, M619/93.
34. Gladwyn, Memoirs, p.308.
35. FO 371/150222, M619/86. The emphasis is in the original.
36. FO 371/153916, WF1052/23, Gladwyn to Heath, 9 Sep. 1960.
37. Ibid. See also minute by Rumbold.
38. FO 371/150222, M619/90, Gladwyn to Sir Frank Lee, 16 Sep. 1960.
39. FO 371/153916, WF1052/23.
40. Ibid.
41. Tratt, Macmillan Government, pp.57–8, 152.
42. Gladwyn, Memoirs, pp.306, 319.
43. Young, This Blessed Plot, p.119
44. Tratt, Macmillan Government, p. 151.
45. FO 371/153885, WF1013/1, minute by Collings, 13 Jan. 1960; LCO 27/140, WF1011/1, report by Gladwyn, 6 Jan. 1960.
46. Gladwyn, Memoirs, p.322.
47. FO 371/150288, M6114/451, conversation between Selwyn Lloyd and German ambassador, 30 Jun. 1960.
48. FO 371/150223, M619/102, minute by Meyer, 18 Oct. 1960.
49. Cited in Young, This Blessed Plot, p.135.
50. O. Bange, 'Grand Designs and the Diplomatic Breakdown', in Wilkes (ed.), Britain's Failure to Enter the European Community, pp.195–7.
51. See for example FO 371/150221, M619/66; FO 371/150222, M619/81 and 84.
52. FO 371/150223, M619/101 and 90.
53. Young, This Blessed Plot, p.119.
54. PREM 11/3325.
55. FO 371/150222, M619/87.
56. FO 371/150222, M619/76.

Reflections on Thirty Years in the Diplomatic Service

ALYSON J.K. BAILES

Starting work in the historic Main Building of the Foreign and Commonwealth Office (FCO) in August 1969 was an exhilarating but also a daunting prospect. Straight out of Oxford University, I was just twenty years old and my family background was about as remote from diplomacy as it could be: my grandfather (whom I greatly respected) had spent all his life as a coal-miner. It was curiously reassuring, therefore, to find that when I reported to the 'German room' of the Western European Department, one of my first duties as the youngest in the team would be to carry fresh coal down the corridor to feed our open fire in winter. Here at least was one task that should be within my capacities and with which I could feel at home.

Selecting a similar, characteristic vignette from my last year with the Diplomatic Service, which I spent as Ambassador to Helsinki in 2001–2002, is not so simple. Diplomatic life in the thirty years intervening has changed almost beyond recognition: but while *tempora mutantur, nos mutamur in illis* and some of the most important changes (especially in intangibles) have crept up almost unnoticed. On reflection, I would select an incident when a senior female official in the FCO made use of the e-mail distribution list linking other senior women at home and abroad to complain about the daily flood of e-mails and how they were making it hard to get on with other duties. Several points are worth noting here, apart from the rise of information technology: including the sizeable number of women now holding ambassadorial jobs or similar rank at home, and the fact that they all (unlike many senior male colleagues) directly answer their own e-mails. Furthermore, none of us felt it wrong to complain and agitate over this problem through the medium of the FCO's own communications network. Altogether, this provides a good illustration of the exhausting, equalising but empowering impact of new technology.

I wish to pick out some generic changes in the work of the FCO and the Diplomatic Service work over the last three decades, based on my own experiences, and to comment finally on some of the virtues and vices that the Service has preserved unchanged. First, though, it is important to remember how remote the world of the FCO was in 1969 from the typical experiences of young people recruited today. We were a generation born around the end of the Second World War and who had grown up with post-war rationing, and many aspects of my own first job kept me focused on the issues and legacies of wartime. We still called the Eastern part of Germany the Soviet occupied zone, although it was during my year in the Western European Department that Willy Brandt became Chancellor in the Federal Republic and began the process that would allow Britain to recognise the German Democratic Republic. Berlin was still a tense, embattled place and the negotiations that would lead to the stabilising Quadripartite Agreement had just been embarked upon. I had to deal with a number of outstanding legal cases left over from the 1945 peace settlement concerning the disposal of property, displaced persons and compensation to concentration camp victims. I also answered hundreds of letters a year about the imprisonment of Hitler's deputy, Rudolf Hess, in Spandau jail.

Beyond this divided Europe, the Commonwealth and a large number of colonies and a large military presence 'East of Suez' were still among the defining features of British interests and responsibilities abroad. We had just one small FCO department monitoring, from outside, an also rather small (in membership and competence) and politically turbulent European Community. Day-to-day trivia also underpinned our links to the past: our stapling machines, hole-punchers and metal-tipped 'Treasury tags' for binding documents together were all of war-time vintage, and our paperwork at working level was exchanged in manuscript written with fountain pens. I was told, perhaps apocryphally, that when Winston Churchill's war-time headquarters under Clive Steps was opened up as a museum in 1984 it only required one raid on the FCO to gather all the necessary 1940s-style desk furniture.

The other dominant reality of my first years in the Service was the threat from the Communist bloc occupying the greater part of Eurasia, and the security disciplines which it obliged us to follow in every department of personal and professional life. I was exposed early to the full implications of being a NATO diplomat in a Communist country when I was posted to Budapest in my second year of service; and later – 1986–89 – I served also in the People's Republic of China. I was fortunate that neither of these regimes was prone to *aggressive* surveillance and active harassment of Westerners at the time that I was there; and as a fairly strong-nerved single person I was stimulated more than intimidated by the constant challenge of trying to protect my work (and my contacts with local friends) from hostile observation. But some diplomats and especially their families found the combination of minimal privacy and permanent vigilance much harder to bear, while all of us were marked by the need constantly to question the genuineness and motives of any local contact who behaved in a half-way decent manner towards us.

On the other hand, I do not think I have ever felt *physically* safer than in my years in Hungary (1970–74), when I travelled alone in the remotest parts of the country and never thought twice about picking up hitchhikers in the hope of some revealing grass-roots gossip. The new generation of diplomats will never experience this particular combination of physical ease and a homely environment with a no-holds-barred ideological threat. With only three 'real' Communist countries left, all outside Europe, most diplomats who still have to work under surveillance do so in a variety of 'rogue' states which are alien and hostile for other more civilisational than ideological reasons. At the same time, all British diplomats – and other civil servants posted abroad – now spend much of their time under physical and mental siege from international terrorist threats of which I remained blithely innocent, at least for my first decade of service. There are more posts than before in which they have to contend with significant levels of violent crime, and they are more likely than before (notably because of the growing emphasis on civilian inputs to crisis interventions) to find themselves in the thick of potentially volatile situations in the name of international conflict management. Such are the human implications of the transition these thirty years have witnessed from a more or less symmetrical ideological confrontation to a unipolar, globalised, but still largely unregulated and untamed world environment.

I would now like to pick out four strands of change in the methods and style of diplomacy which I have witnessed during this time and experienced in my own career. The first is multilateralisation, which took a great jump forward with Britain's entry to the European Economic Community (EEC) in the 1970s but has also been driven by the proliferation of new regional and global fora and the widening of competence of longer-standing ones. The number of issues which Britain can deal with on a purely bilateral basis has shrunk dramatically: when I served on the Sino-British Joint Liaison Group negotiating the future of Hong Kong in 1988–89, I was already aware of the luxury of taking part in one of the last such exercises. There has also been a tendency for issues to move out of the grip of smaller groups into that of larger ones, in such varying contexts as the end of quadripartite authority in Germany, the expansion of specialised export control groupings, and the current sweeping enlargement of the European Union and NATO. Few parts of the world are without their own attempts to build regional and sub-regional cooperation structures, and indeed, one could almost derive a list of 'rogue' states and threats to peace by counting those who remain outside such (often overlapping) groupings.

For all these reasons, if the man-hours spent today by Britain's total diplomatic cadre on work in multilateral fora, and the man-hours which staff in bilateral missions spend on discussing issues which belong to such fora were calculated, both figures would surely come out far higher than in 1969. Such shifts clearly affect individual careers, and during my time I have seen 'multilateral' skills more and more clearly recognised as a legitimate type of career specialisation, joining but not necessarily displacing regional and functional ones. It is becoming harder for diplomats to score well even in bilateral jobs, or FCO geographical departments, without having a working knowledge of at least European Union and United Nations procedures. Another paradoxical effect has been to re-create an almost universal requirement for knowledge of French (because of the way this is used without interpretation in Common Foreign and Security Policy working groups and in European Union caucuses elsewhere).

From my own observation as someone who has done multilateral work intermittently since 1974 (at NATO), British diplomats have generally performed well in these new arenas thanks to their skills in exposition, realistic feel for group dynamics, and the maintenance of high standards in briefing and coordination back home. Their characteristic mistakes are to fail to adapt their use of English to the *lingua franca* of the group (jokes, allusions, idioms and literary references are almost always a mistake) and to understand the importance of the smaller members. More generally, the multilateralisation and especially the Europeanisation of our diplomatic culture may be a problem if it goes faster than the same processes in other parts of the British Establishment and public opinion.[1] That can only serve to resurrect doubts about the FCO's 'soundness' on national interests, especially if playing and scoring in the multilateral game becomes an end in itself where the need for productive outcomes (not just outputs) of institutional work is forgotten. Ultimately, since deinstitutionalisation is neither feasible nor desirable, the only way forward on this is to improve the political legitimacy and operational realism of the multilateral organs as a whole.

Another factor which has helped in practice to ward off cultural isolation for the FCO is the fast-growing direct engagement of British politicians and non-FCO civil servants in the decision-making processes of the European Union and to a lesser extent the work of other international bodies – with the resulting desingularisation of FCO/Diplomatic Service work. In the late 1960s and early 1970s, only the Department of Trade and Industry had a range of overseas experience and contacts comparable with that of the FCO, while some other departments, like the Home Office, still led a purely national existence.

By the time I joined European Communities Department (Internal) in 1976, shortly after British entry to the EEC, the practical exigencies of my work on EEC budgetary and monetary policy dictated such close interdependence with Treasury colleagues that we could toss a coin to see which Ministry should draft a joint brief on any given occasion. It was particularly interesting to observe how the chance to chair EEC Councils and committees during the first British Presidency of 1978 led different Ministers and Ministries to grasp the political reality and potential of Community work, though unfortunately many of them used it to pursue the internal battles of the Callaghan Cabinet over economic policy and the role of the trade unions on a wider stage. During 1979–81, I became one of a still small number of FCO people to spend an 'interchange' posting within the Ministry of Defence (MoD), holding the desk that covered *inter alia* the Soviet invasion of Afghanistan and the Iran-Iraq war, and a few years later as Deputy Head of Policy Planning Staff I had secondees not just from the MoD but from the private sector (Shell) working under me.

For me, this kind of boundary blurring and jumping has nothing but positive connotations. I profited from it to take no less than five temporary attachments outside FCO, in the Brussels organs and the academic world as well as in MoD, and felt each time that I was returning with useful ideas from outside as well as a clearer view of the FCO's own strengths. For the FCO as a whole, the internationalisation of Whitehall has been a source of recurring bouts of concern about losing an original monopoly of foreign policy: then our *primus inter pares* position; and by today, perhaps even our *raison d'être*. As an example, it was thought necessary in 2000 for the modern equivalent of Western European Department to make a study of whether bilateral embassies were still necessary within the European Union.

As ambassador at Helsinki, I was convinced, and still believe now, that the answer is 'yes'. The growing integration of Britain's domestic, as well as foreign policies with European neighbours actually requires more in-depth understanding of 'where they are coming from' (such as only resident observers can provide), and opens up new fields for a good embassy to impact upon and learn from its host society. The concomitant risk is the progressive ring-fencing of groups of staff within the embassy carrying out, for example, commercial, defence or entry clearance functions, so that they directly obey other Whitehall departments' orders on the substance of their work. This could gradually discourage them from sharing burdens, concerns and information with other parts of the post. Such Balkanisation of embassy management could hardly help the development of joined-up British external policies and could probably only be averted by much greater pooling of policies and resources at the Whitehall end. Perhaps, like Britain in Europe, the FCO can only achieve its full potential now through the gamble of a more thorough-going integration with its neighbours?

The third trend of change I have observed could be summed up as professionalisation, though it has several different strands. Over the last thirty years, a combination of public scepticism, Treasury cuts, and the kind of Whitehall infiltration just referred to have kept the Diplomatic Service under constant pressure to prove and re-prove its utility and cost-effectiveness. The FCO and the Diplomatic Service have fought back partly by closing ranks and by adopting more conscious, transparent planning and assessment systems. On the first point, in 1969 the government was still only part-way through combining the former Foreign, Commonwealth Relations and Colonial Services; the 'fast stream' and 'executive' intakes were rigidly segregated; and it was almost unknown for research or legal cadres to contemplate a posting abroad. The homogenising process which followed has been mirrored in labour relations structures, where the Diplomatic Service Association has successfully registered itself as a trade union, opened itself to staff outside the old 'administrative' grades, and is now considering merger with the Whitehall-wide First Division Association. Drastic surgery to the former security officers' and technical officers' cadres has been another step towards a virtually unitary service.

But while the Diplomatic Service itself has been structurally simplified, its management systems have developed through stages of baroque complexity. I cannot remember hearing anything about 'management' as a system or process during my first three jobs in the service, although I was extremely conscious of receiving training in practical professional skills from individuals above me. I could have remained largely ignorant of what the administration did for even longer if I had not worked for the Diplomatic Service Association and Staff Side from 1976 onwards. Nowadays, of course, even the greenest new entrant gets drawn into objective-setting and performance monitoring exercises, is launched on a career-long series of management courses, and has to learn to stare their deficiencies in the face through a fully open individual reporting process.

My own reactions to this evolution have been mixed, and the Service has judged my performance as a manager likewise. I found it easiest to identify with administrative reforms from the early 1990s when management-by-objectives was introduced – realising that this approach has the power to objectify judgements of performance and should thus narrow the scope for prejudice or misunderstanding towards non-typical members of the service, such as women. I was able positively to enjoy 'playing' the management system when good definition of goals and good performance actually attracted more resources to my department or embassy. But this cannot happen all or even most of the time, and the proven achievement of a performance standard cannot guarantee a given reward (promotion or posting) because of what seem to be insuperable inelasticities and inexactness in overall financial and manpower planning. Without such a guaranteed pay-off, today's more complex management processes can easily be felt as a burden for operators at all levels, building animosities between 'us' and 'them' in the administration who are perceived as having imposed them, and perhaps blinding us to the fact of how much might be achieved – as in the old days – just by decent and generous inter-personal relations. In retrospect, all the individuals who made my life difficult in the Service did so because they were the wrong kind of people rather than the wrong kind of managers.

There is another way to justify a systematic and prominent goal-setting procedure, and it relates to my fourth trend, the shorter reaction time and faster turnover for diplomatic decisions. Although my own first three jobs were considered heavily loaded, the tempo of work was amazingly relaxed by today's standards: it was still acceptable to come into the FCO around ten, and we had a half-hour collective tea-break every afternoon. Important diplomatic reporting, even on one-off events like elections, was done in despatches which could take weeks to draft. Telegrams were still reserved for the fastest-moving crises[2] and negotiations, and were themselves carefully drafted in a genuinely terse 'telegraphese'. Telephones were sparingly used for communication with posts, *inter alia* because of security fears, and the fax came into widespread use only in the 1980s. (We were proud to get one of the first highly classified fax machines at Beijing in 1987). Naturally the style of communications affected the whole style of work, and one effect was to stratify the exchange of information so that important messages were exchanged only at high and formal levels – overseas reporting from ambassadors to ministers, submissions at home signed off at Head or Department or higher. A correspondingly great deal of effort went into the *preparation* of documents, which had both its bad and good sides. It was frustrating for a young diplomat to have their drafts criticised and re-written, perhaps several times, and finally signed by another, but when carried out by sympathetic mentors this could be a genuine education in the disciplines of analytical and policy-shaping work.

Above all, there was more time to *think* about what was going on and about how our policy choices related to, and might influence, the broader stream of events. Today when instantaneous communication is possible between not just every post and department but virtually every individual in the Service, the temptation is to prioritise tactical over strategic thinking, articulacy over grasp and expression over substance. Less reflection time makes it harder to look forward and back, to see connections and marshal many-stranded strategies, to think laterally and – since we are only human – to keep our emotions out of it. The setting up of formal, frequently revised objectives for individuals and work units is actually quite a logical response to such an environment, providing some defence against over-instinctive and subjective responses and also against constant, tactically driven changes of course.

Finally, I would like to touch, more briefly, on three virtues which I perceived in the FCO and Diplomatic Service in my early days and which I was still able to appreciate at the time of leaving: plus three equally persistent vices. The first quality which surprised and impressed me among the officials I sat with in my first 'third room' (1969–70) was their creativity and independence of mind, their readiness to ride with and even swim ahead of the tide of history when it might help British interests. This ability to brainstorm, to 'think the unthinkable' in intellectual contexts and 'seize the main chance' in practical ones, is still part of the Service's culture while it remains rather unusual in other diplomatic establishments. Possibly it is an element of balance developed in view of the instinctive conservatism shown by most British professional politicians, and much of the media and public opinion when dealing with foreign affairs.

The second virtue, lack of corruption and partisanship, certainly implies maintaining a distance (in systemic, not personal terms) from the party-political establishment. When I first joined, the political-diplomatic divide was very clear *inter alia* because only top officials had contact with Ministers, and it was standard practice to match a Minister with a Private Secretary who 'leaned' the other way politically. Any aspects of a Minister's work which had party and domestic connotations were strictly siphoned off through Political Advisers. Individuals in the Service who were strongly drawn to political process felt obliged to resign and stand for Parliament, and in at least two cases which I can remember, advanced to ministerial rank. Today, not least because Ministers travel and negotiate so much more in Europe, human contacts are closer between them and diplomats at all levels, and the divisions between 'national', 'government' and 'party' policy cannot in practice be so strictly drawn. Even so, the number of political appointments has remained minimal – often non-existent – even at ambassadorial level and the politicisation of other ranks is unknown. I can hardly over-stress what benefits this brings both to the outward effectiveness and inward cohesion of the Service compared with the opposite pole of practice in the United States. It probably has a lot to do with my third point: the *esprit de corps*, *joie de vivre* and *panache* which still survives in the FCO and Diplomatic Service despite everything, and which – in the most unlikely circumstances – can make diplomatic experience simply and intoxicatingly fun.

What are we still bad at? Developing an appropriate, home grown style of administration (at acceptable cost in time and resources) and identifying and adapting the right technologies to suit the special nature of diplomatic work. Both problems are linked with an uneasy public–private sector relationship which extends far beyond the FCO as such, and with the syndrome to which both Conservative and Labour governments have been prone during these decades: waking up to something useful that the private sector has done and exhorting officials to follow it, but so belatedly that the private sector has already discovered the flaws of the method and moved on before we are halfway through introducing it. Belated and half-hearted imitation of the private sector risks landing the public service with leftover and second-best commercial advisers (and equipment). Thus we had hard-nosed cost-cutting management when industry was getting touchy-feely again; now we have flat information-based hierarchies when industry is re-inventing and disencumbering leadership, and so on. In my possibly heretical view the answer would be not to move further away from business but rather closer to it, to try to find out at any given time where the really smart money is – literally as well as metaphorically.

Any hint of sour grapes can, I hope, be corrected by stressing that I never realised how much the Service had given me until I left it. So many of the things we learn inside are taken for granted – drafting and editing skills, teamwork, communication, languages, time management and planning, value for money – that it can be a revelation to find how they are valued and can be capitalised on in other, including international settings. But the problem is just that these techniques are not exclusive to diplomacy, and can sometimes be practised for more obvious and rapid returns elsewhere. What is not reproducible in (almost) any other career is the experience of dealing with matters of such crucial, often literally life-and-death importance – whether measured by the historical, human or any other yardstick. No other career choice would have allowed me, as a mere twenty-year-old in 1969, to witness and have a hand in the first crackings of the post-war ice that would lead one day to the reunification of Germany. Nor to be the first to hear from a Finnish newspaper editor (before publication of his historic interview) in autumn 2001 that the Russian President, Vladimir Putin, had dropped his opposition to the Baltic States joining NATO. It was worth wrestling with both coalscuttles and computers for that.

ACKNOWLEDGEMENTS

Alyson Bailes resigned from H.M. Diplomatic Service in June 2002 to become Director of the Stockholm International Peace Research Institute SIPRI. This piece is written in a strictly personal capacity.

NOTES

1. As in the joke about a man standing in Great George Street who asks a passer-by 'Which side is the FCO on?' The answer: 'On ours, I hope'.
2. The receipt of a telegram was an adrenalin-boosting event in a way unthinkable now, when even a small post can receive 60 in a day. In my first year at FCO I had literal nightmares about receiving unexpected telegrams in the middle of the night.

Accommodating Diplomacy: The Foreign and Commonwealth Office and the Debate over Whitehall Redevelopment

KEITH HAMILTON

> The construction of our Foreign Service is like one of those old English mansions, complete with tradition and charm, yet unsuited for the amenities of ordinary life.[1]

Students of diplomacy share with its practitioners a penchant for architectural metaphors. The fine addresses once occupied by the foreign ministries of Europe may no longer serve as a convenient shorthand for the decision-making processes of state. But diplomatic structures are still assembled and negotiating gaps bridged, and if the resulting settlements seem sometimes to rest on uncertain foundations time allows them to be viewed and reviewed within infinitely varying perspectives. Buildings *per se*, the places wherein policy is formulated and dialogue conducted, have featured rather less prominently in the writings of international historians. They have not, however, been ignored. The architecture of Britain's missions in East Asia and its embassy in Paris have been the subjects of recent studies,[2] and the so-called 'Battle of the Styles' which preceded the construction of what is now the Main Building of the Foreign and Commonwealth Office (FCO) has been chronicled by Ian Toplis.[3] Another work, that by Anthony Seldon, sets the FCO's restored and redecorated interiors in their broad historical context.[4] This nonetheless touches only lightly upon the debate which engaged many within and beyond Whitehall during the 1960s and 1970s over whether the FCO's present Italianate edifice should be replaced by more functional accommodation better suited to the management of Britain's overseas relations.

Prior to the publication of his book, Seldon addressed this topic in an article in *The Times*. Under the rubric 'Barbarians in Whitehall', he drew upon a letter of November 1963 in which Lord Crawford, then a trustee of the British Museum, protested to the Prime Minister, Sir Alec Douglas-Home, against proposals to demolish the building. It would, Crawford claimed, be 'a monstrous outrage' in which no government of a civilised country could engage 'without being criticised for barbarism'. Seldon then went on to describe how plans to replace the existing structure with purpose-built accommodation were successfully countered by amenity groups and others anxious to preserve Britain's Victorian heritage. Despite the commitment of Harold Wilson's Labour administration to the modernisation of Whitehall, proposals for its physical redevelopment were never implemented and, according to Seldon, after the Conservative victory in the General Election of June 1970, Edward Heath's government announced that the FCO's Main Building would not be demolished but restored. Twenty-five years later its refurbishment was completed at a cost of £100 million.[5] Seldon's brief account is wrong in one particular: it was a Labour, and not a Conservative government that decided to abandon plans to rebuild the FCO. Moreover, he omitted any reference to the fact that plans to raze Gilbert Scott's monumental achievement were dependent upon developments on the other side of Whitehall, and that it was public concern over the work of two other Victorian architects, Thomas Chawner and Norman Shaw, which may ultimately have decided its fate. The case for the barbarians was also significantly understated.

Barbarians have rarely been treated kindly by historians. Architects have hardly fared better when subjected to the scrutiny of penny-pinching politicians. George Gilbert Scott, the architect of the Foreign Office, was from his early involvement with the design and construction of the building at odds with his political masters. The story of the quarrel between Lord Palmerston, who wanted a classical structure, and Gilbert Scott, whose original designs were in the Gothic style, needs no retelling. Gladstone's jibe that 'desiring a classical Foreign Office, the British Government employed the best known Gothic architect of the day to erect it' adequately summarises the outcome.[6] But it is worth recalling that barely six years after its completion, Gilbert Scott was being blamed for serious deficiencies in the accommodation provided. In December 1874, a lift killed a Foreign Office employee, and Gilbert Scott was singled out in the coroner's court for specifying a defective installation, even though it was the Office of Works that had instructed him to use the design in question. Others queried the soundness of the brickwork. There were complaints that the fireplaces smoked or protruded too far into rooms, and about the smell of sewage which seemed to pervade the place. Finally, in 1877, Gilbert Scott was called before a parliamentary select committee for questioning about shortcomings in construction and design, more especially about inadequate lighting, poor ventilation and the excessive cost of decoration.[7] Many of the day-to-day problems with which officials had to cope might equally well be attributed to architectural flaws. Dust and dirt, which seemed so easily to accumulate, were persistent causes of complaint. In March 1871 Edmund Hammond, the first Permanent Under-Secretary (PUS) to occupy the building, took the Foreign Office's housekeeper to task for what he termed its 'generally filthy state'.[8] A more obvious source of the trouble was probably the chimney flues and open fireplaces. And more than twenty years later Francis Bertie, then an Assistant Under-Secretary, could be found wandering the corridors of the Foreign Office scrawling obscenities on its grime-covered window bottoms.[9]

The building was in any case difficult to heat. The rooms were too high and fuel supplies sometimes insufficient. Again, however, it was the servants who took the blame. On Boxing Day 1896, Bertie protested against the laxity of the Office of Works, whose employee, a stoker, had assumed Christmas to be a holiday and failed to maintain the furnaces intended to heat the passages of the Foreign Office.[10] Likewise, when in the autumn of 1883 the Parliamentary Under-Secretary, Lord Fitzmaurice, attributed the 'horrible stenches' then pervading the building to the poor state of the drains and a 'totally unnecessary and most offensive W.C.', he was assured by the Chief Clerk that whilst in the past the unpleasant aroma had been no more than the smell of burnt mutton fat, it had subsequently been due to the failure of the servants to dispose properly of cabbage water.[11] The positioning of the kitchens may indeed have been part of the problem. On 28 January 1898, Sir Thomas Sanderson, the then PUS, was much upset when he found the whole Office was 'pervaded with a smell of onions ... so thick one could cut it with a knife', and the Chief Clerk was required to issue instructions that 'cooking in the Office must be of a kind that does not poison the whole place'.[12] But the servants themselves had good reason to complain. By 1894 the Foreign Office's permanent domestic servants and their extended families totalled thirty-six – a fact which came to light when, following an outbreak of diphtheria, the local medical officer pronounced that the basement rooms occupied by the hall porter and his family would have contravened the Public Health Act had the Foreign Office not been government property.[13] Clearly, even within thirty years of its construction, the building was not considered a salubrious establishment.

Overcrowding soon spread above ground level. After the outbreak of war in 1914, Foreign Office departments expanded in size and number, and additional personnel had to be fitted into ever more confined spaces. Clerical and typing staff were squeezed into a sagging roof-top structure, the Contraband Department occupied the state reception rooms, registry files were stored in the corridors, and a hut was constructed in the courtyard to accommodate the new Cables and Wireless Section. None of this could have enhanced what in 1902 Lord Lansdowne, Queen Victoria's last Foreign Secretary, had damned as the 'hideous Victorian decoration of the F.O.'[14] Nor did it offer any solution to the Foreign Office's long-term accommodation needs. Post-war retrenchment there was, but diplomacy remained a growth industry, and in 1924 the Office of Works sanctioned the extension of the third floor by the addition of a mansard roof.[15] Meanwhile, while the increased use of the telephone may have facilitated speedier communications, it also raised noise levels and impeded concentration in the rooms into which junior staff were crammed.

The Second World War simply exacerbated these problems. The state rooms, renamed the Locarno Suite, were adapted to the needs of the Ciphering Department, and additional property was acquired: the Library and Archives Department was removed to the Old Stationery Office and the Establishment and Finance Department was relocated in Lansdowne House. The end of hostilities brought no peace dividend and space remained at a premium. The end of Empire did, however, afford scope for expansion in Whitehall. The Old Public Offices (OPO), the present Main Building, were in 1945 still occupied by four other departments of state: the India Office, the Colonial Office, the Home Office and the Local Government Board. Indian independence in 1947 allowed the Foreign Office to absorb the accommodation of its former southern neighbour, and prefabricated huts erected in the India Office courtyard, the Durbar Court, provided further space for personnel. The Colonial Office also moved out to make way for the Commonwealth Relations Office and, following the merger of these two departments in 1966 into the Commonwealth Office, a single Foreign and Commonwealth Office was established in 1968. By then the Home Office was the only other occupant of the OPO, but FCO staff were housed in eleven other buildings scattered about central London.

It had long since become apparent to politicians and diplomats alike that drastic measures were required to improve office accommodation. One overseas visitor wrote to *The Times* in June 1946 to protest at the 'slovenly squalor' of the entrance hall, 'dimly lit by a single naked bulb, littered with packing cases, dispatch boxes, and cups of tea', and at the 'squalid' room occupied by the News Department, its floor without carpets, its windows without curtains, its otherwise bare walls rendered in a 'sickly green distemper', and its furniture consisting of an iron bed with a few grubby blankets and some decrepit desks and chairs. 'The acoustics in this large high-ceilinged room are', he added, 'such that if two of the full complement of four Foreign Office officials are talking at the same time – not to mention the unceasing din of telephone bells – it is quite impossible for the visitor to concentrate on what he is being told'.[16] As Foreign Secretary, Ernest Bevin pressed hard for a new building, and Attlee's Cabinet agreed that Carlton House Terrace should be redeveloped so as to provide the Foreign Office with new headquarters behind the existing Nash façade. Detailed plans were prepared and, although it soon emerged that the site would be too small to house a new Foreign Office, this remained official policy for the best part of fifteen years. Alternative projects for the development of the terrace were in consequence effectively shelved, and only in 1960 did Lord Home, the then Foreign Secretary, agree to forego this option and vacate Carlton House Terrace within three years on the understanding that a definite scheme for re-accommodating the Foreign Office would be prepared and put into operation as soon as possible. Nevertheless, modernisation rather than reconstruction was at this stage the preferred government option.[17]

Modernisation, estimated to cost £2 million, was intended to include the installation of new electric wiring, a proper central heating system, and the construction of an additional storey. The space thereby provided would, nonetheless, still have been insufficient to accommodate all the home-based staff of the Foreign Office and the Commonwealth Relations Office.[18] Some within the Cabinet may have regretted the alternative solution, that of demolishing the existing building. Yet, as Lord Home's successor, R.A. Butler, concluded, 'we cannot afford to stable a white elephant in the middle of Whitehall, however sentimentally attached we may be to it',[19] and it was duly announced that the Foreign Office was to be rebuilt on its existing site. This was welcomed by officials who had witnessed a steady deterioration in their working environment and who, like Butler, hoped for a new building tailor-made to suit their requirements. That, however, was not quite how Sir Leslie Martin and Professor Colin Buchanan envisaged Whitehall's future. Commissioned in April 1964 by Geoffrey Rippon, the Minister of Public Building and Works, to report on the redevelopment of the area and related traffic problems, they completed their controversial study in the spring of the following year.[20]

Martin assumed that the Civil Service would wish to reduce its dependence on leased properties, and that the headquarters staff of government departments should, wherever possible, be located in adjacent offices. And to meet these ends he recommended the clearance of sites on the east and west sides of Whitehall to make way for new construction work, including parliamentary offices in Bridge Street, and a gallery spanning Parliament Street and linking both developments. He favoured retaining the original New Scotland Yard, known after its architect as Norman Shaw North. However, amongst the several historic buildings recommended for demolition were its later extension, Norman Shaw South, Thomas Chawner's Richmond Terrace, the Whitehall Club, the OPO, and the Government Offices Great George Street, which house the Treasury. It was important, the report argued, to recognise that administrative requirements could change rapidly and it was therefore questionable whether 'buildings tailor-made to the needs of special Departments should any longer be built'. After all, existing Whitehall buildings wasted space and did not easily lend themselves to alternative uses. The large and lofty rooms of the Foreign Office were an obvious example: only just over a third of the area it occupied was capable of being used as office space.[21]

This vision of a reconstructed Whitehall was one that might have given material meaning to later notions of joined-up government and, as such, it won critical acclaim from senior officials. But, while its implementation would almost have doubled the space available to the Foreign Office in Whitehall, the project had two drawbacks from the department's point of view: it might deprive the department of that distinct physical identity to which many diplomats were attached; and the phased redevelopment of Whitehall implied that work on a new building would have to await the reconstruction of the Bridge Street/Richmond Terrace site. Indeed, Martin specifically referred to rebuilding the Foreign Office/Commonwealth Relations Office block 'later in the 1970s', a phrase which was bound to disappoint those who had hoped that work on a new building would commence within the next five years. As Sir Paul Gore-Booth, the new PUS, recognised, the philosophy behind the proposed phasing was that if too much were attempted at once, there would be no 'decanting' space for staff whilst work was continuing on individual sites.[22] Delayed redevelopment could however mean piecemeal, or possibly no, redevelopment, especially at a time when the recently elected Labour government was reassessing its priorities. Harold Wilson may have been personally committed to shaping a Whitehall 'fit to be the powerhouse of the New Britain',[23] but some of his colleagues seemed set on dispersing its occupants to the outer reaches of old England. True, Wilson's first Foreign Secretary, Patrick Gordon-Walker, was appalled by working conditions in the Foreign Office and, in January 1965, he reminded the Prime Minister of the need for a new building.[24] Nevertheless, one of the earliest pieces of legislation promoted by George Brown's Department of Economic Affairs, the Control of Offices and Industrial Development Act, sought to limit office growth in central London. No wonder that before any decision was taken on the Martin/Buchanan report, Douglas Jay, the President of the Board of Trade, circulated a memorandum urging ministers that its implementation should be deferred so long as the act remained in force.[25]

Already in the previous autumn Sir Harold Caccia, the then PUS, had voiced his concern over the possible impact of the projected legislation on the Foreign Office, whose litter-strewn corridors he likened to the Portobello Road market on a Saturday. 'I have', he objected, 'been to a great number of Ministries of Foreign Affairs in all sorts of one-horse countries, but I would like to place it on record that I have never seen anything so degrading as this building has now become'.[26] Jay's paper provoked an even angrier outburst from Sir Saville Garner, the Permanent Secretary at the Commonwealth Relations Office and head of the newly-unified Diplomatic Service. 'After years of neglect', he asked, 'are we really going to attempt to build a better Britain, modernising our appallingly out-of-date roads and building standards and improving the amenities for our people, or are we going to content ourselves with dreary restrictions, missing our opportunities yet again, so that we become an effete and tenth-rate society?'[27] Gore-Booth was no less worried. Faced by Cabinet dithering over Martin's proposals, he delivered a diplomatic warning to Michael Stewart, Gordon-Walker's successor as Foreign Secretary. He told him that if there were any announcement which suggested 'postponing the supply of modern accommodation to the Foreign Office and the Commonwealth Relations Office, the Government might well be faced for the first time in history with a really "difficult" mood on the part of the Diplomatic Service'.[28] Seldon's 'barbarians' were evidently growing restless when on 19 July the Ministry of Public Building and Works (MPBW) finally issued a statement coupling the Foreign Office and Bridge Street sites as projects on which planning would be set in hand as soon as possible, in accord with the general principles set out by Leslie Martin. 'Arrangements for execution' were, however, to be 'made in the light of the Government's policy of restricting the growth of office employment in London'.[29]

That autumn the MPBW took matters a stage further. A memorandum of 6 October 1965 envisaged the nomination of a distinguished architect to design the new Foreign Office building, with Martin assuming overall responsibility for the co-ordination of Whitehall redevelopment.[30] Further progress remained, however, dependent on the construction of a new Home Office on the opposite side of Whitehall, and could only then begin after staff had been moved into the Old Admiralty Building, a property which, it was assumed, was about to become surplus to Ministry of Defence requirements. An accompanying timetable foresaw the clearance of the Bridge Street/Richmond Terrace site beginning in January 1969, and the demolition of Main Building by the spring of 1974.[31] But, even though this meant the office having to wait another eight years for a new building, there were already indications that this might prove too optimistic a plan. The Ministry of Defence were in no mood to remove their 'Second Eleven' from Old Admiralty Building simply to suit the Foreign Office's need for temporary accommodation.[32] And on 5 November, at a conference hosted by the Civic Trust and chaired by the former Commonwealth Relations Secretary, Duncan Sandys, there were calls for a public enquiry into Whitehall redevelopment and considerable vocal opposition to any idea of demolishing the Foreign Office building. In these circumstances senior officials floated the idea that the Foreign Office should have priority over the Home Office in occupying any new buildings constructed on Bridge Street. This was hardly practical politics, as Home Office mandarins had long been working on the assumption that their new building would allow them to concentrate all their outlying departments in Whitehall. It could therefore have come as no surprise that, in the words of one Foreign Office official, the Home Office 'cut up very rough' on learning of the suggestion. Its Permanent Secretary protested that his department had been in Whitehall since the eighteenth century, and its officials would not even discuss relocation elsewhere unless specifically instructed by ministers.[33]

The timetable remained in place. But the vision of a new Foreign Office building, forecast for the mid-1970s, 'shone only fleetingly', and was soon obscured by a bureaucratic haze.[34] George Brown, Foreign Secretary 1966–68, echoed the complaints of his predecessors. He found the building 'downright inconvenient, ugly and shabby' with people still working 'in what must have been ... intended to be cupboards'.[35] Economic and financial problems were, however, to place severe constraints on government spending in the late 1960s, and targets for Whitehall redevelopment began to slip. In the words of a Deputy Under-Secretary at the MPBW, the office could 'expect to be in its present buildings for at least a decade and probably longer'.[36] The prevailing mood of uncertainty with regard to future accommodation prompted Michael Stewart, soon to become the first Foreign and Commonwealth Secretary, to write to the MPBW on 20 May 1968 to press for a substantial uplift in the accommodation his department would have to occupy in the longer period. The ministry's response was not encouraging. It rejected proposals which included an extensive programme of redecoration, an overhaul of the existing central heating system, the replacement of 350 open solid-fuel fires, the updating of gas and water mains, and the renovation of an overworked and overloaded electric wiring system. Such expenditure, it contended, could not be justified because of the anticipated short lifespan of the building, and it would only agree to redecoration on a piecemeal basis.[37] The FCO responded by resorting to secret diplomacy. Contact was made with lower-grade officials, known to be sympathetic to its plight, and provision for rewiring and new lighting were inserted as maintenance items in plans otherwise dealing with redecoration. Unfortunately, the subterfuge was spotted and on 12 December 1968 the MPBW pronounced against a 'succession of ad hoc improvements' amounting to a full scheme.[38]

That there was a dire need to rescue the FCO from the incommodious conditions in which its officials were expected to work was forcefully stated in a minute drafted only a fortnight later by Donal McCarthy, the newly-appointed head of the Arabian Department.

> We are [McCarthy noted] enjoined to develop a modern image, to be numerate, to approach present-day problems with up-to-date outlook, to improve our managerial techniques, and generally to be (and to be seen to be) with it. I submit that we cannot be really efficient, and certainly seem to the public to be so, if we cannot do something drastic about the conditions in the main building ...
>
> No outside visitor coming deeper into this building than the main entrance, hall and stairway can escape the first impression that the place is tatty, physically dirty and lacking in facilities ... Old cupboards, packages, odd bits of furniture and junk lie around odd places at all times. The sofas on which visitors have to sit in the corridors are often covered in dust

(often broken down). The lifts are often few and inoperative. Most of the lavatories, even when redecorated, are ancient, unreliable and unsalubrious. When the south-west men's lavatory on the second floor of King Charles Street was blocked some weeks ago, the only action taken for a full week was a crude notice proclaiming 'out of use'. Half the rooms are freezing cold if they are not centrally heated (and far from all are centrally heated). If one has a fire instead of central heating, it is often quite a job to get the coal, or the wood, or the fire-lighters; and whether there is to be one at all is a matter of the calendar rather than the temperature ...

The recent process of moving has called attention to shortcomings which we are all conscious of but tend to forget through sheer habit. When I took over my present room, I found months if not years of accumulated dirt behind the telephone's scrambler equipment, and about 1/4″ deep of damp dust which had been hidden by a readily liftable clock on the mantelpiece. The walls were streaked with mud because condensation had descended over picture rails which had not been dusted for months or perhaps years ... I started to move my desk to connect it with the telephone (I was not immediately given the opportunity to site the telephone first) but hastily replaced it when I found that it covered a gaping hole in the carpet, plus another accumulation of dirt.[39]

As was generally recognised in the FCO, there would probably have been more complaints of this kind had it not been for the fact that diplomatic postings in London rarely lasted more than three years. McCarthy's lament was nonetheless welcomed by Gore-Booth, not least because it would assist him in his efforts to persuade the MPBW that Main Building, though under 'condemnation', still warranted minimum renovation. Its sad state was impressed on Sir Michael Cary, the ministry's Permanent Secretary, when on 24 January 1969 he and Gore-Booth, accompanied by Sir Denis Greenhill, his successor designate, toured the building. A programme of redecoration and repair was subsequently agreed. Even this, however, was delayed by the reluctance of Cary's staff to fund accompanying engineering and electrical work.[40] Moreover, while the government remained committed to constructing a new Home Office and the redevelopment of the eastern side of Whitehall, little or no progress was made with planning for a new FCO.[41]

Help was at hand in the shape of Sir Val Duncan's Review Committee on Overseas Representation. The committee's 1969 report is remembered by many for the drastic staff cuts, and consequent early retirements, imposed on the Diplomatic Service after its publication. But the committee also recommended the rebuilding of the FCO 'on modern lines as soon as possible', so as to allow the FCO to 'centralise its London staff ... and to make substantial savings of time and money'. In support of this the committee argued that the FCO in London currently employed 3,050 staff in no less than seventeen buildings and that it would be far more efficient for most London-based staff to be accommodated in one building. 'There is', its report continued, 'no case in our view for perpetuating the present building on aesthetic grounds (which is not the subject of universal agreement), when the accommodation is manifestly unbusinesslike for the conduct of a great Ministry of State ... The present inadequacies of the building cannot be conducive to efficiency, not withstanding the ingenuity of the Foreign and Commonwealth Office in mastering these difficulties'. By contrast, a modern office fitted with the latest communications equipment could reduce running costs by £1.3 million annually. Rented accommodation elsewhere in London could be dispensed with, and even with a capital outlay of approximately £10 million for a reconstructed Main Building, the committee estimated there would be a possible saving to the Exchequer of £1 million per annum.[42]

These recommendations reflected current thinking in the FCO. They were not sufficient to persuade others of the pressing need for new accommodation. There was still concern, evinced particularly by the Royal Fine Arts Commission, over the future of Gilbert Scott's façade, and the local authorities were reluctant to consider the relocation of 2,000 civil servants to an area which was already suffering from acute traffic problems. Nevertheless, on 28 August 1969 the inter-departmental Whitehall Redevelopment Policy Committee took what the FCO's representative subsequently described as a 'small step forward into the 1980s' when it agreed that in consultation with other bodies the FCO should seek to assess its probable staff size in the mid-1970s and identify their special requirements.[43] Planning for the construction of a new Home Office adjacent to the Ministry of Defence was in any case well advanced. Both the Royal Fine Arts Commission and Westminster City Council had approved the project, and Parliament had agreed to the building of new offices on Bridge Street. The Home Affairs Committee recognised that Richmond Terrace and Norman Shaw Buildings North and South would have to be demolished, and John Silkin, then Minister for Public Building and Works, evidently felt no qualms about the removal of 'nondescript' structures which he assumed would 'not be missed'.[44]

Silkin could hardly have been more mistaken. When in December 1969 drawings and a model of the proposed redevelopment of the Bridge Street/Richmond Terrace area were exhibited, first to Parliament and then to the general public, his officials were surprised by the depth of opposition to the clearance of the site. The Victorian Society and other preservationist groups were predictably outraged. True, while there were over 4,000 visitors to the exhibition, no more than 350 letters of comment were received. But half of these favoured the preservation of the existing buildings and a further 110 pressed for a public enquiry. Anthony Crosland, the Secretary of State for Local Government and Regional Planning, felt the government would be ill-advised to resist this demand,

and Tony Greenwood, the Minister for Housing, thought that for the government to proceed without an enquiry would be to set a very poor example to local authorities and private developers. Silkin reluctantly conceded the point,[45] and on 14 May 1970 Crosland announced that Harold Willis QC was to chair an enquiry, which, while accepting the objectives of the Martin plan, was to hear and report on objections to the planned redevelopment of the Bridge Street/Richmond Terrace site. Its hearings were due to begin in Church House, Westminster, on 13 July.[46]

Although the Willis enquiry's remit did not cover the proposed new FCO building, it obviously had a bearing on the matter. Quite apart from the fact that the FCO's rebuilding fell into the second phase of Whitehall redevelopment, the Home Secretary and 400 or so of his staff would have to be re-accommodated before any work could commence. It was also apparent that proposals for rebuilding the FCO were likely to run into similar opposition from a growing conservationist lobby. This was not, however, allowed to impede planning for a new building and in the spring of 1970 an Office working party began upgrading a list of basic assumptions first prepared six years before.[47] A lively debate ensued, particularly at Assistant Under-Secretary level, and a draft of the revised paper was ready for Office circulation in May. It emphasised that because the FCO must remain in close proximity to Downing Street and the centre of machinery of government, it should be established that the existing site must be retained *in toto*; that all FCO departments should be accommodated under one roof, along with the Ministry of Overseas Development and any other government department primarily interested in overseas affairs; and that, given the FCO's representational functions, the new building should in appearance and design enhance HMG's prestige and 'emerge favourably from a comparison with any other Ministry of Foreign Affairs in the world'. Account was also to be taken of advances in communications procedures, both external and internal, the effects of computerisation and the introduction of more advanced aids in the dissemination of information and papers; there must be 'expansion joints' throughout the building to allow for future changes without the wholesale reallocation of rooms; and in this context thought would have to be given to '"open office planning", bearing in mind the special aspects of security and the unique needs of the Diplomatic Service Headquarters'. And, unless satisfactory arrangements had already been made for the establishment of a governmental conference centre in Whitehall or elsewhere, provision should be made in the new FCO building for large-scale conferences.[48]

The MPBW queried only one aspect of the revised paper. Its officials wondered whether it would be physically possible to accommodate the FCO's latest requirements on the existing site.[49] The same point was made by Cyril Lovitt, the outgoing chairman of the Accommodation sub-Committee of the Diplomatic Service Whitley Council. In a letter to Frank Waters, head of the Office Supply and Services Department, he explained that the staff side disagreed strongly with the suggestion that the present site should necessarily be retained for the new FCO. While they accepted that any new building should be within the Whitehall/Westminster area, they regarded it as being 'totally unrealistic to make the assumption that the present building [would] in fact be demolished within the foreseeable future'. However, like the Duncan Committee, they regarded the very early provision of a new building in the interests of efficiency and morale as being so important that urgent consideration should be given to any alternative site on which it could be constructed quickly. In this respect the staff side was possibly more in touch with public thinking than management. Yet, as Waters replied to Lovitt's successor, there was only one vacant plot in the Whitehall area that might be worth consideration. It was the space near Westminster Central Hall where once it had been intended to construct a new Colonial Office, but which was currently used as a National Car Park and upon which it was planned to build the new government conference centre. 'Assuming', he wrote, 'as we all do that, until the seat of Government moves to say Windsor or Windermere the F. and C.O. must be contained within the Whitehall/Westminster area, then a new home cannot be envisaged in either practical or architectural isolation within such geographical limits'. And while he had no illusions about the hazards of timetables, he felt that the FCO could lose more than it might ultimately gain by shifting its united concentration from the problem of rebuilding *in situ*.[50]

Waters still believed a new building could be ready by 1980. Yet, as he was also aware, that must ultimately depend on Parliament, and the Conservative government which emerged from the General Election in June which seemed more likely than its predecessor to lean towards the conservationist cause. The Prime Minister, Edward Heath, wanted to take a 'fresh look' at Whitehall redevelopment, and Lord Jellicoe, who as Lord Privy Seal was responsible for the Civil Service Department, suggested deferring the Willis enquiry in order to allow ministers more time in which to consider existing schemes on their merits.[51] As for the FCO, Sir Alec Douglas-Home, who returned there as Secretary of State, personally favoured the notion of rebuilding within the existing façade 'making use of all the present wasted space in the courtyard',[52] and Julian Amery, Silkin's successor at the MPBW, held similar views. Indeed, almost eighteen months later Amery was to write to Douglas-Home warning him that there would be a 'public outcry' if it were proposed to destroy the historic parts of the FCO building and its Whitehall frontage, and he urged the retention of the 'Locarno Suite, the Grand Staircase and areas to the West'. Concerned also lest the India Office courtyard should disappear in any reconstruction, he further suggested that once Britain's entry into the European Community was complete the government would have an 'even greater need for suitable places for entertainment'.[53] The Durbar Court, which had been regarded as a tribute to empire, would thus serve

Britain's revived European role. Amery nonetheless felt in July 1970 that the government should permit the Willis enquiry to proceed, whilst making it clear that they were not in any way committed to the present redevelopment plans. He advised Heath that if, as he thought likely, the enquiry's findings substantially supported current development proposals, 'we should be able to start work on the project three months after the date on which the final decision is reached'. This was doubtless good news to Reginald Maudling, the new Home Secretary, who considered the accommodation situation of his department 'so serious and so detrimental to efficiency' that they must push ahead with a modern building for their headquarters staff.[54]

On 8 July Heath agreed that the Willis enquiry should proceed, but he insisted that Home Office witnesses 'avoid saying that the scheme under examination [was] the only way of meeting their needs or implying reluctance to consider other possible ways of doing so'.[55] This reservation carried implications which alarmed FCO officials, particularly Oliver Wright, who in May 1970 had been appointed Chief of Administration. Wright had since reverted to calling himself Chief Clerk, but his devotion to nineteenth-century offices did not extend to nineteenth-century buildings. Worried by the prospect of more delay, he explained in a minute to Douglas-Home of 9 July that if the preservationists were to have their way with regard to the Bridge Street/Richmond Terrace site, the FCO would be back where it was when he was last Foreign Secretary.[56] In a letter which Douglas-Home sent to Amery on 28 July, words were not minced. 'When I first became Foreign Secretary ten years ago', the letter stated, 'I found the Foreign Office building inefficient, inflexible and dirty and the prospect of a new building at least ten years away. Coming back as Foreign and Commonwealth Secretary ten years later, I find the Office almost equally inefficient, inflexible and dirty and a new Foreign Office building still not less than ten years away'. But Wright was looking for more than just a renewed commitment to rehousing the FCO. The present building was, he reckoned, 'with certain exceptions, a pretty average disgrace for a major department of state and particularly one with a major representational role vis-à-vis foreign governments'.[57]

Greenhill agreed that if the FCO were going to have to wait until the 1980s for a new building, then 'something drastic must be done'.[58] And Douglas-Home's letter spelt out what immediate improvements were required to make the present building tolerable by modern standards: that is, additional interview and waiting rooms; additional working spaces; improved toilet, lavatory and changing facilities; a thorough external and internal cleaning operation, redecoration and refurnishing; and additional and proximate office space in Great George Street. Douglas-Home was also persuaded to repeat Gore-Booth's tactic of an Office walk-about, but this time at ministerial level, and on the evening of 31 July he and Amery toured the building. The visit, like the previous one, was designed to show off the worst aspects of the FCO's accommodation. Wright was especially anxious that the two ministers should see a 'selection of the filthier lavatories'. 'I am told', he noted, 'the one near the canteen in the basement is particularly revolting'.[59] The itinerary and accompanying speaking-notes prepared by Waters provided ample scope for demonstrating the shortcomings of the building. They might have been prepared by an estate agent determined to undersell the property of a difficult client. 'From the 1st floor, Downing Street West Section of the corridor', the notes began, 'the very lofty rooms can be seen illustrative of the enormous waste of space overhead including that of the Locarno complex, seen from the 1st floor level of the Grand Staircase, and at the same time the very confined space in which the Deputy Under Secretary's PA in Room 39A has to work and the inefficient accommodation arrangements for the departmental ladies in Room 68'. The third floor of King Charles Street was likewise intended to reveal 'the gas fitters who have set up a kind of factory in the corridor', and its second floor was to show the 'untidy, as yet undecorated corridor at the eastern end ... with festoons of wires and cables; the unsightliness of the Durbar Court with the dirt on the roof of the prefab and the ledges and the bad conditions for work in a registry'. The ministers were also meant to be impressed by the 'lack of success in building prefabricated huts in covered courtyards to solve the space problem' and the lavatory at Room K116 which 'in common with all other lavatories is kept clean and hygienic only with the greatest difficulty and tends to resemble a fairly unmodern public convenience'.[60]

The tour did not go quite as planned. The weather and domestic deference combined to limit its impact. As one official subsequently recalled, the tour 'did not show the building in such a bad light as we had, perhaps, expected'! Partly because it was a magnificent day, the sun shining through large windows made many of the remoter offices even look pleasant to work in: and partly also because the office keepers had got wind of the visit and tidied up the piles of rubble and equipment that normally cluttered up the corridors. The accommodation appeared deceptively more agreeable than anticipated, and left some of Amery's officials under the impression that, but for the FCO's special representational needs, it was not very much out of line with general Civil Service standards. Moreover, although Amery admitted that the FCO needed a new building, it was subsequently made known that he thought some concessions would still have to be made to the preservationists and that this would involve at least the retention of the St James's Park façade.[61] Yet, as Wright declared in an Office circular of 14 September, change there would have to be. 'For our own comfort', he observed, 'and to make a psychological break from the old "don't you know there's a war on" attitude, we want to make more space, particularly in registries and typing pools, restore a couple of vanished lifts, improve the lavatories and make some changing rooms for the use of staff and their wives'.[62] Not all such improvements were universally welcomed. Amongst those which were to have priority was

the 'provision of modern toilets for VIP use in strategic areas of the buildings'
specifically intended for foreign dignatories and other visitors. But this was
condemned by John Wilson, head of West African Department, as 'undesirable'.
'The general consensus of opinion within this Department', he objected, 'is that
the provision of "V.I.P. Toilets" is undemocratic'.[63] E.D. Morel could surely never
have dreamt how deeply the spirit of democratic control would one day penetrate
the inner sancta of the office.

More worrying from Wright's point of view was the news that reached him
in October that Amery, now Minister of Construction and Housing, was
contemplating offering the FCO a major upgrade of its present
accommodation and more space in Great George Street in return for its
abandoning all talk of a new building for another ten years. Given that further
delays were likely in planning a new building, there was perhaps something to
be said for accepting this. But as one of Wright's colleagues put it, there was
also the danger that the FCO would thereby abandon its responsibilities in
return for a 'pot of paint'.[64] What Amery had in mind was finally made clear in
a letter to Douglas-Home of 18 November. In this he conceded that ideally
they should aim at providing the FCO with a new building, but that, given
preservationist demands, this would probably mean having to construct it
within the existing façades. This would result in considerable dislocation and,
'worse still', it would cost an estimated £15.5 million. There were two
alternatives: a major face lift, which would include the restoration of the
Locarno Suite and the Durbar Court as well as a new central-heating system, at
a total estimated cost of £1.5 million; and a minor face lift, without new central
heating, at a cost of £700,000. It was an offer that Wright had no doubt the
FCO must reject. On 26 November he explained in a minute to Greenhill that
there was a danger of Amery and Douglas-Home being at cross-purposes.

> Mr Amery [he explained] clearly believes that Palmerston's neo-
> palladian masterpiece is a thing of beauty which should be preserved as
> a joy for ever. But what to Mr Amery is a thing of beauty is for the
> majority of those who actually have to work in it is a bureaucratic slum.
> We must therefore oppose his proposal on the grounds of – in ascending
> order of importance – amenity, economy and efficiency.[65]

Greenhill concurred and in a minute sent to Amery of 30 November Douglas-
Home insisted that the FCO must have a new building as soon as possible.
'When our general policy is to increase governmental efficiency by all possible
modern techniques', he protested, 'we shall be in danger, unless we act urgently,
of allowing the F.C.O. to become a monument to antiquated concepts and
standards'. Steps taken to improve the existing building must go ahead, but this,
he maintained, was not the principal objective. If the FCO were going to have to

be reconstructed within the existing façades, then it would be better to look for a site elsewhere.[66]

This was more a diplomatic ploy than a realistic option. But Willis's report, a copy of which was delivered to the newly-formed Department of the Environment on 9 December,[67] seemed to reinforce the view that it was one the FCO must pursue. It urged the retention of Norman Shaw Building North and the façade of Richmond Terrace, and dismissed preservationist objections to the demolition of the Whitehall Club and Norman Shaw Building South. These recommendations, and their qualified acceptance by Peter Walker, the Secretary of State for the Environment, reopened the whole question of re-housing the Home Office on the eastern side of Whitehall.[68] They threatened to deny the Home Office the single building in which it wanted to concentrate its 4,000 London-based staff and could thereby retard FCO plans for rebuilding on the existing site. Delay was also likely to mean that the FCO would lose the decanting space due to become available in 1976 when the Civil Service Department, the latest occupant of Old Admiralty Building, moved to premises under construction at Queen Anne's Gate.[69] The FCO might then have to wait until the mid-1980s before there was any chance of its being re-accommodated. Wright's reaction was predictable. 'The Report', he complained in a submission of 2 March 1971, 'is a typical British compromise. Nobody gets everything that they want: and progress is effectively blocked'. Once again the FCO was back at square one, and once again the preservationists had won.

> Of course [Wright conceded] aesthetics must play a part in the redevelopment of so central an area of London as Whitehall; but what is so distressing about the nature of the objections is that the objectors' case is almost solely based on considerations of beauty and almost no thought at all is given to the conditions in which people work . . . Unless it is thought that all modern British architects are incompetent (and this it must be admitted, is a perfectly tenable assumption) then it ought to be possible to produce modern efficient buildings that are also pleasant to look at.[70]

Yet there was little the FCO could do beyond pressing the urgency of their case upon the Department of the Environment. Douglas-Home, though personally reluctant to consider relocation,[71] wrote to Walker on 23 March suggesting that their officials 'get down to the task of examining possible new sites' for a new building on the assumption that this at least would remove an alibi for inaction.[72]

Walker was hardly in need of an alibi. Where Whitehall redevelopment was concerned his department's attention was focused, not on the FCO, but on the Willis report and its implications. The nub of the problem was that, while the report's implementation would pose no serious obstacle to the construction of the proposed parliamentary offices, the retention of Norman Shaw North and

Richmond Terrace would reduce by between a quarter and a half the number of civil servants who could be employed on the site. It could also, according to Treasury estimates, add more than £20 million to the cost of rehousing the Home Office. Given these figures it is not surprising that there emerged a rough and ready alliance among the Home Office, the Treasury and the FCO in opposition to the Willis recommendations and their environmental backers. On 15 July ministers meeting in the Ministerial Committee on Regional Policy and the Environment decided that further information was required, particularly regarding costs, and the matter was subsequently referred to an interdepartmental Working Group.[73] Much of its work was concerned with assessing and defining the comparative costs of various options for redeveloping the site. But on 19 October, before there had been any ministerial discussion of its findings, Walker circulated a memorandum restating the largely political case for accepting a modified version of the Willis report. He contended that the full redevelopment of the site would raise the number of civil servants employed in Whitehall beyond the limits previously set by the Prime Minister; that no government had ever previously demolished a Grade I listed building such as the Norman Shaw North; that he had been hard on proposed vandalism by private developers, and must be seen to be no less strict with government departments; and that the Working Group's financial calculations were at fault since they failed fully to take into account the relative cheapness of sites outside the Whitehall area.[74]

In the eyes of FCO officials these arguments were themselves seriously flawed. Walker's paper gave no weight to increased efficiency resulting from the concentration of government departments in single buildings, and included within the projected increased number of civil servants in Whitehall 1,000 FCO staff currently accommodated in Petty France and Regent Street, which lay only just outside the area defined as central London. But the FCO's primary interest in the tussle between Walker and the Working Group related to the effect it might have on the departure of the Home Office from Main Building.[75] Already the evident strength of the preservationist lobby and Walker's own conservationist inclinations had led Wright, albeit reluctantly, to conclude that any rebuild of the FCO would have to be within the existing façades: after all if the government were to insist on retaining Norman Shaw North, it was unlikely to permit the demolition of another Grade I-listed building in Whitehall. 'I think', Wright confessed, 'we shall have to settle for something within the present four walls, simply on the grounds that it would be better than nothing, or rather, like Munich, inevitable'. Wright nevertheless continued to argue that what the FCO really required was a wholly new custom-built structure on its existing site: the present building was 'straining against the upper limits of adaptability' and when, as was planned, the FCO went over to computers for message switching and records there simply would not be room for the new machinery. Whilst a new building would house

4,000 people at a cost of £3,000 per head, 'any spatchcocked affair would house only 2,400 at a cost of £7,000 to £8,000 a head', leaving non-diplomatic staff to be accommodated elsewhere. It would not be able to offer the amenities, the restaurant facilities, shopping and parking that modern office workers deserved, and it would probably only work if the FCO were prepared to accept an as yet unspecified amount of open-planning.[76]

During the 1970s open-planned offices were regarded by some senior civil servants as a way of making more flexible and more economic use of available work space. The notion was not immediately appealing to officials who already considered their room space inadequate, and one of whose prime complaints was the difficulty in finding rooms in which to engage visitors in private conversation. Nevertheless, since the FCO based its case for a new building on the need to modernise, it could hardly ignore the latest bureaucratic fashions. An experimental open-plan office had been established at Kew, and on 6 May 1971 Wright and his colleagues went to examine what was on display. They were impressed. According to William Sharpe, Deputy Head of Accommodation and Services Department, the open-plan concept offered 'distinct possibilities for incorporation in a new FCO building'. He even made enquiries of the Department of the Environment as to what sort of office could be created with about forty per cent open-planning within the existing façades.[77] It had previously been assumed that all staff in economic and political departments required maximum privacy for good working and security; now it seemed worth considering whether with proper office conditions many of these departments could operate with equal success in 'open space or group spaces'. There were obvious drawbacks. 'It must', Sharpe noted, 'be remembered ... that in these Departments a large amount of telephoning and dictation goes on and also that in open space conditions there would be a need for interview and small meeting rooms'.[78] Still, by July 1971 the Department of the Environment, which was engaged in wide-ranging discussions on the accommodation needs of the FCO, appears to have concluded that a large proportion of the staff of the FCO's operational departments would have open plan offices with only departmental heads and their assistants having separate rooms.[79] Evidently, within the context of rebuilding the FCO such abstractions as open diplomacy and policy planning were acquiring new and physical connotations.

This, however, remained an essentially academic debate in the absence of any firm government decision on whether Main Building was to be wholly or partially reconstructed. Throughout the summer and well into the autumn of 1971 the Working Group on Whitehall redevelopment continued to wrestle with the relative costs involved in implementing Willis's recommendations, and as was pointed out by the appropriately named Mr Bunker, the Home Office's representative on the group, if room were not found on the Bridge Street/Richmond Terrace site for 3,100 of his department's staff, the Home

Office would not be moving from its present quarters, and if this delayed FCO redevelopment 'that would be a regrettable consequence of Ministerial yielding to pressure'.[80] There was meanwhile little that the FCO could do to move matters along, beyond an appeal to reason and fair play. Shortly before a ministerial meeting on Whitehall redevelopment, scheduled for 3 November, Wright recited to FCO minister, Joseph Godber, a by now familiar case. The FCO, he reminded Godber, was currently implementing those parts of the Duncan Report which had received ministerial sanction, even though it involved 'sacking a good number of people who joined the Service in an expectation of a full career until 60'.

> It could [he added] create a rather deplorable impression in the minds of government servants if there were too great a contrast between the economies imposed on the manpower of the Service, in the interests of economy and despite the impact in human terms, and a decision on the Willis Report which apparently disregarded cogent reasons of economy in favour of bricks and mortar.

Ministers would in short be discussing the Willis Report 'in the context of their reputation as good employers'.[81]

The ministerial meeting predictably resolved nothing. Doubts were expressed about the bases on which the costs of Whitehall redevelopment had been calculated and the matter was referred back to the Working Group.[82] This, however, did not deter Amery from writing to Douglas-Home on 24 November to express his department's view that 2,500 FCO staff could easily be accommodated in a building constructed within the existing façades, that work on this could start in 1977, and that it could be completed at a cost only £2 million higher than that of a new building on a cleared site.[83] With some justice Maudling protested that Amery's letter was 'premature'. It took no account of the absence of any agreement on the rehousing of the Home Office, and Maurice Macmillan, the Chief Secretary to the Treasury, insisted that before anything was decided about the FCO building the various options must be costed in detail.[84] Disappointed at the prospect of having to make do with a hybrid building which would provide them with less than they needed and less than they had been promised, FCO officials likewise reminded Douglas-Home of the dangers of buying a pig in a poke. They nonetheless recommended conditional acceptance of the offer on the grounds that in the circumstances it was the best they were likely to obtain. As Douglas-Home explained to Amery in a letter of 7 December, he would agree to his terms only if there were no slippage in the timetable, if he were first satisfied that the architects' feasibility studies offered 'real improvements in efficiency and amenity', and on the assumption that the FCO would be 'sole occupants of the reconstructed building'.[85]

With this exchange in mind, Wright responded favourably to a suggestion from the former PUS, Lord Gore-Booth, that he should ask a question in the House of Lords about progress with the FCO building. He thought the moment propitious: Gore-Booth's intervention 'might prod Ministers to make up their minds' and, properly steered, the FCO could use it 'both to get the decision of principle speeded up about the building itself and also, by way of supplementary, get a bit more steam about making the present building habitable'.[86] Unfortunately, from the FCO's point of view, Lord Sandford, the Parliamentary Under-Secretary of State for the Environment, was reluctant either to admit that the matter was 'urgent' or to commit his department to reconstruction in the second half of the 1970s.[87] In reply to the question put by Gore-Booth on 14 December as to what steps HMG were taking to provide the FCO with accommodation 'more consistent with the requirements of modern business practice', he simply explained that Walker was aware that much more needed to be done and that he was considering with Douglas-Home 'how best to proceed in the longer term'. And after assuring the Lords that a programme designed to improve working conditions was being implemented, he added that he was not yet in a position to make any further statement. This was the signal for other peers with diplomatic backgrounds to join the fray. Lord Sherfield who, as Roger Makins, had spent four of his under-secretarial years in what he described as a 'plasterboard "rabbit hutch"' in the Foreign Office, asked whether its 'abolition' would be included in the 'minor works' foreseen by Sandford? For Lord Gladwyn this was going too far. 'My Lords', he enquired, 'is the noble Lord aware that the "rabbit hutch" ... was constructed by me at the end of the war, and was at least greatly superior to the attic in which I worked for two years previously?' In any reconstruction of the FCO he considered it best to think in terms of a headquarters next door to Downing Street, and 'the great bulk of the departments being housed, not in squalor, but in comparative squalor ... somewhere in the suburbs'.[88]

Former colleagues must have hoped this last remark was meant in jest. But, in any event, ministerial indecision over Whitehall redevelopment was itself, as Walker later admitted, fast becoming a joke 'in environmental circles',[89] and another eleven months were to pass before on 20 November 1972 the government announced to Parliament that it intended to preserve the external façades of the OPO together with the fine interiors of the north–west corner of the building, and that proposals would be put to the local planning authorities to reconstruct the remainder so as to provide modern office accommodation.[90] Then on 24 May 1973, Parliament was further informed that the Home Office would be quitting Whitehall and that it would be accommodated in the building at Queen Anne's Gate previously intended for the Civil Service Department.[91] This, however, was by no means the end of the story. The government's announcement on the FCO building still left open the prospect of substantial reconstruction, with new offices emerging within the main courtyard, and behind all but the façades of the old Foreign Office wing. At an estimated cost of about £22 million almost all the FCO's headquarters staff of 3,000 might thereby still be accommodated in one building. But for diplomats the past, more than adequately represented by the Victorian Society, remained a formidable opponent with whom there seemed little chance of their ever being able to achieve a satisfactory *modus vivendi*. Ten years earlier the society had demanded no more than the preservation of the fine rooms and the façades, yet by August 1973 they were insisting that they would challenge any decision to infill the central courtyard, and that all major features of the building must be retained.[92] They were, they claimed, 'shocked' that the FCO's activities should be allowed to take precedence over 'aesthetic requirements'.[93]

The Conservatives yielded no further to conservationist pressures, and the Labour government, formed after the General Election of February 1974, reaffirmed its predecessor's commitment to rebuilding within the existing façades. There was, however, in a statement by Crosland, now Environment Secretary, a hint of future concessions to Victoriana. He told Parliament on 17 December 1974 that a firm of architects had been commissioned to undertake a study to develop and cost the various options for accommodating the FCO 'efficiently in their traditional home, including the practicability of preserving other fine features of the building'.[94] This could be taken as implying the preservation not only of the Durbar Court and the adjacent fine rooms of the former India Office, but also, more ominously, the central courtyard. It was, however, economics rather than aesthetics which finally determined the outcome of this protracted debate. Cuts in government expenditure and other demands on the budget of the newly-established Property Services Agency, including money required for the refurbishment of Richmond Terrace and the construction of a new government conference centre on Broad Sanctuary, meant that by 1976 there were no funds available to cover the costs of any of the proposed architects' options for rebuilding the FCO. Instead, the government decided in May 1976 to spend £3 million over three to four years on a programme of improvement and modernisation. The FCO had in fact to wait another quarter of a century before most of its London-based staff could be housed in two renovated and proximate buildings in Whitehall.[95]

Few now would regret the decision to renovate. Many would consider it incredible that any government could have contemplated the destruction of sumptuous Victorian interiors and the loss of the impressive view of the FCO from across St James's Park. Gilbert Scott's building may not be an architectural masterpiece, but it is an historical monument and a significant feature of the landscape of central London. From an artistic point of view it would be difficult to disagree with Susan Foreman's verdict on plans to redevelop Whitehall in the 1960s. She wrote: 'We know from the history of the then contemporary Marsham Street Building for the Department of the Environment . . . what the fate of Whitehall property would have been. Disaster was only narrowly averted'.[96] Yet it would be inappropriate to dismiss the FCO's reconstructionalists as barbarians. Admittedly, there were barbarians in Whitehall; of that there is documentary proof. In a paper of 15 July 1970 in which he recorded the measures so far implemented in the rejuvenation of Main Building Frank Waters noted that in some of the re-equipped lavatories no sooner had new copper piping been installed than it had been dragged from the wall, and the redecorated spaces filthied: evidence, he observed, that 'vandals exist within our midst'.[97] Those, however, who favoured constructive change, those ministers and officials who preferred rebuilding to renovation, were in many respects the heirs to Victorian reformers who a century earlier had wanted new offices built to suit the needs of more rational and effective government. What was truly remarkable was not their objective, but the slow pace of decision-making in Whitehall and the way in which administrative wrangling and political sensitivities impeded not only redevelopment, but redecoration and refurbishment as well. While Harold Wilson talked of forging a new Britain in the white heat of the technological revolution, his government balked at demolishing structures erected in the age of steam. Edward Heath wanted to abandon the lame ducks of the economy, but presided over the preservation of a white elephant in Whitehall. The metaphors abound and the buildings remain, though the extent to which this has been to diplomacy's benefit or loss is still open to debate.

ACKNOWLEDGEMENTS

The opinions expressed in this paper are the author's own and should not be taken as an expression of official government policy. He is grateful to Heather Yasamee, Head of the FCO's Records and Historical Department, for drawing my attention to the files on which much of the paper is based, and to my colleagues Chris Baxter, Ann Birch and Rachel Cox for their assistance in locating other relevant sources. All references to Foreign Office (FO) or Foreign and Commonwealth Office (FCO) documents relate to materials held at the National Archives, London (formerly the Public Record Office) unless otherwise stated.

NOTES

1. FO 366/1379, XP3884/36/907, memorandum by Ashton-Gwatkin, 4 Jun. 1944.
2. See J.E. Hoare, *Embassies in the East: The Story of the British and their Embassies in China, Japan and Korea from 1859 to the Present* (London: Curzon, 1999); J.N. Ronfort and J.-D. Augarde, *À l'ombre de Pauline: La Résidence de l'Ambassadeur de Grande-Bretagne à Paris* (Paris: Éditions du Centre de Recherches Historiques, 2001).
3. I. Toplis, *The Foreign Office: An Architectural History* (London: Mansell, 1987).
4. A. Seldon, *The Foreign Office: An Illustrated History of the Place and its People* (London: Harper Collins, 2000).

5. *The Times*, 6 Nov. 2000, p.5.
6. Cited in S. Foreman, *From Palace to Power: An Illustrated History of Whitehall* (London: Sussex Academic Press, 1995), p.80.
7. Cecil Derny Highton and Partners, *The Old Public Office, Whitehall: A History of the Building Containing the India Office, the Foreign and Colonial Office, and the Home Office* (bound typescript in the FCO Library: London, 1985), pp.85–7.
8. C. Baxter and K. Hamilton, *The Permanent Under-Secretary of State: A Brief History of the Office and its Holders* (FCO Historians, History Notes No.15: London, 2002), p.7.
9. K. Hamilton, *Bertie of Thame: Edwardian Ambassador* (Woodbridge: Royal Historical Society, 1990) p.7.
10. Ibid.
11. FO 366/678, minutes by Lord Granville to Sir J. Pauncefote and by F.B. Alston (Chief Clerk) to Pauncefote, 17 and 18 Oct. 1883.
12. FO 366/760, minute by Sanderson to Sir G. Dallas, 28 Jan. 1898.
13. FO 366/760, minute by H. Hervey, 13 Mar. 1894.
14. FO 27/3695, note by Lansdowne on letter from Lord Esher, 20 Jun. 1902.
15. E. Maisel, *The Foreign Office and Foreign Policy* (Brighton: Sussex Academic Press, 1994), pp.9–10.
16. *The Times*, 11 Jun. 1946, letter to the editor from J.H. Huizinger.
17. FO 366/00340, XCA 101/1/126, note by Steel, 16 Nov. 1964.
18. Ibid.
19. FO 366/003260, XCA 100/1/7663, memorandum by Butler, 'Foreign Office Accommodation', 13 Nov. 1963.
20. L. Martin, *Whitehall: A Plan for the National Government Centre*, accompanied by C. Buchanan, *A Report on Traffic* (London: HMSO, 1965).
21. Ibid., pp.49–50.
22. FO 366/003445, DSA 10226/06/G, minute by Gore-Booth to Stewart, 28 Jun. 1965.
23. P. Hennessy, *Whitehall* (New York: The Free Press, 1989), p.81.
24. FO 366/003446, PM/65/1, Gordon-Walker to Wilson, 1 Jan. 1965.
25. FO 366/003445, DSA 10226/09/G, minute by Steel to Smart, 1 Jul. 1965.
26. FO 366/00340, XCA 100/1/126, minute by Caccia, 18 Nov. 1964.
27. FO 366/003445, DSA 10226/07/G, minute by Garner to Thomson, 1 Jul. 1965.
28. FO 366/003445, DSA 10226/11/6, minute by Gore-Booth to Thomson, 6 Jul. 1965.
29. FO 366/003445, DSA 10226/26/G, statement by Pannell, 19 Jul. 1965.
30. FO 366/003446, DSA 10227/2A, memorandum by Pannell, 6 Oct. 1965.
31. Ibid.
32. FO 366/003446, DSA 10226/4A and 8A, minute by Steel to Chief of Administration, 11 Oct. 1965, minute by Hardman to Part, 28 Oct. 1965.
33. FO 366/003446, DSA 10226/26H, 2, and 25A, minute by Crowe to Gore-Booth, 17 Nov. 1965, letter by Thomson to Pannell, 25 Nov. 1965, and letter by Cunningham to Part, 12 Nov. 1965.
34. FCO 80/2, XG 4/7, minute by Barnes to Waters, 3 Jan. 1969.
35. Foreman, *Palace to Power*, pp.162–3.
36. See note 33 above.
37. Ibid.
38. FCO 80/2, XG 4/7, minute by Newis to Larmour, 12 Dec. 1968.
39. FCO 80/2, XG 4/7, minute by McCarthy to Waters, 27 Dec. 1968.
40. FCO 80/2, XG 4/7, minute by Gore-Booth to Waters, 1 Jan. 1969, letter by Gore-Booth to Cary, 24 Jan. 1969, and minute by Waters to Larmour, 14 Feb. 1969.
41. FCO 80/3, XG 14/1, minute by Waters to Wilkinson, 30 Dec. 1969.
42. Cmd 4107, *Report of the Review Committee on Overseas Representation, 1968–1969* (London: HMSO, 1969), pp.158–9.
43. FCO 80/3, XG 14/1, minute by Waters to Stanley, 10 Sep. 1969, covering minutes of 10th meeting of Whitehall Redevelopment Policy Committee, 28 Aug. 1969.

44. FCO 80/3, XG 14/1, Silkin to Crosland, 8 Dec. 1969, enclosing draft papers for the Environmental Planning Committee and Defence and Oversea Policy Committee.
45. FCO 80/3, XG 14/1, Crosland to Silkin, 12 Jan. 1970, memorandum (an annexes) by Silkin 80/5, XG 11/1, memorandum by Greenwood (EP(70)6), 26 Jan. 1970.
46. Crosland declared that he was intending to hold a public non-statutory enquiry on 12 March 1970. See Hansard, *House of Commons Debates*, 5th series, Vol.797, col.381, and Vol.801, cols 354-5.
47. FCO 80/5, XG 11/1, minute by Waters to Wilkinson, 5 Mar. 1970. It was also agreed that the MPBW would set up a Working Party to consider the various forms of redevelopment possible on the Downing St./King Charles Street site.
48. FCO 80/5, XG 11/1, 'Basic Assumptions for Planning the New FCO Building', paper covered by minute by Waters to Alston, 14 May 1970.
49. FCO 80/5, XG 11/1, Vickers to Waters, 28 May 1970.
50. FCO 80/5, XG 11/1, minutes by Lovitt to Waters, 18 Jun. 1970, and Waters to. Davies, 24 Jun. 1970.
51. FCO 80/6, XG 11/1, minute, Simcock to Pickup, and letter by Jellicoe to Heath, 6 Jul. 1970.
52. FCO 80/6, XG 11/1, minute by Graham to Waters, 6 Jul. 1970.
53. FCO 80/12, XG 11/1, Amery to Douglas-Home, 24 Nov. 1971 and to Royle, n.d. (Nov. 1971).
54. FCO 80/6, XG 11/1, Amery to Heath, 2 Jul. 1970, and Maudling to Heath, 8 Jul. 1970.
55. FCO 80/6, XG 11/1, minute by Simcock to Pickup, 8 Jul. 1970, and letter by Heath to Maudling, n.d.
56. FCO 80/6, XG 11/1, minute by Wright to Douglas-Home, 9 Jul. 1970.
57. FCO 80/6, XG 11/1, minute by Wright to Douglas-Home, 9 Jul. 1970; FCO 80/8, XG 11/2, Douglas-Home to Amery, 28 Jul. 1970.
58. FCO 80/6, XG 11/1, note by Greenhill, 10 Jul. 1970.
59. FCO 80/8, XG 11/2, minute by Wright to Waters, 29 Jul. 1970.
60. FCO/80/2, XG 11/2, minute by Wright to Douglas-Home, 30 Jul. 1970, and attachments.
61. FCO/80/2, XG 11/2, minute by Wright to Cole, 3 Aug. 1970, minute by Barrington to Cole, 3 Aug. 1970, and minute by Stanley to Waters, 10 Aug. 1970.
62. FCO 80/6, XG 11/1, Circular 'B' 91/30, 14 Sep. 1970.
63. FCO 80/6, XG 11/1, minute by Waters to Lovitt, 4 Sep. 1970; FCO 80/8, XG 11/2, minute by Wilson to Waters, 2 Sep. 1970.
64. FCO 80/7, XG 11/1, minute by Greenhill to Wright, 27 Oct. 1970; Cole minute to Wright, 9 Nov. 1970.
65. FCO 80/8, XG 11/2, minute by Amery to Douglas-Home, 18 Nov. 1970, minute by Wright to Greenhill, 26 Nov. 1970.
66. FCO 80/8, XG 11/2, minute by Douglas-Home to Amery, 30 Nov. 1970.
67. FCO 80/8, XG 11/2, minute by Wright to Waters, 9 Dec. 1970.
68. FCO 80/11, XG 11/1, memorandum by Walker (RE(71)38), 9 Jul.1971.
69. FCO 80/11, XG 11/1, minute by Sharpe to Scott, 14 Jul. 1971.
70. FCO 80/11, XG 10/1, submission by Wright to Greenhill, 2 Mar. 1971.
71. FCO 80/11, XG 10/1, minute by Wright to Greenhill, 22 Mar. 1971.
72. FCO 80/10, XG 11/1, Douglas-Home to Walker, 23 Mar. 1971.
73. FCO 80/11, XG 11/1, Ministerial Committee on Regional Policy and the Environment (RE(71) 4th mtg.), 15 Jul. 1971.
74. FCO 80/12, XG 11/12, memorandum by Walker (GEN60(71)2), 19 Oct. 1971. In a minute of 28 September Heath had recommended that the total number of civil servants in the Whitehall area should not be allowed to rise above the then current level of 14,000, and should if possible be reduced.
75. FCO 80/12, XG 11/1, minute by Sharpe to Scott, 1 Nov. 1971.
76. FCO 80/11, XG 11/1, minute by Wright to Scott, 23 Jul. 1971.
77. FCO 80/10, XG 11/1, Wright to Cary, 11 May 1971, and Sharpe to Johnston, 12 May 1971.
78. FCO 80/10, XG 11/1, Sharpe to Johnston, 17 May 1971.
79. FCO 80/11, XG 11/1, minute by Sharpe to Scott, 8 Jul. 1971.

80. FCO 80/12, XG 11/1, minute by Scott to Sharpe, 19 Nov. 1971.
81. FCO 80/12, XG 11/1, minute by Wright, 2 Nov. 1971.
82. FCO 80/12, XG 11/1, minutes of Cabinet committee meeting (GEN.60(71) 1st meeting), 3 Nov. 1971.
83. FCO 80/12, XG 11/1, Amery to Douglas-Home, 24 Nov. 1971.
84. FCO 80/12, XG 11/1, Maudling to Amery, 1 Dec. 1971, and Macmillan to Amery, 16 Dec. 1971.
85. FCO 80/12, XG 11/1, minute by Wright to Scott, 29 Nov. 1971, and letter by Douglas-Home to Amery, 7 Dec.1971.
86. FCO 80/12, XG 11/1, minute by Wright to Scott, 26 Nov. 1971, and minute by Sharpe to Scott, 6 Dec. 1971.
87. FCO 80/12, XG 11/1, minutes between Scott and Sharpe, 13–14 Dec. 1971.
88. Hansard, *House of Lords Debates*, 5th series, Vol. 326, cols.989–92.
89. CM 37/77, DCA 4424/1, GEN 60(72)3, Working Group on the Redevelopment of RT/NSY, memorandum by Walker, 18 Jul. 1972.
90. Hansard, *House of Commons Debates*, 5th series,Vol. 846, cols 1047–58.
91. Ibid., Vol. 857, col. 149.
92. *The Victorian Society Newsletter*, Feb. 1973, p.2.
93. CM 37/77, DCA 4424/1, draft memorandum by the Department of the Environment, 24 Aug. 1973.
94. Hansard, *House of Commons Debates*, 5th series, Vol. 883, cols 435–6.
95. By 2001 FCO ministers and most home-based senior officials were located in Main Building (the former OPO) and Old Admiralty Building, Whitehall. The *Diplomatic Service List* for that year cites seven other home-based FCO addresses including Apollo House, Croydon, and Hanslope Park near Milton Keynes.
96. Foreman, *Palace to Power*, p.188.
97. FCO 80/8, XG 11/2, paper covered by minute by Waters to Wright, 15 Jul. 1970.

How Did Wilton Park Survive into the Twenty-First Century?

RICHARD LANGHORNE

Wilton Park is a unique institution. It is and always has been a part of the Foreign (and Commonwealth) Office (FCO), but its work from the beginning and through subsequent evolutions has been different in its purpose and intellectually independent from the parent body. It is located not in London but in a magnificent, peaceful, house in the Sussex downs. Its principal task is to arrange international discussions between participants invited from abroad and British representatives of government, civil society and commerce. The topics of its discussions are broad-based and long-term in their scope. National interests seldom intrude and individual, unattributed, contributions pre-dominate. The atmosphere of unconstrained debate enables a thoroughly serious assessment of the fundamental nature of global problems and stresses, actual and potential, to emerge. Thus although Wilton Park does not manage foreign policy or conduct diplomacy in any familiar way, it nonetheless plays a role both in giving a significant depth to British attitudes to the general international and global situation and in creating particular perceptions of the United Kingdom and its ways of thinking among the other members of the international community. It is not surprising therefore that there have been moments, particularly when economies have been required, when it has been easy to ask whether funds spent in either supporting or employing Wilton Park would be better used pursuing the FCO's more obvious primary functions. With that idea has also come the notion that Wilton Park might either be placed in a more purely academic environment or allowed to become a self-financing conference centre like any other. Wilton Park has escaped both fates and succeeded in maintaining its slightly unusual but highly valuable relationships with both the British government and the international community at large. It is in a way a gift from Britain to the rest of the world, a small investment but one with a very large dividend.

Although there have been differences in comparatively recent years about just how Wilton Park should be administered and financed, no concerted attempts have been made to close it down. Indeed, its home at Wiston House in Sussex has been physically improved in ways that imply a long-term future, and in a world which has come to emphasise the significance of public diplomacy its role has become easier to describe and justify. It has by no means always been so. The list of critical moments in its history is a very long one, made even longer by adding in the slightly shorter list of crises over the duties, pay and recruitment of its staff, particularly its head – whether Warden, Director or Chief Executive.

The first crisis was entirely predictable. Wilton Park was set up in 1945 at Wilton Park in Buckinghamshire in War Office accommodation and under War Office administration. This was appropriate enough since the job it was given was to run courses for German prisoners of war who were deemed likely to play a role in a future Germany. Heinz Koeppler, its progenitor and first head, resisted the phrase 're-education', though many used it, because his basic idea was not to prescribe but to reactivate ways of thinking about concepts of democracy and justice by allowing full and free discussion. If there was persuasion, it lay in the method – a distinctively British method involving free discussion – not in the materials. About this, Koeppler was both determined and dictatorial. Right at the beginning, therefore, there was an ambiguity about Wilton Park's role – could it be both gaoler and educator? – and the oddity led to comment. There would also be an obvious end to its task when prisoners of war ceased to exist, at least as far as the War Office was concerned, unless a different focus developed involving civilian participation, as indeed it did. The rehabilitation of Germany and its political system was unlikely to be achieved quickly, and, as rapidly became clear, was powerfully complicated by the onset of the Cold War. This element gave importance from an early date to the addition of German civilian participants to Wilton Park courses, and the courses eventually became purely civilian, thus allowing Wilton Park to escape into a new phase of existence. If the administration of Wilton Park lay with the War Office, the means of achieving its didactic purpose originated with a mixture of authorities: the mix derived from war-time administration, the needs of the Control Office for Germany and Austria and elements at the Foreign Office. Between 1945 and 1947 these began to coagulate at the Foreign Office, though after Sir Robert Birley became Educational Adviser to Sir Brian Robertson, C-in-C and Military Governor in Germany, he was placed above the Foreign Office's Education Department and given charge of Wilton Park from July 1947, which meant that the line of communication was between Wilton Park and Berlin.

Once Wilton Park had become a civilian organisation, the Foreign Office interest and the interest of the allied administration in Germany and Austria became paramount, and the question arose as to whether the War Office's contribution would be supplied from elsewhere. In December 1947 the War Office announced that it wanted the Wilton Park accommodation back. If the Foreign Office had decided not to step in, which it came close to doing, that would have been the end. However, despite misgivings, it was agreed to run Wilton Park for the year 1948–49 and then, as Koeppler was told, it would be closed. By this time, Wilton Park had 'alumni' – a constituency beyond the views of current officialdom in either Britain or Germany. For the first time, but emphatically not the last, Koeppler began to drum up external support, both from former prisoners of war and from the new civilian participants. Robert Birley and the British administration in Germany lent strong support, and it was then agreed to carry on until 1950, to consider agreeing to a longer period in the future and to establishing an Advisory Council. This last was done in 1949 and thus began the long and significant history of the Wilton Park Academic Council. The Treasury nonetheless would consent to one further year only if a commitment to closure in 1950 was given. The Foreign Office, fortified by pressure from Germany, fought back, and won continuation until 1951. But a complication arrived in that the War Office now finally insisted on having its property back, and if Wilton Park was to be found a new home, some suitable accommodation would have to be leased and a longer period of existence would have to be guaranteed. After pressure was put upon the Treasury, the Chancellor of the Exchequer, Hugh Gaitskell, agreed to continue funding until March 1952. This enabled the temporary leasing of Wiston House, a most agreeable and peaceful great English house in the Sussex Downs – ever thereafter to be a significant part of the effect that attending a conference there has had on many individual participants. Later on, the state of the lease from the Goring family – whether a renewal was pending or whether there were many years left – was to have important consequences for the continuation of Wilton Park.

When the government changed in 1951, Winston Churchill's new cabinet demanded economies all round, and the Treasury responded by seeking the closure of Wilton Park in 1952: 'We ought to have another shot at getting rid of this institution'. The Foreign Secretary, Anthony Eden, however, decided to keep Wilton Park running for another year while the Treasury continued to demand its closure, now in March 1953. The same thing happened in the following two years but in all three years Eden carried the day. In 1955, however, a more serious threat appeared: the Foreign Office itself decided that Anglo-German relations had changed and that the particular contribution made by Wilton Park was no longer appropriate. Moreover, the need for economy was if anything greater than hitherto, as the Foreign Secretary,

Selwyn Lloyd, explained. The only possibilities that might change the situation were either that the Germans and/or others might be persuaded to pay for it or a university take it over: both themes that were to recur (and as recently as 1992, to the author's certain knowledge).

By this time, the Foreign Office was all too aware of both the influence of the Academic Council and the significant network that Koeppler himself had created in both Britain and Germany. The decision to close Wilton Park was kept tightly under wraps until the Academic Council was told in 1956 that Wilton Park would close on 31 July 1957 – thus giving more than a year's notice to both the Germans and the staff. This attempt to be fair gave time for a major effort to save Wilton Park to develop. Large numbers of private letters to the Foreign Office were instigated, as also were public ones in the newspapers. Articles appeared in Germany and in Britain, and interventions in Parliament were arranged, much of them inspired by the Academic Council and by Koeppler himself. Out of the brouhaha, one proposition came to the surface as particularly significant. Might it be possible to create a 'new' Wilton Park, on the broad basis of serving NATO rather than just Germany or Anglo-German relations? There was theoretical provision for such a role in the Brussels Treaty, and the idea of a 'new' Wilton Park meant that the Foreign Office could still close the old one at least in formal terms. The whole argument was understandably overshadowed by the Suez Crisis and its aftermath; but it was equally true that the crisis underscored the need for strengthening all and every means for expressing the British point of view. Eventually, the combination of a potential recreation of Wilton Park and much pressure from outside caused the Foreign Office to change its position, and a fierce exchange between the Chancellor of the Exchequer and the Foreign Secretary ensued, leading to a cabinet discussion. There it was agreed to continue Wilton Park for one more year, but to subject it to an inspection by the Chancellor of the Duchy of Lancaster, Charles Hill, who was reviewing all forms of British cultural and information services. He gave approval to Wilton Park, and an extension for two years followed, then three years, then five years on three successive occasions, thus reaching 1978.

What appeared to be a pattern of continuity over twenty years was broken in 1975. The lease of Wiston House was up for renewal in 1978, and Koeppler was due to retire in 1977, carrying with him his personal weight of character, web of influence and undoubted eccentricities. Discussion began in the FCO about the cost and benefit of Wilton Park with a clear sense developing that it was time to close it down. A formidable muddle then ensued. The Academic Council and Koeppler went into action again with their respective constituencies; the government changed in 1979 with the arrival of Margaret Thatcher as Prime Minister; and an outstanding mess was made of the business of appointing a successor to Koeppler – a mess going beyond what might have been expected given the uncertainty about the future of Wilton Park. In the end an extension to 1979 was given, and a future commitment which allowed the lease to be renewed for five years until 1983.

The instincts of the new government were hostile to keeping an entity like Wilton Park within the government machine, and a major review followed in 1982, which was to recommend whether it should be closed or put into the private sector. In the event, the review recommended serious cuts at Wilton Park and altering the way the domestic side was run so as to parallel a hotel in its arrangements. The Director, Tim Slack, obtained the strong support of the Academic Council in resisting what had been suggested, and also what both he and they believed was grossly unfair treatment meted out to him personally. The fight in 1982–83 was a dramatic and highly public affair and ended with the resignation of the Director and most of the Academic Council. These were certainly the darkest moments experienced by the institution since the early 1950s.

In the end, however, the privatising instincts of the Thatcher regime eventually provided a way out. Internal semi-privatisation in the form of the creation of Executive Agencies was spreading across the Civil Service and it was eventually applied to Wilton Park. The FCO was more or less devoid of any part of its operation which could be given executive agency status. But it was clear that all ministers were expected to create as many of these agencies as possible within their departments. The FCO thought of turning the translators into an agency, but then turned to Wilton Park. It would be unlike any other agency – infinitely smaller, delivering an unquantifiable product or service – but it was just plausible, giving the Foreign Office its very own agency and the agency a potential autonomy for which it had often longed. From 1985, Wilton Park had had to make a statement of its objectives; in 1988 this was worked up into a pre-agency status document. Lengthy discussions with the Treasury then ensued, leading to the creation of an executive agency in 1991.

The new situation did not turn out quite as expected – the independence of management did not fully emerge, but additional reporting and auditing obligations did, as the then Director, Geoffrey Denton, complained. After only four years of agency status, the first five-year review asked all the same questions as had been answered in 1991 – Why did Wilton Park exist? Did its work have to be done at Wiston House, even though a 20-year lease had now been taken? The answers were reluctantly supportive, but it was also suggested that Wilton Park should no longer be financed by the FCO at all, while at the same time conforming its programme more to the wishes of FCO departments. There was an obvious difficulty for any reviewer or any other outside observer in trying to quantify the work of an institution that did not make widgets. "How many wars and crises have you prevented?" is not an answerable question. As time went on it became clear that if agency status did not much clarify the necessarily opaque role that Wilton Park had and has, it did remove the uniquely vulnerable position that it had endured as an apparent eccentricity within the FCO. Agency status has also allowed Wilton Park to diversify and increase its sources of revenue thus gaining greater financial stability. Moreover, the increasing importance of public diplomacy, which Wilton Park exemplifies, among the weapons available to states in conducting their foreign relations has given the institution today more security than it has ever before enjoyed. It is a tribute to the old idea that the provisional always survives the longest.

So why, apart from the last consideration, did Wilton Park survive? The answer is not simple. It is true that its very small scale and therefore the relatively trivial amounts of money involved, permitted, however unfairly to its staff, a hand-to-mouth existence when no one was prepared to grant anything more. In the period between the foundation and the creation of the 'new' Wilton Park in 1957, this was plainly significant. Its adaptability helped. What had started for Germans proved to be expandable to fit the needs of NATO countries and then eventually those of the members of OECD. This was chiefly because the importance of Wilton Park, as set out by Koeppler, had always been in its methods rather than its subject matter. The latter was eminently and frequently revisable, the former has remained and gives the specifically useful and specifically British element in its make-up. There are inevitable tensions inherent in an organisation which is part of the government machine but does not represent it; which is located in Britain but is, in practice, a gift from Britain to the international community; which provides a forum for the expression of British views but does not promote them, nor encourage anything except the expression of individual standpoints at its meetings; and which relies on ideas and broad interpretations rather than the technicalities of disagreement. All these things will give it appeal to different interests at different times for different purposes. It has not just had an effective constituency of its own, but it has appealed to many others – to the left for its concern with social justice, to the right for its abiding promotion of democratic freedom, to the underdeveloped world for its willingness to discuss economic fairness, to the developed world for its willingness to look at technological change, to different regions of the world for its enthusiasm for discussing regional issues, and to the military for its readiness to look at security and strategic questions.

Wilton Park has also been extraordinarily well served by the successive members of its Academic Council. Koeppler plainly intended that the Council should be the source of public and private support when push came to shove, and to the frequent exasperation of the Foreign Office it has been so; and both in 1957 and 1978 may have been a crucial element in Wilton Park's survival.

But in the end, what has prevailed is the fairly extraordinary notion, perhaps less so now than it has ever been, that it is actually in the interest of a country to present to the world an organisation that is independent of the national interest narrowly defined but that forms part of the international community as a whole. It is impossible to quantify the advantages this has brought, but however acerbic the arguments have been, it is this argument that has finally triumphed. No other country has a Wilton Park and many regard it with obvious envy: but the fact that Britain does have it and all its attendant advantages is the fortunate result of many skin of the teeth escapes from extinction.

ACKNOWLEDGEMENTS

This contribution relies on personal knowledge and very extensively on information to be found in R. Mayne, *In Victory, Magnanimity, In Peace, Goodwill: A History of Wilton Park* (London: Whitehall History Publishing in association with Frank Cass, 2003). This is a very full account and, apart from some fairly scrappy recollections by others, is the only source for studying the evolution of Wilton Park.

INDEX

Lightning Source UK Ltd.
Milton Keynes UK
UKOW030655050712

195507UK00002B/106/P